Bending the Frame in the German Cyclical Narrative

Bending the Frame in the German Cyclical Narrative

Achim von Arnim's
Der Wintergarten &
E. T. A. Hoffmann's
Die Serapionsbrüder

Vickie L. Ziegler

The Catholic University of
America Press

Washington, D.C.

Library of Congress Cataloging-in-Publication Data

Ziegler, Vickie L.
   Bending the frame in the German cyclical narrative : Achim von
Arnim's Der Wintergarten and E.T.A. Hoffmann's Die
Serapionsbrüder / by Vickie Ziegler.
       p. cm.
   Includes bibliographical references (p.).
   1. German fiction—19th century—History and criticism.
   2. Arnim, Ludwig Achim, Freiherr von, 1781–1831. Wintergarten.
   3. Arnim, Ludwig Achim, Freiherr von, 1781–1831—Technique.
   4. Hoffmann, E. T. A. (Ernst Theodor Amadeus), 1776–1822.
Serapionsbrüder. 5. Hoffmann, E. T. A. (Ernst Theodor Amadeus),
1776–1822—Technique.
   I. Title.
   PT766.Z54 1991
   833'.609—dc20
   90-1652
   ISBN 0-8132-0729-0 (alk. paper)

In loving memory of my grandmothers,
Edrie Thornber LaCroix and Charlotte Oberlies Ziegler

Contents

viii   Contents

Preface

The genesis of this book, though I was happily unaware of the consequences at the time, came from a seminar on the
German *Novelle* given by the late Professor Heinrich Henel dealing with
frame stories. Professor Henel encouraged my interest in the genre,
which I put aside in order to work on my primary field, medieval literature. Later my interest in the frame as a narrative technique as well as
in medievalism led me to *Der Wintergarten*. In examining the use of this
literary form, I had originally planned a much larger work; when the
parameters of that plan had to be scaled back, I decided to examine
two cyclical narratives representative of two traditions, Achim von Arnim's of Goethe, and E. T. A. Hoffmann's of Ludwig Tieck's, and study
the frame-inner story interaction. Both von Arnim's *Der Wintergarten*
and Hoffmann's *Die Serapionsbrüder* had suffered from shameful neglect, though the situation with *Die Serapionsbrüder* has started to
change.

There are many institutions and individuals to whom I owe a great
deal for the completion of this project. Professor Stanley Weintraub,
the director of Pennsylvania State University's Institute for Arts and
Humanistic Studies, has funded grants for travel to archives in Germany and for released time; the Inter-Library Loan Department in The
Pennsylvania State University's Library, particularly Mrs. Nolene Martin and Mrs. Ruth Senior, have rendered invaluable and uncomplain-
ing assistance in running down obscure sources. I would also like to
thank the following libraries and their staffs for helpful assistance and
for allowing me complete access to materials I needed: the E. T. A.
Hoffmann Archiv, Bamberg, Germany; the university libraries of Göttingen, Cambridge, and Yale; the Beinecke Rare Book Library at Yale;
the National Library of Scotland, Edinburgh; the Rare Book Library

of the National Institutes of Health, Rockville, Maryland. Professors Jeffrey Sammons of Yale University and Steven Scher of Dartmouth College provided detailed and helpful suggestions for the final revision of the manuscript.

I would also like to thank the Department of German staff who helped with manuscript preparation before I joined, however ineptly, the computer age; they include Teresa Bowes, Rita Andreessen, Irmgard Lee, Stephanie Jeschke, Julie Koon, and Joanne McGovern. Very special thanks are due Peter Bugbee, whose careful assistance in manuscript preparation was invaluable at a crucial stage.

One of the many dangers attendant upon writing a book is that people close to the author get more exercise in the practice of patience than is perhaps good for them. The members of the German Department and my chairman, Professor Ernst Schürer, have been generous with their time and their help. Other friends and colleagues who have encouraged me during difficult stages that attend the writing of any book include Armin and Barbara Frank, Bridget and Heinz Henisch, Kathleen and David Luft, James Ross Sweeney, and Elizabeth Traverse. Roger Geiger generously provided both moral support and welcome diversion during the final stages. To my parents, who interested me in literature in the first place, and to my brother Bob, a very special thanks for their constant encouragement and support.

A Note on the Translations

The translations that immediately follow quotations, book and article titles, and individual words are meant to serve primarily as a means of understanding for those who do not know German or who feel a bit uncertain of their skills from time to time. Since the goal was to achieve clarity and not a standard version in English of that writer's works, the translation has been guided, above all, by the need to convey meaning and understanding. The translators, who include Beate Engel, Christiane Eydt, Professor Alan Knight (Froissart), and the author, have tried to remain as close to the text as possible; however, when a literal translation would have proved baffling or incomprehensible without extensive notation, they have put the text into a more modern and idiomatic English.

Since many titles and terms reappear frequently, they are translated in the chapter openings or on their first appearance in the text. Book and article titles are translated at their first occurrence in text, but not in notes or the Bibliography. Journal titles are not translated.

Many of the texts involved presented translation problems that my translators approached with sensitivity, flair, and, at times, a sense of extreme frustration. With constraints on their time, they had to deal with archaic syntax, idiosyncratic stylists, and, on many occasions, opaque prose. For the care and conscientiousness they expended on my behalf, I am greatly in their debt. Since I have carefully reviewed all of the translations, any criticism of them should be directed towards me and not towards those who so ably assisted me.

Bending the Frame in the German Cyclical Narrative

Introduction

The frame story, a series of stories presented within a narrative, has been a staple in the catalog of literary genres ever since people started relating tales. Such a development is natural, because it reflects the original storytelling situation, in which disparate groups of people got together through chance, friendship, or threat of danger and told stories to pass away the time, or, as in the case of Scheherazade, to save her life for a thousand and one nights.

Chaucer's *Canterbury Tales* and Boccaccio's *Decameron* show the basic structural outlines common to the first literary frame stories; in Chaucer, the pilgrims are traveling together because of their common goal, and, in Boccaccio, they flee Florence because of the threat of the plague. The advantage of the frame story as a genre is that it enables the writer to integrate a wealth of heterogeneous material. The basic construction of the frame—minimal outer story with numerous inner stories of varying lengths—remained the same until the German writers reintroduced it in the late eighteenth century. Goethe, influenced by his reading of Boccaccio and Cervantes, wrote *Unterhaltungen deutscher Ausgewanderten*, a cyclical narrative dealing with aristocratic refugees from the French Revolution.

After Goethe's work appeared in 1795, other German writers followed Goethe's expansion of the characters in the frame and the manner in which he tied them to the content of the inner stories. They subsequently began to experiment with the genre, making the first significant changes to the structure of the frame story in several hundred years. Instead of constructing a rudimentary, sometimes awkward, outer skeleton, they began fleshing out the characters, often putting a novella within the frame. In addition, they forged complicated relationships among the characters in the frame and those in the inner

1

stories, often arranging the inner narratives in a sequence that itself affected the interpretation of the story.

Achim von Arnim's *Der Wintergarten* (1809) and E. T. A. Hoffmann's *Die Serapionsbrüder* (1819–21), written soon after the Napoleonic Wars, are two of the most important examples that reflect the combination of tradition and innovation so characteristic of the treatment of this genre by these German Romantic writers. Arnim is most famous for his historical novels and several novellas, which are classics in the canon of German Romantic literature; his work has aroused a good deal of critical interest in Germany in recent years, due to a reassessment of the originality of his narrative techniques and a new awareness of the progressive nature of his political writings. E. T. A. Hoffmann has been the focus of critical interest since the 1820s, not only because of the quality of his novels and short stories, but also because of his preoccupation with madness and parapsychology, which have become important themes in both the literary and larger culture. He has also enjoyed a large following outside of Germany, to which numerous translations as well as the ballet, *The Nutcracker*, and the opera, *Tales of Hoffmann*, attest.

In spite of the reputation of these two writers, no one as yet has studied *Der Wintergarten* and *Die Serapionsbrüder*, focusing on the structural unity of the works. This willful decision to disregard the work as the author presented it has blinded critics to the importance of the relationship between frame and inner stories. Previous editors often treated the extensive frames as orange peels, publishing collections of stories with no mention of the enclosing structure. This neglect has given rise to interpretative problems that consideration of the frame resolves.

A major obstacle to critical consideration of these works from the standpoint of their adaptation of the frame story has been the more or less continual controversy among nineteenth- and twentieth-century German critics about the very nature of the novella. Is it a genre that changes in form in the course of its historical developments or is there one ideal and immutable form, inspired by the falcon novella in Boccaccio's *Decameron*? The concept of the frame as a device in the collection of narrative techniques was generally pushed aside or neglected in these debates. What few studies exist of the frame story are either out of date, positivist, fragmentary, or only concerned with the theoretical implications of a frame. No study addresses the specific problem that I analyze: the interaction between the frame and the inner stories.

In spite of their apparent forthrightness in explaining in the text the basic organization of their frame societies and the rationale for telling stories, neither Arnim nor Hoffmann makes it easy for his readers to grasp the underlying significance of the works. The reader must be subjected to the same process of education as the characters in the frames, a process made more immediate by the presence of the frame itself, which lets the reader learn about the effect of the stories upon their fictional hearers. As the reader sees the frame audience draw on their cumulative understanding of the inner narratives as the works progress, he is forced into the same constant reassessment. While the primary nature of the education in each work is different – political in Arnim's, psychological in Hoffmann–there are important similarities in each writer's approach to history. Both men hark back to the national past for sources for their stories, seeing in the chronicles and accounts of earlier centuries a harmony that they felt their own age lacked. Arnim combines a reverential approach with a philologically shocking disregard of textual integrity in his adaptations. Both aspects arise from his desire to use the text for an often transparent moral purpose. Hoffmann uses sources for the most part as a springboard into his own fantasy in order to explain what the psychological dynamics of the past situation were. Yet, for all their obvious differences in their treatment of sources, both men had the same goal: to discover what really happened behind the painting or the text and to lend significance to the apparently insignificant or misunderstood.

The relationship between the frame and inner story in the two works also illuminates some of the differences between the two writers. Arnim's frame contains a narrative which slowly unfolds, a narrative shaped by the inner stories and their effect on the characters in the frame. As the narrative closes, the individuals in the country house end their winter of discontent, ready, each in his own way, to be useful to the nation.

Hoffmann's frame contains no such continuous novella in the frame involving frame characters; with the exception of the Serapion and Zacharias Werner excursuses, there are only bits and pieces of narrative relating to events in the lives of the brothers, which are there, not to develop a story line, but as minimal narrative stock to move to the reading of individual stories or to introduce themes that Hoffmann finds significant. Hoffmann's frame can be seen as an extended interior monologue on the problems of the artist, which are then illustrated by the inner stories and excursuses. It functions as a key to understanding and interpreting the inner stories: the genius of the frame is that it presents, within a fictional framework, an apparently non-fictional intellectual discussion among friends, who were in reality largely Hoffmann's alter egos, of the issues treated in a fictional, artistic manner in the inner stories. Had Hoffmann's frame contained a complex novella, the unique opportunity it presents would have been lost, since it affords us a view into Hoffmann's mind that enables us to see the opinions and ideas which shaped his work. As the subsequent analysis will show, both men developed frame structures which were particularly effective in advancing their literary goals.

Both writers had extraordinary faith in the power of literature to affect people's lives and actions. For Arnim, older literature offered both a means of education and an encouragement to emulation. Written in the depressing aftermath of the Napoleonic wars, *Der Wintergarten* seeks to find both the explanation for, and the corrective of, the great military defeats of the Prussian army and the demoralization of the Germans. It searches for answers in the chronicles and stories of the past, where individuals behaved in a way that ensured a successful outcome. While Arnim used literature to fit an individual for a productive life within society, Hoffmann intended for literature to make life bearable for the sensitive individual mired in philistine surroundings. For Hoffmann, the flight into the nether regions of the mind and the interest in paranormal mental states enabled him, and therefore his readers, to understand the ways in which this unseen world constantly impinged on everyday life, lifting it from the banality that so depressed him.

In both cases, the variety of the material included in the inner sections of the works is astonishing. In addition to the wide variety of sources Arnim uses, he also includes many different kinds of poetry: romances, odes, songs. All of these have a significant bearing on the interpretation of the work. Hoffmann, though he seldom uses verses within the stories, presents a rich variety of narrative forms: novellas, anecdotes, fairy tales, theoretical treatises, and sketches. In this regard, both men take advantage of one of the oldest traditions of the frame stories, the aforementioned integration of heterogeneous material, while expanding the genre at the same time.

Arnim's sources for the inner stories in the *Wintergarten* range from Froissart to eyewitness accounts of the Scottish Rebellion and Bonny Prince Charlie. Arnim's goal, to find material that would have a didactic effect on his readers, shaped his approach to adaptation, already sharpened by his work on *Des Knaben Wunderhorn*. His reinterpretations emphasized retention of positive character traits and events and elimination of those details which put individual characters in a negative light, such as Philander's collusion with the brigand soldiers in Moscherosch's *Soldatenleben*. In his adaptations, Arnim often joins totally different sources, such as Moscherosch and Grimmelshausen's *Springinsfeld* in the fourth evening, and novels by Weise and Reuter in the seventh. Not only does the study show that Arnim employed considerable skill in his stylistic adaptations, but it also delineates underlying parallels in works that he joined.

Der Wintergarten stands most clearly under Goethe's influence, as Arnim's frame characters try to confront the reality of the Napoleonic wars and their significance for the Germans. Arnim's response differed from Goethe's attempt to recreate the pre-revolutionary aristocratic world. Arnim, confronted with a defeated and disoriented nation, found models in the German past for the qualities necessary to regenerate German life and culture; in his stories he brought those qualities before the eyes of his countrymen. Since no thorough study has ever been made of Arnim's sources and his use of these sources in *Wintergarten*, the significance of this work for literary and cultural history has remained hidden.

Although Hoffmann's *Die Serapionsbrüder* contains a number of his major novellas, such as "Die Bergwerke zu Falun" and "Das Fräulein von Scuderi," it has never been analyzed as a work complete in itself with special emphasis on the frame and the relationships of inner stories to the frame. Major Hoffmann themes such as madness, the problems of the artist, and extrasensory phenomena appear in discussions in the frame and then in the inner stories. For example, material in the frame about magnetism and metals throws new light on the controversial figure of Cardillac in "Das Fräulein von Scuderi." Literary historians have ignored important theoretical excursuses which Hoffmann made about the scientific material underlying some of his most significant literary creations.

The treatment of *Der Wintergarten* and *Die Serapionsbrüder* as unified works demands, like the telling of tales in a cycle, patience and attention on the part of the reader. Like the cycles themselves, this treatment cannot be undertaken hastily. It is definitely worth the effort, however, since it will lead to an enhanced understanding of two major works of prominent German Romantic writers and the context of political and intellectual issues of the day in which the works arose.

I

Achim von Arnim's
Der Wintergarten

Introduction

Es müßte sonderbar in ihren Winter hinein blühen, wenn ihnen so der
Sinn für das Große eines Volks aufgehen sollte und für sein Bedürfnis.

—*"Von Volksliedern,"* 1805

"Things would have to flower remarkably in their winter, if for them
the sense of the greatness of a people and its needs were to open up."

—*"On Folk Songs,"* 1805[1]

While the works of Achim von Arnim often seem like the forlorn stepchildren of German Romantic literature, even within a mistreated family, one child may suffer more from misunderstanding and neglect than the others. The condescending dismissal that *Der Wintergarten* has suffered is probably due in large part to the dependence of the work on sources, which is initially its most striking characteristic. With the exception of Wulf Segebrecht, most critics have not been willing to look more deeply at this narrative.[2]

---

1. *Achim von Arnims Sämmtliche Werke* 6 (Berlin, 1857), p. 450.
2. Brian Rowley, "The Novelle" in *The Romantic Period in Germany*, ed. Siegbert Prawer (New York, 1970), p. 141. Most critical comments on *Der Wintergarten* have been negative in nature, as a brief and representative survey of the critical literature of the past fifty years will show. Gertrud Hausner, "Achim von Arnim und die Literatur des 17. Jahrhunderts" (Diss., Vienna, 1934), p. 44, says that *Wintergarten* merely adapts and links together older German stories. Werner Vordtriede, "Achim von Arnim," *Deutsche Dichter der Romantik*, ed. Benno von Wiese (Berlin, 1983), p. 319) is also somewhat condescending about the work. In his Princeton University dissertation of 1968, "Achim von Arnim, Writer in Transition: Themes and Techniques in Short Prose Narratives," Hermann Weiss refers to Arnim's work in *Wintergarten* as merely editorial (p. 1). A new evaluation of Arnim's work, Roland Hoermann's *Achim von Arnim* (Boston, 1984), mentions *Wintergarten* only in passing (pp. 6, 89). Much recent research about Arnim's political ideas centers on the *Wunderhorn* or other essays and stories without analyzing *Wintergarten*, but Bernhard Gajek's article, "Achim von Arnim: Romantischer Poet und preußischer Patriot (1781–1831)" in *Sammeln und Sichten: Festschrift für Oscar Fambach zum 80. Geburtstag*, ed. Joachim Krause, Norbert Oellers, and Karl Konrad Polheim (Bonn, 1983), pp. 264–82, contains much interesting material about Arnim's thoughts and plans for *Nationalerziehung*. Jürgen Knaack, in his dissertation, "Achim von Arnim—Nicht nur Poet: Die politischen Anschauungen Arnims in ihrer Entwicklung" (Hamburg, 1976) mentions *Wintergarten* only briefly, p. 28. Knaack says that Arnim chose exemplary stories from German history to avoid censorship.
   Vordtriede, "Achim von Arnim," notes that in his later works Arnim took from older sources (p. 326).

Wintergarten deserves a better fate than an airy dismissal as a badly seasoned rehash of older material, not only because it was important to Arnim's own development as a writer, but also because Arnim had to examine problems similar to the post-World War II German political situation. In both cases, Germans had experienced the capitulation of their country in the face of a devastating defeat as well as the total collapse and decay of value systems in the personal and political spheres. Seen as a linchpin in Arnim's early development, *Wintergarten* takes on added significance. *Wintergarten* was not simply a futile literary exercise from a man who read too much; it was Arnim's attempt to advance his own deeply held beliefs about the interdependent role of literature, political action, and religious belief.

In 1808, when Arnim began collecting materials for this cycle, he had already immersed himself for years in the study of older German literature, the first fruits of which were the *Wunderhorn*.[3] There are two main streams apparent in this pursuit: the belief, which was with him from the very first, that art is a means for all sorts and conditions of men to come together and the didactic, exemplary value of older literary works.[4]

See also Bernd Fischer, *Literatur und Politik. Die 'Novellensammlung von 1812' und das 'Landhausleben' von Achim von Arnim* (Frankfurt, 1983).

The most recent and most welcome contribution to an understanding of *Wintergarten* comes from Wulf Segebrecht, in an article, "Die Thematik des Krieges in Achim von Arnims Wintergarten" in *Aurora* 45 (1985), pp. 310–16. Segebrecht was not the first to write positively about the work; in the notes to his edition of von Arnim's works, Walther Migge, in *Achim von Arnim: Sämtliche Romane und Erzählungen* 2 (Munich, 1963), p. 870, saw Arnim's own original contribution quite clearly. All subsequent quotations from *Wintergarten* and other works by Arnim will be from this edition and will be in the text.

Research of Arnim's sources has been unsatisfactory for various reasons. Anton Reichl's catalog, "Über die Benutzung älterer deutscher Literaturwerke in Achim von Arnims 'Wintergarten,' " in *Schulprogramm Arnau* (Böhmen), 1889–90, I, II, overlooks a great deal and in addition, contains mistakes. Reichl seldom analyzes, preferring a mere register of variations. Konrad Kratzsch's work, "Untersuchungen zur Genese und Struktur der Erzählungen Ludwig Achim von Arnims" (Jena, 1968), contains some interesting observations in spite of its clumsy Marxism. In another article, "Die Vorlagen zu Achim von Arnims 'Wintergarten' aus den Beständen der Arnim Bibliothek in der Zentralbibliothek der deutschen Klassik," in *Marginalien: Blätter der Pirckheimer Gesellschaft* 29 (April 1968), pp. 29–44, Kratzsch expands the material in the above mentioned dissertation.

3. See Jörn Göres, "Das Verhältnis von Historie und Poesie in der Erzählkunst Achim von Arnims" (Diss., Heidelberg, 1956). In Arnim's preoccupation with the past, Göres sees a high degree of continuity; for him, *Wintergarten* represents part of an unbroken line in Arnim's intellectual development, a line that began with the publication of *Wunderhorn* and continued through the writing of *Die Kronenwächter* (pp. 145–46).

4. Helene M. Kastinger Riley, *Achim von Arnim* (Hamburg, 1979), p. 45. See also p. 44, where she notes that a lecture Arnim gave just after he left secondary school deals

Because of this didactic tendency, Arnim's goals differed from those of the philologically inclined literati. Johann Friedrich Voß, for example, the renowned Homer translator, blasted Arnim for the liberties taken with original texts.[5] Clemens Brentano wanted to restore an old folksong; Arnim wanted to change the points of emphasis. The purpose of this new version was to make material from the past accessible to his contemporaries so that it could have the desired exemplary effect.[6] Arnim believed that it was the mission of art to present this material in such a way that those in a different age understood it and learned the necessary lessons.[7]

Drawing the appropriate conclusion from the past to affect one's behavior in the present seemed particularly crucial to Arnim in the early years of the nineteenth century as Napoleon stormed through Europe. His concern with the fate of his countrymen was already apparent in the important essay, "On Folk Songs," written in 1805. This work contains numerous passages lamenting the spiritual decline of Germany from its earlier greatness, implying the existence of a more propitious period in Germany history.[8] The belief in a Golden Age was one that Arnim had in common with other Romantics; Möllers notes that he agreed with Grimm's concept of a paradisical time which

---

with the belief that art is part of humanity's birthright. See also Knaack, *Achim von Arnim*, pp. 24, 26.

5. See Riley, *Achim von Arnim*, pp. 52–53; Gerhard Möllers, "Wirklichkeit und Phantastik in der Erzählweise Achim von Arnims" (Diss., Münster, 1971), p. 37.

6. See Werner Hoffmann, *Clemens Brentano: Leben und Werk* (Bern, 1966), p. 230; Heinz Rölleke, "Anmerkungen zu 'Des Knaben Wunderhorn' " pp. 276–94, especially pp. 283 and 287, in *Clemens Brentano: Beiträge des Kolloquiums im Freien Deutschen Hochstift*, 1978, ed. Detlev Lüders (Tübingen, 1980). Rölleke criticizes Arnim's mixing of old and new and brings up the problems Arnim had with Brentano because of their different approaches.

7. Cited by Riley in *Ludwig Achim von Arnims Jugend- und Reisejahre* (Bonn, 1978), p. 62. For a historical account of the situation in Prussia, see Karl Otmar Freiherr von Aretin, *Vom Deutschen Reich zum Deutschen Bund*, pp. 515–672, esp. "Der Untergang des alten Preußen," pp. 599–602, in *Deutsche Geschichte*, 2, *Frühe Neuzeit* (Göttingen, 1985). Reinhold Steig, *Achim von Arnim und Clemens Brentano*, (Stuttgart, 1894), 1, provides much material about Arnim's anguish over Prussia's collapse. In a letter to Brentano on September 8, 1806, he wrote: "Wer des Vaterlandes Noth vergißt, den wird Gott auch vergessen in seiner Noth!" (p. 191). See also pp. 207–24, especially pp. 207–9. Here Steig describes how Arnim rode in a transport with wounded soldiers and how Arnim watched Hohenlohe's surrender in Stettin after the event. In a letter to his aunt, written on November 18, 1806, Arnim wrote: "Sie erinnern Sich vielleicht meiner ruhigen Überzeugung, die ich in Strelitz oft streitend vorgelegt, daß ohne eine innere höhere Staatsentwicklung kein glücklicher Krieg möglich sei" (p. 209). This comment of Arnim's reflects once again his conviction that the inner disposition of a people has a significant bearing on events.

8. See Arnim, *Sämmtliche Werke*, 6 (Hildesheim, 1982), pp. 452, 474.

marked the beginning of human history, when God's will and man's were identical. Arnim's own adaptation of these ideas differed from those of other Romantics. Unlike Novalis, who projected human wishes into the past, Arnim believed in the continual presence of this primordial time in human history.[9] Another passage from the folk song essay bears this belief out: "Und als ich dieses feste Fundament noch unter den Wellen, die alten Straßen und Plätze der versunkenen Stadt noch durchschimmern sah,. . ." ["And as I saw, still under the waves, this firm foundation, the old streets and squares of the sunken city still gleaming through the water. . ."].[10]

If the primordial time still exists buried in the events of the day, then a way must be found to bring it to view in the present. Like other Romantic writers, Arnim saw art as an intermediary between different worlds, but he connected it with other purposes. Novalis saw art as a passport to the past that never was, while E. T. A. Hoffman used literature as a means to explore the mysterious demi-mondes of the subconscious existence. But for Arnim, art was to be the midwife to a rebirth of the best of the German spirit into a present which sorely needed it.[11]

Even in the poem "Zueignung" (Dedication), which appears at the very beginning of the work and which dedicates *Wintergarten* to Bettina, Arnim brought in the theme of preservation of the inspirational.[12] (Bettina Brentano, whom Arnim would later marry, was the sister of Clemens Brentano.) The setting of the poem was an orangerie in Aschaffenburg in mid-September, 1808, where Arnim and Bettina

9. Gerhard Möllers, "Wirklichkeit und Phantastik in der Erzählkunst Achim von Arnims" (Diss., Münster, 1971), pp. 32–33.

10. Arnim, *Sämmtliche Werke* 6, p. 446.

11. See Möllers, "Wirklichkeit," pp. 31–35; Knaack, *Achim von Arnim*, pp. 23–24; Göres, *Verhältnis*, pp. 17–21, on the relationship of poetry and history for Arnim.

12. Irmgard Berchtenbreiter, *Achim von Arnims Vermittlerrolle zwischen Jakob Böhme als Dichter und seiner Wintergartengesellschaft* (Munich, 1972), p. 282, says that Arnim took from the *Orangengarten*, ". . . einen Vorsatz mit, der als stilistisches Programm verstanden sein will." On p. 283, she suggests links between this poem and other parts of *Wintergarten:* "Vom 'Orangengarten' her ließe sich sagen: sie preist den alten, schöngeschmückten 'Helm' und kann nichts finden an einer zeitigen 'Frucht', wie sie der Ankömmling schätzen gelernt hat. Allerdings lebt sie in einer Epoche, die nicht die 'rechte Zeit' ist, daß das Schöne klinge. Es wird noch einen 'Winter' lang dauern, ehe ein Neues, eine 'Frucht' keimt, die der Kunst der Vergangenheit an die Seite zu setzen wäre. So ist es dann auch, als man sich endlich-am 'Schluß'-trotzdem im Sehen zu ertüchtigen versucht, eines jener 'alten Kunstwerke', dem die 'Wintergesellschaft' ihre Aufmerksamkeit schenkt."

parted and where he watched the stagecoach disappear.[13] Arnim uses the real situation to introduce an artistic allegory grafted onto the orange tree, which bears blossoms and fruit at the same time.[14] Just before he introduces the picture of the gardener picking the flowers and the fruit, he says of the spirit: "Der Geist sich offenbart in Frucht und Blüte" ["The spirit reveals itself in fruit and blossom"] (125), while the fruit of the orange tree is "schöner Künste Frucht" ["The fruit of beautiful arts"] (126). The gardener lets the fruit that spills out of the rusty helmet fall, since he has an abundance, but as it falls, it hits a tambourine lying in the grass and produces music:

> Ich fand das Tamburin mit Wohlgefallen,
> Das unten lag, worauf sie (Frucht vz) tönend fiel,
> Das Schöne ist auf Erden unverloren,
> Es klingt zur rechten Zeit, den rechten Ohren. (126)

With joy I found the tambourine which lay below, on which the fruit fell with a ringing sound. Beauty is not lost on earth if it resounds at the proper time to the right ears.

These lines could be read as an announcement of Arnim's plans for *Der Wintergarten*: He would like to ensure both that the fruits are not lost and that the appropriate ears hear the sounds.[15] In both cases, in the orangerie and in the *Wintergarten*, the garden does serve as a sort of refuge where art may fulfill its role.

While the image of the helmet in the poem is problematical, the description of it implies a positive disposition towards it on the part of the author:

> Es war ein Helm von altem, rost'gen Eisen,
> Worin der Gärtner seine Frucht gepflückt,

---

13. Steig, *Achim von Arnim und die ihm nahe standen* (Stuttgart and Berlin, 1913) 2, p. 192, as well as Otto Betz/Veronika Straub in *Bettina und Arnim: Briefe der Freundschaft und Liebe 1806–08*, 1, pp. 303–4, say that this parting was at Aschaffenburg in mid-September, 1808. Thomas Sternberg, *Die Lyrik Achim von Arnims* (Bonn, 1983), places the parting at Aschaffenburg in one place (p. 219) and in Augsburg at another (p. 260).

14. Sternberg, *Lyrik*, says that Arnim liked to place reality and poetry in a continuous dialogue, with poetry firmly planted in reality, while those unusual events in reality should be poeticized. He sees this process at work in the "Zueignung" poem (see pp. 219, 260, note #21). See also Berchtenbreiter, *Achim von Arnim*, pp. 282–83, who says that the poem has connections between the opening scene with the lady of the house and the final one in *Wintergarten*.

15. Sternberg, *Lyrik*, pp. 219, 116. Sternberg sees the garden as "privates Freudenreich."

Manch schwerer Hieb ließ sich darauf noch weisen,
Doch schwerer hat ihn schöne Frucht gedrückt;
So mußt der Helm vor meinen Augen reißen,
Der fest geschmiedet schien und reich beglückt:
Der alten Waffen schwer errungner Segen,
Und schöner Künste Frucht, läßt sich nicht hegen. (126)

It was a helmet made of rusty old iron, which the gardener used for picking fruit, many a heavy blow had left a mark which still remained, yet beautiful fruit had weighed down more heavily upon it; so before my very eyes, the helmet had to split, which seemed so strongly forged and richly graced: The hard-won blessing of the old weapon and the fruit of beautiful arts cannot be contained together.

The helmet could well be a symbol for Prussia: the battle scars, the appearance of strength and wealth, the advantages that were won with old weapons. Yet this helmet cannot hold the fruits of art, which could be a disguised call on Arnim's part for a Germany that could learn from the fruits of the spirit.

Arnim's intent to hunt for such fruits is apparent at the very beginning of *Wintergarten*, when he cites Ritter von Thurn, a figure out of French didactic narrative (127), in an idyllic and idealistic introduction, linking the records of the past with service to God and their relationship to the present.[16] This quiet prelude contrasts sharply in form and content with the reference to current events which comes immediately after the remarks of Ritter von Thurn:

Diese guten Worte eines alten Ritters mögen in diesem verdrießlichen, immer wiederkehrenden Winter, wo allen schönen Kindern Zeit und Weile lang wird, *wohl zur rechten Zeit wiederholt werden;* doch *keinem geziemen sie besser, als der nun zerstreuten, übellaunigen Wintergesellschaft,* zu deren Unterhaltung die folgenden Geschichten zusammengebracht wurden, *die sehr unzufrieden mit der ganzen Welt,* doch immer etwas Neues von ihr wünschte, endlich aber mit al-

16. See also Migge, p. 887. See Hermann F. Weiss's perceptive article, "Achim von Arnims Harmonisierungsbedürfnis: Zur Thematik und Technik seiner Novellen" *LWJB* 15 (1974), pp. 81–99, esp. p. 95, for comments on the role of Divine Providence in Arnim's work. For an informative survey of interest in older German literature from the seventeenth to the early nineteenth century, see Gisela Brinker-Gabler, "Tiecks Bearbeitungen altdeutscher Literatur: Produktion, Konzeption, Wirkung" (Diss., Cologne, 1973), pp. 12–100, esp. 19, 25, 29, 49–50, where she deals with patriotic motivation for the study of older literature. See also Migge, *Achim von Arnim* 1, pp. 1074–78. Möllers, "Wirklichkeit," pp. 36–37, analyzes Arnim's goal of national regeneration through examples from the past.

lem, was bloß erzählt und nicht geschehen, ganz nachsichtig, aufmunternd, wohlwollend und zufrieden schien. (127) (emphasis mine)

These good-natured words from an aged knight could certainly be repeated at an appropriate time in this vexatious winter, which keeps returning, where for all handsome children time and leisure seem long; yet for no one are they more suited than for the distracted, ill-humored winter gathering, for whose entertainment the following stories were collected, people who were very dissatisfied with the entire world yet who always wanted something new from it, who however seemed finally forebearing, well disposed, indulgent, and satisfied towards everything that was merely told and did not occur.

The stormy style of this description reflects the miserable morale of the Prussians in their winter of discontent, a situation to which Arnim alludes when he introduces the only rule for the stories, namely to make no specific references to current events, but rather to collect stories from other times and countries (132).

The majority of these inner stories deal with the manner in which the individual, faced with a personal or political crisis, behaves; it must have seemed particularly crucial to Arnim in 1808 to improve the present by analyzing the past. Prussia had capitulated to Napoleon's forces during the campaign of 1807 and lost territory west of the Elbe. Frustrated by the prostration of his country, Arnim had no ready outlet for his overwhelming desire to help. Military service as well as the bureaucracy were out of the question, the latter partly because of Arnim's ideas about a new social order.

In addition to urging the citizenry to defend their country in his short-lived periodical "Der Preuße" "The Prussian," Arnim also wrote political articles and essays. One of the most famous, "Was soll geschehen im Glücke" ("What should happen with a fortunate turn of fate") contains valuable insights into Arnim's ideas about Napoleon[17] as well as thematic parallels with some of the *Wintergarten* material. The opening lines of the essay reveal Arnim's ideas about Napoleon's place in history and the formation of a new nobility through education.[18] The problem with Napoleon, as Arnim saw it, was that he had betrayed the goals of the French Revolution; however, because the uprising was a

---

17. In the article in which Arnim's essay is printed " 'Was soll geschehen im Glücke' Ein unveröffentlicher Aufsatz Achim von Arnims" *Jahrbuch der deutschen Schiller-Gesellschaft* 5 (1961), pp. 196–221, Jörn Göres writes about Arnim's attitude toward Napoleon; see pp. 208–9.

18. Göres, "Glücke," p. 199.

movement of the people, the death of Napoleon would not end it. Arnim's solution to the issues raised by the French Revolution was a radical one and would not have been much appreciated by the ruling classes of this time: "Das ganze Volk muß aus einem Zustande der Unterdrückung durch den Adel zum Adel erhoben werden" ["The entire nation must be elevated by the aristocracy from a condition of oppression to nobility"].[19] Behind these remarks stands Arnim's love for and almost messianic belief in the value of older literature in forming this new chivalric order.[20]

The onslaught of the current national catastrophe brought on by the French caused Arnim's earlier ideas about the didactic value of art and its connection with religion, history, and politics to express themselves in *Der Wintergarten*. The preceding discussion has shown that *Wintergarten* had to be didactic and had to depend heavily on sources for Arnim to achieve the goals most dear to him. Many of these sources were, as Göres points out,[21] not originally moral stories per se, but Arnim changed their focus in his adaptation and made them exempla for the characters in the frame. This process is at work in the story of the first evening, "Die Liebesgeschichte des Kanzlers Schlick und der schönen Sienerin" ("The love story of Chancellor Schlick and the beautiful Sienese"), which Arnim changed from a rollicking and bawdy Renaissance novella into a more idealized love story. In it he analyzes the importance of faithfulness and the effect of European politics on love; both of these themes relate to the situation of the lady of the country house, madly in love with a French officer.

Arnim chose the frame story genre because it offered several advantages, such as introducing material from widely different sources. Another attraction for him was that the gathering of a group of people listening to someone else provides a setting that lends itself to didactic purposes, a tendency that becomes apparent as the guests are mustered in the initial frame. The meeting of well-bred friends and strangers in an isolated house was already well known to Arnim through Boccaccio and Goethe. However, although the country houses in Boccaccio and Goethe are places of refuge either from the plague or from the French Revolution, Arnim does not intend for his Germans to enjoy the privileges of class and position; leisure and solitude available to them in this

---

19. Göres, "Glücke," p. 200.　　20. See also Göres, "Glücke," p. 215.
21. Göres, *Verhältnis*, p. 63.

house should make it easier for them to receive the lessons of the stories, so that they, as they do at the end, can make their contributions to rebuilding German society.

The plague that threatens the *Wintergarten* guests is neither bubonic nor revolutionary, but a disease of the soul. Arnim's guests have no names, but this anonymity does not serve to flatten them out into mere stereotypes or to mint them as coinage of representative ideas. This namelessness rather serves to emphasize the connection between these people and Arnim's readers, particularly when it becomes a matter of the lessons that Arnim wants to convey. The inner stories function either as positive, negative, or analogical examples that can work directly on the guests and Arnim's readers.

The only figure who does not fit the description of the frame characters as outlined is the first one to appear, the half-allegorical, half-real Winter. We see him at the beginning and at the end as a bent, gray, aged man and, in between, as a season. Arnim's integration of Winter in these two guises into the narrative is as pervasive as the snow that Winter brings along. As Migge points out, Arnim loved to let allegorical or mythical figures assume a real shape in his stories, with enough of their transcendental nature showing to disquiet the other characters.[22] He uses this procedure with Winter; although we first see him as a freezing gray old man in need of a ride, the narrator himself seems to doubt his existence as a real person (130). Rather, he encourages the reader to believe that the character symbolizes the frozen passiveness of Prussia after the departure of the victorious French troops:

So zog also der Winter ein, wo die Feinde ausgezogen, und meine frohen Erwartungen und Gedanken erstarrten wie der lebendige Strom, der durch die Straße floß. Alles besetzte und bewachte dieser traurige Winter mit seiner langweiligen Heerschar, selbst wo die kaufmännischen und adligen Häuser ihre hohen Stirnen, mit mancherlei Bildwerk gekrönt, erheben, hing er seinen weißen Glanzteppich auf, und selbst an dem Boden knirschten die gejagten Füße noch unwillig, daß auch der treue Boden, den selbst die Feinde mußten stehen lassen, seine Farbe angenommen. (130)[23]

Thus the winter moved in, where the enemies had evacuated, and my joyful expectations and thoughts grew stiff like the lively stream which flowed

22. Migge, pp. 876–77.
23. Segebrecht, "Thematik des Krieges," pp. 311–12, comments on the significance of this mood and its relation to the allegory of Winter; he sees winter as an allegory not

through the streets. With his tedious legion, this dismal winter occupied and guarded everything. Even where the houses of the merchants and the aristocracy raise their high foreheads, crowned with various kinds of sculpture, he hung up his glistening white carpet, and even on the ground the driven feet crunched resentfully, because the faithful earth, which even the enemies had to leave alone, had also taken on his color.

The narrator continues with this militaristic tone in the frame of the second evening, but after that, there is only one reference to winter. It comes in a comparison of avalanches with people's moods in the seventh evening, before the reappearance of Winter as the fiancé of the lady of the house in the eighth evening. When Winter returns in human form, the first signs of spring, warmth, and light, also arrive (347). This appearance of the sun parallels the inner story of Jacob Böhme and Aurora, with the emphasis on the dawning of God's revelation to him. Since it is the lady of the house who will eventually see the error in her choice of lovers, it is she who has preoccupied herself with the study of Böhme and who in some way serves as the model reader Arnim wished to have. Well educated, sensitive, and sensible, she needs only exposure and help to understand.

The central position of the lady of the house in this cycle reveals itself immediately in the narrative. After Winter is introduced, she appears in the unusual guise of a motionless statue covered with snow, who runs in alarm at the narrator's unexpected arrival. Her position and the fact that she appears blanketed in snow underscore her central role in the novella in the frame and foreshadow her engagement to Winter. Hopelessly in love with the French officer, the lady accepts Winter's suit out of resignation and despair.

The narrator entreats the inhabitants of the country house to let him in and, as he arrives on the scene of their future evenings, several elements appear in the description that are of significance to the major themes of the story. The room to which he is led has been redone in the Gothic manner (131), indicating the importance of an older period in German history, as well as the interest of the estate's owner in this time. The first object he sees upon entering the room is the painting of the French officer, standing in a place of honor with flowers before it; that, plus the sighing of a flute clock, indicate that there is a melancholy

_____

only for the postwar period, but also for the frozen social situation, which Arnim's work tries to address.

aspect surrounding the picture. The lady of the house confirms this impression in saying that her nerves are on edge because she has suffered greatly and that the snow covers many painful memories (131). Because of her misguided choice of admirers, she has no real sense of direction and purpose, since personal inclination and national loyalty do not coincide. However, she has in her personality those traits that make change possible, and she likes the older periods of German art, which pleases the narrator (131).

The succession of other guests and members of the group follows much more briskly, without the lingering attention that Arnim devotes to the lady. Her sister, an intelligent, sensible woman who has never fallen in love, spends most of her time embroidering and pouring tea.

The young invalid with a wooden leg attracts the reader's attention immediately; his character description is perhaps the most positive of any in the group.[24] The invalid, unlike the others present, has suffered in the service of his country; for this reason, Arnim assigns him a didactic role vis-à-vis the others in the group, with special attention paid to his assault on the lady's misplaced affections. This role comes quickly to the fore in the frame for the first evening, as the invalid tells the love story of the Chancellor Schlick and the beautiful Sienese, relating it to her love for the French officer. While his overriding interest lies in winning the lady for himself (and thereby for their country), he also exemplifies the sort of self-sacrificing bravery that should inspire some other members of the circle (the narrator clearly describes this function at the beginning of the fourth evening, which deals with war) (211). In the frame of the sixth evening, the envoy tries to induce the invalid to write his memoirs, ". . .Warum lassen Sie untergehen was Sie allein berichtigen können?" ["Why do you let perish what you alone could correct?"] (303) since memoirs are the most valuable kind of history.

The envoy, unemployed due to the German defeat, is the next guest to make his appearance. He remains a shadowy figure until the third evening's frame, where the reader initially sees him in an unimportant role. (The invalid and the narrator, mentally lamed by the cold, begin to dissect the personalities of the colony members in such a way that they distort reality [196].) Yet the first appearance of the envoy in cen-

24. Ibid., p. 312, interprets the role of the *Invalide* in a manner similar to that of this study. In n. 4 on the same page, Segebrecht remarks on the frequency of appearance in Arnim's work of invalids, who symbolize for those around them the cruelty of war.

ter stage reveals his importance, as the narrator's preface implied that it would. The envoy makes an elegant, eloquent, and forceful speech, reflecting many of Arnim's own ideas about the connection between blood revenge and piety, the German's adulation for anything foreign, and the ensuing inability to sacrifice for the common good. Because of his experience abroad and his proximity to the government, he sees his countrymen both as individuals and as citizens of the state. The envoy performs an extremely important function in the frame, providing an intellectual counterweight to the invalid, whose long-standing passion for the lady of the house often softens his sharp mind or sinks him into the sloughs of despond. The envoy's return to the diplomatic service of his country provides an example to the other members of the circle, such as the *Geniale*, who comes with him, and the readers.

Both the invalid and the envoy have served their country in their respective spheres. For this reason, each of them operates some of the time in a different didactic role, functions that set them apart from the other frame characters. While the invalid can bring home to the hearers the real dimensions of military courage and the cruelty of war, the envoy can teach the guests about the essence of history and the value of the past for the present. Because he is an envoy, he has an important double perspective: he sees himself not only as a German among Germans, but also as an observer of Germans abroad.

Neither the actress who accompanies the envoy nor the sister of the lady of the house plays a real role in the frame. However, the last three women to appear figure in several evenings: the *Geniale* (the ingenious woman), the *Gesunde* (the healthy woman), and the *Kranke* (the sick woman). The *Geniale*, who makes her entrance by graciously pressing snowballs into the hands of her acquaintances (132), reappears in the seventh frame, *Winterlaunen* (Winter moods), which offers a light-hearted pause between the stories about Jacob Böhme and Prince Charles. The pause, "Die drei Erznarren" (The three notorious fools), is intended to drive away the depressing mood of the *Winterlaunen*, caused by the depressing situation in which they find themselves. Although many of the frames deal with the intellectual problems confronting the Prussians because of Napoleon, this one concentrates on the group's mood and emotion. No member of the company registers mood changes as quickly as the mercurial *Geniale*. Her perverse humors call forth all sorts of criticism from the others, which she takes to heart. She ends the story by going off with the envoy to help her country.

The *Gesunde* and the *Kranke* appear as a pair in the introduction and in the fifth frame. One immediately senses some of the liberated woman in the *Gesunde*, a quality reinforced during her major appearance as a sort of Amazon in the fifth frame (132, 249). Her vigor manifests itself in a kind of aggressiveness. The *Kranke*, on the other hand, participates in only passive activities. A gossip, she introduces the fifth frame "Mistris Lee" story, saying the English lord entertained her with it (250). The balancing of these two opposites in the fifth frame, their only major appearance, shows a certain deftness in Arnim, not only because of their opposite natures, but also because "Mistris Lee" has qualities in common with both of them.

As he develops the story about the lady of the house and the French officer in his description of the frame society, Arnim gives definite hints as to how he intends to apply the examples of the inner stories to the characters in the country house. Naturally, Arnim did not intend to reach only those Prussian women in love with French officers, but all those less devoted to their nation than they could be.

Arnim's choice of a cyclical frame as the vehicle to present his lessons from older literature enables him to bring his intelligent and sensitive countrymen right into the country house, where they may feel affinities with certain characters and expose themselves to the benefits of the stories as well. The conventions found in the *Decameron*—the isolated society in which each individual tells a story and the rule which forbids reference to the events of the day—these Arnim retained as had Goethe before him.[25] He kept as well something much more important from Goethe, something which characterizes the German cyclical narratives: the interaction between the inner stories and the frame. Like Arnim, Goethe depended heavily on sources for his inner stories. Unlike Arnim, the novellas that Goethe took from sources have often been exhaustively and exhaustingly analyzed, while in Arnim's case, most critics have ignored his adaptations and the reasons for them. Most of Arnim's inner stories were not originally intended to function in the specific, applied manner for which Arnim used them.

25. See Wolfdietrich Rasch, "Achim von Arnims Erzählkunst," *Der Deutschunterricht* 7 (1955), pp. 38–55, p. 42; Göres, *Verhältnis*, p. 63.

He cut them loose from their literary moorings, not because he was insensitive to the artistic unity of the original, but because he saw in that original what Göres refers to as the "verdeutlichende Exempel" (elucidating model).[26]

In order to understand more fully how Arnim developed the network of relationships between the frame and the inner stories, one must examine the technical aspects of various elements of the frame and inner story as they appear in the *Wintergarten*. The frame itself was not a means to ban threatening forces from a group escaping from the current crisis.[27] While that was true in the *Decameron*, and partially true in Goethe's *Unterhaltungen* (Conversations), it is not the case with *Wintergarten*, though it may seem that the ban on stories of the present places it in this category. The rule serves two functions: it creates an oasis, and banishes the distracting present with its nefarious tendency to preoccupy totally the minds of the audience (132). The rule serves not to provide the opiate of oblivion, but to offer mental space for those lessons from the past helpful in coping with the present.[28] Arnim's use of the frame structure for mastery of a situation rather than for escapism has an antecedent in *Unterhaltungen*; we find a similar function in Hoffmann's *Die Serapionsbrüder*, particularly in those stories dealing with madness.

Unlike Goethe and Hoffmann, Arnim uses a first-person narrator, who has many apparent similarities with himself.[29] Like Arnim, the narrator has been on a research trip looking for old songs and he enjoys older art as much as his creator (127, 131). In his introduction to the Concordia story, he refers to his writing it down on the basis of other stories (161). The frame of the eighth evening contains the narrator's account of his own interest in Böhme and his collection of Böhme materials (348).[30] Arnim chose a first-person narrator very like himself

26. Göres, *Verhältnis*, p. 63.
27. Weiss, *Achim von Arnim*, p. 44, writes: ". . . earlier proponents of the frame ban the threat of tragedy from both the frame and the stories," implying that this situation obtains for *Wintergarten*.
28. Weiss's analysis in *Achim von Arnim* of the relationship of politics to *Wintergarten* seems to deal only briefly with the relationship. "The frame narrator alludes to the depressing political situation in Germany . . . , but never elaborates on it, merely informing us that the group was very dissatisfied with life" (p. 56).
29. Weiss, *Achim von Arnim*, notes that all of Arnim's cyclical narratives have first-person narrators, p. 49.
30. See Migge, p. 875. Arnim made a thorough study of Böhme and had an unfinished biographical manuscript, which was lost after an auction of Arnim's *Nachlass* (literary remains) in 1929.

because of his deep, personal involvement with the major themes of the work, the degree of intimacy that such a narrator brings, and the added realism in the reproduction of an oral narrative situation. In addition, the narrator, who is part of the colony, yet outside it, can stand aside and comment on events in a more impartial way than some members of the group.

In Goethe's *Unterhaltungen*, the inner stories fall into thematic groups, a convention that probably came from Boccaccio, who had a subject for each day. Since *Wintergarten* has never been taken seriously as a successor to *Unterhaltungen*, the existence of a definite thematic pattern has not received the attention it deserves.[31]

Table One shows that the most important narrators are the invalid, the envoy, and the narrator.

Table One

First Winter evening	Schlick	invalid
Second Winter evening	Concordia	narrator
Third Winter evening	Altdeutsche Landsleute	envoy
Fourth Winter evening	Philander	invalid
Fifth Winter evening	Mistris Lee	Ariel
Sixth Winter evening	Froissart	envoy
Seventh Winter evening	Schelmuffsky	*Geniale*
Eighth Winter evening	Böhme	narrator
	Pelia	lady of the house
Ninth Winter evening	Charles Stuart	narrator

The invalid, the envoy, and the narrator reveal their worries about the spiritual state of the German people, concerns that appear in the frame as well as in the older exemplary material. The inner stories circle round the interrelated themes of national history, love, and the inner man.

The Schlick story portrays the hopeless conflicts engendered when adulterous love runs afoul of national and political allegiance. "Albert und Concordia" and "Altdeutsche Landsleute" (Compatriots from an earlier age) describe marital love in the context of constancy to ethical and religious norms of conduct. In each, the love story takes place against the backdrop of a political situation: in "Albert und Con-

31. K. Kratzsch, in his dissertation, "Untersuchungen," p. 7, notes that the order of the stories has not been examined and believes that Arnim had a plan he did not follow.

cordia," the formation of an ideal society in the wilderness; in "Alt-deutsche Landsleute," against the fidelity of Germans to each other in occasionally hostile foreign courts.

The theme of war, begun in "Altdeutsche Landsleute," reaches a peak in the fourth evening. Here the invalid's rules for soldiers in the frame and the Philander story from the Thirty Years' War appear, as well as the discovery of Ariel sleeping on the desecrated *Viktoria* monument. Affairs of state predominate in the Jean Froissart chronicle of the sixth evening, as they do also in the account of Charles Stuart in the ninth. However, "Mistris Lee," the middle story and frame five, concentrates on right and wrong behavior, particularly in the person of Mistris Lee, the enigmatic "neue Amazone" ("new Amazon"). Negative and positive examples also appeared in the stories of the second and third evenings, but always in conjunction with general or abstract themes, such as the ideal society or the conduct of war.

The Schelmuffsky story forms a pleasant interlude before the dawning of a new day, heralded in the eighth evening, which is devoted mostly to Böhme. The inspirational quality of Böhme's life can, as Arnim presents it, herald the beginning of a new dawn for Germany; attendant on the advent of this time of light is the death of Winter, announced in the frame, a death that occurs on several levels.

Erster Winterabend
(First Winter Evening)

Arnim's first adaptation, "Die Liebesgeschichte des Kanzlers Schlick und der schönen Sienerin" ("The love story of Chancellor Schlick and the beautiful Sienese") takes the rather bawdy Renaissance novella of Aenas Silvius Piccolomini (later Pope Pius II), a novella of passionate love, political ambition, and betrayal, and changes it into an idealized love story of faithfulness ruined by fate in the form of European politics.[32] This inner story has intimate connections both

32. See p. 28, *Translationen von Niclas von Wyle*, ed. by Adelbert von Keller (Stuttgart, 1861). All subsequent Wyle quotations come from this volume and will appear in the text.

to the frame triangle of the lady, the French officer, and the invalid, and to the political goals that Arnim hoped to advance in the *Wintergarten*. The invalid tells the story, preceding it with an impassioned plea for the lady of the house to give up her love for a French officer whom she has sheltered and to love him instead. This Frenchman's conquest of the lady was apparently complete (134, 135); although he promised faithfulness to her when he left, he has not kept his word and the lady, rejected and defeated, retains only a shadow of her former beauty.

The parallel between the lady's situation and that of the German nation lies close at hand. The feelings of loneliness and disorientation she suffers correspond to the dark night of the spirit that overshadows the nation (135). The present time bears little resemblance to the age of chivalry, a period more favorable to love since there was a happy conjunction of the demands of politics and love (135). Though the *Wintergarten's* time, unlike the Middle Ages, did not easily reconcile the demands of state and the desires of the individual, it was not unique; there have been many such times in the past, among them the period in which the Emperor Sigismund's chancellor fell in love.

However, the invalid, along with his desire to comfort the lady, has another motive in mind in the choice of the story: not only to win the lady for himself but also to meld personal love with patriotism (135). Arnim's adaptation reflects this goal, since he left out the bawdier parts, such as the detailed praise of Germans as lovers. The point he is making in his adaptation is that the spirit of the age in which the lovers lived made it impossible for them to maintain their international love affair. Their adultery did not create this situation; it was rather a symptom of the underlying problems of the age. Like Lukrezia's affection for Eurial, the love of the lady for the French officer is impossible. The adulterous nature of Eurial and Lukrezia's passion foreshadows its eventual demise. Its inability to overcome the constraints of Lukrezia's marriage to an imperious husband symbolizes, especially for Arnim, the impossibility of the relationship in the larger world. By contrast, the capacity of marriage to bring about a real paradise plays an important role in the companion story to Eurial and Lukrezia, the story of the second *Winterabend*, Albert und Concordia, "Das wiedergefundene Paradies" (The rediscovered paradise).

To fit the text to his desired goal, Arnim had to change the original emphasis of the story. While he used more sophisticated techniques in other stories, such as the integration of very different sources, here he accomplished his ends by simply leaving out material that detracted from the example he wanted to portray. Reichl notes only the excision of mythological and bawdy material,[33] but his comments shed little light on why Arnim changed what he did; nor do they reveal the care and consistency of his adaptation.

So that this story might serve as a warning to people in the country house who might have identified with the main characters, Arnim had to excise sections of the Piccolomini novella that show Eurial and Lucrezia in an especially negative light. Lucrezia's remarks as she tries to justify her adulterous desires—"Niemant straffet den Irrenden der mit vil Irret" ["No one punishes the one who goes astray if he strays a lot"] (Wyle, 26)—do not appear in *Wintergarten*. Nor do the extreme condemnations of the reluctantly helpful servant, Sosias (Wyle, 29). Since the invalid wants to persuade the lady to see herself in the story, he smoothes off many of the rough edges of the two main characters. Nor did Arnim feel it appropriate to include some of the more rollicking bedroom scenes in Wyle's translation. In spite of Arnim's disclaimer about the cleric Piccolomini's avoidance of anything unseemly (135), it was Arnim who left out the indecent.

Arnim's attention to detail in focusing emphasis where he wanted it was apparent at the very beginning. He shortened the description of Sigismund as well as the description of the women. His main purpose here was to motivate Eurial's interest in Lukrezia through the emperor's attention to her. Therefore, passages about honors offered to the emperor, the location of the church in Siena and the emperor's delight in women (Wyle, 21–22) were shortened or cut.

Since the invalid wants to win the lady over, Arnim was particularly careful in his adaptation of Lukrezia. He retained some of the medieval imagery in the description of the women (136, 137) but muted other passages that hint at the destructive power of love, especially on the part of the woman, preferring to emphasize her transforming power (Wyle, 22, and Arnim, 137). One medieval belief that Arnim left intact is the convention that outer beauty symbolizes inner worth: "Ihre äußere Gestalt gab zu merken, die Geschicklichkeit ihrer innern Form und Vernunft,. . ." (137) ["Her shape and figure let one recognize the

33. Reichl, I, pp. 4–5.

fitness of her inner form and good sense,] (Wyle, 23). Not only does this statement help to establish Lukrezia as an unusual person, but it also indirectly flatters the lady of the house.

The care in the portrait of Lukrezia delineated by these small details runs through the entire story. Arnim eliminated much of the long passage where she debates about taking Eurial as a lover, especially those that are more overtly sexual or calculating, as when Lukrezia coldly considers the advantages and disadvantages of an affair (Wyle, 26). Instead of dwelling forcefully and at length on Lukrezia's potential problems, as Sosias in Wyle's translation does, Arnim's Sosias sums it up in a few words (139). When Wyle's Sosias warns her that no great love remains long undiscovered and that it is easier to break the affair off in the beginning (Wyle, 29), Sosia's speech has the effect of making Lukrezia seem more willful and, in a sense, more deserving of her fate. Sosias's brutal condemnation, "Du enteerest und verlümdest din huse, und wirst allain sin ain eebrecherin dines geschlechtes" ["You dishonor and insult your house and will be the only adulteress in your family"] (Wyle, 29), and his graphic description of the practical difficulties (29) create the same effect, that the punishment was deserved. Such a condemnatory note in Arnim's adaptation would have alienated the lady rather than convinced her.

Arnim left out or softened certain parts of the section with the procuress, among them the part where Lukrezia scolds the messenger for trying to incriminate women of a good reputation and the one in which Lukrezia threatens her life (Wyle, 34; Arnim, 140). While it may be necessary for Lukrezia to display some sort of apparent outrage about the procuress's visit, Arnim seemed anxious not to overdo her anger, perhaps for two reasons. The minimal display of displeasure makes Lukrezia seem less hypocritical and the hasty threat to what was probably a minimal hairdo (140) makes Lukrezia appear more refined and more, in the final analysis, a victim. Once again, Arnim adapted the source so that Lukrezia does not seem so different from the lady in the frame.

Arnim also omitted or toned down the passages that deal with women's sex drives. It was a common belief in the Middle Ages that women were more highly sexed than men[34]; Piccolomini still makes references

34. See James A. Brundage, "Prostitution in the Medieval Canon Law," pp. 149–60, in *Sexual Practices and the Medieval Church,* ed. by V. L. Bullough and James A. Brundage

to this belief at numerous points, saying that a woman is a wild sexual animal that no bridles can restrain (Wyle, 38–39, 43). Arnim's excision of this material not only reflected changed attitudes but also was in keeping with a presentation of a Lukrezia more sympathetic to his audience.

Arnim also showed a similar concern with Eurial's character, though not to the same degree. Wyle's Eurial resembles Arnim's except for the traits that Arnim left out, a coarser sexuality and a more calculating temperament in regard to his political prospects and Lukrezia. For example, Arnim not only deleted descriptions of Eurial in Lukrezia's chamber (Wyle, 52–54), but he also cut much of the scene between Eurial and his servant, in which Eurial describes Lukrezia's charms (Arnim, 149). Wyle's Eurial dwells awhile on this subject, better able now to understand the behavior of King Candele, who liked to have his companions watch him and his wife make love so that his own pleasure would be increased (Wyle, 55).

In Wyle, Eurial shows a great deal more concern with his own material prospects vis-à-vis Lukrezia, such as when he lists the numerous ways in which the emperor could damage his career (Wyle, 53–4). Arnim left out all of Eurial's self-seeking concerns (152); he apparently did not want to show Eurial in a bad light, because he would be unsympathetic to his listeners. A Eurial with all warts showing would not have the desired didactic effect, because listeners would not identify with him and the point would be lost; consequently, Arnim's Eurial is less openly calculating.

Although Wyle's Eurial has promised earlier to remain with Lukrezia as long as she wants him, he finds all kinds of reasons why he has to leave her. In Arnim the final reasons for parting remain indefinite (156), while in Wyle, the reasons are more concrete: he cannot see her: "und zu letscht als er sach Im all zugeng genomen und abgestellt sin do verkundt er der liebhaberin sin hinschaiden" ["And finally when he found all access taken from him and shut off, then he informed his mistress of his departure"] (Wyle, 76). The implication here is that Eurial gives up when he cannot express his love as openly as

---

(Buffalo, 1983), on the sexuality of women. He notes that women were thought to be naturally warmer than men and sexually mature at an early date (p. 152). Women were thought to be unable to resist sexual temptation and thus were considered highly sexed (p. 152).

he wants. The preoccupation with their sexual relationship that played such a powerful role in Wyle seems only to be implied here.

The invalid's warning, "Welche dieses lesen wollen lernen sich zu warnen" ["Whoever wants to read this should see it as a warning for themselves"] (157), has a special point. Although it is in the source, it appears here as an admonition to the lady and serves as a piquant bridge to the frame. Its primary function seems to undercut Göres's emphasis on the comforting aspects of Eurial and Lukrezia's love.[35] Göres did not make direct comparisons with the source and consequently missed those changes of Arnim's that tied directly into the invalid's attempts to convince the lady of the wrongness of her love for the French officer. Göres was right in noting Arnim's emphasis on the positive aspects of love, but he ran into trouble when he tried to establish a dichotomy between love as a transcendental force with a connection with the absolute and with demands of space and time on individual human beings. Had Göres carried his thoughts on the redemptive aspects of Arnim's work a little further, he might have observed that medieval historical thought offered a paradigm for a solution to his critical dilemma of trying to make a more positive interpretation than the text warrants. Medieval historians interpreted both pagan history and the Old Testament as anticipations of the fulfillment of God's promises; each embodied some good, which was incomplete, yet which in some way reflected the coming perfection. Such an approach would seem to offer a solution to the problems that the Eurial-Lukrezia story presents within the context of the frame. There are certainly positive aspects to their love, but because of its adulterous nature and the fact that it occurs between citizens of different countries with demands that sometimes run counter to the goals of the individual it could not succeed. Given this story's position as the first in a series and its particular significance for the invalid, we are perhaps justified in seeing in it both a promise and a warning. For love to develop fully, one should choose one's partner from one's own countrymen and, as the second story shows, develop the relationship in marriage.

Arnim's position in *Wintergarten* on the issue of loving one's countryman versus a foreigner differed sharply from his treatment of the problem in *Die Novellensammlung von 1812* (the novella collection of

35. See Göres, *Verhältnis*, pp. 64–67.

1812). In the stories "Seltsames Begegnen und Wiedersehen" (strange meeting and reunion) and "Der tolle Invalide auf dem Fort Ratonneau" (the crazy invalid at Fort Ratonneau), German women fall in love with or marry Frenchmen. In both cases, this love for a foreigner causes them painful rejection by their compatriots, but the relatives and friends who denounce Lilie and Julie appear in a negative light. Lilie's mother, a woman of dubious virtue who gives her daughter into the Devil's grasp in "Der tolle Invalide," and Constanze's patriotism that hides darker motives in "Seltsames Begegnen," receive much criticism from the narrator.[36] The image of the French that emerges in these two stories is much less one-sided than that in *Wintergarten*, though the element of patriotism is still strong (see, for example, the comments on Julie's father, 768). Perhaps these stories, written when Arnim had some distance from the war, represent a perspective that was more concerned with the individual's development than with the fate of a nation.

Further evidence of the exemplary intent of the narrator appears in the frame, when various characters make moral judgments on the behavior of the main figures in the story. In the course of this discussion, they extend the story, finding it impossible that the chancellor could forget Lukrezia.[37] Arnim's addition to what he found reflects one of his favorite approaches to older literature, to develop a story from a brief reference. The fantasy about Eurial and his beautiful wife of noble birth, whom he marries after Lukrezia dies, serves to give the invalid an opportunity to press his suit towards the lady of the house. The addition ends with a monument, a literary motif often employed by Clemens Brentano, as, for example, in his "Geschichte vom braven Kasperl und dem schönen Annerl." The chancellor and his wife stand alongside this monument with respect and devotion. The invalid draws up several captions, of which only the sad one appears:

> Viele würden tot ihn nennen,
> Doch an seiner Seite wachet,
> Seine Frau als Todesengel
> Seine Lebensflamm anfachet,
> Hält die Fackel treu in Händen, (158)

36. See pp. 737–38, pp. 787, 777–89, 794. See also Migge, p. 919, who believes that Constanze represents the kind of blind chauvinism that Arnim was against.

37. Weiss, *Achim von Arnim*, has misinterpreted the function of the frame and the purpose of the inner stories when he maintains that the audience is there to furnish "a light-hearted sequel to the sad tale . . . ," pp. 13–14.

Many would say he was dead, yet at his side, his wife keeps vigil as an angel of death, fanning the flames of life, faithfully holding the torch in her hands . . .

The invalid suggests that he would like to be in the position of the young wife if the lady of the house were the chancellor, so that he could bring her back to life. Like the chancellor, the lady should overcome her own hopeless love affair, make a good marriage and return to life. Arnim ends the evening on the same note with which it began, with the wasted appearance of one who has loved in vain and the possibility of regeneration through the right kind of love.

Zweiter Winterabend
(Second Winter Evening)

Like the story of the first winter evening, those of the second also come from old stories, but the moral element in these narrations, which comes under the subtitle of "Das wiedergefundene Paradies" is much stronger, as is the emphasis on religious devotion. It would certainly fulfill even the demands of the Ritter von Thurn (127). While the emphasis on marriage as the basis for social order is an important theme in this inner story,[38] it forms part of a larger pattern of exempla offered by the lives of the three major model males in the work, Albert, Schaffgotsch, and Captain Wolfgang.

As in the frame of the first evening, there is an allusion to current events, but in the second night the reference is veiled. The assembled guests, given emergency quarters by the lady of the house because of the ferocity of the winter weather, gradually drift off to sleep in the great hall. Only the narrator is restless and wanders outside. A fire

---

38. Göres, *Verhältnis*, makes little effort to compare Arnim's adaptation with the source or to understand the function of the Schaffgotsch story (pp. 74–77). He suggests that moral behavior in regard to marriage determines the success or failure of the island community and is therefore of the greatest importance (p. 75). Göres connects, though with insufficient research to make his point, the theme of adultery and Romantic theories of the state, especially those of Adam Müller, a friend of Arnim's. In his rush to emphasize the sanctity and value of marriage, which are certainly important to Arnim, he overlooks much of the story. Kratzsch, p. 10, sees parallels between Schaffgotsch and Albert but does not see the larger implications of this connection for the inner story, for the story as a whole, or for Arnim's adaptive technique.

breaks out in the stable; the narrator and the stableboy extinguish it with snow thrown into its center. The manner in which the narrator describes the fire seems to indicate that it bears some relationship to recent events; if the fire represents the Napoleonic wars and their threat to German society and culture, as symbolized by the country house, the narrator's role, with his attempt to extinguish the threat of the fire, corresponds to his efforts to snuff out the threat to German society posed by the foreign conqueror.

The narrator's strenuous efforts on the group's behalf cements his position within the group and, as a celebration of his reception into it, he is supposed to tell a story. He further reinforces the possibility of didactic influence when he says that the narrative will concern a colony similar to theirs (161). The mention of love shows the connection between the story of the first evening and this one, but also foreshadows, as does the remark of the lady of the house, the love interest in the frame. Both the colony of the frame, and that of the inner story are marooned, forced, under widely varying times and circumstances, back onto their own resources.

Joined by Arnim, there are two stories that make up this inner narrative, the "Amtsbericht vom Tode des Generals Grafen von Schaffgotsch" (Official report of the death of general count Von Schaffgotsch) and parts of the first volume of Johann Gottfried Schnabel's *Wunderliche Fata einiger Seefahrer, absonderlich Alberti Julii, eines gebohrnen Sachsens* (The unusual fortunes of some seafarers, especially Albert Julius, a native Saxon), often referred to as *Die Insel Felsenburg* (The Isle of Felsenburg). Migge notes that Arnim liked to link old stories and here used the history of Albert's family as the connecting point.[39] However, neither Migge nor Reichl realized that the story of Schaffgotsch has very striking parallels with the life history of Albert's father as related in *Felsenburg*.[40]

Arnim made a number of overall changes in the narrative structure of his adaptation in comparison with the *Felsenburg* original. Some of these changes came about because of the difference in format; since Armin was not planning a long Robinsonade, much material in *Felsenburg* could not be included. In *Felsenburg*, the main narrator is Eberhard

39. Migge, 2, p. 872.
40. Migge, 2, pp. 872–73; Reichl, 1, pp. 8–9.

Julius, a nephew of Albert Julius, who founded the colony. Captain Wolfgang, who has been in a shipwreck off the coast of Felsenburg, owes his life to Albert Julius and his colony. He promises to come back to Europe to find an honorable Julius and bring him to Albert before he dies. Schnabel's interest in portraying the life of this idealized colony and the roles of Albert's relatives was of no interest to Arnim, so he had to change the narrative plan to permit compression within a short space of the material most important to him, the founding of the colony. This section would have been of the most immediate interest to the *Wintergarten* group. The easiest way to do that was to choose a narrator who had only been to the island once. Although in *Felsenburg*, Captain Wolfgang does return to the island and marry, it was easy for Arnim to present him as a retired sea captain to whom Albert told his story.

The presentation of Wolfgang as the informed authority shows Arnim's more original approach in this adaptation when compared to his treatment of the Eurial story. This freedom is apparent at the outset, when he suggests with tongue in cheek that proof must be supplied, since we would not want to be taken in by some lazy fellow who just dreamed it up (161).[41] The informed authority, Captain Wolfgang, will satisfy the audience's needs and cover Arnim's own changes.[42] Because of the structural alterations Arnim made, he began with Wolfgang's story of his past, not Eberhard Julius's account. Reichl gives his usual thorough listing of the elements Arnim kept or changed, including the shift of birthplace and the absence of details about Wolfgang's life up until his graduation from the university.[43] He does not analyze these modifications or the passage Arnim added, in which he described the paradise-like landscape Prenzlau in the Uckermark, where the captain plans to spend the rest of his life (161). This idyllic landscape is filled

41. In a letter to Brentano written on November 14, 1808, Arnim suggests what he found attractive about the *Insel Felsenburg*, giving some indication of what elements he would emphasize in his reworking: "Schaffe Dir *Die Insel Felsenburg* an, es giebt vielleicht kein unterhaltenderes Buch, besonders den ersten Theil so romantisch und nationell und religiös lutherisch" (Steig, *Achim von Arnim*, 2, p. 264). This letter also provides an example of how Arnim tended to see relationships between sources such as the *Insel Felsenburg* and Schelmuffsky (p. 264).

42. Much to the despair of the brothers Grimm, Arnim was not concerned with philological exactness but with what he considered to be transmission of an inner truth; see Möllers, "Wirklichkeit," p. 37.

43. Reichl, 1, p. 7.

meadows continually "greening," and forests standing for centuries. However, the most prominent element in the landscape (*vor allem eingedenk*) (to be mindful above all) is the elegant church. The *Säulenwalde* (forest of columns) will replace the *Buchenwälder* (beech forest) until the Last Judgment. Wolfgang's future holds no surprises and he can meet it with steadfast fortitude, a state of affairs that contrasts sharply with that of the *Wintergarten* group. As if to emphasize the contrast Arnim added, immediately after the above description: "heute ist aber bei uns ein schreckhafter Sturm und mancherlei Weissagung" ["However, our condition today is one of terrible storm and sundry predictions"] (161).

The narrator breaks the group's rule here, as will often be the case in the course of the cycle. The storm refers not only to the season but, more importantly, to the political situation, the uncertainty of which is apparent in the numerous prophecies about it. Wolfgang has found his paradise; Albert has found his; even Schaffgotsch, in the hour of his horrible death, is certain of his own reward. Arnim's interjection of this remark just after the description of Wolfgang's gives the reader one quick glance at the tack Arnim will be taking in these stories, a direction that fits with the title "Das wiedergefundene Paradies" (Paradise regained). How did each man find it? Part of the answer lies in their relationship with God. In this story, Wolfgang, Albert, and Schaffgotsch all live in such a way that they will not be afraid to die; each suffers tests of faith and endurance.

In order to make Wolfgang's character parallel that of the other two men, Arnim had to leave out certain events of Wolfgang's youth. In *Wintergarten* the captain's university career involves a sober approach to his studies, a way of life broken only on the day he becomes a doctor when he overindulges himself (161). Schnabel's version is somewhat less exemplary. In *Felsenburg*, Wolfgang begins his drinking education with the support of an allowance his prospective father-in-law gives him. He had indeed been industrious and temperate prior to that happy change in his fortune, not out of virtue, but out of necessity. With ample funds at his disposal, Wolfgang begins the pursuit of debauchery with the same energy he previously devoted to his studies (*Felsenburg*, 31).[44] In the *Wintergarten*, Wolfgang's single drinking bout arises out

44. See Johann Gottfried Schnabel's *Wunderliche Fata einiger See-Fahrer, absonderlich Alberti Julii, eines gebohrnen Sachsens* (Nordhausen, 1736–52), p. 31. All subsequent quo-

of a pardonable excess of joy at finishing his education; in Schnabel, it is part of the regular routine. When the *Felsenburg* Wolfgang meets the *Eisenfresser* (fire eater), Schnabel made a connection between his drunken state and the murder (31); Arnim did not, perhaps because he was anxious to clean up this part of Wolfgang's life. At this point, Arnim left out great chunks of the captain's career, because they have little to do either with positive character development or with bringing him close to Albert and Felsenburg. For example, his almost successful seduction of the Javanese mistress of an Italian living on the Cape does not qualify as an appropriately Lutheran approach to life.[45]

Arnim's portrait of Wolfgang as a dependable and upright man is consistent with much of Schnabel's account.[46] When Schnabel left Wolfgang stranded on Felsenburg, he prepared to meet his death as a faithful Christian, praying continuously. But in *Wintergarten*, Wolfgang only suddenly begins to pray, remembering the prayers of childhood (162). Yet the idea of some sort of metanoia is present in this section of *Felsenburg*, when Schnabel noted that the feeling of abandonment and guilt lead one to God (*Felsenburg*, 85). Arnim built on this and emphasized the suddenness of the change because he did not have the time that Schnabel did to build up Wolfgang's character. The portrait of Wolfgang that appears in the *Wintergarten* shows that, far from being merely a careless translator, Arnim could change both structure and characterization in support of a goal. Wolfgang becomes a parallel figure to Albert and Schaffgotsch through the elimination of biographical details that do not fit, through the description of Prenzlau and through his sudden return to the prayers of his youth on the island.

With a similar intent in mind, that of drawing parallels between the earthly and heavenly paradise, Arnim changed the description of the first sight of the inner part of the island. He referred to this area as a "paradisical plain" (162), full of brooks, fruit, and flowers; Schnabel's account confines itself generally to details about the waterfall, only briefly mentioning the extraordinary beauty of the place (*Felsenburg*, 87). Arnim added other religious elements such as the detail about the cathedral-like appearance of the avenue of trees. This underscores the

---

tations are from this edition, which is referred to as *Felsenburg*. The quotations are in the text.

45. See note 41 for reference to Arnim's letter to Brentano, November 14, 1808.
46. See Albert's letter praising Wolfgang, p. 24; also pp. 32, 85.

religious nature of the place, as does the presence of Albert, who sits in the church like the vicar of Christ.[47]

In *Felsenburg*, Albert tells his relative Wolfgang and the newly-arrived Lutheran pastor the story of his life and the settlement of Felsenburg. He tells these stories in evening installments after they visit his various children. Since Arnim presented the story as a tale brought back in its entirety and left out mention of his descendants and other relatives, he told it at one fell swoop, not in pieces. But he did take over from the source the idea of dictating it, of it being written down. Occasionally Arnim makes use of one of Albert's interruptions in narrative to provide a transition of his own, as in the middle of the description of Albert's voyage with the Van Leuvens. Where Albert breaks off the story in the original (*Felsenburg*, 133), Arnim inserted a comment that sums up the material unnecessary for him to relate, such as some of the events on the voyage. This transition is somewhat abrupt, yet not out of place in an account that is told, not read: "Was soll ich Euch mit Reisegeschichten aufhalten, lieber Capitän, Ihr habt wohl deren schon zu viel selbst erlebt . . ." ["Why should I detain you with travel stories, dear captain, you have probably experienced too many of them . . ."] (174).

When one examines Albert's account of his early life, the similarities of Stephanus Julius's career with that of Schaffgotsch are quite striking (*Felsenburg*, 110–11). The major outlines of Julius's life, his career in the service of the state, the attempts of enemies during wartime to frame him, and the decapitation, can all be found in the Schaffgotsch story.

Although the similarities between the lives of the two men undoubtedly made a substitution seem appropriate to Arnim, one wonders if he would have chosen the Schaffgotsch narrative if there had not been important differences as well. Through his substitution of Schaffgotsch for Albert's father instead of Stephen Julius, he intimates that Albert was of noble birth (163).[48] Since Arnim had deleted those parts of *Felsenburg* that dealt with Eberhard Julius, he was able to give Albert

---

47. The reawakening interest in Gothic architecture in the eighteenth century often compared it with trees and other natural forms. See W. D. Robson-Scott, *The Literary Background of the Gothic Revival in Germany: A Chapter in the History of Taste* (Oxford, 1965), pp. 96, 103.

48. Reichl notes Arnim's departure from the *Felsenburg* narrative at this point, 1, p. 8.

aristocratic parentage. This motif is a common one and helps to increase narrative interest. Another difference that certainly attracted Arnim would have been Schaffgotsch's piety. While Schnabel mentions Stephen Julius's unwillingness to be untrue to his religious beliefs, Schaffgotsch's behavior presents detailed information on this point (169). Schaffgotsch's pronounced Lutheran beliefs may also have attracted Arnim to this story, since he praised that quality in Schnabel. Upon being asked if he wants a Lutheran pastor or a Jesuit, Schaffgotsch replies: "Wollte Gott, . . . ihr solltet lutherischen Schriften gelesen haben, ihr würdet nimmermehr einen Jesuiten begehren" [". . .you should have read Lutheran writings, then you would never again want a Jesuit"] (168).

With this story, Arnim shows that Schaffgotsch, Albert's father, was able to maintain his constancy to his beliefs under the most trying of circumstances, as his son later does. Much more than the Stephen Julius story could have done, the dramatic account of a steadfast aristocrat unjustly condemned strengthens the exemplary value of Albert's life by "doubling" it in the person of his father. This didactic underpinning appears in a story with a certain amount of narrative interest: the astrological prophecy whose truth is proved in an extraordinary way and the tension about Schaffgotsch's fate hold the readers' interest.

Arnim made further changes in young Albert's autobiography that show his careful attention to his source. Arnim left out Albert's happy sojourn with a Lutheran pastor found in Schnabel, but combined some elements of that with Albert's stay with the *Amtsmann* (official) (*Wintergarten*, 172; *Felsenburg*, 112).[49] For the sake of brevity, Arnim had the official's wife perform some of the functions of the pastor's wife in *Felsenburg*, preserving the contrast between the good and the bad woman but condensing the account of two families into one. Arnim also made the contrast between the teachers more definite. His tutor at the official's house gives him instruction in those subjects pleasing to the Almighty (172).

The kind woman who took Albert in dies. In her place comes the new wife of the official, a young woman who dislikes Albert. Because

---

49. Reichl is inaccurate in his discussion of this section. He writes: "Von dem Aufenthalt bei dem Prediger weiß Arnim nichts;" 1, p. 9. The comparison of the pertinent passages from the two works shows that Arnim did use the stay with the pastor, but in a more subtle way.

of the stepmother's cruel treatment of his charge, the honorable tutor leaves (172). The student tutor who replaces him finds his private lessons with the official's second wife most rewarding. Arnim left out Schnabel's wittily bawdy comments, perhaps to portray Albert as exceptionally shy in sexual matters, so as to make his behavior towards Concordia more credible.

In his portrayal of Lemelie, Arnim modified his source in a unique way, in contrast to his treatment of the other major male characters. In the case of Wolfgang and Albert, he left out those parts of the original that might have reflected badly on them. For Lemelie, Arnim did the opposite, except in Lemelie's final speech, where he avoided the sort of grisly or coarse detail that he characteristically omitted in adaptations. He deleted those parts of Lemelie's speeches that did have the effect of veiling Lemelie's lechery to some degree, as in the scene about a month after Van Leuven's death. In the original, Lemelie offers to care for Concordia's unborn child as he announces he is going to exercise the rights of a husband in three days (*Felsenburg*, 208). Arnim left this detail out. He also excised Lemelie's flowery remarks about fate and their future (*Felsenburg*, 207–8), perhaps because he thought both elements were incompatible with Lemelie's true character.

In his efforts to put his own stamp on Lemelie, Arnim motivated his behavior more consistently than Schnabel did. As he recovers from his illness, Lemelie pretends he is sicker than he is, so he can stay alone with Concordia (*Felsenburg*, 192; *Wintergarten*, 182). Schnabel went into more detail about Lemelie's attempts and had him promise never to say anything more if Concordia does not tell her husband. When Schnabel's Lemelie senses that Van Leuven knows about his behavior, he tries to improve and succeeds to a great extent (*Felsenburg*, 193). Had Arnim included such an apparent change of heart, it would have weakened the perception of Lemelie as the Devil Incarnate (see 185), which Arnim apparently wanted to maintain for him. In this role, Lemelie in *Wintergarten* can serve as the most negative counterpart possible to Wolfgang and Albert, emphasizing their good qualities through his negative ones. Arnim did not let Lemelie realize that Concordia had told her husband. Arnim motivated Lemelie's changed behavior through his hope of avoiding betrayal, a more probable reason for Lemelie than repentance (182). Arnim also foreshadowed Van Leuven's murder more effectively than Schnabel, who sent Lemelie out an hour before Van Leuven goes (*Felsenburg*, 199); Arnim had him depart directly after Van Leuven has left (*Wintergarten*, 183).

Arnim shortened the gruesome catalog of Lemelie's crimes (incest, whoring, patricide, matricide, poisoning), all of which Schnabel dwelt on in rather extensive detail (*Felsenburg*, 213–5).[50] This tendency repeated itself again and again in Arnim's adaptations and should not be interpreted as an attempt to spare Lemelie, especially since Lemelie himself recounts the details of Van Leuven's murder (185–86) and since Arnim paraphrased or left out the most moving part of Lemelie's final speeches. The following section shows how differently Arnim approached Lemelie:

"Dann bat er um einen tödlichen Gnadenstoß: bei Gott wäre für ihn keine Gnade, er müsse ins Reich des Teufels, dem er lange ergeben, ewig verbleiben" ["Then he begged for a fatal finishing blow: as there was no mercy for him from God, he would have to go for eternity to the realm of the Devil, to whom he had long ago yielded"] (Arnim, 185).

. . .mithin meiner Leibes-und Gewissens-quaal [sic] ein Ende machen, denn ihr seyd dessen, eurer Rache wegen wol berechtiget, ich aber will solches dannoch vor eine besondere Gnade der Menschen erkennen, weil ich doch bey Gott keine Gnade und Barmherzigkeit zu hoffen habe, sondern gewiß weiß, daß ich in dem Reiche des Teuffels, welchem ich mich schon seit vielen Jahren ergeben, auf ewig verbleiben werde. (*Felsenburg*, 212)

Therefore make an end to the torment of my conscience and my body, because you are certainly justified, on the grounds of revenge, to do so; I, however, would look upon such an end as a special act of mercy by others, since I have no hope of finding pardon and mercy with God, as I know for certain that I will have to remain for eternity in the kingdom of the devil to whom I yielded myself many years ago.

Lemelie's final speech, which shows some glimmering of repentance, does not appear in *Wintergarten* (*Felsenburg*, 218). In *Wintergarten*, Lemelie's parting words are more reminiscent of the spirit of the chapbook Faust:" . . . ich aber muß fort zu des Teufels Quartieren!"

---

50. Weiss, "Harmonisierung," notes that Arnim generally seems reluctant to depict violent actions and death, citing Lemelie as an exception (p. 85). Even here, though, as the analysis has shown, Arnim tones down his version from the original. Lemelie, although not a major character, helped Arnim to dramatize the themes of marriage and the earthly paradise.

["... I however must go away to the Devil's quarters!"] (186). This adaptation continues the consistency with which Arnim developed his characterization of Lemelie.

The last major group of changes that Arnim made from his source centers around Albert and his relationship to Concordia. Schnabel's portrait of Albert just before Concordia releases him from his oath differs sharply from that of Arnim.[51] The treatment of one minor incident, the sighting of a ship, shows how different Schnabel's Albert is. In Schnabel, Albert wants to leave the island, but Concordia is not at all interested in attracting the ship's attention.[52] In Arnim, the ship sighting comes much later, as Albert composes a poem. The feelings that Schnabel discussed at great length in the following quotation are only hinted at in the song ("Die Sehnsucht hat es hergeschickt, die Sehnsucht hat es fortgetrieben") ["Longing has brought it here, longing has driven it away"] (191). Schnabel's Albert is young and rich and wants to return to a well-ordered society to find a wife instead of waiting for little Concordia to grow up (*Felsenburg*, 249). These practical and reasonable thoughts, which would be considered a normal reaction to the situation, find no place in Arnim. His Albert is hopelessly in love; social position and a new life in Europe apparently do not enter his head. The introduction of this section of the story in Arnim is quite abrupt, in part because Arnim had left out passages, but also to some degree because he changed Albert's character. Reichl notes that Arnim's Albert is more sentimental,[53] but does not examine what function this sentimentality has, which is to show that steadfastness and courage are worthy qualities and to demonstrate that not just for this story, but for the work as a whole and the society that hears it. Lukrezia's constancy brought her misery and death, perhaps because she practiced it in the wrong context. Schaffgotsch dies as a result of his faithfulness, but with the promise of a heavenly reward; Albert's courage brings "das wiedergefundene Paradies." Herein lies a message for the *Wintergarten* society.

51. In a perceptive remark, Reichl notes the changes: In *Felsenburg*, Albert wants to leave so that he can marry; in Arnim, Albert thinks only of Concordia (Reichl, 1, pp. 14–15).

52. As Reichl points out, 1, p. 14, this state of affairs makes it natural for Albert to discuss his feelings.

53. Reichl, 1, p. 15.

Near the end of Arnim's adaptation, Albert's longing for Concordia conflicts so sharply with the promise he has made not to take advantage of her that he releases his feelings in a song that has a significantly different tone than *Felsenburg*. The two versions are as follows:

Felsenburg

Ach! hätt ich nur kein Schiff erblickt,
So wär ich länger ruhig blieben
Mein Unglück hat es her geschickt,
Und mir zur Quaal zurück getrieben,
Verhängniß wilst du dich denn eines reichen Armen,
Und freyen Sclavens nicht zu rechter Zeit erbarmen?

Alas! If I had only not caught sight of the ship, then I would have remained at peace longer. My misfortune has sent it here and driven it back to torment me. Destiny, would you not like to take pity at the right time on a rich poor man and a free slave?

Soll meiner Jugend bester Krafft
In dieser Einsamkeit ersterben?
Ist das der Keuschheit Eigenschafft?
Will mich die Tugend selbst verderben?
So weiß ich nicht wie man die lasterhafften Seelen
Mit größrer Grausamkeit und Marter solte quälen.

Should the best strength of my youth fade away in this solitude? Is that characteristic of continence? Does virtue itself want to destroy me? Then I would not know how one could torment blasphemous souls with greater cruelty and agony.

Ich liebe was und sag' es nicht,
Denn Eyd und Tugend heißt mich schweigen,
Mein ganz verdecktes Liebes-Licht
Darff seine Flamme gar nicht zeigen,
Dem Himmel selbsten ist mein Lieben nicht zuwieder
Doch Schwur und Treue schlägt den Hoffnungs-Bau darnieder.

I love something and do not mention it, because oath and virtue call me to silence. My entire hidden light of love may not show its flame. To Heaven itself my love is not offensive, yet vow and fidelity destroy the edifice of hope.

Concordia du Wunder Bild,
Man lernt an dir die Eintracht kennen,
Doch was in meinem Hertzen quillt

Muß ich in Wahrheit Zwietracht nennen,
Ach! Liesse mich das Glück mit dir vereinigt leben,
Wir würden nimmer mehr in Haß und Zwietracht schweben.

Concordia, you are a marvelous image, one learns to know harmony from you, yet what gushes up from my heart I must truthfully describe as discord. Alas, if fortune would let me be united with you, we would no longer be suspended in hate and disharmony.

Doch bleib in deiner stillen Ruh,
Ich suche solche nicht zu stöhren;
Mein eintzigs Wohl und Weh bist du,
Allein ich will der Sehnsucht wehren,
Weil deiner Schönheit Pracht vor mich zu kostbar scheinet,
Und weil des Schicksals Schluß mein Wünschen glatt verneinet.

Yet remain in your hushed peace, I do not seek to disturb something like that; you are my only happiness and sorrow, I just want to restrain longing, since the magnificence of your beauty seems too precious for me and since the decision of fate flatly denies my wishing.

Ich gönne dir ein beßres Glück,
Verknüpft mit noch viel höhern Stande.
Führt uns der Himmel nur zurück
Nach unserm werthen Vater-Lande.
So wirst du letzlich noch dies harte Schicksal loben,
Ist gleich vor deinen Freund was schlechteres aufgehoben:

I wish for you a better fortune, linked with a much higher station in life. If Heaven only brings us back to our dear Fatherland, then you will in the end praise this hard fate, even though for your friend something worse is provided.

(255–56)

Wintergarten

Ach hätt ich nur kein Schiff erblickt,
So wär ich länger ruhig blieben,
Die Sehnsucht hat es hergeschickt,
Die Sehnsucht hat es fortgetrieben,
O Liebe willst du dich denn eines reichen Armen
Und freien Sklaven nicht zu rechter Zeit erbarmen.

O, if only I had not glimpsed a ship, then I would have remained longer at peace. Longing has sent it here, longing has sent it away. O love, do you not want to take pity in time on a rich poor man and a free slave?

Ich liebe was und sag es nicht,
Denn Eid und Tugend heißt mich schweigen,
Mein ganz verdecktes Liebeslicht,
Darf seine Flamme gar nicht zeigen,
Zum Himmel treibt es seine reinen hellen Strahlen,
Die Sonne ist ein Widerschein von meinen Qualen.

I love something and do not say so, because oath and virtue call me to silence.
My completely hidden light of love may not show its flame, it sends its pure
bright beams towards heaven; the sun is a reflection of my torture.

Ein Fruchtbaum, der von Früchten schwer,
Hängt seine Früchte zu der Erden,
Kommt starker Wind von Osten her,
Er kann nicht froh erschüttert werden,
Er stürzt herab die Früchte und die schwachen Blüten
Und meine Träume, die mir Nachts so herrlich glühten.

A fruit tree, heavy with fruit, bends down towards the earth with its fruit. If a
strong wind comes from the east, the tree cannot rejoice at being shaken. It
loses the fruit and the tender blossoms and my dreams, that gleam so wonder-
fully to me at night.

Den trägen Tag verfolgt der Mond,
Er atmet Ruh auf alle Wesen,
Das Meer ist keiner Ruh gewohnt,
Zur Unruh bin ich so erlesen,
Mein einzig Glück, den Traum muß ich voraus schon hassen,
Im höchsten Glück wird er mich wiederum verlassen.

The moon pursues the languid day. It breathes peace on all creatures. The sea
is not used to peace, I too have been singled out for disquiet. My only happiness, the dream, I must hate in advance, for at the moment of greatest happiness it will leave me again.

Concordia bleib in Deiner Ruh,
Nie werd ich Deine Entracht stören,
Mein einzig Wohl und Weh bist Du,
Dir will ich ew'gen Frieden schwören,
O süßer letzter Augenblick, da darf ich sprechen,
Da wird der Liebe Strom durch Aug und Lippen brechen (191–92).

Concordia, remain in your peace, I will never seek to disturb your harmony,
you are my only joy and sorrow, I want to swear eternal harmony to you. O
sweet final moment, then I may speak, then the torrent of love will break
through eye and lips.

The sighting of a ship occasions the song in both instances, but the reactions of the two Alberts are quite different. Schnabel's character (lines 3–4) reflects Albert's intense longing to leave; the corresponding lines in Arnim's poem reflect the ambiguity in Albert's mind—an inchoate desire for a beginning elsewhere coupled with a strong wish to remain there with Concordia in a deeper relationship. Schnabel ascribed his character's fate to destiny (line 5); Arnim imputed it to love.

Arnim left out Schnabel's second stanza, in which Albert complains of loss of youth and personal ruin through virtue, since it runs counter to the portrait of Albert that Arnim had drawn. Arnim moved Schnabel's third stanza into second place; this strophe makes the general message of the first stanza more particular. Arnim changed the last two lines of Schnabel's version, taking the idea that heaven approved of this love and making part of heaven a reflection of his devotion. His version does not have the hopelessness of Schnabel's last line.

Schnabel's fourth and sixth stanzas also fall away, since they deal with the strained atmosphere between Albert and Concordia due to his desire to return to Europe. Neither discord nor a strong longing to leave appear in Arnim's version, so he replaced them with two stanzas that use nature symbols and conditions to express his mood.

The third stanza describes Concordia as a tree, full of fruit and tender blossoms, ready to bear an abundant harvest. The harvest will be destroyed by a strong wind from the east—Albert's passion—that will ruin the fruits, blossoms, and his dreams. In the fourth stanza, Albert, like the sea, has no peace (line 21).

Arnim kept the first half of Schnabel's fifth stanza (lines 25-28) but changed the last three lines, which in Schnabel emphasize the hopelessness of his love (lines 28–30), to an avowal of love. In Arnim's Albert, there is no thought of self-preservation or of the difference in their social class. Arnim's changes in Schnabel's poem reflect these differences and also support the portrait of Albert that *Wintergarten* has been at pains to draw.

Arnim's sense for the literary taste of his time reveals itself in the adaptation of Concordia's letter and subsequent betrothal scene in the *Wintergarten*, which show marked improvement in literary quality over the Schnabel version (*Felsenburg*, 262–63).[54] Upon its receipt,

54. Reichl, 1, says, ". . . an Stelle der Galanterie hat er auch hier das Gefühl gesetzt" (p. 17).

Felsenburg's Albert has an attack of pomposity (*Felsenburg*, 264); Arnim's Albert simply plucks up his courage and goes to Concordia, saying, "Was bin ich gegen Euch" ["What am I compared with you?"] (193).[55] Arnim also shortened and improved Concordia's speech, allowing the tenderness to come through.

The contrast between the love affair of Schlick and Lukrezia, and that of Albert and Concordia, could hardly be greater. In the first instance, an illicit relationship takes place at the highest levels of Italian society, in the appropriate luxury, with no religious considerations playing a role. In the second, Albert and Concordia, through the purity of their characters, their ideals, and their determination to behave in a manner consonant with their religious beliefs, bring about the destruction of evil and the establishment of a paradise. The figures of Captain Wolfgang and Schaffgotsch reinforce the value of moral example. Schaffgotsch's story, while meant to foreshadow Albert's own faithfulness in a difficult situation, also provided yet another opportunity for Arnim to present a picture of a German who remained true to his principles even when his life was in danger, an example that, from the context, would seem to be salutory for the assembled company. The emphasis on marriage is an implicit criticism of the lady of the house, while at the same time, it holds out a goal to be strived for as she makes difficult emotional adjustments in the course of the work.

Dritter Winterabend
"Altdeutsche Landsleute"
(Compatriots from an Earlier Age)

Arnim's source for the story of the third winter evening, Thomas Lirer's *Schwäbische Chronik* (Swabian chronicle), marked the first time that Arnim used a chronicle, as opposed to purely fictional accounts,

---

55. Weiss, "Harmonisierung," notes that Arnim, in contrast to other Romantic authors such as Tieck and Hoffmann, reunites lovers, usually in marriage (pp. 82, 83). The fact that Arnim not only separates Eurial and Lukrezia but also dwells on their separation is an indication of how seriously he viewed the idea he was trying to put across, since his treatment of Eurial and Lukrezia differs so markedly from his usual tendencies.

as the basis for his inner stories in the *Wintergarten*.[56] Arnim's "Alt-deutsche Landsleute" is the first of a series of narratives in the frame that have as their bases military-political chronicles. This story is followed by Moscherosch's account of the Thirty Years' War in the fourth evening, Froissart's description of the turmoil in fourteenth-century France and, finally, the history of the Scottish Rebellion in the ninth evening. The preponderance of chronicles as sources should not be surprising, given Arnim's ideas on the didactic and inspirational possibilities in these materials (see the frame discussion for the sixth evening). The "Altdeutsche Landsleute" story makes a good transition to the political and military themes of subsequent evenings, since it continues the love interest that figured prominently in the first two inner narratives, yet lends emphasis to martial episodes as well, such as the numerous campaigns in Germany and those against the heathens.

Lirer's work is full of inaccuracies and belongs more in the realm of fiction than history.[57] He seems to have lived at the same time his chronicle was printed and not in earlier centuries, as he himself maintained. He was from Vorarlberg and was in the service of the counts of Werdenberg. He probably was a member of the class of well-to-do free peasants and may have obtained the knowledge he displays in the chronicle on numerous military campaigns.[58] At the end of the first part of his chronicle, Lirer claims that he went with the lords of Werdenberg as a servant on their trip to Portugal and that he wrote these events down on St. Oswald's Day, 1133.[59] His chronicle purports

56. Monty Jacobs, in "Arnims 'Altdeutsche Landsleute,' " *Euphorion* 16 (1909), pp. 179–80, shows that Arnim's purported source, the *Zimmerische Chronik*, was not what Arnim used . His library in Weimar contains the 1761 edition of the *Schwäbische Chronik*, edited by Johann Reinhard Wegelin. I have used Wegelin for information about the introduction and notes that Arnim would have had at hand; however, since this chronicle is scarce, I have used Eugen Thurnher's edition, *Thomas Lirer: Schwäbische Chronik* (Bregenz, 1962), for purposes of quotation.
57. See Thurnher, *Lirer*, pp. xiii–xxii.
58. Thurnher, *Lirer*, pp. x, xiv.
59. Lirer says, "Und ich Thoman Lirer gesessen zu Ranckweil das do gehört zu dem Schloß und herrschafft Felltkirch hab diese ding den merern tail gesehen. und auch vil an frumen leuten erfragt und erfarn. an warhafften herren rittern und knechten die mich des gar warlich underricht habent. dann ich auch meins gnädigen herren von Werdenberg knecht bin gewesen und mit ym außgefaren gen Portigal. und mit ym wider haim kumen. Und ist das buch zum ersten abgeschriben worden in dem als man zalt von der geburt Christs xj. hundert und im xxxiij. iar an sant Oßwalts tag." Thurnher, *Lirer*, p. 52. Thurnher points out that the counts of Werdenberg did not exist before the middle of the thirteenth century. Since there was no kingdom of Portugal in 1133, a trip there seems unlikely (p. xiii). As Thurnher notes, such inconsistencies were not uncommon in medieval and late medieval chronicles (p. xiii).

to be a history of the development of Swabia from the time of the fictional Roman emperor Curio, who settled the territory up to the year 1462. The work was extremely successful and, within a few years, there were three editions. Since Wegelin reissued it, it must have remained popular through the sixteenth and seventeenth centuries.[60]

Although Lirer's veracity had been under attack even during his lifetime, his inconsistencies did not trouble his eighteenth-century editor.[61] Wegelin's attitude most probably influenced Arnim; Wegelin believed the chronicle deserved attention, not only because of the dialect, but also because of examples of Swabian simplicity and honesty.[62] In Wegelin's approach there are affinities with Arnim's own ideas about the value of the preservation of the past, since it emphasizes the virtuous character of the Swabians, whom Arnim refers to as *altdeutsche*.

An additional aspect of Lirer's chronicle that may have appealed to Arnim is that Lirer, like Arnim, used historical events for ends that transcended the events themselves. Lirer's work still stands under the influence of the tendency of medieval historical writing to see temporal events in the context of their relationship to Christ's life and Passion, how such events relate to that and to the Last Judgment;[63] Arnim, as we have seen, sought inspiration for a dismal German present in a past where life, religion, and nationalism were more coherently and effectively linked.

One of the most striking aspects of the part of the chronicle that Arnim used is the ethnic consciousness among the Germans abroad and their willingness to help one another. When Von Wolffegk and his nephew Arbogast flee to Portugal, a resident German, Oswald von Hatstadt, helps them to make their way at court.[64] Arbogast, even though imprisoned, refuses to reveal his identity to anyone but Germans, saying only in response to questions that he himself is a German.[65] This fidelity to their countrymen and their willingness to help

60. Thurnher, *Lirer*, p. xi.
61. Thurnher, *Lirer*, p. xi.
62. Quoted by Thurnher, *Lirer*, p. xi. See also Wegelin, *Schwäbische Chronik* (no page numbers).
63. Thurnher, *Lirer*, pp. xvii–xxv. A useful essay for literary scholars on medieval historiography is Herbert Grundmann's *Geschichtsschreibung im Mittelalter* (Göttingen, 1965).
64. Thurnher, *Lirer*, p. 40; Arnim, *Wintergarten*, p. 199. Arbogast, even though imprisoned, refuses to reveal his identity to anyone but Germans, saying only in response to questions that he himself is a German.
65. Thurnher, *Lirer*, pp. 41, 47; Arnim, *Wintergarten*, pp. 201, 205.

each other stand in sharp contrast to the behavior portrayed in the frame by the envoy, as he describes the deportment of many Germans abroad:

Nie habe ich gesehen, daß diese Leute als treue Landsleute einer für alle und alle für einen und für die Ehre ihres Landes gestanden, wie oft habe ich ihnen einzelne verunglückte Landsleute empfohlen, die mit Aufopferung eines Vergnügens errettet werden konnten, aber umsonst, sie konnten Vaterland, Ehre und Leben wie Spieler aufgeben, nur nicht einen Tag des Vergnügens. (198)

Never have I seen that these people have stood as real compatriots one for all and all for one and for the honor of their country, how often have I commended to them unfortunate fellow countrymen, who could have been saved with the sacrifice of one pleasure, but in vain: they could give up their country, their honor and their lives like gamblers, just not one day of self-gratification.

In "Altdeutsche Landsleute," Oswald von Hatstadt not only helps Germans who come to the court, but also lies in prison for the abduction of the king's daughter, a deed he did not commit. Albrecht von Werdenberg makes two trips to Rhodes to rescue a compatriot, and another to Portugal, in part to get von Hatstadt released from prison. Walter von Wolffegk cares for the nephew he has taken from an unworthy mother. All of these examples of Germans ready to sacrifice for their countrymen must have seemed an especially attractive part of the story to Arnim.[66]

Another element in the chronicle that might have appealed to Arnim was the readiness of some of the Germans to take blood revenge; once again, the envoy's remarks offer a clue as to how we are to interpret the significance of the chronicle. In a significant passage, the envoy notes that Germans in the present age seem incapable of "Blutrache aus Frömmigkeit" (a pious blood revenge); in the proper context, revenge is not a vice, but the sword of divine justice. Rejection of such vengeance separates the individual from God (196–7). This kind of blood revenge appears in the chronicle excerpt that Arnim used. Von Lirer's account is little more circumspect than that in *Wintergarten*: ". . . ward der hertzog von Schwaben erschlagen von seinem diener

66. Göres, *Verhältnis*, p. 71, reaches a similar conclusion; he points out that, after Napoleon's defeat of Prussia, a sense of community among the Germans was lost. He believes that Arnim chose the story because it offered corrective examples for the present age and offered Arnim a means to teach through contrast what his contemporaries lacked (pp. 71–73).

aim der was sein vogt hieß Walther Wolffegk. der fand yn bei seiner
swester" [". . . the Duke of Swabia was killed by his retainer . . . who
was his overseer and was called Walther von Wolffegk. He found the
duke with his sister"].[67] Arnim gave a little more detail, motivating von
Wolffegk's revenge with his strong emotions: "Als er die Stiege seines
Hauses schnell hinauf gegangen um seine Schwester, die Frau des von
Andelon, Landvogts zu Straßburg, zu begrüßen, da fand er seinen
Herrn bei ihr, in unziemlicher Vertraulichkeit. Der Schimpf übernahm
ihn so heiß, daß er ihn und seine Schwester erschlug . . ." ["When he
went up the steps of his house in order to greet his sister, the wife of
von Andelon, the provincial governor of Straßburg, he found his own
lord with her in unseemly intimacy. The affront overpowered him so
strongly that he killed him and his sister"] (198–99).

In interpreting this passage, Göres says that, in Arnim's eyes, such
terrible revenge is allowed because marriage is God's will; the execution of such retribution, therefore, reflects the seriousness with which
God wishes men to regard the breaking of marriage vows. As a consequence, Göres sees the alienation of the Germans from God in the envoy's remarks about shutting oneself off from God when one is incapable of revenge.[68] The Germans' lack of interest or inability to seek
revenge is a sign of their deficiency of faith,[69] a failing that paralyzes
them at the present. The envoy brings this indictment of his countrymen in connection with their behavior towards the French. Many
Germans have collaborated with the enemy, a dishonorable act for any
German, if he lets himself be used by foreigners against Germans (p.
197). The behavior of the Germans in the chronicle is quite different,
since they stand with their countrymen in adversity; as such, they function as role models for the Germans of Arnim's day.

The envoy brings other criticisms of the Germans to the attention of
his hearers, remarks that have an implicit connection to the theme of
the inner story. The mocker of all things German, who scorns his native
country, has plagued the envoy in his foreign posts. While the figures
in "Altdeutsche Landsleute" are not chauvinistic, they scorn neither
nationality nor their fellow countrymen in need, and they have a good
reputation abroad (200, 201). Germans who denigrate their own nation give up any attempt of changing things for the better, saying that

67. Thurnher, *Lirer*, p. 39.   68. Göres, *Verhältnis*, p. 72.
69. Göres, *Verhältnis*, p. 72.

their only hope is in their children. The envoy seems to speak for Arnim when he says that no child will be educated without a living example; such education consists of the family's transmission of the historical wealth that has been given to them as an inheritance to their children (197). Without knowledge of their past, Germans are doomed to the same sort of destructive behavior that those collaborators with the French perpetrate. Part of this unwillingness to sacrifice for the German nation lies in the mistaken belief that a foreign education is better for a child, with the result that the child knows and cares little about his native land (197–98).[70]

Because the story as it stands provides the kind of exemplary material Arnim needed, he changed little, though he used some of the adaptive techniques that cropped up in other stories. He maintained the unreflecting, brisk tone of the narrative, with little interest in the characters' feelings. As in other adaptations, Arnim did leave out many of the tedious and extraneous details, such as the account of the quarrel between Albert von Werdenberg and his brother.[71] Lirer's version of the aftermath of the slaying of von Wolffegk's sister is more diffuse and less effective. He had von Wolffegk flee, than let him go through negotiations that lead to his journey to Portugal. Only at this point did Lirer mention anything about a son but his account has two sons, Arbogast and Andelon.[72] Arnim mentioned only one son, Arbogast von Andalon, whose father was Landvogt of Straßburg. Lirer seems to alternate between one son and two sons, a situation that distracts the readers and dilutes attention to the fate of Arbogast, the story's main focus—the readiness of Germans in earlier times to help each other. Arnim added a motif of fidelity and self-sacrifice that is not in the original and that supports the connection made earlier in the discussion of interaction between the frame story and the inner story. When Wolffegk prepares to be banished from Swabia forever, Arnim makes the following remark, which is not in Lirer: "Walther unterwarf sich diesem Urteile gegen den Willen des Grafen von Werdenberg, doch aus

70. The ambassador's remarks about education in one's native country foreshadow the conversation in the frame of the sixth evening, where the value of memoirs figures prominently.

71. Thurnher, *Lirer*, pp. 42–43.

72. Thurnher, *Lirer*, p. 40, gives only the following terse reference: "Und nam mit ym seiner swester sün Arbogast und Andelon." We hear no more about Andelon until Albrecht von Werdenberg arrives at the court of Portugal (p. 44). Instead of Arbogast, Andelon appears in prison (p. 47).

Liebe zu ihm . . ." ["Walther submitted himself to this verdict against the will of the count of Werdenberg, yet he did it out of love to him"] (199).

The next group of departures from the source occurs in the final section, in which Arbogast and the Portuguese princess are reunited. Arnim's account of their falling in love in Portugal, their separation when Arbogast is captured during a battle with heathens, his abduction to Rhodes, all remain close to Lirer. The account of Albrecht von Werdenberg's first visit to Rhodes to get a likeness for the princess's identification was also close to Lirer. But after the secret departure of Princess Elisa with Werdenberg and Amisa, the lady-in-waiting, Arnim made several additions and changes, among them Arbogast placing his head in the mysterious lady's lap (205–6) and the medieval love poem, translated by Arnim from Reinmar von Hagenau's "Hôhe alsam diu sunne stêt das herze mîn" [As high as the sun stands my heart].[73] Arnim's readiness to add this song, which is not in Lirer, though the singing itself is mentioned, undoubtedly reflects his love of older German poetry.

The major change that Arnim made was that of marriage partners. The late medieval original thought it entirely appropriate that Arbogast defer to Albrecht von Werdenberg in regard to Elisa's hand and marry instead Amisa, who was more suited to him in background. Arnim felt rightly that this turn of events made a bad story, since the reader was not prepared for it. Graf von Pfirt comes with a solution, a change of roles, and everyone is happy, including the king of Portugal, when he gives over his kingdom to a boy who is his grandson in name only.

Perhaps Arnim made this change, not only because the original version's ending was unsatisfying from the point of view of narrative structure, but also because he wanted to show that Arbogast's fidelity to his compatriots as well as that of Albrecht von Werdenberg was rewarded. In this sense, the story is, as the envoy says in introducing it, "trostreich" (full of comfort) (198), not only because it shows Germans who do help each other, but also because they are happier for it in the end.

The preceding discussion has shown that Arnim's purpose in adapt-

73. Reichl, 1, p. 22, wrongly identifies the song as one of Friedrich von Hausen's. In Hugo Moser, Helmut Tervooren, *Des Minnesangs Frühling* (Stuttgart, 1977) it is listed in the Reinmar section, 182, 14, pp. 353–54.

ing this story seemed to lie not so much in the changes he made in it (which in many ways are less significant than they are in other inner stories in the frame) but in its implicit relationship, one of contrast, to the outer frame. The story as it was preserved in the chronicles suited its purposes, though the alterations he made improved the story and, therefore, made it a more effective vehicle for the transmission of the ideas he wanted to emphasize.

The closing remarks of the envoy hold up as an ideal the positive behavior of *Landsleute* who remain faithful and ready for sacrifice for their countrymen: ". . . als treue Landsleute einer für alle und alle für einen und für die Ehre ihres Landes gestanden" [". . . stood as faithful compatriots one for all and all for one and as well for the honor of their country"] (198). The repeated references to *Landsleute* (compatriots) in this paragraph echo the title of the third evening, "Altdeutsche Landsleute," in which many Germans are ready to sacrifice for their countrymen. This repetition of *Landsleute* referring both to the Germans of Arnim's time as well as medieval ones underscores the connections Arnim was trying to make in *Wintergarten* between the German present and the German past.

Vierter Winterabend
(Fourth Winter Evening)

The transitional nature of the third story, which dealt with both amorous and military themes, points ahead to the concerns of the fourth evening, entitled "Der Krieg / nach alten Erzählungen" (the war / according to old tales). Perhaps more than on any other evening, the events of the present continually impinge. The deliberate ambiguity of the title hints at what is to come: does it refer to war in general, the Napoleonic wars, or earlier conflicts? As the ensuing discussion will show, the title concerns all three categories.

The evening belongs to the invalid, since he is the only veteran and the only one who has really suffered because of the war and his devotion to his country. His patriotism has already appeared in the first evening, when he remonstrated with the lady of the house about her love for a French officer. The patriotism of the invalid is larger than, but inclusive of, military service. He understands the horrors of war but is no pacifist; although his own life attests to the necessity for personal bravery in the face of attack, his goal for his nation seems to be larger than reaction to an invasion, as his role in both earlier and subsequent evenings shows.

The invalid opens this section with a rather grisly account of a soldier who used his detached arm as ammunition in a cannon. When the soldier could no longer shoot, he began to write, one of his efforts being a list of rules for soldiers. The personal bravery and sacrifice of this individual for a cause foreshadow a major theme of this section on war: the horrors of battle and the real bravery it demands. In some respects, both this figure and the invalid reflect Arnim, who did not fight but who wanted to be helpful to the cause through his writing.

The *Kriegsregeln* (rules for war), which appear almost at the beginning of the fourth evening, have some parallels to an inspiring speech that General Blücher delivered to his men in Göttingen in 1806. Arnim, who heard the speech, was zealously distributing leaflets meant for use by the soldiers in the singing of patriotic songs. Because of this well-known interest of Arnim's in such music, the general assumption has been that Blücher's speech was his only inspiration for prefacing his story with a series of rules in verse form for soldiers.[74] Arnim's tendency to include his own poetry in his works has seemed to confirm this supposition. Yet, examination of Moscherosch's *Soldatenleben* (Soldiers' life), the source for the Philander section, suggests otherwise, for Moscherosch's description of Philander among the brigands came directly after a section on the conduct of soldiers. This section includes rules for their behavior, the last part in verse.[75]

74. Migge, 2, p. 873. W. Kosch, *Deutsches Literaturlexikon* 1 (Bern, 1968), notes that Arnim was in Göttingen in the summer of 1806 with Blücher's troops, distributing fliers of his war poems (p. 152). Steig, in *Achim von Arnim*, 1, p. 196, gives an account of Blücher's visit.

75. The work from which the *Soldatenleben* comes was a somewhat disparate collection of translations and original material. Its title varies; the edition used here, *Wunderliche Wahrhaftige Gesichte Philanders von Sittewald, das ist Straffschriften* (Straßburg, 1666), is one of the four authorized ones. See Curt von Faber du Faur, *German Baroque Literature: A Catalogue of the Collection in the Yale University Library* (New Haven, 1958), p. 113–4, and Artur Bechtold, *Kritisches Verzeichnis der Schriften Johann Michael Moscherosch* (Munich, 1922). See also Steig, *Achim von Arnim* 1, pp. 196–206, which includes the songs he passed out. All quotations from Moscherosch are in the text and come from this edition.

Neither Migge nor Reichl seems to have been aware of the existence of the *Vorrede* (Preface) to the *Soldatenleben*. Migge apparently did not examine the edition he cites, that of 1643, because the *Soldatenleben* was not published until 1644 in Strasburg. Reichl did not know of its existence, because he used the truncated version in the Deutsche National-Litteratur series, which cuts out the Preface.[76] Bechtold's description of the Moscherosch editions reveals that Arnim could have used only one edition, the *Ausgabe letzter Hand* (final edition supervised by author) of 1665–66, which contained the Preface. Bechtold notes the following differences that separate the 1665–66 edition from the earlier ones (the major one being the changes in names). In all editions preceding the 1665–66 edition, the vowels in the Croatian names were missing: Lffl, Bttrwtz, Bbwtz; Moscherosch spelled out the names in his final edition; so does Arnim. Even more significant is the fact that Arnim knew the name of the city's military commander; all editions prior to this one had simply identified him with initials "D. V." Arnim refers to him as Gordon, the same last name Moscherosch uses in this edition.[77]

Moscherosch's Preface (546–75) contains a lengthy discussion of the justification for the military as well as a criticism of its shortcomings. It also includes five pages of rules for the soldier written in verse,[78] introduced in a manner similar to Arnim's Preface (571); *Wintergarten* (211). Arnim, as he did with the Schaffgotsch story in the *Insel Felsenburg* adaptation, made a substitute different in circumstance but similar in spirit. The rules of war based on General Blücher's speech offered several advantages to Arnim. It provided an opportunity to draw parallels between the present and the past, an opportunity Arnim saw as vital to his poetic mission. Arnim's "Von Volksliedern" essay gives a significant clue regarding the importance of war songs, when it notes that earlier German military ballads were magnificent because they

76. *Gesichte Philanders von Sittewald*, von Hanß Michael Moscherosch, ed. by Felix Bobertag (Berlin and Stuttgart), Vol. 32, *Deutsche National-Litteratur*, ed. by Joseph Kürschner. The 1643 edition from Straßburg was identical to the Straßburg 1642 and did not contain *Soldatenleben*: see Bechtold, *Verzeichnis*, pp. 14–17.

77. Bechtold, *Verzeichnis*, p. 26.

78. Some of this verse is apparently not his; the name Zincgres appears in the second poem, p. 573, and Weckerlin in the third, pp. 574–75. See also p. 657 and Reichl, 1, p. 28. Zincgres's poem was one of the *Kriegslieder* Arnim distributed; see Steig, *Achim von Arnim* 1, pp. 196, 198–99.

involved a common effort. He contrasted that earlier situation with the more negative present one, where empty war songs prevail.[79]

When Arnim wanted to present elements of Blücher's speech in this section of *Wintergarten*, Moscherosch's example offered a ready precedent with which he was familiar. Arnim's verses are full of wholesome suggestions for daily living, appeals to honor, and promises of reward in this life and the next, but, at the end, the invalid says ". . . klingt das aber nicht ganz menschlich, und doch ist viel des Entsetzlichsten geschehen!" [". . .however, doesn't that sound altogether human, and yet, a lot of terrible things happened!"] (214). Though the content of the verses and this comment seem to reflect contradictory attitudes, on the one hand approving of war, and on the other rejecting it, they are very much in the spirit of Moscherosch's *Soldatenleben*. Moscherosch certainly does not try to cover up the horrors of war; Baroque scholars have pointed out that his graphic report is one of the few eyewitness accounts of the most terrible war fought on German soil up to Arnim's time.[80] Moscherosch criticizes the criminal activities of the soldiers and takes a strong position against the plundering and destruction of innocent lives and of property, elements that Arnim retained in the Philander episode (552). But he also defends the profession and criticizes his civilian contemporaries because they do not pay the soldiers enough, therefore making the temptation to plunder greater (551, 557–59). He also brought in precedents from German history, where soldiers behaved with honor towards God and their emperor, sacrificing themselves to the common good, demonstrating a sense of historical perspective that would also have been appealing to Arnim (563–66).[81]

---

79. Arnim, *Sämmtliche Werke* 6, (1857), p. 465.

80. See Faber du Faur, *German Baroque Literature*, p. 112. See also Stefan Grunwald, *A Biography of Johann Michael Moscherosch (1601–69)* (Bern, 1969), p. 55. Brinker-Gabler, *Tieck*, p. 17, notes that Moscherosch's writings were attractive because of the detailed picture of Germans in a time that was felt to be late medieval and that emphasized model behavior. Moscherosch wrote at a period in which there was a strong cultural reaction in German intellectual circles against French cultural hegemony. That, in addition to the exemplary portrayal of German character evident in the work, probably attracted Arnim as much as the depiction of Germans struggling against an occupying enemy. See also Wolfgang Harms, "Das Interesse an mittelalterlicher deutscher Literatur zwischen der Reformationszeit und der Frühromantik," *Akten des VI. Internationalen Germanistenkongresses* (Basel, 1980), Part I, pp. 60–83, p. 60, where Harms makes a similar point about Moscherosch.

81. See, for example, his discussion of the soldiers' loyalty and readiness to work together under Charlemagne, pp. 563–66.

There were other obvious points of attraction to Moscherosch for Arnim. The Thirty Years' War took place on German territories and was waged by outsiders who fought there; consequently, it furnished a good comparison with the Napoleonic wars, where the German lands were once again the card table for the poker players in European politics. The patriotic note that Moscherosch strongly strikes in the preface would also have appealed to Arnim (546).

Loyal service and deep patriotism portrayed by Moscherosch probably drew Arnim to the work, but he clearly planned to leave his own stamp upon it. As he wrote in a letter to Brentano in June, 1809:

Ich glaube gerade darin die eigentümlichste Kraft bewährt zu haben, ohne den Erzählungen von ihrer ersten Ausbildung zu nehmen, ihnen neue Organisation und Beziehung zu geben. Du magst in dieser Hinsicht besonders den Philander von Sittewald vergleichen.[82]

Without detracting from their original formation, I believe that I have preserved their peculiar power in giving these tales a new structure and new connections. In this respect, you may especially compare Philander von Sittewald.

The "neue Organisation und Beziehung" of which Arnim speaks seem to consist largely of a change in the character of Philander vis-à-vis the soldiers and in the changed sequence of events. Arnim was not interested in one of Moscherosch's major points, the improvement of the soldiers' behavior, for which the brutality depicted in *Soldatenleben* offered ample documentation. Arnim would not have advanced his goal of patriotic inspiration by concentrating on the heinous acts of renegade soldiers. His focus lay elsewhere, as the invalid reveals when the *Kranke* begins to boast of her own bravery against the enemy. The invalid, tired of civilians who turn a minor incident into an invitation to be cited for courage under fire, silences her by stating that he is going to tell a story about the Thirty Years' War, which will reveal the real damage armed conflict causes (214).

The invalid has really suffered in the war, unlike the other members of the circle, who sort out their petty contributions to the national effort in order to assuage their own guilt and mask their cowardice. The lack of understanding about the dangers of war that the invalid mocks here and that forms the major thrust of the Philander account appears again after the inner story with the brief encampment in the snowy night.

82. Steig, *Achim von Arnim* 1, p. 281.

The inability of the assembled company to endure the fairly mild winter night (241) stands in the strongest possible contrast to the invalid's own experience and that of Philander. In addition to instructing his hearers, the invalid naturally has a vested interest in putting the dangers of war in stark relief, since he could hope thereby to incline the lady favorably towards him.

Because Arnim wanted events to dominate, he had to change the character of Philander, who in Moscherosch's scenes has something of a Picaro on the road to reform about him. Conversions to Christian behavior detract from the emphasis on the rigors of war. Arnim also dropped Philander's mentor, Expertus Robertus, as well as the characters from the other *Gesichte* (visions) who do not like Philander. He built, as he often did, on references in Moscherosch's text that indicate that Philander was a professional scribe, such as Moscherosch's reference to accusations of slander against Philander because of his lampooning of the syndics (Moscherosch, 579–80). Arnim used Philander's writing as the motive for his leaving the city and as the occasion for his employment by the queen of the gypsies, who wants a clerk to answer the attacks of Philander (237). Since the gypsy section came from Grimmelshausen's *Springinsfeld,* Arnim had to find a way to link the two stories; he employs Philander's literary talent. He mentions that Philander wrote a eulogy in honor of the soldiers and a diatribe against the gypsies (215).

Arnim's consistency in adaptation of the character of Philander belies those critics who charge him with a confused and indiscriminate approach. Throughout this section, he deleted numerous passages that show Philander in obvious collusion with the brigands or in the grasp of a prickling conscience. (See Moscherosch, 663, for example, where Philander admits he behaved exactly like his captors.) In contrast, Arnim's Philander says little about his own attitude, registering at various points his great pity for the peasants (217, 220). Arnim's Philander seems to be a careful prisoner, not compromising himself as Moscherosch's did, and waiting for his chance to escape. Because Arnim omitted the development of Philander's religious consciousness, he changed Philander's motivation of escape. Instead of being touched by the religious song of the city watchman (Moscherosch, 691), a song that Arnim kept (234–35), Arnim's protagonist sees his father and his father's house from a distance (234). If Arnim had not changed the

character of Philander from a reformed adventurer to a reluctant prisoner, it would have been more difficult to integrate the gypsy scene
from *Springinsfeld*.

The adaptive techniques Arnim used here are reminiscent of some
seen in the second winter evening in the Albert and Concordia story.
In the original, just before the duel between Philander and the doctor
on the one side and Laffal and Bobowitz on the other, the former two
discuss their plan of attack. The doctor is all for a stab in the back; in
Moscherosch and in Arnim, Philander is against that, but in Moscherosch he cites Julius Caesar to reinforce his position, telling a story
about how Caesar, knowing the vanity of Pompey's soldiers, tells men
to hack at their faces, whereupon all run away (Moscherosch, 730–
31). Arnim omitted the story, but added a remark to Philander's comment that reveals his knowledge of Moscherosch's anecdote: "Pfui das
ist ein häßlich Stoßen, von hinten zu, hauet und stoßt ihm nach dem
Gesicht, so wird er fliehen" ["Phooey, that is an ugly thrusting, from
behind, hit and stab at his face; then he will flee"] (231). Reichl misses
this reference and says Arnim left out the incident.[83]

Arnim rearranged the sequence of events fairly freely as he got closer
to the point where he wanted to tie in the Grimmelshausen story. Once
he reached the duel, he jumped back to two previous scenes he had
skipped over and brought them in after the fight. To some extent, his
changes make a more coherent narrative than Moscherosch's account
does (Moscherosch, 696–710, Arnim, 232–33; Moscherosch, 690–
95, Arnim, 233–37). In order to get Philander back to his home town
without the commander recognizing him, Arnim had Gordon expelled
for collusion with the brigands to fleece the peasants. The mayor of
the city in Moscherosch's version writes a letter complaining of this
collaboration while Gordon is still in town (Arnim, 233; Moscherosch,
702–10). Arnim had taken the scene from Moscherosch where the
brigands eat and drink with the townspeople (Moscherosch, 663–685;
Arnim, 224–230). When he shifted Moscherosch's sequence of events
after that, he made a consistent involvement with the townspeople in
order to release Philander without the necessity of converting him, for
which there is no need.

At the point where it becomes necessary to return Philander to an

83. Reichl, 1, p. 30.

ordered life, Arnim made a break with the Moscherosch account and switched to Grimmelshausen's *Springinsfeld*.[84] Perhaps the invalid's remark in the frame about the *sonderbare Verhältnisse* (peculiar circumstances) (214) that crop up in wartime offers a clue why Arnim chose Grimmelshausen's account of a brief sojourn with gypsies; although both works deal with life in the German lands during the Thirty Years' War and its aftermath, facilitating integration of the narratives, there are other elements in Grimmelshausen's work that probably made it seem a natural choice to Arnim. Just as Moscherosch's work in its entirety, with its concern with both the problems of soldiers and the ravages of war, had attracted Arnim, so did the much smaller *Springinsfeld*. Philander and the narrator of *Springinsfeld* are both writers who have gotten into trouble because of their work. The latter had written critically about Simplicissimus and Springinsfeld; when the three meet by chance in a tavern, the other two men want to know what induced the narrator to write in such a negative manner about men he had never met (22). As explanation the narrator relates his sojourn among the gypsies. In Grimmelshausen's account, the queen of the gypsies is none other than Courasche who figures prominently in other Grimmelshausen works. Arnim had apparently no interest in expanding the renown of that lady, so his gypsy queen is just that, though traces of Courasche come through: "sie . . . hatte nicht wie die andern ein pechschwarzes Haar, sondern etwas falb. . ." ["she . . . did not have jet-black hair like the others, but rather somewhat dun-colored. . ."] *Wintergarten* (236), that is a direct quote from *Springinsfeld* (25). In Grimmelshausen, Courasche is anxious to obtain the services of the young student to set down her life's story so as to spite Simplicissimus (29). In his adaptation, Arnim naturally had to motivate the gypsy queen's need for a clerk in another way. He prepared for this situation at the outset of the story, with the two commentaries by Philander, one about the gypsies and the other about soldiers.

Philander's encounter with the gypsies is morally neutral, providing a good basis for integration with Arnim's dispassionate portrait of Philander among the soldiers. The gypsy interlude helps to ease Philander's transition back to a lawful society in several ways. Like the brig-

---

84. The edition used is a reprint of the 1670 edition of Hans Jacob Christoffel von Grimmelshausen, *Der seltzame Springinsfeld* (Tübingen, 1969). All quotations will come from this edition and will be in the text. See also Migge, p. 873.

and soldiers, the gypsies are thieves, who stand outside ordered society not only because of their behavior, but also because of their race and their life style. Because Philander in both cases had to stay with these asocial groups in order to survive, he is exonerated of blame for active participation in their misdeeds. The real impossibility in spite of appearances, of Philander becoming a part of the gypsy group parallels Philander's apparent lack of complicity with the robbers. The stealing of the gypsies received little emphasis in *Wintergarten*, in contrast to the torture and other violence inflicted on peasants. Their theft is not connected with the war and it does not result in the death or maiming of the victim; for these two reasons, Arnim probably gives it less attention. Philander does not return to society directly from the soldier group, which might have looked questionable, but from a period of forced detention in a society which was racially and professionally closed to him.

As in the story of the first evening, Arnim took out some of the overtly sexual material. In Grimmelshausen, the delousing salve of the gypsies can only be applied when the sufferer lies naked in front of a fire. The beautiful young gypsy offers to do this task for the scribe; he is afraid that the salve may change him into an animal and eventually agrees to the treatment on the condition that she let him do the same thing to her. They do this, and as he awakens to find himself black the next day, he learns from Courasche that he is engaged to the girl (36). Arnim simply says that they became engaged according to gypsy custom, consisting of running after the girl until he caught her. Philander was then given a salve with which he was to smear himself against vermin (238). The gypsies plan to treat Philander just as they do all their other victims; he awakens in the morning after the application of the salve, to find that the whole pack of them are gone. He learns from children, not from the gypsy queen, that he has turned black.[85] Philander, under the care of a pastor, learns that the robbers with whom he has traveled were betrayed by the doctor and will be condemned to death in a few days (238–39).

85. In Grimmelshausen, the desertion by the gypsies comes after Courasche has shown the student in a mirror that his complexion is now so black he can pass as a gypsy and that this anointing with salve serves the same function as circumcision. The applicator of the salve must become his wife whether he likes it or not. The student presses Courasche for payment for his services, she puts him off, promising him it after his wedding. A few days later they desert him in the night (pp. 36–38).

Immediately upon completion of Philander's adventures, the *Gesunde* runs to the piano and plays Schiller's "Reiterlied" (Song of the horsemen).[86] Since she has never been in battle, she has no idea of the emotional reaction that song might unleash and consequently reacts in a uncomprehending manner when the invalid insists that she quit. He has prefaced his story with the remark that it will reveal the real horrors and dangers of war, without those present being able to figure out the worth of their contributions, implying, as he begins, that they understand little of what war is really like. The *Gesunde*'s behavior underscores the truth of this supposition, as does the excursion into the winter weather in the latter part of the frame of this evening. The cloud of unknowing that blinds them to the nature of war and the bravery and fortitude necessary to wage it still dominates, until they make camp in the snow and cannot stand it even for half an hour.

On their way back to the estate after the short-lived foray into the snow, they pass through the Brandenburg Gate. Arnim used this rather awkward transition to introduce another character, Ariel (who has many similarities with Arnim himself) and Ariel's poem, "Träume" (dreams). Both the character and the poetry mention, either directly or by strong implication, the political difficulties of the day. (Both "Träume" and "Nelson und Meduse," at the end of the fifth evening, violate the rule of the lady of the house not to mention current events.)

Ariel has slept on the gate since Napoleon carried away the statue of the goddess of victory.[87] While he waits for the statue's return, he writes poetry to make himself fall asleep (242). "Träume" is, as Stern-

86. The "Reiterlied" was one of the songs Arnim distributed to Blücher's troops. See Steig, *Achim von Arnim*, 1, pp. 196, 202–3. Segebrecht, "Wintergarten," says, in regard to the reaction of the invalid, p. 240, that the singing of this song seemed particularly out of place to the invalid because it showed him that his contributions to the conversation have had little effect. The only way he can drive the reality of war, as opposed to the distortion that verbal descriptions often bring, home to them is through a demonstration. See also note 5, p. 313, in the same article. It is important to note that the invalid's negative reaction to the song is based on the horrible waste of war, but does not condemn war outright as a means of national policy. He describes his feelings as follows, "Diese ganze Last von armen Seelen, die sich an dem Liede begeisterten und entgeisterten, die alle von mir gerissen wurden, die macht mich wasserscheu, liederscheu, kameradenscheu, reiterscheu, und um aller armen Menschen willen, die unnütz gestorben sind, singen Sie nicht weiter in diesem fürchterlichen Geisterchore" (239). What the invalid is protesting against is the *Gesunde*'s description of the song as "ein schönes Kriegslied" (p. 239), an entirely understandable reaction from one who has been through what the invalid has.

87. Migge, 2, p. 889, says that Napoleon took the Victoria with the Quadriga to Paris as spoils of war.

berg noted, in many respects a summary of early Romantic ideas about art.[88] The first part, based on Winkelmann's lectures on Greece, contains a yearning for the dream which begets oblivion, an understandable wish in the political situation of the time,[89]

> O so seid dann gelobt ihr holden Gespinste der Träume,
> Die Vergessenheit treibt, wie den Sommer der Herbst,
> Denn ihr kehret zurück und bringet eure Gespielen,
> Denen ihr gerne gesagt, wie ich dem Eigensinn folg'.
> Seiet vor allen gesegnet, ihr Träume schönerer Künste,
> Als mir die kriegrische Kunst, Vaterland, Freunde geraubt, . . . (243)

O so be praised then, you dear webs of dreams that forgetfulness drives as the autumn does the summer because you return and bring along your playmates whom you gladly told how I follow my own mind. Be blessed before all, you dreams of finer arts; when the art of war robbed me of homeland and friends, . . .

These lines could certainly be autobiographical, since Arnim did feel the loss of friends such as Brentano during the battle with Napoleon, as well as the devastating defeat of Prussia. Even in the dream, as he turns to Greece for solace, he is still tied to his homeland: "Ach und wie tief ich grabe im Sande von Brandenburgs Erde, Immer nur find ich den Sand und er ist mir so lieb, . . ." ["Alas, no matter how deep I dig in the sand of Brandenburg's earth, I find always only the sand, and it is so dear to me, . . ."] (243).[90] During the dream, the narrator is transported from Prussia to ancient Greece and the studio of Phydias, where he witnesses an exchange between a barbarian who worships Radegast and Phydias.[91] The two cannot find a common ground where they understand each other, but the Brandenburg Gate itself is a symbol of the connection between the two races, as is Winkelmann's book (247).[92]

88. Sternberg, *Arnims Lyrik,* pp. 158–60, believes that the poem as it stands in *Wintergarten* is a compilation from various writings of Arnim's, some dating back to his London period. He suggests that the first forty-one lines are primarily a summary of early Romantic ideas about the work of art and the artist.
89. See Migge, 2, p. 889.
90. Sternberg, *Arnims Lyrik,* p. 87, notes that the Mark of Brandenburg is full of sand; this image appears at several places in Arnim's poetry.
91. Migge, 2, p. 889, says that Radegast was a Nordic god much honored by a Wendish tribe in present-day Mecklenburg, p. 313.
92. Migge, 2, p. 889, notes that the builder took as his model the Propyläen in Athens. Segebrecht, "Wintergarten," p. 313, says that the dream deals with the spirit of

The last thirty-six lines of the poem (247–48) are rather autobiographical; they describe the building of the Brandenburg Gate, which Arnim saw as a child, and the invasion by the French (248). The portrait Arnim painted of the Brandenburg Gate, symbol for Prussia, comes at the approximate center of *Wintergarten*. It has a strong connection with the theme of war, which has dominated this fourth evening, though it transcends the battle with the French:

> *Und die Victoria sank nieder am herrlichen Tor,*
> Das ich erbauen gesehn und steigen die Göttin auf Säulen,
> Warnend steht es nun da ohne den göttlichen Schmuck;
> Die Erhabene lag vorm Fenster so schmählich gestrecket,
> Sarg und Wagen dabei, der die Leiche entführt.
> Wie der Wagen entdonnert, da meint ich sie gänzlich entführet,
> Doch in der Enge des Tors schloß sich die Göttin noch an,
> Größer sie war, als Brandenburgs Tor sie konnte erfassen,
> Und so stand auch mein Volk, größer als Brandenburgs Land.
> Stürzt auf uns Toren dies Tor, fort wollt ihr die Göttin uns rauben,
> Und vernichtet auch uns, da ihr vernichtet den Ruhm.
> Brandenburg, Tor des Sieges, wie bist du also gefallen,
> Ein Jahrhundert erwarb, was ein Tag dir geraubt. (248)

And Victoria sank down at the magnificent gate that I saw being built and where I saw the goddess climb onto columns. As an admonition, it stands there now without the divine adornment. The majestic woman lay shamefully stretched out in front of the window; close by are the coffin and the carriage, which takes away the corpse. As the carriage thunders away, I believed she was really abducted; yet, in the narrow passage of the gate, the goddess grasped the walls once more. She was too great for Brandenburg's gate to contain her. And thus my people stood too: greater than the country of Brandenburg. Hurl down this gate upon us fools; you want to steal the goddess from us, and you destroy us too since you obliterate the glory. Brandenburg, gate of victory, how did you thus fall? That which one century earned, one day robbed from you."

The Brandenburg Gate without Victoria stands there in a warning manner after she was taken away as a corpse in a coffin. The absence of part of the stolen monument stands as an admonition and exhortation to the Prussians, reminding them of what they lost and urging them, through its incompleteness, to a regeneration that would bring the statue back again. The goddess of victory and the gate, symbols

---

Greek art that the barbarians never appreciated; however, with the Victoria there is an indissoluble union with the spirit of the Mark of Brandenburg.

of freedom and of the Prussian people, stand for things greater than themselves, entities that are capable of inspiration, so that what was lost in a day after being built up over the years could be regained.

The fourth evening is one of the most complex units in the entire *Wintergarten*, of particular importance since its theme is war, a subject central to Arnim during the difficult time in which he wrote and, as we have seen, to the *Wintergarten* group as well. The *Kriegsregeln*, which began the work, offer a picture of the model soldier, a picture inspired by the German past, which stands in stark contrast to the renegade soldier brigands depicted in the Philander episode. The juxtaposition of the *Kriegsregeln* and the episode describing the rapine violence of Battrawitz and his friends pointed up the differences between what could be and what is. In this regard, it parallels the "Reiterlied," which presents a sentimental picture of war that differs from its reality, a reality for which the assembled guests in *Wintergarten* are not prepared. Why is the invalid so concerned to show them what war is really like? The answer goes beyond a pro-war or anti-war stance; rather, it concerns the future of the German nation. If the assembled company cannot understand the horrors of war and the sacrifice which some have made for their nation, then they are ill-prepared to rebuild, to gain back that which "ein Jahrhundert erwarb, was ein Tag dir geraubt" ["That which one century earned, one day robbed from you"] (248).

Fünfter Winterabend
(Fifth Winter Evening)

In the critical miasma that has surrounded *Wintergarten,* the one breath of fresh air critics admit to inhaling has been Arnim's inner story for the fifth evening, "Mistris Lee." Although Migge and others imply it is the only original narrative in the collection, our analysis of the Johann Beer story shows otherwise. But because Arnim's friends immediately knew that this narrative was not only an original novella, but a very fine one, the story has attracted attention. Brentano and Goethe's verdicts differ very little from the assessments of contemporary critics.[93] After receiving Brentano's favorable opinion of "Mistris Lee," Arnim wrote him about the source of the story. Like many in Goethe's *Unterhaltungen* or Hoffmann's *Serapionsbrüder*, the story rested on an anecdote or an event that the writer had heard about, an English legal case that featured the Gordons and Mistris Lee.[94]

The account Arnim gave Brentano of what actually happened in the Gordon-Lee incident differs considerably from that in his novella. The real Mistris Lee was a trollop bent on attracting sensational attention to herself and willing to carry on numerous affairs. Her true character was so much in evidence that her estranged husband was only too glad to use the public opprobrium to his own advantage by divorcing her. Her unsavory reputation probably helped the Gordon brothers to be acquitted, even though they themselves were rather disreputable fortune hunters. The actual situation offered little opportunity either for complex character description or enigmatic character development. Mistris Lee was thrown out on the street with the Lockhart brothers, ready to hunt other gulls.

Arnim's narrator, who is suddenly German (in spite of the fact he was introduced as an English lord), tells a closed-frame story. He opens with an incident at Covent Garden where Mistris Lee excites attention and admiration and leads the German to question his English friend over negus in New Bond Street. The narrator relates excerpts from his friend's account, which frames the inner story. His sympathies lie with the brothers, as where he says: " . . . weil ich sie lieb hatte . . . " ["because I liked them"] (273). He notes that they have sat in this cafe countless times. Arnim's Mistris Lee presents an unsettlingly ambiguous face to the world, while the Gordon brothers appear as men of good faith with some of the less scandalous English vices. Laudon has been discharged from the army because of his debts but is prepared to marry Lee in spite of the loss of her fortune; Lockhart is the very model of a late-eighteenth-century cleric whose parishes were the hunt and London balls. What did Arnim have in mind? One must assume that there was a purpose in both his changes and the inclusion of the story in the *Wintergarten* collection.

One might well begin from the other end and ask what sort of story

93. Steig, *Achim von Arnim* 1, p. 283; Migge, p. 886.
94. Migge, p. 884.

Arnim would have had if he had related events the way they had happened. It would have been an entertaining account of how a trio of scoundrels were hoisted on various petards. Such a story would have had little application to the country-house audience, since no one in the group bore any resemblance to the three major characters in the story. Nor did the events in which these people found themselves have any bearing on the present situation in Germany or on the cultural history of the German people. Had Arnim not changed the account, one could indeed have reproached him with including material with no connection to anything else.

The title of the fifth evening offers a clue to the relationship of this story with contemporary political and cultural problems: "Die neuen Amazonen" (The new Amazons). This theme appears in the frame sections, in Mistris Lee and in the long romance, "Nelson und Meduse." Like the Amazons, Meduse destroys men.

The legend of the Amazons is supposedly related to the old tale of a far country where everything was done backwards; in this instance, the women, not the men, fought. Certainly Arnim's Germany would have had, to judge from the criticisms of it in the frame, affinities with that legendary land of topsy-turvy behavior. Destructive behavior on the part of females clearly interested Arnim; he explored it further in the 1812 collection in the novella, "Melück Maria Blainville, Die Hausprophetin aus Arabien."

If one examines Arnim's presentation of the Amazon theme, we see it operating, as is often the case in *Wintergarten*, at various levels and in several permutations. The appearance of the *Gesunde*, fresh from ice skating and wearing a helmet, causes the invalid to voice his regrets that his injury kept him off the ice: ". . . denn das ist geringe Ehre, das jetzige Männergeschlecht zu überwinden, wo die Besten vor dem Feinde erschlagen sind . . . " ["because it is now a thing of little honor to overcome the present representatives of the male sex, now that the best men have been killed facing the enemy"] (249). He calls the *Gesunde* "meine schöne Amazone" (my beautiful Amazon), a theme that the *Gesandte* picks up as he notes that the newspapers announce only the birth of girls, and that a kingdom of Amazons, of which she must be queen, is on its way; she is "die neue Amazone" (249). The narrator hints that these flights of fancy were to have some connection with the evening's conversation (249).

The second major element in the inner story, England, appears in the frame in the person of a lord, who turns out to be none other than Ariel from the fourth frame. Posing as a gallant Englishman, he says he has rescued the *Kranke* from an afternoon of interminable boredom by telling her all his family scandals. Beneath the *Kranke's* frivolity runs a current of criticism, which ties in with some of that appearing in the frames of other evenings. The young people who are her contemporaries have another similarity with that backwards land from which the Amazons come: instead of being ready and able to endure discomfort because of their youth, they demand the creature comforts requisite to an eighty-year-old before any undertaking (250–51). Apathy and lack of engaged action on the part of the Germans, which the invalid criticized in the frame of the fourth evening, again figure in the frame discussion. There seems to have been little interest or enthusiasm for anything, even for intrigue (250). This lack of passion as a criticism of contemporary young people reappears in the description of Mistris Lee:

. . . daß sie in die allgemeine Abteilung von gut und böse nicht passen will, denn beides hat doch einen festen Grund, aber das Wunderbare in ihr, diese Mischung von Talent und Beschränktheit, von scheinbarer Bosheit und mitleidiger Güte, so etwas ist nur in einer Frau unsrer Tage zu finden, wo der Enthusiasmus früherer Jahre an der kalten Gleichgültigkeit der Mehrzahl aufbrennt, und die Luft, die daraus sich entwickelt, ist nun einmal wie alle Luft gestaltlos und unatembar, weil sie verbrannt ist. (253)

. . . that she will not fit into the general division of good and bad because, after all, both have a firm foundation. Yet, the incredible quality in her, the mixture of talent and limitation, of seeming malice and compassionate kindness, something like that is to be found only in a woman of our time, where the enthusiasm of earlier years burns up at the cold indifference of the majority. And after all, the air that develops from this fire is as formless and unbreathable as all air because it is burnt.

The striking parallels between parts of the above description of the capricious Englishwoman and the young Germans give a clue to the relationship between the frame and the Lee story, as did the invalid's criticism of young men. Common to all three descriptions is the inability of the generation of young adults, to which Arnim at that time belonged, to fill their roles. Second-rate weaklings among the men, women in their topsy-turvy behavior without a sense of commitment to act as a guide, are cause for alarm, especially in the present political situation.

Arnim's three major characters, Lee, Laudon, and Lockhart, serve as foils for comments on the Germans. Arnim's portrait of Mistris Lee reveals a woman full of whims, with no inner principles to guide her unethical irresponsible behavior. In an early meeting with Laudon and Lockhart, she asks about their mother, who had also taken care of her as a child, and adds: ". . . es ist eine ausgezeichnete Frau, aber gestehen Sie, ihre Grundsätze sind allzu streng" ["She is an excellent woman, but you must admit, her principles are much too strict"] (258). Lee is also a sceptic in religious matters, a negative character trait in Arnim's eyes (256). Upon seeing Laudon for the first time in seven years, she is sure that the old affection that existed between them as teenagers is still there in full force. Then she wants to see Lockhart and ignores Laudon, then showers Laudon with attention. They plan to elope. Subsequently, on the advice of her lawyers, she renounces the plan, a decision she immediately gives up when Laudon comes. After the abduction and after she has spent the night with Laudon, she decides it is Lockhart she really wants. Since she cannot have him, she betrays Lockhart and Laudon to the police. In a telling passage, Arnim describes her approach:

. . . Sie seufzte jetzt über dem Abgrunde wunderbarer tiefer Irrung, in den sie immer tiefer hinabsank; da war kein Ausgang, sie wünschte sich beleidigt zu sein, um sich rächen zu können. Die Launen sind des Teufels Gewalt auf Erden, . . . (271)

Now she sighed over the abyss of the amazingly profound aberration into which she sank more and more deeply; there was no exit. She wished to have been insulted so that she could avenge herself. Moods are the devil's power on earth, . . .

Her confusion and lack of principle bring her under the influence of evil.

The two brothers receive much more sympathetic treatment, though each has faults that lead to their banishment (among them, taking such a woman seriously). Laudon is good-hearted, though often undecided, while Lockhart has a more complicated character. A member of London's racier sets, Lockhart was no worse than the others. He was happy to be of service to anyone, so long as he did not have to commit himself to one person in particular. His well-meaning advice to friends often turned out badly, since his friends did not have his own superior gifts of execution (253).

Both brothers, however, have an inner sense of what is right and wrong, as evidenced by Lockhart's answer to Mistris Lee's remark about his mother's principles (258). The experience with Mistris Lee brought about a realization that their mother was right, since the way they decide to live their lives in exile reflects her ideas. Laudon himself, probably the less ethically inclined of the two brothers, sees through Lee's character:

... und so kam es, was unglaublich scheinen möchte, bei so treu bewahrter alter Anhänglichkeit, daß Laudon in Mistris Lee endlich nichts als die schändlichste Wollust sah, die genießen wollte ohne abhängig zu werden, und wie *die alten Amazonen der Fabelwelt nach dem Genusse mordete.* (273)

... and thus it happened, which may seem incredible in the light of such long-standing devotion, so faithfully maintained, that at last Laudon saw nothing but the most shameful sensual wantonness in Mistress Lee, who wanted to enjoy without becoming dependent and who killed after consummation of her pleasure like the old Amazons of the fable world.

The contrast that the story makes is not between young German women and Mistris Lee, but between young Germans and the Englishmen, who, though not without fault, are ready to risk their honor and futures for love.

Through his description of the enigmatic Mistris Lee, Arnim also presented a warning to his readers of the fate of a woman who wants to enjoy with no sense of commitment. Such actions can lead to behavior reminiscent of Amazon women because it is a savage attack on the other person's sense of worth. Such irresponsible lust can destroy the other person, not only in a material sense but also in an emotional one. The readiness of such an individual to treat the other person as an object for gratification damages his sense of self-worth. Arnim would probably not have seen it in those terms, but rather in the damage such behavior causes to those family and personal relationships on which a stable and responsible society depends. He also makes it clear that the offender loses as well. As he notes later in the frame of the story, "Wenn ein Mensch in seinem Leben je ganz Tier sein kann, so kann er nie wieder ganz Mensch werden, . . . " ["If a human being can ever be all animal in his life, then he can never become all human again"](274). Mistris Lee, though reconciled with her husband, has to pay a high price for her treachery, since she falls into a sort of witless state.[95]

The moral point that Arnim seems to be making may lie behind his decision to change the fate of the brothers. Instead of having them acquitted, he sends them to Botany Bay in Australia. Along with others who are banished, they flee to an island where they set up quite a different sort of society, having learned from their mistakes:

... sie sollen kurz nach ihrer Ankunft in Botany-Bay mit andern Verbannten entflohen sein, und eine Insel unabhängig beherrschen; sie sollen gegen die Gewohnheit jener Länder eine furchtbare Sittenstrenge eingeführt haben, um mit ihrem warnenden Geschicke ein ganzes Volk zu bilden. (273)

... they are supposed to have escaped together with other banished people shortly after their arrival in Botany Bay and to rule an island independently. Contrary to the customs of these countries, they are said to have introduced a terrible moral rigorism in order to educate a whole people with their fate, which should serve as a warning.

There are certain parallels here to Albert's island paradise of an ideal society, where a moral life of the highest probity is maintained.

The Preface to "Nelson und Meduse" picks up themes from the frame at the beginning of the fifth evening, but also has connections to the story. The symbolic, elliptical language of the poem introduces the themes of real bravery versus that of mock courage in the face of a safe situation. Arnim's ironic portrait of the tourists on the beach who cut up a dead whale is an allegory for those Germans who fight the enemy only when there is no need to or no risk in it. The invalid comments on this trait in the frame of the fourth evening and in the fifth when he complains of the state of the current generation of men, as does the *Kranke* (249–50). Once the whale that washed up out of the sea is safely dead, a tailor sits on him and boasts that he has caught him to sell (276). The whale's last gasp frightens the brave adventurers, but then, assured that he is indeed dead, they cut him up. Arnim's disapproval of their acts is apparent in comments like the following: "Rippen

95. Möllers, "Wirklichkeit," gallantly defends Mistris Lee as a victim of youthful idealism nourished by Richardson's novels. In his interpretation, he disregards passages where the narrator makes negative comments and, with one exception, neglects the frame, thereby ignoring the connections with the Amazon theme, which appears both implicitly and explicitly in the inner story (i.e., on p. 273). See pp. 72–84.

sind der Helden Beut, / Sich ein Denkmal draus zu bauen" ["Ribs are the heroes' booty to build themselves a monument"], and "Nun er also ist zerstücket, / fassen ihn die Herrn der Kunst," ["Now that he is finally cut up in pieces, the masters of art seize him"] (277). Arnim contrasts their empty heroism with the real bravery of soldiers in battle (277). The tourists are now scared to bathe in the sea, because they fear revenge from other whales. Their panic increases at the sight of a black elephant running towards them; at this, the sea seems the lesser of two evils. Subduing the elephant does not occur to them. "Keiner denkt ihn zu bezwingen. / In das Meer die meisten springen" ["Nobody thinks of subduing him. Most of them jump into the sea"] (278).

In contrast to the cowardly tourists stands the figure of Nelson in the beginning of the "Erste Romanze" (First romance), on board his ship on the sea in the setting sun. Through times of terror, Nelson brought the French to surrender, never losing his courage (279). Nelson's bravery diverges sharply from the cowardly, self-seeking behavior of the bourgeois tourists, who look only for material gain without risk. Nelson's valor against the French, which Arnim holds up for admiration, could be a model for the Germans.

The second romance continues with the attack on those who stay at home safe by the fire, from which vantage point they criticize the Nelsons of the world, imputing their deeds to chance and not to the character of the outstanding individual (280). These stanzas show how skillfully Arnim sustained his treatment of the theme of accountability and bravery in defense of one's country while giving his own interpretation of historical events, as, in this case, Nelson's death.

The second romance introduces the singer Meduse, whose first appearance to Nelson awakens reactions in him that foreshadow the unlikely course of their relationship:

> Eine Frau so götterhold,
> Daß er gleich den Blick gewendet,
> Um nicht in dem Strahlenmeere
> Zu versinken ohne Ehre. (280)

A woman so lovely and divine that immediately he turned away his glance in order not to sink without honor in the ocean of light.

Ohne Ehre (without honor) here would indicate that he surrendered without a struggle, without fighting, which Nelson would never let himself do, though he little suspects the nature of the battle now before him, that with Meduse.

The end of the second romance mentions the bright coasts of the south, a theme that carries over into the Columbus allegory at the beginning of the third romance. Just as Columbus hardly dared believe he had discovered paradise after the long voyage, so Nelson, at sea since his boyhood, has also seen beauty only from a distance, as something against which he must arm himself (282).

As Nelson goes for the first time to Meduse's house, with more difficulty than he went to battle, he finds a rather exotic scene replete with apes and parrots, echoes of the south, the home of magic and danger (283). Tempted by Meduse in her morning gown, he kisses her bosom, but Meduse simply asks in a friendly way if he could wait until after the opera performance. As she and the musician prepare for the performance, the musician warns that there is a plot against her as many believe she is a magician; but Nelson, intoxicated by love, does not hear this warning and intends to defend her against such insults.

The subtle hints about danger from dark forces of magic become very clear at the beginning of the fourth romance, when Nelson is warned against the artful snares of the dancer (285). This warning continues through a series of admonishments directed not only at Nelson, but at his countrymen: "Ließ sich je ein Volk noch warnen, / Lernt es je durch andrer Not" ["Did a people ever allow itself to be warned, does it ever learn from the plight of others"] (286), cautioning them to stay away from the siren-like attractions that served to hide the dark power within.

Ready to strike to the ground all who do not admire Meduse, Nelson waits impatiently at the beginning of the fifth romance for Meduse to appear. During this time, he overhears two men nearby talking about the snake Meduse carries in her bosom. They said the snake practices magic with the Devil, in spite of a holy picture full of sorrow standing hidden in her room. Meduse, they say, often forgets this picture and lets it collect dust. Nelson, outraged at this insult, calls them liars. At this point, the picture of the Virgin Mary dominates the poem before Meduse appears and before the terrible incident in her chamber. It functions here both as a foreshadowing of hope and also as backdrop for understanding the subsequent bedroom scene. Mary shines out and through the curtain; the singer cannot completely reject her. At night, when the face of the picture shines forth, Meduse weeps, as the snake gnaws at her heart. Because of this pain, she hates to sleep alone. The snake devours young boys, whose blood it sucks, keeping Meduse young and enabling her to sing so beautifully (289–290). Consequently, her art rests on dangerous supports, which probably help to make it so entrancing, since they are supernatural.

This series of revelations about Meduse's secret life culminates in the stanza describing the role of her *Amme,* who stands behind these nefarious events. Hungry for money, the wet nurse forces Meduse into complicity.

During her role as Proserpine in the opera, Meduse seems to carry on a struggle with Pluto, the god of the underworld. When the god of death seizes her, Nelson, unable to contain himself, jumps on the stage to take her away, as she sighs in his arms that her power is broken and she will sing no more.

Nelson takes Meduse home, where a Cupid-like figure opens the door. Upon undressing the unconscious singer, Nelson finds the snake and chain on her breast. He chops up the chain, Meduse awakens, and the picture of Mary seems to send forth approval. Meduse at first sings a mass, beats her breast, and wrings her hands. But these meditative moments soon give way to an overwhelming desire to seduce Nelson, "den frommen Held" (the innocent hero) (294). Her aggressiveness puts the sea lord off: "Sie so männlich, er so weiblich / Scheint ihm in dem Streit unleidlich" ["She so manly, he so effeminate it seems insufferable to him in the fight"] (295).

The picture of Mary beckons sadly and Nelson jumps up from the bed: ". . . der Unschuld Kräfte / Siegen über Zaubersäfte ["the powers of innocence win over magical potions"] (295). He dashes from the room where Meduse sits as the love in her heart changes to feelings of blood revenge: "Und sie bricht des Weibes Schranken / Mit entsetzlichen Gedanken ["And she transgresses a woman's limits with terrible thoughts"] (296). The narrator's perturbed disapproval at such role reversal is readily apparent as he describes Meduse's Amazon-like behavior.

In order to avenge her wounded pride, Meduse incites discord and fighting among the nations, leading Nelson to the battle of his life, Trafalgar, in which he received the wound that killed him. Meduse, lying at the feet of the dying man, confessing her guilt says, "Alles Unheil von mir stammet" ["All disaster stems from me"] (299). Nelson and Meduse marry, and he dies in her arms.

With the conclusion of the *Romanze*, Arnim ended the series of portraits of Amazon-like women who dominate the frame of the fifth evening, beginning with the *Gesunde* and progressing to the most fearful, Meduse. In order to understand both the moral and the political significance in Arnim's treatment of the frame, one must look at the important material in the frame conversation between "Mistris Lee" and "Nelson und Meduse." In this talk, the Englishman (who is really Ariel) and the narrator discuss women and political developments. The Englishman asks if his partner believes that " . . . die Nationen nur als Repräsentanten der verschiedenen beiden Geschlechter nationell gegen einander kämpfen, z.B. Engländer und Franzosen" ["the nations only fight against each other as representatives of the two different sexes on a national level, for instance the English and the French"] (274). The narrator's answer tells the reader how to understand the recent past as well as the relationship of that past to the Amazon theme:

Warum sollte ich es nicht auch so ausdrücken können, es wird sich am Ende zeigen, wer männlicher gefochten, es sei denn, daß in Europa endlich eine Herrschaft der Weiber alles vereinte, was mir sehr wahrscheinlich wird, wenn ich sehe, wie die Weiber seit der Mistris Wolstonecraft über der Männer Ungerechtigkeit klagen, und sich so schön auswachsen und ausbilden gegen die Männer, die ihr Dasein gar keiner Verschönerung und körperlichen Vollendung mehr kräftig und wert achten. (274)

Why should I not be able to express it in this manner? In the end, it will be apparent who fought in a more manly way, unless a rule of women would unite everything. This possibility seems very likely to me when I see how the women since Mistress Wolstonecraft complain about men's injustice and grow up so nicely and develop in comparison with the men, who no longer see their existence as powerful and worthy of any beautification and physical perfection.

In the romance and in the frame conversation (274), England is clearly the masculine nation. Since the romance purports to explain the death of Nelson, which came about in a battle with the French, and since the tone of *Wintergarten* is predominantly anti-French, it would seem plausible to view the killing of Nelson, the prototype of the incorruptible hero, as yet another reason to dislike the French. In any case, at a time that Arnim, at the end of the fifth evening describes as "dieser wunderbare Zustand ohne Gegenwart" ["this strange condition without a present"] (301), Nelson's death bears witness to a world not structured as it ought to be; Meduse becomes an agent of this disorder, as she "bricht des Weibes Schranken" ["transgresses a woman's limits"] (296).

The major thematic complex representing this theme in the fifth evening is the Amazon myth.[96] Central to it is the absolute power that women have over men. It is a power that corrupts in either sex, as it does the Amazons, who kill their lovers after sexual pleasure (273). From the potential victim's point of view, the injustice of this approach needs no further elucidation; however, Arnim saw therein a danger for the perpetrator as well. Mistris Lee becomes the victim of an inner perversion, ". . . die schändlichste Wollust sah, die genießen wollte ohne abhängig zu werden" [". . . the most shameful sensual wanton-ness, which wanted to enjoy without becoming dependent"] (273). Mistris Lee and Meduse are both punished; Mistris Lee loses her senses, while Meduse loses the man she loves to a death she has caused.

The orchestration of the Amazon theme on three different levels, the frame, the Mistris Lee story, and the long epic poem, reveal early in Arnim's development the ability to integrate themes and symbols on many levels, a talent apparent in *Isabella von Ägypten* (from the 1812 novella collection) and *Die Kronenwächter* (The crown guardians). In the context of the *Wintergarten,* this emphasis on the Amazon theme gave Arnim another viewpoint from which to criticize his weak con-temporaries who capitulate to Napoleon. *The Wintergarten* is a criticism of German men as much as German women; the invalid at the begin-ning castigates the current breed of men (249), as does the *Kranke.*

Sechster Winterabend
(Sixth Winter Evening)

In his commentary, Migge has rightly noted the importance the conversation in the frame of the sixth evening has for an understanding of Arnim's views on history, particularly the significance of memoirs.

96. See Thomas Bulfinch, *Bulfinch's Mythology, The Age of Fable* (New York, no date given), p. 119. The Amazonian kind of woman sees to predominate in the description that the Englishman gives of women: "Es ist ein entsetzliches Geschlecht, die Weiber . . . und wie sie so prangen in Gesellschaft mit prächtigen Zeugen, leuchtenden Metallen und Steinen; erkennt und seht nur an den schwarzen Haaren, sie mögen sie noch so

Arnim's envoy says, after discussing Massenbach, "Memoiren im weitesten Sinne sind das Wesen, das Höchste der Geschichte" ["Memoirs in the broadest sense are the essence, the epitome of history"] (303).[97] Because of the envoy's position, he is able to observe the great events of the time and know that what is usually written about them is deficient in both quantity and quality. The only worthwhile parts, the details, are thrown away like lemon peels (303). Precisely these details, the ones that only the king or participants in these events know, are the "geheime Geschichte," (secret history) the sort that one finds in memoirs. That is the history that alone can ensure both immortality and instruction (302).

The didactic element that surfaces in the envoy's speech underscores once again Arnim's hopes that through contemplation of a proud and worthy past, his contemporaries could bring the necessary virtues to bear to rid themselves of their hated enemy. Arnim explains the values of memoirs in his preface to *Die Kronenwächter,* with which he was also occupied when he wrote *Der Wintergarten:*

> . . . so läßt sich die Geschichte mit der Kristallkugel im Auge zusammenstellen, die nicht selbst sieht, aber dem Auge notwendig ist, um die Lichtwirkung zu sammeln und zu vereinen; ihr Wesen ist Klarheit, Reinheit und Farbenlosigkeit. Wer diese in der Geschichte verletzt, der verdirbt auch Dichtung, die aus ihr hervorgehen soll, wer die Geschichte zur Wahrheit läutert, schafft auch der Dichtung einen sichern Verkehr mit der Welt. Nur darum werden die eignen unbedeutenden Lebensereignisse gern ein Anlaß der Dichtung, weil wir sie mit mehr Wahrheit angeschaut haben, als uns an den größern Weltbegebenheiten gemeinhin vergönnt ist.[98]

> . . . thus history can be put together with that crystal ball in the eye that does not see by itself, but which is necessary for the eye to collect and unite the light effect; this crystal ball's essence is clarity, purity and colorlessness. Whoever violates these qualities in history also spoils the poetry that is to emerge from it; whoever purifies history into truth also creates a secure intercourse with the

---

herrlich mit Perlen durchwinden, die fleischfressenden Raben, die über dem Meeresstrudel schweben, und in anscheinender Gleichgültigkeit auf Opfer warten, die ihnen die Gesellschaft herbeizieht" (273–74).

97. Christian Massenbach was a colonel who was implicated in the defeat at Jena and wrote several volumes of memoirs, in part to justify himself, which were published in 1809–10. Migge, *Arnims Werke* 2, pp. 890–91.

98. Migge, *Arnims Werke* 1, p. 520. Migge notes that the source study and preliminary writing go back to the time during which Arnim was preparing *Wunderhorn,* 1804–08. He seems to have been working on *Die Kronenwächter* in 1810; by 1812 a large part was finished; in 1817 the first section appeared (Migge, 1, p. 1078).

world for poetry. The insignificant occurrences of our life tend to become an inspiration of poetry only because we looked at them with more truth than we are usually granted concerning the greater events of the world.

These truths that the accounts of individual lives reveal from times past have value for the present, for the individual who reads them and who, if he is a poet, creates "ahndungsreiche Bilder" (pictures full of presentiments) for posterity.[99] As this book's Introduction pointed out and, as we have seen in the earlier inner stories, Arnim never lost sight of the present. Indeed, the envoy makes a direct connection between his account from Froissart and present events when he urges the invalid to write his memoirs, saying that Froissart is the model for a secret history of the present age, which is yet to be written (303–4).

In his remarks about Froissart, the envoy notes that he made use of all kinds of material, as did Herodotus. Froissart used anecdotes from travelers, court assemblies, what he was able to hear and see on the spot, for he traveled a great deal. While Arnim could not return to earlier centuries to interview people, he did have a similar approach to sources.

In his urging of the invalid, the envoy asks him to do for his time what Froissart did for his. At the same time, he gives the audience a picture of the time Froissart chronicles, in which there were men who could accomplish the deeds the times demanded of them, giving the society of the country house, surrounded on every side by the enemy, "ahndungsreiche Bilder."

Just before he begins his story, the envoy says he is not interested in historical comprehensiveness but rather in giving a "Bild der Zeit" (image of the time).[100] In this effort, he admits that he was not as true to his sources as Froissart was to his; he chose only that which was useful to him. When one looks at Arnim's adaptation of Froissart, one finds that the envoy's statement does indeed reflect Arnim's approach: not perhaps in the sense to be expected, that he has changed circumstances and relationships, but in his excision of much of Froissart's detailed commentary about the political and economic manoeuvering behind the events Arnim does relate.

Arnim did not seem to permit himself the sort of liberties that he

99. Migge, *Arnims Werke* 1, p. 519.
100. Migge, *Arnims Werke* 1, pp. 519–20.

does with a literary text, such as *Insel Felsenburg,* or *Springinsfeld,* where he made major changes in identities and events. When one reads Froissart's account one no longer has the feeling, as one does with Arnim, that it is primarily a story of two men, Olivier Clisson and the duke of Brittany. Froissart's account shows Craon's attempts to prepare asylum and support for his cause from the duke of Brittany; it reveals some of the reasons for the enmity of the dukes of Burgundy and Berry towards Clisson. The extravagant duke of Berry had lost his unscrupulous treasurer, Bétisac, when the latter's extortions and cruelty became known, in part because of Clisson and de la Rivière's influence.[101] Nor do we have such a complete picture of King Charles VI's recurrent madness and the instability that it brought about.

One might ask why Arnim did not consider such events important in the "Bild der Zeit" (image of the time) that he said he would give through Froissart. It is certainly not because Arnim had read only a very little of the chronicles; piecing together anecdotes from earlier times in Clisson's life, his adaptation shows a wide-ranging knowledge of them. The answers can perhaps be found in Arnim's own ideas about history, some of which he shared with his contemporaries. Some were peculiarly his own, as in the narrative situation in which he sets the excerpts from Froissart's chronicle. In a discussion of Arnim's own ideas about the Golden Age, G. Möllers notes that, for Arnim, the concept of the "seltsame Urzeit" (peculiar primeval age)[102] was one in which God's will and man's were the same.[103] Arnim makes this point in a passage from the *Kronenwächter* introduction:

. . . wie die Eindrücke der Finger an harten Felsen im Volke die Ahndung einer seltsamen Urzeit erwecken, so tritt uns aus jenen Zeichen in der Geschichte das vergessene Wirken der Geister, die der Erde einst menschlich angehörten, . . .[104]

. . . as the imprints of fingers on hard rocks awaken the notion of a peculiar primeval time in the people, thus the forgotten influence of those spirits that once belonged to earth in a human way appears to us from those signs in history.

101. Bétisac's actual story is told in Vol. 14, pp. 58–71, of Baron Kervyn de Lettenhove's edition of works of Froissart, entitled *Oeuvres de Froissart* (Brussels, 1872). All quotations in French from Froissart's works will come from this edition, and will appear in the text with volume number and page.
102. Migge, *Arnims Werke* 1, p. 519.
103. Gerhard Möllers, "Wirklichkeit," p. 32.   104. Migge, *Arnims Werke* 1, p. 519.

Arnim believed in the continuous presence of the *Urzeit* (primeval age) in history, in spite of what the written chronicle of that time said.[105]

The discussion of the first evening's story has already shown that Arnim saw the late Middle Ages as a time in which it was easy to find men who knew what they were meant to do and did it. In the life of Olivier Clisson, Arnim must have seen such a figure. He made Clisson the centerpiece of his story: Clisson's bravery, his fidelity under pressure, the devotion of his vassals, and even of those who were not. Such a figure demands to be seen against a canvas of large dimensions, which Arnim provided from Froissart: the magnificent entry of Queen Isabella into Paris, as well as several other descriptions of life at court.

For Arnim, Clisson could have also been a model figure whose deeds could serve as an example for future generations, as the envoy has remarked in regard to historic personages at the beginning of the evening. There would be some obvious parallels between the situation in which Clisson found himself and that of many Germans in Arnim's time. The government was in unfriendly hands, collaborators betrayed countrymen for their own advancement, and protracted struggle was necessary for a victorious outcome. The envoy stresses the fact that he does not want to provide a history as such, since that is forbidden, but a picture, a picture that is meant not only to entertain but also to inspire.[106]

The preceding discussion has already hinted at the possible reason behind Arnim's beginning his adaptation with Queen Isabella's luxurious entry into Paris, a pageant that, even for Froissart's experienced eyes, was extraordinary.[107] Arnim followed Froissart closely to the meeting with the king, except for the verse which the choirboys, dressed as angels, sing to the queen at the gate of St. Denis:

> Dame enclose entre fleurs de lis,
> Reine estes vous de Paris,
> De France et de tout le pays;

105. Möllers, "Wirklichkeit," p. 33.

106. See Möllers, "Wirklichkeit," pp. 36–37. In describing Arnim's purpose in using old chronicles, Möllers suggests that they enabled him to present a pre-existent, yet dormant, historical possibility that might improve the present situation.

107. F. S. Shears, *Froissart: Life and Work*, (London, 1930), p. 57. Arnim gives the date of the triumphal entry as June 21, 1389; the actual date was August 22, 1389 (see Lettenhove, 14, p. 394). T. Johnes, *The Chronicles of Froissart* (London, no date), notes that manuscripts differ on this point (vol. 2, p. 398). Arnim's use of the June date offers one clue as to which manuscript he might have used.

Nous en ralons en Paradis,
(Froissart, XIV, 10)

Lady, surrounded by fleurs de lis, You are Queen of Paris, of France, and of the whole country. We now return to Paradise.

Schönste Lilie unter Lilien,
Königin des Paradieses,
Sieh wir bringen dir die Krone,
Gib uns einen Blick zum Lohne.
(Arnim, 306)

Most beautiful lily among lilies, queen of paradise, see, we bring you the crown; give us a glance as reward.

The differences between the two verses are an excellent contrast on a small scale of the difference in approach and emphasis of the two men. Froissart's verse emphasizes the temporal role of Isabella as Queen of France, with its mention of the fleur-de-lis and the geographical extent of her power. Arnim likens Isabella to the Virgin Mary, with his Queen of Heaven reference, as well as to a courtly lady, with its *Minnesang* phraseology (the reference to the lily and the requesting of a glance as a reward). Arnim's verse is typical of the idealized level at which he maintains much of his account.

In Arnim's adaptations, he often supplies an apparent motivating action or leaves out approaches that would reflect unfavorably on his hero. For example, in order to justify Craon's hatred of Clisson, Arnim used the arrival of Queen Isabella to provide the occasion for an indiscretion of the duke of Touraine, Charles the VI's brother. Froissart did not make this connection. It probably seemed to Arnim one of those events that could have happened but were never written down. Arnim also makes the duke's infidelity a little more palatable by making his acquaintance with the woman the result of a coincidental fall (307). The duke's liaison affords another point of comparison between Froissart and Arnim: Froissart, in introducing Craon's treachery, puts it in terms of power politics and human failing. He describes the great influence of both men, their allies, and Craon's desire to cause trouble, adding a trenchant comment about the frailty of human nature: "Ainsi les envies qui tousjours couvertemènt ont long temps régné en France, se couvrouient et dissimuloient, mais elles vindrent à trop mauvaise conclusion ["Thus the grudges that, always secretly, have long held sway in France were concealed and disguised, but they led to a very bad conclusion"] (xiv, 317).

Arnim has no such deliberation on politics or Gallic lack of virtue. Were he to do so, he would by implication weaken his portrait of Clisson. Froissart (XIV, 318) makes no mention of why Craon told the duchess of Touraine about her husband's passion; for Arnim, that apparently offered a chance to supply a motivation, the securing of her friendship and support (308).

After Peter Craon's treacherous attempt to assassinate Clisson, King Charles is determined to punish him and leads a large army to Brittany to do so. Arnim leaves out much of the political background, including the family ties between the houses of Burgundy and Brittany as well as the behavior of the dukes of Berry and Burgundy, who were the king's uncles. The conflict between these dukes and the four ministers of Charles' father, King Charles, was long-standing. The ministers had curbed the power and therefore the access to the royal treasury that the princes were glad to enjoy. The king had rewarded them handsomely; it is against this background that the jealousy of Berry and Burgundy must be seen when they complain in Arnim (312) that Clisson has too much money and must have swindled and extorted to acquire it. Since that is how Berry got what monies he did to squander, he assumes that Clisson did the same. However, that did not seem to be the case with Clisson. Both Berry and Burgundy are anxious to regain the influence they had when Charles VI had just been crowned.[108]

Arnim's omission of this background helps to keep attention centered on Clisson and the campaign to avenge him. The next group of excisions, including those relating to Charles VI's chronic madness and his weak character, serve another function, that of idealizing the king. Froissart's criticism of the king's refusal to take advice, his youthful imprudence that costs him his sanity and almost his life, is dampened considerably in Arnim's version. Arnim also condensed the medical details; though he notes that the king's doctors had advised against the march on such a hot day, one has the impression that the king is impatient with the attempts at delay by Berry and Burgundy (312). Froissart says quite bluntly that the accidental blow that led to the

108. See Lettenhove, 15, pp. 53–54. Also A. Coville, "France: Armagnacs and Burgundians (1380–1422)," in *A Cambridge Medieval History* 7, pp. 368–92, esp. pp. 368–72.

king's derangement was said by some to be the king's own fault (XV, 39). Arnim adds, "Strafen konnte man ihn nicht . . . " ["One could not punish him . . ."] (315), while Froissart says only, "On ne le povoit amender, ne faire autre, puisque Dieu vouloit que il fuist ainsi" ["One could not help (cure) him or do anything, since God willed that he be like that"] (XV, 43). Arnim weakened or left out parts of the two papal criticisms: Boniface in Rome said the king deserved his affliction for supporting the Pope at Avignon while Pope Clement at Avignon said that Charles had not kept his promise to destroy Boniface and that his madness was a punishment (XV, 50–51). Arnim kept only elements of Clement's comments about the king's mental condition, that the illness was a result of intemperate exertion and that those who did not teach him better in his youth should be punished (316). Froissart was more critical, quoting the remarks of the people who are tired of the king's irresponsibility and the threat it poses to the kingdom (XV, 90–91). Arnim, however, ascribed the king's narrow escape as a third sign that he should not indulge his youthful spirits (318).

Arnim may have had several reasons for giving the portrait of the king a somewhat different accent than Froissart. In Froissart, Charles VI is not at all unhappy at having a good reason to fight the duke of Brittany, who has been a most undependable peer, continually aiding the English, who helped him to get the duchy. Arnim presents the campaign as a fight to vindicate Clisson. It raises Clisson's stature to be defended by a dashing, recklessly brave young king rather than by a man teetering on the edge of madness who cannot cope with the various political pressures being brought to bear on him and who takes flight in dangerous pleasures of the moment. When the king loses his senses, the dukes of Berry and Burgundy rule France and take advantage of their power to rid themselves of Clisson (Arnim, 316). The rest of the *Wintergarten* reworking of Froissart concentrates on Clisson and his victory over some of his enemies, especially the duke of Brittany and Peter Craon. The ways in which Arnim describes Clisson leave no doubt as to the exemplary value of his character. They include passages on Clisson's bravery in battle (310, 318, 320), his popularity in France (318, 319), and his sense of justice (319).

Because Clisson had freed another Breton duke from an English prison and married him to his daughter, the duke of Brittany invited Clisson to his new palace. After asking Clisson to inspect the construction of a tower there, he locked him up in it and nearly put him to death. For this unpleasant memory and his sheltering of Craon, Clisson intends to pay the duke back. His resolute purpose, his bravery, his willingness to stand against an enemy and his good character all recommended him to Arnim as a good example for the Germans of his day. The other reason for the inclusion of an excerpt from Froissart's chronicles was to give a vivid example of the value of memoirs as discussed in the frame. Not only can such memoirs provide inspiration for the present, but they can also encourage others to do the same for the present age. As the envoy remarks in the frame at the beginning of the seventh evening, ". . . warum lassen Sie untergehen was Sie allein berichtigen können?" ["Why do you let perish what you alone can correct?"] (303).

The importance of the invalid's memoirs for the present age become clear when we look at the stirring example of Olivier Clisson. Memoirs are vital not only to the intellectual life of a nation, but also to its political and spiritual development. The envoy has already referred to the necessity of contemporary examples in the frame of the third evening: "Aber wisset, daß die Kinder noch dreifach schlechter als wir geraten, wenn wir uns zum Besseren aufgeben, denn nur das lebendige Beispiel erzieht, . . . " ["But know that the children will turn out three times worse yet than we if we neglect the better way, because only the living example educates"] (197). Through access to contemporary memoirs, present and future generations can find examples that not only explain what Arnim called *die geheime Geschichte* (secret history) but that also provide models worthy of emulation. There are significant parallels between Olivier Clisson and Prince Charles in the ninth evening, showing once again the consistency of theme and purpose that underlies *Wintergarten*.

Siebter Winterabend
(Seventh Winter Evening)

The seventh evening represents a sort of pause in the midst of weighty meditations on the significance of history (sixth evening) and the life of Jakob Böhme (eighth evening). Arnim tended to concentrate on one or two members of the *Landhaus* (country house) society in each frame. Here we have the enigmatic figure of the *Geniale* (ingenious lady), a woman whose moods change like quicksilver and who here seems to have no definite intellectual and spiritual mooring. Arnim began the section with a discussion of *Launen* (moods), noting that although *launig* (whimsical) meant "lustig unterhaltend," (amusingly entertaining) *Launen*, the noun, always meant bad moods (324). Such moods, the *Gedankenlaunen* (contemplative moods) are very like the Swiss *Schneelaunen* (avalanche),[109] since both could be set off by the most unrelated causes. While Arnim listed loud talking or bird flight as causes for an avalanche, his list of the bringers of bad moods contains more substantial elements, such as a bad period in history, or a longing for the ascent of a ruler loved by the people from one's own country, or a puzzling aspect of history that one cannot resolve (324). These causes indicate that political concerns, both past and present, are never far away. This situation seems to depress the ingenious lady, because when the ambassador says he luxuriates in her originality, she reproaches him, saying that that expression is an empty one, since it no longer fits the times (325). In her sense of personal inadequacy, the *Geniale* is much like Ariel, who reappears at the end of the seventh evening with his autobiography.[110]

The song that the *Geniale* plays reflected the current political mood and was taken from a letter Arnim wrote to Bettina on January 15, 1809, in which he shows signs of being depressed about the political situation in Berlin.[111] The poem reflects a mood in Arnim's letter that has some similarities with the mood in the frame. In his letter, Arnim, disconsolate about current events and saddened at being far away from Bettina, wrote a song that reflects the unease he felt at how much the times were out of joint; it appeared with few changes in *Wintergarten*.[112]

109. Arnim notes in the frame that in Swiss dialect (he does not indicate which ones), avalanches are *Schneelaunen*.

110. Arnim comments on the deleterious influence of the times on *Genialität* in "Von Volksliedern,": "Es wurde das Leben verachtet, der Tod gefürchtet, und die Genialität bei dieser Ärmlichkeit in Völlerei geseßt" (*Werke* 6, p. 452). Berchtenbreiter, *Achim von Arnim*, p. 86, says that Bettina was the model for the *Geniale*. Although Berchtenbreiter does not cite the letter to Bettina in which Arnim includes the poem that the *Geniale* uses as a song to support her point, it would have strengthened her interpretation.

111. Steig, *Achim von Arnim* 2, pp. 247, 248.

112. Steig, *Achim von Arnim* 2, p. 248. In line six of the second stanza, the letter has "Und was wir Großes thun"; Arnim probably changed *Großes* to *Geniales* (ingenious things) to fit in with the ingenious character in the frame.

The tone of the poem, with its disillusionment with the current state of things and its criticism of God for his role in events, parallels the mood of the letter as well as of the frame. The first two lines of the second stanza reflect the *Geniale's* comment that *Genialität* (ingenuity) is no longer suited to the time.

The first stanza of the poem helps to prepare the way for the inner story to follow, since it speaks of a rather disorienting state of affairs in the world. The Schelmuffsky character, with his extravagant tales and strange manner, produces such an effect, though in a much less threatening manner than contemporary political events do. The *Geniale* says as an introduction, that she has a story that will ". . . allen Streit und bösen Launen ableiten" [". . . deflect all controversy and bad moods"].

This story, which is a combination of two sources, seems to come at this juncture precisely for that purpose.[113] Arnim certainly gave evidence in the various aspects of his adaptation of having had a rather rollicking time integrating the two works and adding motifs of his own. The two sources he used, Christian Weise's *Die drei ärgsten Ertz-Narren in der ganzen Welt / aus vielen närrischen Begebenheiten hervor gesucht / und allen Interessenten zu besserem Nachsinnen übergeben [The three worst archfools in the whole world / sought out from among many foolish events / and handed over to all those interested in salutory reflection]* (1676) and Christian Reuter's *Schelmuffskys wahrhaftige, curiöse und sehr gefährliche Reise: Beschreibungen zu Wasser und Lande in Zweyen Theilen curiösen Liebhabern vor Augen geleget, und mit zweyen Lust und Trauerspielen versehen [Schelmuffsky's true, curious and very dangerous journey: descriptions on water and land presented to the eyes of curious connoisseurs, and equipped with two comedies and tragedies]* (Frankfurt und Leipzig, 1750) are sharply satirical.[114]

Weise was primarily an educator but wrote many plays for his students. He was most successful with this narrative. Weise, whose models were Grimmelshausen and Moscherosch,[115] provided the framework for the beginning and end of Arnim's inner story. It must have seemed natural to Arnim to use Schelmuffsky, since Reuter's works

113. See Hausner, *Achim von Arnim*, p. 57, who notes that seventeenth-century novels traditionally included a *Schwank*. Perhaps Arnim wanted to imitate this tradition with the tale for the seventh evening.
114. These editions of Weise and Reuter will be used for quotations.
115. Faber du Faur, *German Baroque Literature*, pp. 412–13.

were still read in the eighteenth century.[116] The free-wheeling tale of Schelmuffsky, the consummate opportunist, whose egotism is matched only by his naiveté, gave Arnim a chance to maintain the Weise framework but use Schelmuffsky as a stellar example of a much more amusing fool than anything Weise had to offer. The *Geniale* notes that, for reasons of decency, she has to leave out much of the story; certainly the lusty Charmante has been cleaned up a bit prior to her appearance in *Wintergarten*.

Reichl's account of the differences between Arnim's version and his sources is one of his most dependable efforts.[117] Because Reichl's description of Arnim's changes is very detailed, this analysis will deal primarily with the elements significant in Arnim's development of dramatic structure.

In contrast to inner stories where Arnim concentrated on more serious topics and presents his characters as more obviously exemplary figures, the moral point is made lightly and indirectly here, with a lot of irony, much of which is present in Reuter, but which Arnim also obviously enjoyed and augmented. The tone is very reminiscent of his "Wunder über Wunder" (Miracle after miracle) parody of Wilhelm Meister in *Landhausleben* (Country house life). Because he wanted to make his point with a light touch, he took out much of Weise's moralizing tone. Weise clearly intended the story to have a didactic cast. In his preface, he expresses the hope that, however amusing his readers find the fools in the story, they still consider the wise teachings that lie therein.[118] In his adaptation, Arnim left out many of Weise's aphorisms that mark Florens's path to wisdom and his inheritance.[119] The section from Weise's novel, which appears on pages 326–28 in *Wintergarten*, remains in many regards very close to Weise. Arnim's major efforts to tighten the narrative include the retention of the *Grillenfänger* (capricious person) as a companion on the trip and the deletion of Weise's painter and the rest of the entourage, because they are not needed. The painter had accompanied the group in Weise's work to paint the portraits of the fools they met.

In a very skillful manner Arnim joined the Reuter narrative with

116. Faber du Faur, *German Baroque Literature*, p. 306, notes that Goethe wrote a farce based on Reuter's *Harlequinades*.

117. Reichl's analysis fills all of the last part of his article, pp. 1–8, part II.

118. Weise, *Ertz-Narren*, p. 6.

119. Weise, *Ertz-Narren*, pp. 10, 14, 16.

Weise's through the introduction of Schelmuffsky, the loquacious guard "dog." One of Reichl's best contributions was his discovery of Armin's source for this idea.[120] Near the end of the first part of Reuter's work, Schelmuffsky returned to London, robbed of the treasures the great mogul of India gave him. He refuses to throw himself upon the mercy of his former noble friends and, instead, earns his passage from London to Hamburg by guarding the wagons at night.[121] Arnim changed the location of Weise's travelers to Hamburg and put Schelmuffsky in an inn with a similar position available, except that he guards the wagons by barking like a dog (328).

Hamburg is not only the scene of Schelmuffsky's strange employment when Arnim introduces him to his readers but also, in the Reuter novel, the place where Schelmuffsky makes the acquaintance of Charmante. Her character in the original was considerably more salacious. In the Reuter version, she does not ask Schelmuffsky to accompany her to a dance, but to come with the messenger to her room. After demanding that her visitor make himself comfortable on her bed and tell her the story of the rat and his birth once more, Charmante expresses her utter admiration in a scene that Reuter describes quite graphically. Reuter's Charmante does take Schelmuffsky to a ball, but only after the duel. In the original, this is with a Dutch nobleman, and in Arnim (337) it is with the count himself, who is angry that Schelmuffsky has taken his trousers to go to the ball.

Arnim left out Schelmuffsky's journey to Stockholm and his return to Amsterdam, when a shipwreck claims Charmante's life, as well as his own success in London. In a manner characteristic of Arnim's adaptive style, he took elements of the journeys to Stockhom and Amsterdam and combined them with the voyage to India.

Arnim's delight in continuing in Reuter's manner shows itself in the way he handled Schelmuffsky's return to Europe. In the original, Schelmuffsky was not planning to go back to India, but Arnim motivated his departure from the Mogul in an addition that was very like the original in tone:

. . . ich aber entschuldigte mich sehr artig, wie daß ich zwar ein brav Kerl wäre, der sich was Rechts versucht, aber in Hamburg hätte ich ein zwilchen Schnupf-

---

120. Reichl, 2, p. 7, discusses Arnim's adaptation of his sources in some detail in the pertinent section.
121. Reuter, *Schelmuffsky*, p. 102.

tuch vergessen, worin alle meine Sachen eingewickelt, und da nun der Herr Bruder Graf jetzt wohl schon verfault wäre, so wollte ich mir den erst holen und dann wieder kommen . . . Als ich über die Altonaische Wiese zurück kam, stieg der Geist des erstochenen Herrn Bruder Grafen, der Tebel hol mer, aus der Erde und verlangte seine schwarzen Samthosen. (343)

. . . however, I excused myself very politely, saying that, though I was a good fellow, up for trying anything exciting, I had left behind in Hamburg a handkerchief made of ticking in which all my things were wrapped. Now that my lord brother was already rotted in his grave, I wanted to go back and get it first and then come back . . . When I came back across the Altona meadow, the ghost of my stabbed lord brother, may the devil take me, rose from the earth and demanded his black velvet pants.

A comparison with the part of the original text from which Arnim made his break shows how ably he continued it so that the reader of *Wintergarten* would not realize that a change had been made unless he had the original at hand:

Ich antwortete ihm hierauf wieder und sagte, wie daß freylich was rechts hinter mir steckte, und daß ich der bravste Kerl mit von der Welt wäre, und weil ich mein Herze nur daran gehänget hätte, fremde Länder und Städte zu besehen. . . . [122]

I answered him on that point and said that of course I had courage and that I was one of the best fellows in the world, and because I had set my heart on seeing strange countries and cities. . . .

Arnim's freedom with his sources becomes more and more evident as he installed Schelmuffsky at the inn. The *Wirt im grünen Samtpelze* (innkeeper in the green velvet fur) is a recurrent figure in Schelmuffsky's adventures at the inn in Reuter. Here he pops up again, as does Dame Charmante, who reappears to Schelmuffsky in Reuter, but only as a ghost.[123] Here she is obviously still alive (343).

At this point, Arnim brought back Weise, albeit in a very loosely related way. The end of Weise's book involves the resolution of the problem of the fools, which is done through a *Collegium prudentium*. While their resolutions are sententious and full of uplifting thoughts, there are other attempts at humor in Weise's novel, so that Arnim's

122. Reuter, *Schelmuffsky*, p. 86.
123. Reichl, 2, p. 7, notes the similarity of Arnim's adaptations with the original, saying that among other things, the ghost of the brother, the count, was probably inspired by the specter of Charmante in the original.

frolicking irony is not wholly foreign to the original.[124] Arnim's synthesis of these two works shows two of the major adaptive techniques he used: rearrangement of events and invention of new ones, which have some relationship to the source.

The ending of the seventh evening, entitled "Ariel," is not an anecdote or story, as it may appear to be. Rather, it is a revealing passage that seems at least partly autobiographical and hints at certain parallels between the inner story and Ariel's. Because Ariel listens to the account of Schelmuffsky in a very thoughtful manner, the lady of the house asks Ariel if he has found such a Schelmuffsky since that evening on the gate, a person who could distract his thoughts as Schelmuffsky has done. She adds that his *Ahndung* (premonition) has not quite come about, which seems to be a reference to the dream he had the night the *Wintergarten* society discovered him on the Viktoria gate, in which Viktoria returned to him (242). Ariel tells her she is right about the dream but that it may have been induced by his terrible hunger, since it has vanished with the arrival of a friend who supplied food and clothing.

With this oblique reference to his dream, we are once again back in the uncertain atmosphere of the *Wintergarten* society, an atmosphere that the beginning of the frame in the seventh evening emphasized. Ariel remained true to his oath in spite of his present physical well-being and begins to relate his past, just as Schelmuffsky did. While the fight with the dog for a piece of meat and his avoidance of his rich friends because of his poverty have some superficial similarities with Schelmuffsky's life, it seems that these similarities are there only to point up the differences between the two. The story of Schelmuffsky's career is a diversion; Ariel wants to dedicate his life to a noble cause: "Dienen konnte ich nicht, wo ich nicht sicher war zu nützen . . ." ["I could not serve where I was not sure to be of use"] (345).

With Ariel's account, we see some of the strains of the war on those who cannot fight but who want to serve; this passage makes a parallel to those sections of the frame that have concentrated on the invalid. Like Ariel, Arnim, in the end, did not fight; like Ariel, Arnim was disillusioned with the government. Arnim's efforts to serve his country during the war years were unceasing, though frequently frustrated. Already in 1805 he had tried for military duty, but it did not work out.

124. Reichl, 2, p. 8.

His periodical "Der Preuße" (the Prussian) was almost as short-lived as his hopes for experience at the front. His brief time in Königsberg, where the Prussian court had flown, convinced him there was little hope for political activity for someone of his convictions.[125] He hoped to influence others with his work in older literature, the study of which is not an end in itself:

... ich wählte das Buch statt des Schwertes. Was mich ergreift, dem ergeb ich mich ganz, meine ganze Lebensweise entwickelte sich darnach, meinen Büchern, dieser lieben Gesellschaft aus alter Zeit zu leben. . . . Bald genügte es mir nicht, dies allein in mir zu treiben, ich fühlte einen Drang andre damit zu ergreifen und zu durchdringen. . . . wir hofften auf eine schöne Zeit für Deutschland. (345)

... I chose the book instead of the sword. I dedicate myself completely to whatever stirs me. My whole way of life developed according to the aim of living for my books, this dear company from an earlier age. . . . Soon it was not enough for me to pursue this alone in myself; I felt an urge to touch and pervade others with it. . . . We hoped for good times for Germany.

Because of Arnim's critical political writings that advocated a different social order in Germany and because of his dissatisfaction with the organization of the Prussian army, the chances for him to serve in the military were reduced. He advocated, among other things, merit promotions for army officers.[126]

125. Helene M. Kastinger Riley, *Achim von Arnim in Selbstzeugnissen und Bilddokumenten* (Hamburg, 1979), pp. 99, 54–63; Segebrecht, "Thematik des Krieges," p. 314. See also Helene M. Kastinger Riley, *Ludwig Achim von Arnims Jugend- und Reisejahre* (Bonn, 1978), pp. 58, 84–86. See also Migge, 874–75.

In a letter written in Göttingen to Brentano, September 8, 1806, Arnim wrote: "Soldat fürchtest Du daß ich werden möchte? Es wäre freilich das einfachste, aber wahrscheinlich auch das nutzloseste bei meiner Unkenntniß und Ungewohnheit in tausend nothwendigen Dingen. Aber was eben allein Werth hat in mir, was ich jedem mittheilen kann, ist diese selige Beschränktheit, die mich hier fest hält, und laut und vernehmlich will ich reden und will kein Blatt vors Maul nehmen, und mag das Wort wie leerer Wind tausendmal gesprochen worden sein, ich will es doch thun, mitfreuen, mitleiden, mitfallen, aufmuntern und trommeln, während andere fechten; kommt mir aber der Feind zu nahe, so schlage ich ihm die Trommelstöcke um die Ohren" (Steig, *Achim von Arnim* 1, p. 191).

In a letter from Berlin, Arnim wrote to Bettina on March 10, 1809: "Dieses neue Edikt macht es endlich den Menschen fühlbar, daß dieser jetzige Zustand gänzlich unerträglich ist, daß kein Krieg so verderblich wie dieser Friede, der bis zum Ärmsten selbst das Nothwendigste des Lebens aufzehrt. . . . Mich ergreift meine alte Trauer, die mich in Königsberg quälte, das Gefühl, vielleicht etwas Unrechtes aus Versehen ergriffen zu haben. Statt des Buches hätte ich das Schwerdt nehmen sollen, jetzt ist es doch eigentlich zu spät, . . . " Steig, *Achim von Arnim* 2, p. 268.

126. See Riley, *Jugend- und Reisejahre*, pp. 85–86.

Ariel's devotion to a better future for his country, like Arnim's, had to show itself in other ways. He says at the beginning of this section that he has remained true to his oath (apparently to wait for the return of Viktoria) and has given away a small silver lamp that came back from the Crusades with an ancestor. Arnim's choice of this particular antique serves to draw a parallel between the Crusades as a holy war and the current struggle; even such a revered possession must be given up, though that is little enough (345).

Ariel's depression had reached such depths that he was tempted to destroy himself and the city with fires and explosions. Just at this point, an old friend, revealed later as the invalid, appears and rescues him from his physical and spiritual misery. Ariel sees the hand of God in this rescue (346); his triumphant certainty contrasts sharply with the attitude towards God in the song at the beginning of the seventh evening.

Ariel's account ties in much more strongly with other parts of the *Wintergarten* than the ending that Migge suggests that Arnim had planned before the Ariel character was introduced.[127] One of Ariel's functions in the frame is to serve as a counterpoint to the invalid, who has done what Ariel and Arnim could not manage. This connection surfaces in this section, when Ariel hints broadly that it is the invalid who has rescued him from the demoralizing burden of his physical needs. In a larger sense, however, only the invalid can rescue the Ariels. Only someone who has made the sacrifice of fighting can, in a sense, save those who have not.[128]

Achter Winterabend
(Eighth Winter Evening)

The end of the frame in the seventh *Winterabend* emphasizes the beneficent role of Divine Providence and how conviction comes after long preoccupation with a subject. This religious note carries over into

127. See Migge, 2, p. 877–78, where the original ending is reprinted.
128. Weiss, *Achim von Arnim*, does not analyze the function of the Ariel excursus and implies that it is out of place, p. 57.

the eighth *Winterabend*, with a reference to church attendance and to Jakob Böhme, in whose works the lady of the house is immersed when the narrator finds her. She is perplexed, because she has heard so many conflicting opinions about Böhme from people who have never read him (347). The narrator explains that he came to Böhme in a manner similar to hers (348).

The narrator's experience parallels that of Arnim, who apparently changed the disparaging opinion of his youth in regard to Böhme.[129] Böhme's standing among Arnim's contemporaries also provides a means for taking the intellectual temperature of his countrymen, this time on a spiritual level. In speaking about those Germans who regard enthusiasm for Böhme as a *Modekrankheit*, the narrator says that if a fashionable mental disease were possible, it would help the country. A general spiritual movement would revive it, and those who survived would finally be healthy (347). The implication here, that a spiritual awakening would help the country, relates closely to previous remarks in the frame on the condition of the German nation and foreshadowed the coming individual decisions to change the directions of their lives.

In order to fight the frequent tendency to mock any kind of enthusiasm (347), the narrator takes Böhme as an example of how such an attitude can block a real appreciation of his works and proceeds to justify the man. Because of the confusion about Böhme, where some think him mad, others holy, the narrator advocates an examination of his life (348). This conviction, that only biography can reveal the inner man, reflects the earlier frame conversations, where memoirs and their value are discussed. The narrator indicates that he himself has collected anecdotes and material about Böhme's life in the form of a poem about them that he will read that evening.

Arnim's own notes on a manuscript, "Aus dem Leben Jakob Böhmes" (from the life of Jakob Böhme), now lost, indicate that he compiled this biography at the time he was writing the *Wintergarten*.[130] Migge notes that his source was Abraham von Frankenberg und Ludwigsdorf, whose biography of Böhme is the major source for the mys-

---

129. Sternberg, *Arnims Lyrik*, pp. 179–81, discusses Arnim's changing opinion of Böhme. Sternberg cites two letters of Arnim's, one to Winckelmann, September 14, 1801, and the other to Brentano, July 9, 1802 (Steig, *Achim von Arnim* 1, pp. 24, 38) with negative comments about Böhme. Sometime before 1809 his opinion altered dramatically.

130. Migge, 2, p. 875.

tic's life.[131] Migge's evaluation of Arnim's use of his source, though accurate, did not have the space to show Arnim's originality.[132] An examination of the Frankenberg biography and comparison of Arnim's reinterpretation proves that Arnim's originality has been undervalued. Arnim not only reworked the prose text, weaving incidents and events from Frankenberg's account into his own fictionalized verse frame, but he also expanded the brief remarks about Beer into a narrative and created striking parallels with the frame within the poem. The character of Sela seems to be fictional,[133] but the story of Sela, the apprentice sent by the Jesuits to spy on Böhme, contains many biographical details from von Frankenberg's own background. Through his uncle, Abraham von Sommerfield, Frankenberg as a young man became interested in Böhme, whom he met in 1622, just two years before the mystic's death. Like Sela, he devoted himself to the master as a young man.[134] The identity of Sela is not as important as what he represents: the effect of Böhme on younger people. Arnim seems to have used the Sela section as a positive example of Böhme's influence on youth, connecting it with the didactic concerns of the narrator in the frame, so as to help in the spread of an appreciation of Böhme. Sela is a beneficial model for the confused and unknowing individuals in Arnim's contemporary society, an interpretation that receives added support when the Aurora incident at the end of the poem is also considered.

In the poem, Aurora is Böhme's daughter, who inflames Sela so that he finally sees the inner sense of the master's teaching. Arnim's own poetic imagination is at work here, since Böhme had only four sons. However, his first important work, *Morgenröte im Aufgang* (1612) (Au-

---

131. Migge, 2, p. 875; Faber du Faur, *German Baroque Literature*, p. 31.

132. Migge, 2, p. 875. Reichl did not have access to a copy of Frankenberg, II, p. 8, so he has little to contribute. The only other work that has dealt with Arnim and Böhme is Irmgard Berchtenbreiter's *Achim von Arnims Vermittlerrolle.*

133. See Sternberg, *Arnims Lyrik*, p. 181; See also Hans Grunsky, *Jacob Böhme* (Stuttgart, 1956), whose biography contains a list of individuals whom Böhme knew personally (pp. 345–47); there is no Sela among them.

134. See Grunsky, *Böhme*, p. 50, 42. Grunsky also refers to a letter of Böhme's detailing his spiritual developments (p. 42); it can be found in *Theosophia Revelata oder Alle Göttlichen Schriften Jacob Böhmens* 9 (1730), edited by Will-Erich Peuckert (Stuttgart, 1956), xxi, pp. 29–41. Arnim could have found other parallels for Sela in Frankenberg's biography, men such as Dr. Balthasar Walther, a physician whom Frankenberg mentions. Well traveled in the Orient, Walther had dabbled in the Cabbala, in magic, and in chemistry, but had not found what he searched for until he read *Morgenröte*. He seems to have come to Görlitz after he read it and spent several months with Böhme. See Grunsky, *Böhme*, pp. 37–38.

rora. That is the day-spring or dawning of the day in the orient), was soon called *Aurora* by Dr. Balthasar Walther.[135] Aurora seems to function both as an allegorical presence as well as a real one, paralleling the figure of Winter, who reappears immediately before the narrator recites his poem. These two figures show a tendency that becomes characteristic of Arnim's later work, to make figures from legend appear in everyday life, a technique that Hoffmann also used, but for different reasons. In juxtaposing the two figures of Aurora and Winter, Arnim has provided a skillful contrast by example. Both of the allegorical characters figure in love relationships, but, while the coming marriage of the lady of the house to Winter is a sign of her depressed and desperate feelings since the departure of her French officer,[136] the marriage of Aurora and Sela demonstrates Sela's desire to grow and expand his horizons. Winter dies when Spring comes, while Aurora, whom Sela marries in a garden in spring, is a continual source of inspiration.

Another example of the contrast between Aurora and Winter comes near the end of the poem, as Böhme speaks to Sela, his new son-in-law, after Sela's marriage to Aurora:

> Du hast mit ernstlichem Bemühen,
> Mit frischer Kraft zusamm' gelernt,
> Der Tag wird heiß zusammenglühen,
> Was winterlich getrennt entfernt. (360)

With serious effort and fresh strength, you have learned all sorts of things; day will bring together in rapture what was separated and put at a distance by winter.

135. Abraham von Frankenberg's biography of Jacob Böhme comes at the beginning of the 1682 edition of his works, published in Amsterdam, and has as its title, *Bericht von dem Leben in Abschied des in Gott selig-ruhenden Jacob Böhmens, dieser Theosophischen Schriften eigentlichen Authoris und Urhebers*. Since the pages either are not numbered individually or are numbered only on the right-hand side, with the number preceded by two asterisks, I have adopted the following method of citation: if **2 is on the right, a quotation from the page on the left will be noted as facing p. **2. On the page that faces p. **3, Frankenberg notes that Böhme had four sons. On the page facing p. **5, Frankenberg says that Dr. Balthasar Walther called *Morgenröte Aurora*. In the 1682 edition, the word *Aurora* stands on an introductory page with a picture before the title page. See also Grunsky, *Böhme*, p. 29, who notes that Böhme had only three sons and not the daughter whom legend accords to him. J. Hoffmeister, *Der ketzerische Schuster: Leben und Denken des Görlitzer Meisters Jakob Böhme* (East Berlin, no date), says, p. 34, that Böhme had no daughters, though another Böhme in his village did.

136. Migge, 2, p. 877.

A union with Winter is not the proper one for the lady of the house, as the end of the story will show, nor is a condition of the winter of the soul a good one for the Germans.

The middle section of the poem deals with material that Arnim took, though not without some rearrangement and adaptation, from Frankenberg's *Lebenslauf* (biography).[137] Arnim changed from the third person narration of the biography to first person as Böhme related his life to Sela. The poem indicates Böhme worked for a herdsman,[138] but the reference to his wages and his wish "Um wenig Kost und Weihnachtgabe, Und wünschte einst mir Flügelein" ["For a bit of food and a Christmas gift, and I wished one day for little wings"] (352) are Arnim's invention.

Arnim's addition of miraculous details, making Böhme into some sort of half-divine child, appears in his treatment of the cave incident. Although Frankenberg, unlike Böhme, was partial to miracles,[139] Arnim went far beyond his sober account that described the open entryway that Böhme found in the mountain. This space contained a large tub full of money that Böhme left untouched.[140] In the poem, Arnim has an eagle grasp his clothing and carry him to Landeskron, where an old man sits in the cave with the treasure. In contrast to Frankenberg, Arnim's Böhme feels at home in the cave; he even plays with the treasure and plaits the old man's beard (353). Perhaps Arnim wanted to heighten the contrast between this cave and the one that Johann Beer finds with criminals. If he intended this incident to have that function and that with the eagle to prefigure the sense of the divine blessing and protection, he would capture the spirit, if not the exact sequence of events, of the Frankenberg biography. Frankenberg shows us Böhme's presentiment of evil; not only does Böhme sense horror in the cave, but an artist who took the treasure a few years later dies a horrible death.[141] Frankenberg does not use the dramatic device of an eagle swooping down out of the sky to lift the child as a sign of divine

137. The events in Böhme's biography that appear on p. 354 in *Wintergarten* are taken from the page facing p. **3 through the page facing p. **5 and the page facing **6 in Frankenberg, *Bericht*, but they do not always appear in the order in which they do in the Frankenberg biography.

138. Frankenberg, *Bericht*, facing page **2.

139. Faber du Faur, *German Baroque Literature*, p. 31.

140. See Sternberg, *Arnims Lyrik*, p. 181–82, for comments about Arnim's changes from Böhme's mother imagery to his own daughter personification.

141. Frankenberg, *Bericht*, facing p. **2.

predestination, but he does see the cave incident as a sort of prefiguration of Böhme's spiritual entry into divine secrets.[142] The eight stanzas
that Arnim devotes to the cave incident foreshadow the Johann Beer
story. It takes up far more space than any other biographical anecdote
that Böhme relates in this section.[143]

It is striking that the only section of the biography in which he felt
impelled to make major changes was the one concerning the cave, yet,
as has been indicated, he seemed to have definite reasons for doing so,
as he wanted to set up a contrast with his version of the Johannes Beer
story. It is greatly expanded from the account in the source, so much
so that, instead of being called an adaptation, it should be viewed as an
original piece.

After the end of the verse biography, Ariel relates an incident that
parallels in a prosaic way Böhme's discovery of the door. This factual
recounting in the frame of a device treated poetically in the inner story
is a device we find used in a much more extensive way in *Die Serapionsbrüder* (see Chapter Two, the discussion on "Fräulein Scuderi"). The
narrator notes the frequency of such anecdotes, with which comment
he introduces the anecdote entitled "Johann Beer." It comes from
Frankenberg, who cites a number of other miraculous incidents involving sudden discoveries of caves before relating in more detail the
incidents surrounding Beer.[144]

Arnim took four major elements from Frankenberg's account: the
piety of Johann Beer, the treasure in the cave, the three doomed souls,
and Beer's conversations with them. In Frankenberg's biography, both
caves have an evil aspect about them; in Arnim, as we have seen,
Böhme's did not. In both accounts, Beer seems to have run into a spot
where evil permeates the atmosphere. But in Armin's account, we feel
it much more palpably, from the beginning of the story. Resolved to
act upon his discovery of the cave, Beer feels a powerful wind with a
terrible hail or downpour. This natural warning terrifies him so much
that he retreats from the cave. After a number of weeks, he decides to
try again, on the first Sunday after Easter, a time with symbolic significance. This time he finds a narrow passage with no wind, which is

142. Frankenberg, *Bericht*, facing p. **2.
143. The rest of Arnim's account of Böhme's life stays quite close to Frankenberg,
although Arnim does change the order of the pewter plate revelation and the visit of the
mysterious stranger to the shop, reversing Frankenberg's sequence.
144. Frankenberg, *Bericht*, p. **2.

strangely lit. He knocks on the door to gain entrance to a compartment. There he finds three emaciated men with old-fashioned skullcaps who flounder in the sloughs of despond. Their appearance bespeaks punishment and guilt, as does the black velvet book that lies open in front of them: *Buch des Gehorsams* (book of obedience) (362). Surrounded by the murderous weapons that were the tools of their damnation, they wait for the Last Judgment. They know they have done evil, but they do not repent; nor do they have any hope that they will be able to perform good works in the future. Theologically speaking, they are in a fairly desperate state, since they cannot repent and have no hope. Since they do not will to do good, they cannot know God, who, as the narrator says, is the highest good (362). Beer brings them to the point where they feel they are changing, yet they are not sure whether they can find the necessary will and desire in themselves to complete the process.

In some respects, given the season of the liturgical year and the remark of the narrator that the hour of revelation is at hand, this scene is reminiscent of the story of Christ on the cross and the two thieves. In the Beer account, however, Beer has to leave before complete repentance is assured, with the promise that he will come back. From Beer's son-in-law, who is a minister, the narrator learns that Beer visited these condemned men and perhaps was able to bring them to repentance (363).

The ending of the Johann Beer anecdote contains the presence of an unusual glow around the bed of Beer and his wife; he says it is a guardian angel sent from God. The effect of this angel is to make her more devout and more attentive to her own behavior, as she tries to build a peaceful Christian marriage (363). The tone of the ending, as well as the presence of the angel, indicate the exemplary nature of Beer's life, which his wife echoes. They stand in sharp contrast to the lost souls in the cave. Just as Böhme's cave served as a sign of his special favor and foreshadowed his election to a special mission for God, Beer's cave serves as an inner space where the redemptive powers available to the committed Christian could be exercised. While this section provides further evidence of Beer's sanctity, it also reinforces Arnim's portrayal of marriage, which he explored more fully in Albert and Concordia's lives in the second *Winterabend*.

The theme of marriage, which also figured in the poem about

Böhme, has significance for the story that the lady of the house tells to fill the rest of the evening. The tentative change of heart of the men in the cave parallels the change in Polia, who turns her hatred of Poliphil to love. However, the subtle and extensive connections between the Poliphil and Polia story and the frame reach far beyond this obvious parallel. The romantic interest in the story corresponds to that of the lady of the house, who knew the invalid before the war (368), fell in love with the French officer, and has now decided to marry Winter. Through the lady's decision to marry a half-allegorical figure, she parallels Polia's decision to serve Diana. Marriage to an allegory enables her to remain faithful in her memory to the French officer.

Another similarity between the lady of the house and Polia in the first part of the story lies in the hardheartedness they show towards their admirers—the lady towards the invalid and Polia towards Poliphil. Poliphil falls dead after she has made her vows to Diana (365); the narrator refers to his body as *erstarrt* (stiffened) (366). When the lady announces in the frame following the story that she will marry Winter, her statement has a similar effect on the invalid, who becomes stiff and pale (367). The story serves as a two-part foreshadowing of events in the frame that include the marriage to Winter, the despair of the invalid, and the hints that the lady will perhaps marry him (435).

The *Polifilio* of Francesco Colonna, an Italian monk, is a rambling Renaissance account of the search for an ideal love among tableaux both pagan and allegorical.[145] The shortened French translation from 1804 contains two books, the first dominated by Poliphil's long and eventually successful search for Polia. The second book presents Polia's account of their trials, with additional accounts by Poliphil. While Arnim's version leaves out many of the allegorical trappings and scenes, his retelling does retain the unreal feeling that permeates the original. The cloud of dust that seizes the hard-hearted Polia , the strange scenes she sees in it, her resurrection of Poliphil, all add to the atmosphere of fantasy. The sustaining of this imaginary world in the adaptation was important to its function in the frame.

An examination of Le Grand's version shows that Arnim changes the character of Polia from the original account, chiefly through addi-

---

145. Migge, 2, p. 875. He notes 2, p. 876 that Arnim used the 1804 French translation. The edition cited here is *Le Songe de Poliphile*, traduction libre de l'italien, J. G. Le Grand (Paris, 1804).

tions that cast her in an initially less favorable light. In Arnim's version, Poliphil is an architect who comes to Polia's street to see her family's palace and ends up falling in love with her when he sees her at the window. Since Poliphil annoys her, Arnim's Polia greets his repeated forays into her street with a turned back. The original Polia is less aware and hence less malicious (115). Colonna's Polia seems to sin against love through ignorance and not through willfullness. Colonna seems more interested in symbolic representations than in individual interaction. This tendency sets his story apart from some of Arnim's changes; Arnim's Polia resembles the lady of the house much more than does her prototype.

While the original Polia scarcely remembers what Poliphil looked like (117), Arnim's Polia stares at her admirer in horror and thinks she hates him when she sees him again (364). In the original, this reaction only comes after Poliphil's many attempts to see her after she has taken her vows to Diana (119). Arnim condensed this section, letting her rejection happen on the day she enters Diana's service (364).

Since the original Polia did not wilfully dismiss Poliphil's attentions when he first saw her, she was quicker to realize the error of her ways. Arnim's Polia realizes the enormity of what she has done only after the terrible vision of the beasts who cannot eat the hard hearts of the cruel women they had torn apart. Although Arnim shortened this part of the original, he added another section to this vision, in which the wild animals force Polia in a dream to eat the stone hearts of these women, causing her to lose her teeth. Previous analyses have shown that Arnim liked such additions; they helped to emphasize a point but were so closely integrated into the original that the seam was not visible, thus increasing the didactic value of the older material.

Arnim retained the scenes with Polia's nurse, shortening and adding, as he had done before. The description of the supremely revolting man whom one sinner against Venus received as a husband is Arnim's addition (366); the original refers to him concisely as a *malotru* (lout, 129). Arnim chose to end his account at the point when the lovers are driven out of Diana's temple into the realm of Venus. This love story in the inner frame foreshadows the love interest that dominates the closing frame of the evening.

Immediately after this story, the lady announces her engagement to Winter. The invalid's reaction reveals to the reader the longstanding attachment between them, since he had courted her already before the war (368). Feeling herself forgotten by him because of the fighting, she fell in love with the French officer. With this background, we can understand the feeling of personal betrayal that causes him so much anguish. Not only has he been crippled physically in the service of his country, but he has also been damaged emotionally:

Was jammern doch die Menschen jetzt soviel über die Münzscheine für echtes Gold und Silber, wer gibt mir auch nur einen Schein für meine Hoffnungen, die andern erfüllt sind, für meine Wünsche, die andern gewährt, für meine Dienste, die alle verloren, für meine Erfahrungen, die mir alle unnütz, für meine Zuneigungen, die außer Kurs gesetzt sind. . . (368–69)

What are people now complaining about paper money instead of real gold and silver? Who will give me only one bank note for my hopes that have been fulfilled for others; for my wishes that others have been granted; for my services that have all been lost; for my experiences that are all of no use for me; for my affections that have all become worthless.

The narrator, impressed with the goodness of the man, becomes angry about the war, since it disrupted the couple's attachment (368). This scene proves once more that it is impossible to keep the recent past from the *Wintergarten* society, since this past permeates every relationship.

In order to comfort the invalid, the narrator includes two poems to close the eighth evening, both love songs. The first song, an account of a celebration before a wedding on a cold winter night, ends with the death of the bride and the man she loved; he catches her wreath on his sword and kills himself because she is dead. The invalid protests that such a song will not help him, since the love is mutual. However, the second song, "Frühlingsnacht," has a similar theme, which brings the two lovers to their death once they were reunited. Unlike the previous "Winternacht," these two rise again as larks (377).

The coming of dawn in the poem, with its reunion of the two lovers and the mention of Aurora, echoes the Böhme poem, in which Aurora symbolized the advent of wisdom and happiness in love. Perhaps that is why the invalid remarked, before he heard the poems, that "Wer in der Liebe lebt, der lebt in Gott, wer ungeliebt hier lebt, den holt der Teufel" ["Whoever lives in love, lives in God; whoever lives here without being loved, may the Devil take him"] (368). Every section of the eighth evening has reinforced the message that love of God and love between man and woman are connected: the marriage of Sela and Aurora, Venus's aid to Polia and Poliphil, and the resurrection of the dead lovers as larks. Arnim integrated the main theme of these inner stories with the novella in the frame, the private affair of the lady of the house and the invalid, that is in turn connected with the events of the day. The eighth evening is particularly significant because the lady of the house decides to marry Winter, making it ultimately possible for the frozen *Wintergesellschaft* (winter society) to make personal decisions about individual courses of action.[146]

Neunter Winterabend
(Ninth Winter Evening)

The ninth evening, the last in the series before the conclusion, Arnim once again returned to the theme of war, this time the 1745–46 Scottish Rebellion led by Bonny Prince Charlie. Migge believed that Arnim probably became acquainted with the legends about Prince Charles on his trip through Scotland in 1804.[147] His source, *Ascanasius Or The Young Adventurer; Containing an Impartial History of the Rebellion in Scotland*, which Arnim frequently translated word for word, shortens, and to which he makes frequent additions, is a curious mixture of pro-Georgian sympathies for the victory over the rebels and definite personal admiration for the prince, particularly in the second part, which deals with his escape. Arnim couples this excursus with an ode on the adventures of a young Celtic hero attempting to avenge a long-standing offense. Unlike the earlier evenings, this Scottish account is not prefaced by a frame giving clues to its function. The first and most obvious reason for its inclusion was its connection with the military and political events that dominated the fourth and sixth evenings and made their appearance in the third and the fifth. Another factor that might have drawn Arnim to the magnetic prince was a fallacy, wide-

146. Segebrecht, "Thematik des Krieges," p. 314, says that though this union devastates the invalid, yet it ushers in the end of the period of numbness.
147. Migge, 1, p. 876.

spread since the mid-eighteenth century, that the Celts were Teutonic.[148] In their fate he might well have seen a warning for their putative cousins, the Germans. But, in order to understand what appealed to Arnim, we have to consider the story itself and the changes he made in his adaptation.

The figure of Prince Charles Stuart understandably greatly attracted Arnim, particularly at the time in which he was writing *Der Wintergarten*. Charles was a young man who could act courageously and was willing to sacrifice himself for his country.[149] He did not give up, even in his desperate plight, hunted by the king's men. Arnim also devoted considerable space in his adaptation to the brave Scots who aided the prince in his flight, including one young woman, Flora Macdonald; these people risked their lives and many were imprisoned for aiding the Pretender. This behavior contrasts with that of many Germans, whom Arnim criticized throughout *Wintergarten*, as he accused them at various times of cowardice, inadequate sacrifice, and collaboration with the enemy. Much of the material in Arnim's source came from contemporary eyewitnesses, which, given Arnim's own preferences for the value of such accounts as shown in the sixth evening of Froissart, must have seemed valuable and of interest to him.

The changes Arnim made in his source lay largely in romanticizing the Scots' cause and adding sections that did not exist in the original text but that Arnim skillfully integrated to make his point. In adapting his source, Arnim tended to leave out all praise of English valor, which the *Impartial History* includes. This tendency is particularly noticeable when one compares the account of the Battle of Culloden in the English account and in *Wintergarten*. Here Arnim completely ignored the praise of the duke of Cumberland that abounds in his source.[150]

Arnim's reluctance to praise the English probably has several

---

148. Robson-Scott, *Literary Background*, p. 39, in discussing Klopstock's fascination with Ossian, notes that P. H. Mallet's history of Denmark had put out the notion that the Celts were Germanic, an idea that was very popular.

149. See Charles's speech during his flight on p. 405: "Kapitän, ich hätte gut Leben gehabt, wenn ich ruhig geblieben, aber ich wollte vielen andern ein gutes Leben geben, wenn ich König würde. Ein guter König ist der größte Sklave in seinem Reiche, keine Stunde gehört ihm, was ich erlitten, ist nichts gegen das, was mir bevorsteht, . . . Jetzt kenne ich Elend, jetzt kenne ich Menschen, das sollte jeder kennen, eh' er herrschen will."

150. See pp. 70–72 of *Impartial History*.

sources.[151] One of the most obvious reasons he did not is that he wanted to glorify the Scottish people, particularly the Highlanders as they used to be. An examination of Arnim's additions make this tendency clear. He expanded and changed the source in portraying Prince Charles and the Scots as an ethnic entity. One of the first instances of his idealization of the prince comes early in the report, where the English source mentions only that after the victory at Prestonpans, Charles lived in Holyrood House.[152] Arnim used Charles's stay in Holyrood as an opportunity to link him to Scotland's past and to inspire him to brave efforts through the influence of the great events to which the rooms of Holyrood bore witness (375).

The memories that haunt Holyrood prove a foreshadowing of Charles's personal courage. After the English defeat at Falkirk, Charles and the Highlanders want to press on to further victories, but the Lowlanders, alarmed by the English reinforcements, long to surrender. In reference to Charles Arnim commented that the strength of youth that a great man possesses expects more than the mixed masses of mankind can achieve (378). The most telling comment that Arnim made on Charles's bravery came in his comment on the end of the Battle of Culloden:

Als Gott die Hochländer verließ, die sich in blinder Furcht über die Heide zerstreuten, als jeder seiner selbst nur gedachte und jeder sein Elend fühlte, da stand der Prinz noch unbeweglich bei Culloden. (385)

When God abandoned the Highlanders, who dispersed across the heath in blind fear, when everybody thought only of himself and everybody felt his misery, the prince still stood fast at Culloden.

Part of Charles's problem is that he gains his reputation in the manner in which he loses, while his opponent, the duke of Cumberland, al-

151. Anti-English sentiments appear in Steig, *Achim von Arnim* 1, in a letter which Arnim wrote to Brentano on July 5, 1803, where he criticizes the state of the arts in England and notes: "Sind auch die Engländer seit Elisabeth stets gesunken, . . ." (p. 95). In this same letter he mentions in an approving manner Walter Scott's *Minstrelsy of the Scottish Border*, which had just appeared earlier in the year, and criticizes the English (p. 95). Both here and in the text of the ninth evening (381, 402), Arnim expresses a love for Scottish folk music. It is easy to see from the adaptation of the text of the ninth evening that he was quite pro-Scottish; one interpolation that bears this out and has nothing to do with politics appears on p. 404, during the foot-washing scene; Arnim comments on the custom of Scottish girls of washing the feet of strangers, an extraordinary kindness in his eyes.

152. *Impartial History*, see p. 10, "He now returned in triumph to Edinburgh, where he took up his residence in the palace at Holyrood House."

ready enjoyed considerable renown. Because of the high regard in which the duke is held, he can turn a defeated army into a pursuant, victorious one. Arnim noted that a young man like Charles too easily discounted the value of reputation, assuming that it must grow bigger (378–79). Charles maintains his bold courage even throughout a long and dangerous flight from his would-be captors. Arnim followed the source fairly closely here as well, though he often added elements that reinforced this quality; he revealed at the same time Charles' consciousness of his lineage. When Charles and his helper think they may be forced into hand-to-hand combat with four pursuers, they discuss how many each could kill. Charles says he would not want to bear the name he does if he could not kill two himself. Arnim also could not resist portraying Charles in a kingly manner not found at that point in the original. In one such meeting, the English source says only, ". . . where everything necessary was concerted"[153]; Arnim added,

Sie fand ihn auf dem Hügel: den Königssohn, wie den ärmsten seines Volks in jeder Beschwerde; aber ruhig und standhaft, als ruhte noch des Landes Schicksal in seinem Herzen; sie begrüßte ihn ehrerbietig, er empfing sie gnädig. (391)

She found him on the hill: the son of a king, in every discomfort, like the poorest of his people, yet calm and steadfast, as if the fate of his country still rested in his heart. She greeted him respectfully; he received her gracefully.

Such regal pose and bearing, even in the midst of adversity, increase the value of Charles as a model worthy of imitation.

Sometimes Arnim's desire to make Charles seem kinglike went to rather extreme lengths. When Charles is hiding at John McKinnen's house, the maid, according to ancient Scottish custom, washes his feet. She does it so energetically that, in the original, Charles asks that she not ". . . go so far up with her hand, he having only a philibeg (kilt) on."[154] Arnim, unwilling to resolve the question of what a Scottish prince wears under his kilt, says: ". . . nicht so weit hinauf mit der Hand zu waschen, weil sie an sein Degengefäß stoße" [". . . not to wash so far up with her hand because she was bumping against his sword guard"] (404).

Arnim encouraged the reader's sympathy for Charles not only

153. *Impartial History*, "She accompanied O'Neil to the Prince, where everything necessary was concerted" (p. 121).
154. *Impartial History*, p. 149.

through admiring descriptions of his personal valor, but also through addition of details that added to the poignancy of Charles's defeat. A good example is the comment he made when Charles, in flight, leaves Scotland from the same place he landed to lead the rebellion; Arnim noted that he arrived with almost the same small number of men, but with the confident warmth of youth (386). After the battle of Culloden, where the English text says simply, "Here it was the Prince first despaired . . ."[155], Arnim expands the thought:

. . . ernst gab er da sein Unternehmen auf, entließ alle, damit jeder auf den mannigfaltigen Wegen die Verfolger irrte und entkäme; der Zukunft warf er seine Krone zu. Die treuen Freunde . . . brachten nach allen Richtungen die traurige Friedensbotschaft durch das Land. (385)

. . . there he gave up his enterprise in a grave manner, dismissed all, so that everyone could confuse the pursuers and escape; he entrusted his crown to the future. The faithful friends . . . took the sad message of peace in all directions through the country.

Such additions arouse the readers' attraction not only to the prince but also to his cause.

Prince Charles, as the rightful king of Scotland and a man of great personal valor, provides an example of courage in the Rebellion and bravery in defeat, but he was also of interest to Arnim as the representative of the Scottish people. For Arnim, the Scots as a group, though not as individuals, have fallen away from their former greatness. Again and again in his adaptation, Arnim added not only comments about the bravery of individual Scots, but also reflective passages on the historical development of the Scots. In order to build up the desired ethnic portrait, Arnim left out details that did not fit, such as attention to the bravery of the Scots who sided with the English. He lists only those prominent Scots who were against the prince (375).[156] Even in short phrases, Arnim tried to put the Scots in the best possible light. Where the English source says, "a few Scots"[157] Arnim wrote, ". . . der Rest treuer Schotten" [". . . the remnant of faithful Scots"] (385). The additions that Arnim made elaborated on the differences between the Scots of old and those now, and helped to explain the terrible debacle. Per-

155. *Impartial History,* p. 98.
156. *Impartial History,* pp. 11, 14–15.
157. *Impartial History,* p. 98.

haps Arnim, looking for reasons for German defeat, found it here in the Scottish decline from earlier times. In a significant passage, Arnim described the outcome of the Battle of Culloden as ". . . die letzte Hoffnung der alten vordeutschen Zeit" [". . . the last hope of the old pre-German time"] (381). Up to the time of the battle, Arnim criticized the caution of Charles's advisors, who wanted to hold back when he should have risked everything: "Im Kriegsrat drängten nun die Häupter seiner Partei zum Rückzuge; sie waren nicht für das Außerordentliche geschaffen, und hatten es doch unternommen" ["In the war council, the leaders of his party pressed for retreat; they were not made for the extraordinary, and yet had undertaken it" (376). The Lowlanders were afraid to fight, while some of Charles' adherents deserted him after Culloden and recanted their support during the post-Rebellion trials. Arnim condensed some of the trial material, which was extensive in the source, but described in detail the Earl von Kilmarnoch's and Lord Balmerino's deaths. The former, in a craven way, recanted his support for Charles, while the latter, blessing King James to the end, went to his death with a gallantry and grace that moved even his executioner to lose his nerve (382–84).

When the cause of a Balermino and a Charles Stuart was lost, then there was no longer any hope for the Scots as a race. Arnim described their rapid descent from their earlier greatness in terms of the decay of tribal customs and the adoption of a new economic order imposed after the defeat by England:

Das innere Gesetz, das die Herren mit ihren Stämmen verbunden, die Ehre der Gewalt über Menschen, mit denen sie bis dahin wie die Könige alter Zeit, als Häupter der Familien verbunden, verschwand; es blieb nur noch der Reiz des Eigentums . . . die armen Hochländer mußten aus dem Lande wandern, das ihre Voreltern gegen zwei Jahrtausende mit ihrem Blut geschützt hatten, viele gingen nach Amerika und fochten da für die Freiheit; die Fragmente der Lieder, von Macpherson gesammelt und verbunden, tönten wie ein Nachhall ihres Todesseufzers durch ganz Europa. (381)

The inner law that had bound the lords to their tribes vanished, as well as the privilege of power over people by which, like the kings of old, they had been bound together until then as heads of the families; only the attraction of property remained. The poor Highlanders had to migrate from the country that their ancestors had protected with their blood for nearly two thousand years; many went to America and fought for liberty there. The fragments of the songs, collected and joined together by Macpherson, sounded through all of Europe like an echo of their final sigh.

Because their inner law had gone, the Scots could no longer function as an entity. Like the Germans who collaborated with the French, they now sought to carve out positions of prestige with the enemy.

In his juxtaposing of the cowardly Lowlanders versus the brave individuals who stood by Charles, the timid counselors who were less courageous than the simple foot soldier (376), the craven Kilmarnoch over against the doughty Balmerino (382–84), Arnim wanted to accomplish two ends: to explain the German defeat by Napoleon in terms of the lack of personal courage of the part of too many people and also, through the examples of individual bravery, to show what could be accomplished and to what nobleness of character it could lead. The report stood also as a warning: if the Germans did not pull themselves out of their hibernation and regenerate their nation, they would suffer a fate similar to that of the Scots.

Part of the appeal that the Scots had for Arnim lay in their poetry, which reflected their greatness. Even before he went to Scotland, Arnim had read Walter Scott's *Minstrelsy of the Scottish Border*. At the inclusion of a folk song in the ninth evening text (401), Arnim said it had a Scottish parallel and referred to the work of Henriette Schubart in translating Scottish folk songs. However, the most important body of poetry to Arnim for understanding the Scots was that of Ossian; the preceding quotation referred to MacPherson's work and its importance, reflecting as it does the valor of a vanquished race. Prince Charles, who represented the finest Scottish virtues of courage and ardor, stood alone and could not save his nation, suffering the fate of defeated Scottish chieftains of old.

Since Arnim saw Charles as the last representative of an earlier age of Scottish chieftains, it would be only natural for him to look to Mac-Pherson for the song that closes the inner story of the ninth evening, "Das Lied von der Jugend" (The song of youth). A large part of this lay comes from MacPherson's *The War of Inis-thona*, from the poems of Ossian.[158] *The War of Inis-thona* begins with reflections on the youth of the poet, a reference to Selma, the conversation between Oscar and his

158. See *The Poems of Ossian*, translated by James MacPherson (New York, no date), pp. 280–84.

grandfather Fingal, the decision to go to Inis-thona, the tale of the deaths of the king's sons, Argon and Ruro, Oscar's revenge and his triumphal return to Selma. In the Appendix of the present book, Mac-Pherson's *Inisthona* stands side by side with Arnim's poem, showing that Arnim followed his source closely except for a few additions in the middle. The most important change he made probably came from a little clue in the text, a reference to Lano's water, which sends forth the vapor of death (see Appendix, p. 286). From this reference, Arnim developed a spirit, who warns Oscar not to fight Cormalo because the spirit likes both him and Oscar. The brave Celt disregards this advice but, in a larger interpolation, he finds that Cormalo's widow, the daughter of the king of Inis-thona, loved the man who killed her brothers and dies of grief at her husband's death, cursing Oscar (419). Oscar realizes that he loves her and his spirit is broken by the vapors of the deadly water (419). Oscar's depression is so great that he disappears in his ship and is not found again (419–20), a fate that seems more appropriate to a Romantic hero than to Ossian's son.

The only other source in MacPherson that might have had some connection to Arnim's additions was a poem called *The Death of Oscar,* which was not considered authentic and did not appear in most editions. It was an alternate version of his death that was also depicted in Book I of Temora. In the alternate version, Dermid and Oscar kill Dargo, and both fall in love with his daughter, just as the daughter of the king of Inis-thona falls in love with Cormalo, the murderer of her brothers.

In addition to his own predilection to add to and adapt a source (already in evidence in *Wunderhorn*), Arnim could also have been influenced by the example of Walter Scott in *Minstrelsy of the Scottish Border.*[159] Part three of this book, *Imitations of the Ancient Ballad,* which Arnim mentioned in his letter,[160] included songs that combined old

---

159. *Minstrelsy of the Scottish Border* (New York, no date given) by Sir Walter Scott, edited by Thomas Henderson. In Hermann F. Weiss's edition, *Unbekannte Briefe von und an Achim von Arnim aus der Sammlung Varnhagen und anderen Beständen* (Berlin, 1986), he cites two letters from Henriette Schubart, whom Arnim mentions in a note on p. 402 of *Wintergarten* in conjunction with a love song that Arnim presents as a Scottish folk song on the same page. In her letter of May 1818 to Arnim she replies to his request to send some of her *Übertragungen* of Scottish folk songs (p. 167). Weiss mentions in note 2 on the same page that several of her adaptations from Scott's *Minstrelsy of the Scottish Border* appeared in the *Zeitung für Einsiedler* in 1808. See also, Weiss, *Briefe*, pp. 174–75, and Migge, 2, p. 893.

160. Steig, *Achim von Arnim* 1, p. 95.

material with new and others that were entirely new but based on legend or tradition.[161] Like Scott, Arnim too was motivated by the desire to preserve this material as well as to bring it before a larger audience. However, as we have seen in previous examples in *Wintergarten*, such adaptations had functions within the work as well. The relevance of the connection between Oscar and Prince Charles, the young hero out to keep up the family tradition and ready to prove himself with great deeds, is clear; this parallel extends to their respective fates as well, since both are broken men after their efforts. Another major theme in *Das Lied von der Jugend* (The song of youth), which was in the source but which Arnim expanded upon, is the problem of aging. The original begins and ends with references to growing old (see Appendix). Arnim expanded on this theme in his interpolations at the end, where he connected the fate of the individual with that of "Geschlechter" (generations) (421).

The elegiac quality of the lay, which Arnim expanded, commemorates the passing of the old Celtic order. Ossian is old and will not live long; Oscar is dead, and new generations will arise and decline. The death knell for Celtic poetry has its parallels in the political situation of the Scots as well, since the outcome of the Battle of Culloden ended their hopes of regaining Scotland. Arnim's additions at the end, which intensify the tone of lament, form a fitting ending to Prince Charles's attempt as he sailed away to France and a wasted life .

Since the frame in this ninth evening gives us no help, either at the beginning or the end, as to how this section is to be interpreted, it is necessary to examine it in the context of the preceding evenings. Because Arnim saved it for the last evening, one must assume that it either sums up or develops certain themes.

In its concentration on the behavior of the individual during times of stress, the episode serves a didactic purpose for Germans in the post-Napoleonic era. Not only the leading figures but also the average individual could find in this account people worthy of emulation. For Arnim, the source that provided these details proved once again that "Memoiren im weitesten Sinne sind das Wesen, das Höchste der Geschichte" ["memoirs in the broadest sense are the essence, the best of history"] (303). The reactions of the Scots against their occupiers,

---

161. See, for example, Scott, "Thomas the Rhymer," pp. 577, 605, esp. pp. 580, 600–601.

the English, offered certain striking parallels to the German political situation, though the response of the Scots differed from that of the Germans in many cases. Arnim in this section resumed the concerns of the third, fourth, and sixth evenings, where individual courage in the face of danger made a much different response possible than cowardice could have done. It is important to note that he celebrated not only Charles's efforts to regain his kingdom, but also the bravery of individuals during Charles's flight, who had everything to lose by helping the hapless Stuart and nothing to gain, except a sense of having done the right thing.

Schluß
(Ending of Wintergarten)

The final section, entitled *Schluß* (Conclusion), falls into two parts: "Der Eisgang," (The breakup of the ice), the first deals with the upheaval in the change of seasons that led to the dissolution of the ice floes and the rescue of the orphaned child, as well as the examination of the courtly novel at the country house; the second, entitled "Der Wintergarten, Taufe, Hochzeit" (The winter garden, baptism, wedding) resolves certain elements of the frame plot and points ahead in new directions made possible by the influence of the inner stories and their tellers on the listeners in the frame.

Just as the *Wintergarten* began with a powerful storm announcing the presence of Winter, so it ends as well with a forceful natural upheaval, the breaking up of the ice. This event, which, like the arrival of winter, operates on literal as well as symbolic levels, functions as a sign that the grip that the spiritually numbing season of winter has on their daily lives must pass. The quickening spirit of the populace, which shows itself in the nature of their attack on the ice, which they approached as if it were their country's enemy, foreshadows the renewal of national spirit sought throughout the work and now manifesting itself at the end (422). Winter, like the French army it followed, is leaving, enabling the population to bestir itself from the spiritual hibernation that has gripped it during the occupation. The comparison of Winter to an occupying enemy was apparent at the beginning, when Arnim used militaristic terms to describe Winter's appearance (130).

Now, as the vanquished begin to bestir themselves, the invalid provides yet another example of selfless behavior in the rescue of an orphan from the flood waters. The desperately depressed state of the invalid may well have induced him to attempt this daring feat; however, it is also consistent with the portrait of the invalid that has appeared throughout the book. Among all the characters of the frame, he is the one who has consistently risked his life and shown the most personal courage. The rescue of the child is a means to reestablish contact with the lady of the house. It is also a new beginning, both on a national and a personal level, a beginning that will come after Winter's death.

The decision to give the child to the lady of the house also necessitates a return of the *Wintergarten* group to the country house, where the envoy encourages the ladies to examine closely pictures from a courtly novel; while there, others remark that no books have been so useful to Germany as these chivalric romances full of earlier strength and glory (426). The remarks advocating the reading of medieval literature hark back to the beginning of the work, just as the reference to Winter did (see 127).

When Ritter von Thurn describes the advantages of reading older literature at the beginning of the work, he actually is revealing Arnim's intentions for the *Wintergarten*. He suggests the study of older histories in order to devote ourselves to good, to flee evil, and to direct heart and thought to the service of the Almighty (127). The scene with the courtly novel at the end has obvious parallels as well as differences. In the final section, we hear about one book, not many. More significantly, the comments are from members of the group, who have now learned enough about their past that they can appreciate the value of such literature. Their reaction confirms the success of Arnim's use of older German literature throughout the work: as they examine the book, they are able to make the connection between art of the past and the present: while it fulfilled contemporary artistic demands, it also carried in itself the dignity and truth of older art (426). Arnim took the old material, restored it, and amplified it, just as he hoped his countrymen will do when confronted with the need to integrate the past and present.

While much of the book's description expressed Arnim's beliefs about the value of older literature, there is a picture at the end that points to the future: "Nur das letzte Bild, weil es die Geschichte des Tages und unsres Kreises näher berührt, sei erlaubt mit Worten, so wenig Worte auch vermögen, hier vorzulegen und zu erklären" ["Perhaps it may be permitted to present and explain in words, though words can achieve little, just the last picture, because it touches closely on current history and on our circle"] (426). This comment offers further proof that the courtly novel has definite links to the *Wintergarten*. The narrator describes an idealized picture of a joyful entry of a young aristocratic couple towards a castle, with happy peasants welcoming them, knights following, along with wild animals. The lady, sitting behind her knight on a white horse, carries in her hand a banner, on which is written, "Die Zeitenlose" (The timeless woman). This picture of harmony of all classes represented the goal for which the guests in the *Wintergarten* society should aim (427). Since Arnim and his contemporaries were from a later age, they must have viewed the whole from a somewhat different perspective (427–28). From the higher point, from the vantage of later time in history, the narrator can see the unsuspected harmonies that those in the procession are not in a position to see (429). Their sense of contentment and sufficiency did not rest on self-satisfaction, but on the singular harmony of the times in which they lived. There was no national crisis revealing unsuspected weakness and disharmony. The view from the peak symbolized the interval in time between the Middle Ages and the Napoleonic wars and the necessity to see the past in the larger context of the present.

This experience of harmony recalled to Arnim the Rhine trip with Clemens Brentano when he felt such harmony (428).[162] The tableau continues into the poem, which describes the procession as well as the life of the aristocratic couple. The banner, which the lady carried in the procession, "Die Zeitenlose," (The timeless woman) reappears here and represents love that endures (431). This song, which is sung by the members of the procession to portray the future life of the couple, returns the narrative to the theme of love. This theme figures prominently in the last section in the ending of the *Wintergarten*.

The final section of the *Wintergarten*, entitled "Der Wintergarten, Taufe, Hochzeit" weaves the theme of love through the events and

162. See Göres, *Verhältnis*, p. 59, who comments on the characteristic overlapping of space and time that is expressed here in the pictures of nature and history.

decisions surrounding the invalid, Winter, the lady, and the conservatory itself. The lady receives the child, left secretly by the invalid, as a sign of hope for the future. She marries Winter, who drops dead on the spot. The invalid comes to say goodbye to her before leaving on a long journey with Ariel and she gives him the wedding ring that she has just received. At this point, the lady of the house has finally come to realize where her love belongs; not to a foreigner and not to an allegorical figure, but to a brave and loving fellow countryman. She opens the doors of her conservatory to the cold winter air and the foreign plants, which Arnim describes in somewhat decadent terms (". . . jener verruchten wollüstigen Pflanzen") (". . . of these odious and lascivious plants"] (432), immediately die. Their death signals the end of foreign influence, both on a personal and on a national level: ". . . die aufgehende nordische Sonne beschien ein untergehendes Südland" [". . . the rising sun of the north shone upon a country of the south going down"] (435). The lady of the house sends the French officer's portrait back to the "feindlichen Freunde" ("the hostile friend") (435) and devotes herself to the child, while awaiting the return of the invalid. As Segebrecht notes, she overcomes her paralysis of spirit through actions that call for self-sacrifice, a recurrent theme in the inner stories and in the behavior of the invalid.[163] After the education that the stories and the conversations in the frame have brought about, she has reached the point the invalid, at the beginning in his letter (136), hoped for. The lady shows in her behavior the didactic value of art.

The death of the plants in the conservatory applies not only to the death of the lady's love for the French officer but to the tendency of many Germans to appreciate foreign culture more than their own. Since the conservatory is an enclosed place, one's sphere of action is limited,[164] especially as it must be shielded from the environment. The groups assembled at the lady's house must break away from this existence, as she has done. As Segebrecht notes, there are several possibilities of action ranging from active encouragement and support of revolution (the princess, the envoy, and the *Geniale*); using this time to educate oneself (Ariel and the invalid); and the collection of the *Wintergarten* stories for other readers.[165]

163. Segebrecht, "Thematik des Krieges," *Aurora* 45 (1985), p. 315.
164. Segebrecht, "Thematik des Krieges," p. 316.
165. Segebrecht, "Thematik des Krieges," p. 315–16.

Through the direct influence of the stories and the events surrounding them, the members of the *Wintergarten* group are ready to go their separate ways. The role of art in bringing them to this point has not been, as the princess says, to hide from the ugly realities of war,

... wie ist die Kunst zu schwach den Abgrund zu bedecken mit schönem Schein, doch diese Kunst ist schrecklich, die betrügt, die rechte Kunst ist wahr, sie heuchelt nie den Frieden, wo sie ihn doch nicht geben kann. (434)

... though art is too weak to cover the abyss with beautiful pretense, yet art which deceives is terrible. Good art is true; it never feigns peace where it cannot provide it after all.

Arnim has not shrunk from letting the grim realities behind the stories of individual bravery show through. He has not used art as an escape from daily reality nor has he distilled from it one truth, one course of action that he wants all to follow. He has instead offered art as a means of individual inspiration just as his inner stories portrayed a variety of people who chose many different ways to deal with the problems at hand. He avoided giving prescriptions, asking only that the individual respond to art in an individual way. Only in this way can the integrity both of the work of art and the human being be preserved.

II

E. T. A. Hoffmann's
Die Serapionsbrüder

Introduction

At the hands of most critics, the frame of E. T. A. Hoffmann's *Serapionsbrüder* (The Serapion brotherhood) has suffered the fate of derelict relatives in a respectable family. Like those hapless brothers, sisters, and cousins whose presence raises awkward moments, the frame has been misunderstood, castigated, and, in some instances, disowned and cast out.[166] Individual stories, such as "Das Fräulein von Scuderi," (Mademoiselle von Scuderi), "Rat Krespel" (Councillor Krespel), and "Die Bergwerke zu Falun" (The mines of Falun) have rightly attracted critical adulation and analysis, but the only part of the frame that has received much attention until recently has been the *Serapionsprinzip* (Serapiontic principle); it has often proved to be rather elastic when cut off from its moorings in the frame.[167] In his recent

166. Perhaps the most savage judgment on the *Serapionsbrüder* frame, to discard it, was made by Hans von Müller and Walther Harich. See von Müller's discussion, pp. 676–77, in Hans von Müller, *Gesammelte Aufsätze über E. T. A. Hoffmann*, ed. by Friedrich Schnapp (Hildesheim, 1974), in an article, "Die neueren Sammlungen von E. T. A. Hoffmanns Werken und Privataufzeichnungen nach Inhalt und Anordnung untersucht," first appearing in *Zeitschrift für Bücherfreunde*, Neue Folge, vol. 18, no. 1 (Leipzig, January 1926). See as well Harich's Afterword to *Die vier großen Gespräche und die kleinen Schriften über Literatur und Theater* (Weimar, 1924), pp. xv–xvi. For other negative verdicts, see René Wellek, "German and English Romanticism," in *Confrontations* (Princeton, 1965), pp. 17–18; Ilse Winter, *Untersuchungen zum serapiontischen Prinzip E. T. A. Hoffmanns* (The Hague, 1976), p. 66, 67; H. von Müller, "Aus der Einleitung zum Kreislerbuch," *Gesammelte Aufsätze* (Leipzig, 1903), p. 64; Nino Erné, "Zu dieser Ausgabe," in *Hoffmanns Werke* 1 (Hamburg, 1964), pp. 9, 10–11.

167. The *Serapionsprinzip* has attracted much attention, with the following critics giving a representative range of opinions. See Winter, *Untersuchungen;* Jean Ricci, *E. T. A. Hoffmann: l'Homme et l'oeuvre* (Paris, 1947); Siegfried Schumm, *Einsicht und Darstellung: Untersuchung zum Kunstverständnis E. T. A. Hoffmanns* (Göppingen, 1974); Volkmar Sander, "Realität und Bewußtsein bei E. T. A. Hoffmann" in *Studies in Germanic Language and Literature,* ed. R. Fowkes and Volkmar Sander (New York, 1967); Walter Müller-Seidel, "Nachwort," pp. 999–1026; E. T. A. Hoffmann, *Die Serapionsbrüder* (Munich) (All quotations come from this edition and will be given in the text with page numbers); Christa Karoli, "E. T. A. Hoffmann und Zacharias Werner: Ein Beitrag zum romantischen Genieproblem," *Vergleichen und Variationen: Festschrift für H. Motekat,* ed. A. Goetze and G. Pflaum (Munich, 1970), pp. 147–69; Wulf Segebrecht, *Autobiographie und Dichtung: Eine Studie zum Werk E. T. A. Hoffmanns* (Stuttgart, 1967); Hans Joachim Kruse, "Wirkung," pp. 631–46, in *E. T. A. Hoffmann, Gesammelte Werke,* (Berlin-Weimar, 1978) (subsequently referred to as *Aufbau* in notes); Hans Mayer, "Die Wirklichkeit E. T. A. Hoffmanns," (originally published in 1958), in *Romantikforschung seit 1945,* ed. Klaus Peter, (Königsstein, 1980), pp. 116–44; Thomas Cramer, *Das Groteske bei E. T. A. Hoffmann* (Munich, 1970); Christel Schütz, "Studien zur Erzählkunst E. T. A.

biography, *E. T. A. Hoffmann oder die Tiefe zwischen Stern und Erde: eine Biographie* (E. T. A. Hoffman or the chasm between star and earth) Eckhart Kleßmann says the collection must be seen as a unique and unified work of art because it contains in concentrated form major elements of his art and, therefore, his world view.[168] Renewed appreciation of Hoffmann's achievement dominates Lothar Pikulik's commentary on the *Serapionsbrüder, E. T. A. Hoffmann als Erzähler* (E. T. A. Hoffmann as narrator). This work, which was originally intended for an edition, still retains that format to a large degree. Pikulik's book gives the reader detailed background information and a summary of each story containing comments about major themes and good insights into the individual works. It does not treat the interaction between frame and inner story as a continuous web, which sets it apart from my interpretation.[169] *Bending the Frame* shows that both the frame and the narratives form an artistic unity, with frame and story sequence providing important clues to the understanding of inner stories.

Due to its unique position among Hoffmann's works and, indeed, within Romanticism, the frame deserves attention, not only for the light it can throw on the inner stories in the collection as well as other works of Hoffmann, but also for its own sake.[170] One of the great advantages of the *Serapionsbrüder* frame is the unique perspective it affords of a theoretical discussion of ideas such as the role of madness in the development of the artist and the nature of the artist's relationship to life, juxtaposed with stories that deal with these problems. While Hoffmann sometimes did include such discussions of theories and ideas with stories like "Der Magnetiseur" (the magnetizer) and "Dichter und Komponist" (poet and composer), there is nowhere else in his work such an extended treatment of concepts central to his

Hoffmanns" (Diss., Göttingen, 1955); Friedhelm Auhuber, *In einem fernen dunklen Spiegel. E. T. A. Hoffmanns Poetisierung der Medizin* (Opladen, 1986), pp. 27–35; Hans Toggenburger, *Die späten Almanach-Erzählungen E. T. A. Hoffmanns* (Bern, 1983), pp. 38–56.

168. Eckart Kleßmann, *E. T. A. Hoffmann oder die Tiefe zwischen Stern und Erde: Eine Biographie* (Stuttgart, 1988), pp. 430–31.

169. Lothar Pikulik, *E. T. A. Hoffmann als Erzähler: Ein Kommentar zu den 'Serapionsbrüdern'* (Göttingen, 1987). While Pikulik gives a useful general introduction to the frame in the *Serapionsbrüder* (pp. 14–19), he does not deal in detail with correspondences between the frame and the inner stories, nor with the interpretative clues for the stories that are hidden in the frame.

170. See Pikulik, *Erzähler*, p. 22, who notes that the *Serapionsbrüder* contains all of Hoffmann's major themes.

thought. The frame also provides critical judgments on his own and other writers' works.

The frame functions as a storehouse of information on a wide variety of topics and also provides by turns a bulwark, as well as a trap-door vis-à-vis threatening outside forces, such as the uncanny powers of the *Magnetiseur* or the omnipresent threat of madness.[171] The conversations in the circle of friends, whether they are composites of Hoffmann's acquaintances or primarily alter egos,[172] give the frame characters the chance to discuss troubling or difficult problems in a secure setting. This device lends a certain amount of distance to the question at hand. The inner stories that deal with the themes discussed in the frame provide the opportunity to examine the question or problem in ways that give the emotions expression that a rational discussion does not, yet the fictional nature of the stories helps to keep the issues at a safe distance.

For all of the above reasons, an examination of the thematic correspondences between the frame and the inner stories, and the other complex relationships on various levels that exist between outer and inner stories, needs to be undertaken. This analysis will show that an understanding of the frame/inner story connections reveals both unsuspected unity and new insights on interpretation of the individual stories. Walter Müller-Seidel and Wulf Segebrecht noted the unity of the frame in pregnant remarks, though the contexts in which they did so precluded a detailed analysis.[173]

Examination of earlier critics' cursory dismissals can help to ad-

171. See Horst Conrad, *Die literarische Angst: Das Schreckliche in Schauerromantik und Detektivgeschichte* (Düsseldorf, 1974), p. 76, who remarks in connection with "Sandmann" that the narrator likes to juxtapose strange events with the opinions of educated people, a tendency that, according to Conrad, leaves the reader suspended between logic and irrationality. This remark can also be applied to the frame and offers another example of the interrelatedness of the inner and outer sections of the work.

172. See ensuing discussion.

173. Walter Müller-Seidel, *Nachwort* (Winkler), pp. 999–1026, especially pp. 1001, 1014; Wulf Segebrecht, *Autobiographie*, pp. 59, 152. See also Bernhard Casper, "Der historische Besen oder über die Geschichtsauffassung in E. T. A. Hoffmanns *Serapionsbrüdern* und in der katholischen Tübinger Schule," in *Romantik in Deutschland,* Sonderband der DVJS (Stuttgart, 1978), pp. 490–501, p. 491, who notes that the frame story contains much reflection by Hoffmann on his own work and on literature in general. N. J. Berkowski, *Die Romantik in Deutschland,* translated from the Russian by Reinhard Fischer (Leipzig, 1979), p. 591, notes the significance of the collection. In their book *E. T. A. Hoffmann: Epoche-Werke-Wirkung* (Munich, 1986), Brigitte Feldges and Ulrich Stadler note, p. 55, that the nature of the inner stories changes because of the context of the frame conversations.

vance this interpretation, because in understanding and countering them, we reach a much deeper comprehension of this idiosyncratic work. One of the linchpins in the argument against serious consideration of the frame has been Hoffmann's apparently casual attitude towards it, shown in his initial dealings with his publisher, Georg Reimer. In answer to a previous letter of Reimer's in 1818, Hoffmann, agreed to Reimer's suggestion about a collection of short pieces, discussed the stories to be included, and then asked for advice.[174] The letter also shows that Hoffmann's plans were as yet still vague; he was obviously thinking in terms of only one book. Not until the following summer did Reimer and Hoffmann put in writing the decision to publish a second volume.[175] These facts make it impossible to argue that the frame and the stories stand in the same relationship to the story as the frame in works such as *Unterhaltungen deutscher Ausgewanderten* (Conversations of German emigrés).

In addition to this letter, critics hostile to the frame have seized on the fact that all of the stories, with the exception of "Die Bergwerke zu Falun" (The mines of Falun) and "Die Königsbraut" (The king's bride) were published elsewhere;[176] René Wellek's negative attitude is typical of such comments: "[A]ll of Hoffmann's *Serapionsbrüder* is an external device which brought together stories published independently and does not distinguish the stories collected in *Serapionsbrüder* from stories collected without any framework."[177]

The implication in the preceding quotation is that the stories were published before Hoffmann wrote the frame, mitigating against serious consideration of it. In actual fact, only eleven of the twenty-six pieces included in the collection were written before Hoffmann began the frame for the first volume.[178] Since over half of this material was written

174. Hans von Müller and Friedrich Schnapp, *E. T. A. Hoffmanns Briefwechsel* 2 (1814–22) (Munich, 1968), p. 156. Harvey Hewett-Thayer, *Hoffmann: Author of the Tales* (Princeton, 1948), p. 101, says that the success of the *Fantasiestücke* and the *Nachtstücke* must have tempted Reimer.
175. The letter makes it clear that he was thinking only of a one-volume collection at the outset (Müller, *Briefwechsel* 2, p. 156); see also p. 157).
176. See Müller-Seidel (Winkler), pp. 1032–34.
177. René Wellek, *Confrontations*, pp. 17–18.
178. Segebrecht (Winkler), pp. 1032–34, lists the first publication dates of the items included in the collection. Friedrich Schnapp, in the series *Dichter über ihre Dichtungen: E. T. A. Hoffmann* 13 (Munich, 1974) in his extensive chronology, pp. 312–86, gives additional information on the times of composition. Schnapp lists the publication date of "Ein Fragment aus dem Leben dreier Freunde" as 1817 instead of the 1818 date that the Winkler edition gives (Schnapp, p. 360; Segebrecht, p. 1032), but on p. 1048 Sege-

while he was composing the frame,[179] one must at least admit the possibility that some of the same themes that found their expression in the stories might also have appeared in the frame. The stories in the third and fourth volumes, with the exception of *Erscheinungen* (Apparitions), were written concurrently with the frame. To refuse to see inner relationships because the composition time of some frame parts was not contemporaneous with that of the stories is tantamount to saying that an author's revisions of or additions to a work have no value. Approximately one-sixth of the total is the frame, a percentage high enough to suggest that Hoffmann ascribed some significance to it. If he were concerned only with money, as detractors of the frame and of some of the stories in it have maintained, he would have devoted neither the time nor the energy to write so much about the problematic topics that dominate it.[180]

---

brecht explains that Hoffmann wrote the story in the fall of 1816 in its first version, which differs markedly from the one in the *Serapionsbrüder*. Kruse, *Aufbau 1*, says it was first published in 1818 (p. 675). For our purposes, it is important to know that it was written before Hoffmann began work on the frame in February 1818, since he does list it in his letter to Reimer as one of the stories available. Those stories and essays that appeared before February 1818 are (in the order of their appearance in the *Serapionsbrüder*): "Rat Krespel" (written in 1816, published in 1818); "Die Fermate" (written in 1815); "Der Dichter und der Komponist" (written in 1813, published in 1813); "Der Artushof" (written in 1815, published in 1817); "Nußknacker und Mausekönig" (written 1816, published 1816); "Der Kampf der Sänger" (written in 1817, published 1819); "Die Automate" (written in 1814, published 1814); "Doge und Dogaresse" (written 1817, published 1819); "Das fremde Kind" (written and published in 1817); "Erscheinungen" (written 1814, published 1817). For the above information see Segebrecht (Winkler), pp. 1032–34, 1038, 1043, 1045, 1048, 1053, 1057, 1062, 1065, 1076, 1109; Schnapp, p. 354.

I include "Alte und neue Kirchenmusik" taken from the review of Beethoven's Mass in C major and the essay "Alte und neue Kirchenmusik," written in 1813–14, as part of the frame, since it is not fictional and since more than one person speaks. The Winkler edition does not set it off from the text (p. 406), while the *Aufbau* edition does (p. 491). See also Kruse, *Aufbau 1*, p. 731.

This table shows that Ricci, *Hoffmann*, is wrong when he says that all of the works in the *Serapionsbrüder* appear in the order in which Hoffmann wrote them (p. 443).

179. Hoffmann seems proud of the fact that he is bringing new material into the collection; he says that the fourth volume, except for "Formica" and "Zusammenhang," contains only new stories (Müller/Schnapp, *Briefwechsel 2*, p. 269).

180. Jean Mistler, *Hoffmann le Fantastique* (Paris, 1950), says that the conversations of the frame are worth more than some of the stories (p. 205). Further indication of the importance of the topics in the frame to Hoffmann lies in the fact that it gave him an opportunity to answer his critics. Hartmut Steinecke, in an article, "Der beliebte, vielgelesene Verfasser . . . : Über die Hoffmann-Kritiken im 'Morgenblatt für gebildete Stände' und in der 'Jenaischen Allgemeinen Literatur-Zeitung,' " MHG, 17 (1971), pp. 1–16, says on p. 15, n. 8 that Hoffmann used the Serapion conversations for that reason.

Hans Mayer discusses the attraction of the frame for Hoffmann because of his need to present the real and the mythical worlds simultaneously: see "Wirklichkeit," pp. 121, 122.

Another problem that has further damaged the literary standing of the frame has been the aura of biography that surrounds it. In the attempt to identify the *Serapionsbrüder,* questions of literary values have been ignored, as the frame was demoted in the eyes of some critics to a thinly disguised description of the *Seraphinenorden* (Seraphian order). This group of literary friends began to meet once a week shortly after Hoffmann's arrival in Berlin in September, 1814.[181] At first, they gathered in the Café Manderlee, then in Hoffmann's apartment, with occasional meetings elsewhere. The most important members of the circle included Hoffmann's friend and biographer Julius Edward Hitzig, Baron Friedrich de la Motte Fouqué, Carl Wilhelm Salice Contessa, Adelbert von Chamisso, and David Ferdinand Koreff.[182] Until the fall of 1816, the group met in a fairly regular pattern to listen to new writing by the members. At that time, there was a long interruption in their meetings due to the departure of Chamisso in July, 1816 and Contessa's move from Berlin later that year.[183] On November 14, 1818, Hoffmann, Contessa, Koreff, and Hitzig, among others, began meeting again. The formal name of the group came once more from a liturgical calendar, this time a Polish one which commemorated Serapion Sindonita. According to Schnapp, the circle met until sometime in the spring of 1820.[184] During this period of revival of the club, Hoffmann was at work on the frame and the collection of stories that was to be the *Serapionsbrüder,* started about ten months before he and his friends reorganized.[185]

181. The name *Seraphinenorden* (Seraphian order), by which the group is generally called, does not appear in Hoffmann's diary. Attribution to Hoffmann as its originator appeared in a letter of Georg Seegemund to Wilhelm Neumann on March 14, 1815. See Friedrich Schnapp, "Der Seraphinenorden und die Serapionsbrüder E. T. A. Hoffmanns," *Literaturwissenschaftliches Jahrbuch* 3 (1962), pp. 99–112, p. 101. The name came from the Roman Catholic liturgical calendar, which celebrated St. Seraphinus von Montegranaro on that day. Schnapp, p. 101; Segebrecht (Winkler), p. 1035.

182. The von Pfuel brothers, Ernst and Friedrich, participated in the circle; guests included Theodor G. Hippel, Hoffmann's lifelong friend Ludwig Robert, and Werner von Haxthausen. Seegemund was apparently a member for a very brief time (Schnapp, "Seraphinenorden," p. 102). According to Schnapp, pp. 102, 103, 106–7, there is some variation in regard to the composition of the group. Hoffmann, for instance, does not mention Koreff, but Koreff became a member only after Hoffmann no longer kept a diary. Segebrecht, *Autobiographie,* lists Ludwig Robert as a member, not a guest, p. 22. See also Segebrecht (Winkler), p. 1035.

183. Schnapp, "Seraphinenorden," p. 102.

184. Schnapp, "Seraphinenorden," pp. 104–5, 110. At that time, in the fall of 1818, Hoffmann changed the preliminary title of the book from *Die Seraphinenbrüder* to *Die Serapionsbrüder* (Schnapp, "Seraphinenorden," p. 105). See also Pikulik, *Hoffmann,* pp. 12–13.

185. Segebrecht (Winkler), pp. 1031–32.

Repeated attempts have been made to identify the six *Serapions-brüder*, Theodor, Ottmar, Lothar, Cyprian, Sylvester, and Vinzenz in the frame with specific members of the *Seraphinenorden/Serapion* group. One of the most recent appeared in the *Aufbau* edition of the *Serapionsbrüder*, where Kruse says there was unanimity about the identification of the characters.[186] The issue is not as clear-cut as Kruse implies; Segebrecht, like Hoffmann's earlier biographer, Ricci, tends to avoid matching specific characters with Hoffmann and his friends. Segebrecht notes that Hoffmann brought almost all his acquaintances into his work in various ways. However, that fact does not justify taking a character in a frame that is the creation of a poet and matching him with a historical person.[187] Life experiences pass through Hoffmann's fantastic and ironic prism, flashing a light that reminds us fleetingly of one of his friends, then of Hoffmann taking the opposite side of the argument, a process reflected in the following quotation from Hoffmann's diary: "Ich denke mir mein Ich durch ein Vervielfälti-

---

186. Kruse's comments, *Aufbau*, 1, pp. 626–27, are typical of a number of critics' identification of the brothers in the frame. Lothar Köhn, *Vieldeutige Welt: Studien zur Struktur der Erzählungen E. T. A. Hoffmanns und zur Entwicklung seines Werkes* (Tübingen, 1966), p. 109; Carl Georg von Maassen, *E. T. A. Hoffmanns Sämtliche Werke* 5 (Munich, Leipzig, 1912), pp. ix–x, identifies Hoffmann as Lothar and Theodor. W. Harich, *E. T. A. Hoffmann: Das Leben eines Künstlers* (Berlin, 1923) also splits Hoffmann's identity among Theodor, Lothar, and Cyprian; Karl Ochsner, *E. T. A. Hoffmann als Dichter des Unbewuß-ten: Ein Beitrag zur Geistesgeschichte der Romantik* (Frauenfeld, 1936), p. 12, says that Lothar often speaks for Hoffmann; Segebrecht cautions against such attempts in the notes to the Winkler edition (pp. 1035–36). Hans Georg Werner, in *E. T. A. Hoffmann: Darstellung und Deutung der Wirklichkeit im dichterischen Werk* (East Berlin, 1971), p. 53, says that Lothar represents Hoffmann. Schnapp, "Seraphinenorden," goes very far in his biographical speculations, even to placing dates on the later meetings of the group, pp. 108–10. See Friedrich von Oppeln-Bronkowski, *David Ferdinand Koreff: Serapionsbruder, Magnetiseur, Geheimrat und Dichter* (Berlin, 1928), pp. 72–78. Pikulik, *Hoffmann* takes the position that all of the characters are fictitious and reflect Hoffmann, though he may have borrowed traits from his friends (pp. 13–14). See also Kleßmann, *Hoffmann*, p. 429, and Klaus Gunzel, *Die Serapionsbrüder: Märchendichtungen der Berliner Romantik* (Cologne, 1986), p. 576.

187. Segebrecht (Winkler), 1035–36; Segebrecht, *Autobiographie*, p. 22, n. 83. See Ricci, *L'Homme*, p. 442, who says that each character represents one facet of Hoffmann's personality. Coming at this question from a different approach, Manfred Momberger, in his book *Sonne und Punsch: Die Dissemination des romantischen Kunstbegriffs bei E. T. A. Hoffmann* (Munich, 1986), arrives at the same opinion as Segebrecht, namely, that none of the characters in the *Serapionsbrüder* are identifiable with Hoffmann. He notes the inclusion of parentheses by the author in a speech of Lothar's (p. 527). Momberger says that the speaker in the parentheses is obviously not the character in whose speech the parentheses occur and that the author is not identical with any of the narrators (see pp. 121–22). See Pikulik, *Hoffmann*, pp. 13–14, who agrees with Segebrecht and James M. McGlathery, *Mysticism and Sexuality: E. T. A. Hoffmann, Part 1: Hoffmann and His Sources* (Las Vegas, 1981), p. 70.

gungsglas—alle Gestalten die sich um mich herum bewegen sind Ichs und ich ärgere mich über ihr tun und lassen" ["I think of my ego through a multiplying glass—all figures moving around me are egos and I am annoyed with what they do and do not do"].[188] This famous passage seems to justify a certain amount of caution on the part of the critic in the area of easy biographical assumptions.

While Segebrecht and Pikulik have correctly seen what many critics have overlooked in this question of character identity in the frame, their observations have some bearing on the thematic concerns of the frame as well. If the figures in the frame are merely descriptions of Hoffmann's friends and their ideas about art, madness and contemporary life, then they have less significance for the stories and for the development of ideas in the frame. Certainly we would expect to find some memories of the *Seraphinen* evenings in the brothers' conversations, but they are refracted and transmuted by Hoffmann's artistic vision and are not the work of an Eckermann recording conversations for posterity. As the result of Hoffmann's meditations on major themes that dominate his work, the frame offers important clues in understanding some of the problems of artistic perception and creation that preoccupied him.

The encounter of the artist with the seen and unseen world, with outer reality and internal vision and its artistic presentation, fill the conversations in the frame. The first of such confrontations occurs early in the frame with the unforgettable figure of the mad count who is convinced he is the early Christian martyr Serapion wandering around the desert outside of Thebes and Alexandria. Hoffmann, who wrote the story about Serapion to motivate the choice of the name day,[189] incorporated in that story and the subsequent frame discussion some of his most deeply held beliefs about art and reality. Consequently, Serapion's significance is central to an understanding of frame-inner story relationships. However, the *Serapionsprinzip* has often become a critics' catchall, isolated from the frame and frequently distorted.

The three major groups of critics of the *Serapionsprinzip* generally divide themselves into the following: those critics who see Serapion as an unqualifiedly positive model for the poet, such as Peter

---

188. E. T. A. Hoffmann, *Tagebücher*, ed. Hans V. Müller and Friedrich Schnapp (Munich, 1971), p. 107.
189. Müller-Schnapp, *Briefwechsel I*, p. 180, note 1.

Matt[190]; those who see *Gemütlichkeit* (congeniality) as an overriding theme of the frame and try to integrate Serapion into it; and those who see him as the incarnation or representative of one important quality but deficient in other respects. The advocates of *Gemütlichkeit* downplay the threatening elements in the Serapion story and sometimes turn that account into a sort of idyll. As might be expected, these critics, with their emphasis on sociable evenings by the fire, tend to take a more biographical approach to the characters in the frame, though that does not seem to be their major goal. Köhn, in *Vieldeutige Welt* (Ambiguous world) interprets the frame as a bulwark against threatening forces, with *Gemütlichkeit* as its major structural element. He sees Serapion's existence as an ideal state in which man lives in innocence and at peace with things around him. His emphasis on a quiet and happy atmosphere leads him to the conclusion that many of the stories do not conform to the Serapion principle. His position makes him undervalue the significance of the frame for understanding the problems of the artist and for interpretation of the individual stories. Like Köhn, Winter, in *Untersuchungen* (Investigations), does not give the frame the importance it deserves. Her superficial understanding of it causes her to dismiss parts of it, such as the Zacharias Werner episode, as insignificant.[191]

In light of the textual evidence, the view that sees Serapion as a significant but flawed figure seems most convincing. Lothar's remarks on the personality of Serapion support this interpretation. While he

190. For Peter von Matt, *Die Augen der Automaten: E. T. A. Hoffmanns Imaginationslehre als Prinzip seiner Erzählkunst* (Tübingen, 1971), p. 16, Serapion represents the ideal artist.

191. See Köhn, *Vieldeutige Welt*, pp. 136, 115, 125, 137–38; Winter, *Untersuchungen*, pp. 67–68. Other interpretations besides that of the *Gemütlichkeit* theory range from the very general, such as the remarks of Horst Dämmrich about the importance of critical reflection for the artist (Horst Dämmrich, *The Shattered Self: E. T. A. Hoffmann's Tragic Vision* [Detroit, 1973], p. 36), to the bizarre: Jacques Wirz, "Die Gestalt des Künstlers bei E. T. A. Hoffmann" (Diss., Basel, 1961), pp. 56–57, maintains that Serapion was an example of decadence because of the deception of his existence. Hans Georg Werner's "Der romantische Schriftsteller und sein Philister-Publikum: Zur Wirkungsfunktion E. T. A. Hoffmanns," originally appeared in *Weimarer Beiträge* 24, Heft no. 4 (Berlin, 1978), pp. 87–114, and was reprinted in *Zu E. T. A. Hoffmann* (Stuttgart, 1981), ed. Steven P. Scher, pp. 74–97. Werner sees Serapion's principal value as one of disquieting the assembled group (p. 84). Kenneth Negus understands the importance of the inward vision that Serapion demonstrates but applies Lothar's remark about the *Hebel* (lever) (p. 54) to Serapion, a surprising approach, since the text expressly states that Serapion's failure lies in his inability to perceive the external world. Kenneth Negus, *E. T. A. Hoffmann's Other World: The Romantic Author and His New Mythology* (Philadelphia, 1975), p. 74.

believes that Serapion was a real poet, because he really had seen what he proclaimed, he also describes Serapion's madness as the result of the loss of a sense of the real outside world that gives us entrance into the spiritual one (54). The real artist must strive for a synthesis of the outer tangible world and the inner spiritual one; Hoffmann elaborated on this theme at other points in the *Serapionsbrüder* (599, 709). Serapion has certain qualities of a real poet but, because he does not admit the existence of an outer world, he cannot serve as an unqualifiedly positive model for the writers in the frame. Because this outer world controls what we perceive, it must be taken into account.[192]

While there is a relationship between madness and poetry, Serapion does not represent the embodiment of Hoffmann's theories about art. Müller-Seidel connects the Serapion principle to an anecdote about the Kantians that preceded it in the narrative. These men, interrupted in the middle of their quarrel, resumed it again at the same place twenty years later. Their behavior reveals a discrepancy between the inner and the outer world, which Serapion in his madness also displays, since he ignores the external world completely.[193] He exalts himself above space and time; while exaltation is an attribute of true poetry, this negation of space and time has serious effects and, when confronted with the uncanny, leads to the two conditions Hoffmann feared most: philistinism and madness.[194] Although Serapion is a true poet, we hear none of his stories; he cannot understand *Duplizität*, which conditions all earthly existence. Serapion cannot develop the principle that bears his name, because he is unaware of *Duplizität:* the members of the circle must do it.[195]

Serapion's insanity blurs and distorts the boundary between real and unreal so much that criticism and analysis become impossible. Siegfried Schumm believes this mental state disqualifies Serapion as an ideal, because unlike the members of the *Serapionsbrüder*, he cannot

192. Major Hoffmann critics since the second World War have inclined to this view. See Ricci, *L'Homme*, p. 427; Mayer, "Wirklichkeit," p. 137, discussion of the *Serapionsprinzip* on pp. 136–40; Sanders, "Realität," pp. 117, 121; Müller-Seidel, *Nachwort* (Winkler), pp. 1003–4; Pikulik, *Erzähler*, pp. 26, 58; Kleßmann, *Hoffmann*, pp. 431–32.
193. Müller-Seidel, *Nachwort* (Winkler), pp. 1003–4. See also Pikulik, *Erzähler*, p. 26.
194. Müller-Seidel, *Nachwort* (Winkler), p. 1004.
195. Segebrecht, *Autobiographie*, pp. 94, 133; "E. T. A. Hoffmann," in *Deutsche Dichter der Romantik*, ed. Benno von Wiese, (Berlin, 1971), pp. 391–415, p. 400.

accept criticism.[196] Schumm cites Serapion's belief that he sees the towers of B and believes that they are the skyline of Alexandria. If his listener tried to tell him it was more likely B—, this disagreement would upset his equilibrium, insofar as it penetrated it at all. Yet, precisely in this labile condition, Serapion, as Friedhelm Auhuber suggests, in *In einem fernen dunklen Spiegel: E. T. A. Hoffmanns Poetisierung der Medizin* (In a distant, dark mirror: E. T. A. Hoffmann's poetizing of medicine), represents the openness of the *Serapionsbrüder* to eccentrics and outsiders, in order to show the complex and inevitable intertwining of normal daily existence with the nether world of dark forces.[197] Auhuber's insight takes on special significance when the cast of characters in the inner stories is taken into account. As subsequent analyses will show, the themes of madness, psychic phenomena such as magnetism, and the problems of a heightened sensibility dominate the inner stories.

While the preceding discussion of recent Serapion criticism has brought out important aspects of the nature of Serapion's relationship to Hoffmann's work as a whole, Serapion's importance to the major themes of the frame and the inner stories has not been analyzed in detail, perhaps because he has been seen as the embodiment of a principle he himself did not formulate. As the incarnation of an abstract idea, he has been forgotten as an individual who has a certain function within the work itself. Serapion's ensuing madness because of his fail-

---

196. Schumm, *Einsicht*, pp. 119–20. Other critics who represent positions similar to those of Ricci, Sanders, Segebrecht, Preisendanz, and Schumm include Christel Schütz, *Studien*, pp. 65–67, and Helmut Pfotenhauer, "Exoterische und esoterische Poetik in E. T. A. Hoffmanns Erzählungen," *Jahrbuch der Jean-Paul-Gesellschaft* 17 (1982), pp. 129–44, esp. pp. 130–31. See also Feldges and Stadler, *Hoffmann*, pp. 57–58. Segebrecht, in his article, "Krankheit und Gesellschaft: Zu E. T. A. Hoffmanns Rezeption der Bamberger Medizin," in *Romantik in Deutschland*, ed. Richard Brinkmann (Stuttgart, 1978), pp. 267–90, sees Hoffmann's portrayal of Serapion reflecting Hoffmann's reading in medical theory, pp. 281–82. Wolfgang Nehring, in his article, "Die Gebärdensprache E. T. A. Hoffmanns," *Zeitschrift für deutsche Philologie*, 89 (1970), pp. 207–21, p. 211, says that the intellectual content of Hoffmann's stories has dominated critical discussion so completely that the importance of the external world to the artists in the stories has not been fully appreciated or understood. See also Jutta Kolkenbroch-Netz, "Wahnsinn der Vernunft-juristische Institution-literarische Praxis. Das Gutachten zum Fall Schmolling und die Erzählung 'Der Einsiedler Serapion' von E. T. A. Hoffmann," in *Wege der Literaturwissenschaft*, ed. Jutta Kolkenbroch-Netz et al. (Bonn, 1985), pp. 122–44, especially pp. 138–44. Kolkenbroch-Netz sees definite connections between the Schmolling legal brief with which Hoffmann was involved and the Serapion story.

197. See Auhuber, *Spiegel*, p. 120.

ure to incorporate external reality into his world view figures in the considerations of artist's problems which, in one way or another, dominate the entire frame.

The section in the conversation between Serapion and Cyprian, in which Serapion proves to his own satisfaction that Cyprian, not he, needs the help of a doctor, provides an unsettling situation that confirms the fluid boundaries between the sane and insane. This subject figures again and again in the inner stories and the frame.[198] The position of the Serapion anecdote in the introduction to the collection of stories underscores the importance of the relationship of madness to intensified perception and understanding and its implicit value for the artist. Cyprian, the character in the frame perhaps most interested in abnormal mental states, justifies this interest by maintaining that his association with mad people has animated and strengthened his own mind (29). There are two major reasons for engrossment with madness: revelation of nature's inner depths and the inspiration such revelations bring to the artist.[199] Therein lies the significance of Cyprian's remarks, in which he implies that abnormal states of consciousness offer the greatest opportunities for this inner sight.[200] For this reason, Serapion, who has artistic vision, must be at least partly mad.[201] His dementia is both requisite for and warning to the artist; as such it figures prominently in the *Serapionsbrüder*.

198. Auhuber, *Spiegel*, pp. 136–42, goes over the conversation between Serapion and Cyprian in some detail. Auhuber sees this undermining of the norm as a therapeutic process for the brothers. See esp. p. 141. See also Pikulik, *Erzähler*, pp. 58–59.

199. Helmut Motekat, "Vom Sehen und Erkennen bei E. T. A. Hoffmann," MHG, Vol. 19 (1973), pp. 17–27, p. 21, where Motekat suggests the significance of the right kind of artistic vision. Hoffmann was perhaps influenced in his emphasis on the importance of inner vision by Gotthilf Heinrich Schubert; a pertinent passage in Schubert's *Ansichten von der Nachtseite der Naturwissenschaft* (Darmstadt, 1967), stresses the importance of visions of primeval harmonies: "Sie wurden allem Anschein nach im gewöhnlichen Sinne weder gelehrt noch gelernt; sondern ein Abbild der alten Naturoffenbarungen, mußte das Verstehen aus der Seele des Schülers selber, als Begeisterung kommen" 84–85. See also W. Segebrecht, "E. T. A. Hoffmanns Auffassung vom Richteramt und Dichterberuf," *Jahrbuch der deutschen Schillergesellschaft* 11 (1967), pp. 62–138, p. 135.

200. Matt, *Augen*, p. 38, testifies to the importance of this inner vision.

201. Schubert, in his *Ansichten*, suggests that moments of perception and exaltation appear in deranged people: "Aber die Augenblicke jener höheren Begeisterung, welche das menschliche Daseyn zu seinem höchsten Gipfel zu führen, und unser eigentliches Wesen erst zur Blüthe zu bringen scheinen, sind unserer Natur nichts Fremdes, und öfters werden sie selbst in einer sonst irren und wüsten Natur gesehen" (p. 321). Ronald Taylor, "Music and Mystery: Thoughts on the Unity of the Work of E. T. A. Hoffmann," *J.E.G.P.* 75 (1976), pp. 477–91, notes the positive aspect of madness for the artist (pp.

Striking examples of people with artistic sensibilities who are threatened with madness occur near the beginning and the end of the frame (Serapion, Rat Krespel, and Zacharias Werner). Other artists in the inner stories are directly threatened by madness, such as Heinrich von Ofterdingen in "Der Kampf der Sänger" (The singers' contest), Berklinger in "Der Artushof" (Arthur's court), Cardillac in "Das Fräulein von Scuderi," and the Baron von B. Characters who were not artists but whose personalities were attacked by outside forces that altered their states of mind include Ferdinand in "Die Automate" (The automaton), Elias Fröbom in "Die Bergwerke zu Falun," Angelika in "Der unheimliche Gast" (The uncanny guest), Marie in "Nußknacker" (Nutcracker), and Graf Hyppolit in "Vampirismus" (Vampirism). In addition to these characters from the inner stories, there are numerous examples in the frame of victims of madness and strange psychic forces. The plethora of figures related to the themes of artistic vision and altered mental states would seem to justify a detailed examination of these topics in the *Serapionsbrüder*.

Hoffmann's flirtation with the nether side of human consciousness caught the censorious attention of one of his earliest critics, Ludwig Börne, who wrote that the *Serapionsbrüder* was a scientific work rather than a political one. Börne described it as a textbook on madness that could prove dangerous for one's mental health, and the Zacharais Werner section in the frame gives important information on this point.[202] Evidence of Hoffmann's own concern with his mental state was revealed in a diary entry of January 5, 1811, in Bamberg; there he says that he thinks about madness much of the time, whether awake or asleep.[203] R. Mühlher notes that part of Hoffmann's worries about his mental health arose as a result of the fact that he knew that he was predispositioned by heredity to mental problems.[204] Due probably to

---

485–86). Toggenburger, *Almanach-Erzählungen*, p. 51, notes that the dangers of madness are especially acute for the artist.

202. Ludwig Börne, *Gesammelte Schriften* 6 (Vienna, 1868), p. 57ff. Cited in *Aufbau* 1, p. 632.

203. E. T. A. Hoffmann, *Tagebücher*, Müller, Schnapp, p. 112.

204. Robert Mühlher, *Deutsche Dichter der Klassik und Romantik* (Vienna, 1976), pp. 275–76. Herbert M. Mühlpfordt, "Vererbungs- und Umwelteinflüße auf die Brüder J. L. und E. T. Hoffmann," *Jahrbuch der Albertus Universität zu Königsberg* (Würzburg) 17, (1967), pp. 80–146, p. 101. Christa Karoli, "E. T. A. Hoffmann und Zacharias Werner," MHG 16, (1970), pp. 43–61, p. 55.

his own personal concern, Hoffmann was one of the first to discuss the theme of hereditary insanity in literature.[205]

Hoffmann's gnawing worries about his own precarious mental balance fed on the interest among doctors and writers at that time in madness.[206] This new evaluation of insanity first arose from the ideas of the Scottish physician John Brown (1735–88) and their influence on German Romantics and German physicians, among them Hoffmann's medical acquaintances in Bamberg, especially his close friend, Dr. Adalbert Marcus.[207] Brown believed that there were two general diseased conditions, the sthenic state, a condition of overexcitement, and the asthenic state, one of nervous weakness. From this basic concept, others were quick to draw analogies between body and soul, the inner and the outer world.[208] Such comparisons provided a basis for finding a positive quality in madness, since the asthenic person quickly became a positive symbol of the romantic movement, a representative of higher motives. The night was also considered to be asthenic and the imprudence that often overcomes people at that time of day, while madness was the noble form of this recklessness.[209] Nervous illnesses, in which emotions were easily stirred, were thought to be capable of refining an

205. Karoli, "Hoffmann," p. 46.

206. Klaus Dörner, *Bürger und Irre: Zur Sozialgeschichte und Wissenschaftssoziologie der Psychiatrie* (Frankfurt, 1969), p. 252. Wulf Segebrecht in his article "Krankheit," says that for both doctors and writers, the study of the abyss of mental illness is both dangerous and necessary (p. 274). Segebrecht's remarks parallel those of Cyprian on p. 29 of the *Serapionsbrüder* about the advantages of looking into the depths.

207. See Dörner, *Bürger*, pp. 254–55. See also Friedrich Roth, "Dr. Adalbert Friedrich Marcus, der erste dirigierende Arzt des allgemeinen Krankenhauses zu Bamberg." *Festschrift zum 100jährigen Jubiläum des allgemeinen Krankenhauses zu Bamberg* (Bamberg, 1889), pp. 21–34; Nelly Tsouyopoulos, "Die neue Auffassung der klinischen Medizin als Wissenschaft unter dem Einfluß der Philosophie im frühen 19. Jahrhundert," *Berichte zur Wissenschaftsgeschichte*, 1 (1978), pp. 87–100, pp. 89–94, who notes a new attitude toward sickness as a result of the influence of Brown and others, namely that there was unity and not antithesis between the healthy and the pathological state; Friedrich Speyer and Carl Moritz Marc, *Dr. A. F. Marcus nach seinem Leben und Wirken* (Bamberg, 1817); Karl Rothschuh, "Naturphilosophische Konzepte der Medizin aus der Zeit der deutschen Romantik," in *Romantik in Deutschland*, pp. 243–66, esp. p. 248. Segebrecht, "Krankheit," gives extensive background on the medical world in Bamberg during Hoffmann's sojourn as well as on Hoffmann's medical reading. See also Kleßmann, *Hoffmann*, pp. 223–25.

208. Franz G. Alexander and Sheldon T. Selesnick, *The History of Psychiatry: An Evaluation of Psychiatric Thought and Practice from Prehistoric Times to the Present* (New York, 1966), p. 123; Werner Leibbrand, *Romantische Medizin* (Leipzig, 1939), pp. 145–46. See also Gesa Wunderlich, "Krankheits- und Therapiekonzepte am Anfang der deutschen Psychiatrie" (Diss., Berlin, 1981), pp. 7–14.

209. Dörner, *Bürger*, p. 255.

individual; madness was "indirekte Asthenie" (indirect asthenia).[210] A large group of physicians devoted their interest to manifestations of the subconscious, including such men as Gotthilf H. Schubert, Johann Christian Reil, and Carl Gustav Carus.[211] Their interests strongly paralleled those of many Romantic writers, Hoffmann included. Schubert, in his *Ansichten von der Nachtseite der Naturwissenschaft* (Views from the night side of natural science), seemed to believe that the sick individual came closer to union with its own inner spirit:

> Es werden zwar die noch ungeborenen Kräfte eines künftigen Daseyns vornehmlich in einem krankhaften oder ohnmächtigen Zustand des jetztigen sichtbar, . . . mag auch im gesunden und wachen Zustand der vollkommeneren Organe, jene dunklere Sympathie entfernter Wesen immer wirksamer seyn, sie vermag aber erst in solchen Momenten wie die des magnetischen Schlafs, des Nachtwandelns, Wahnsinns und andern ähnlichen krankhaften Zuständen hervorzutreten.[212]

> Although the yet-unborn powers of a future existence become visible predominantly in a diseased or unconscious state of present existence, . . . that darker sympathy with more distant beings may always be more effective in the healthy and awakened state of more perfect organs, yet, that darker sympathy can only emerge in such moments as those of magnetic sleep, sleepwalking, madness and during other similar diseased states.

This attitude towards madness found its way into the works of Hoffmann, among others, and resulted in the frequent portrayal of madness as a condition with positive as well as negative aspects.[213]

Philippe Pinel (1745–1826) and Reil (1759–1813) had a profound influence on Hoffmann's ideas about mental illness. Both men broke

---

210. Dörner, *Bürger*, p. 256.

211. Rothschuh, "Naturphilosophische Konzepte," p. 244.

212. Schubert, *Ansichten*, pp. 302, 363. See also p. 204. The portrait of Serapion owes much to Schubert's idea of the "versteckten Poet." A survival of this Romantic concept, that the individual came closer to essential truths about himself in a more irrational mental state, seems to survive even in Freud, who says that the illness of depression brings on rather accurate self-criticism, insights accessible only to the ill person (see *Collected Papers* [1917], trans. Joan Riviere, 4 (1959), Ch. 8, pp. 155–56. Armand DeLoecker, *Zwischen Atlantis und Frankfurt* (Frankfurt, 1983), p. 24, notes that Schubert's ideas on the weakened power of reason in a sick individual influenced Hoffmann.

213. Dörner, *Bürger*, p. 256. Segebrecht, "Krankheit," p. 268, says that Hoffmann was exceptionally well read in the psychiatric literature of his day. (See also p. 281.) See J. C. Reil, *Über die Erkenntniß und Cur der Fieber* 4 (Vienna, 1802) in a section on *Geisteszerrüttung* that describes what happens when the imaginative faculty becomes ill. Reil writes: "Die Phantasien bekommen die Stärke der Anschauungen, betäuben die übrigen Kräfte des Seelenvermögens und associiren sich nach falschen Regeln" (p. 53).

with the mechanistic approach to mental illness popular in the earlier eighteenth century. Pinel saw mental illness resulting from heredity and emotional experience; consequently, the only doctors who could understand it were those who had some concept of the workings of heredity and of the human heart. His descriptions of psychological disorders, which we find reflected in Cyprian's and Theodore's remarks on Serapion, were detailed and careful.²¹⁴ Reil's *Rhapsodien über die Anwendung der psychischen Curmethode auf Geisteszerrüttungen* (1803) (Rhapsodies on the application of the psychological method of therapy to derangements of the mind) offered a systematic approach to treating mental illness, as where he carefully lists rules to be followed in treatment.²¹⁵ If psychological influences can cure emotional illness, they can also cause them, a situation encountered repeatedly in the *Serapionsbrüder*, as in the case of Elis Fröbom and Heinrich von Ofterdingen.

This tendency towards clinical observation of madness, an approach that appears in other sections of the frame, particularly in the discussion on magnetism, may mask an attempt on Hoffmann's part to deal with the threat of madness as well as his interest in and attraction to

214. In J. C. Reil's *Rhapsodien über die Anwendung der psychischen Curmethode auf Geisteszerrüttungen* (Halle, 1803), there is a passage that describes an approach similar to that of Cyprian: "Bey der psychischen Kur dieser Geisteszerrüttung (i.e., idée fixe) kömmt es bloß allein darauf an, die fixe Vorstellung zu tilgen. Mit ihr schwinden alle Triebe, Begierden und unstattliche Handlungen, die von ihr, als von ihrer Quelle, ausströmen" (p. 324). See also p. 329, "Zuweilen kann man den Kranken überreden, er habe seinen Zweck erreicht, oder ihn durch lebhafte Vorstellungen von der Absurdität seiner Vorsätze überzeugen."

Phillipe Pinel, in his *Traité médico-philosophique sur l'Aliénation mentale, ou la manie* (Paris, 1801), also gives advice similar to that which Cyprian follows: "L'art de consoler les aliénés, de leur parler avec bienveillance, de leur donner quelquefois des réponses évasives pour ne point les aigrir par des refus, de leur imprimer d'autres fois une crainte salutaire, et de triompher sans aucun sorte de violence de leur obstination inflexible" (pp. 46–47). Cyprian gives Pinel and Reil as sources of his medical knowledge in his account of Serapion (p. 20); Theodor mentions Pinel and fixated ideas as well (p. 29). See also Alexander and Selsnick, *History of Psychiatry*, pp. 112–13, 135–37; Annemarie Leibbrand-Wettley, "Die Stellung der Geisteskranken in der Gesellschaft des 19. Jahrhunderts," in *Der Arzt und der Kranke in der Gesellschaft des 19. Jahrhunderts* (Stuttgart, 1967), pp. 50–69, p. 57.

215. J. C. Reil, *Rhapsodien*, pp. 218–21. Reil devotes a considerable amount of space to the *idée fixe*, pp. 305–364. Kruse, p. 653, cites only an anecdote on p. 316 of Reil, but there is much material of interest in this section. Reil defines the *idée fixe* as follows: "Der fixe Wahnsinn besteht in einer partiellen Verkehrtheit des Vorstellungsvermögens, die sich auf einen oder auf eine Reihe homogener Gegenstände bezieht, von deren Daseyn der Kranke nicht zu überzeugen ist, und die daher die Freiheit seines Begehrungsvermögens beschränkt, . . . Beide Merkmale, fixe Ideen und subjektive Überzeugungen, daß der Wahn Wahrheit sey, gehören wesentlich zur Charakteristik dieser Krankheit" (pp. 307–8).

it. The conflicting ideas about insanity become apparent in the frame discussion. Ottmar's reaction is extreme and fearful; he rejects Cyprian's fervent desire for madness (29), while Ottmar criticizes Cyprian's earlier book (Hoffmann's *Die Elixiere des Teufels*) (The elixirs of the devil) for dealing with the topic (28).[216] Theodor takes his usual more cautious and reasoned approach, advising those who know they have a weakness in this area to keep away from the topic, so as not to bring madness upon themselves.

This fear of complete madness, which the Serapion story illustrates so well that Theodor's hair stood on end (29), appears again and again during the course of the frame because of its importance for the artist.[217] As Cyprian indicated (29), the artist can be inspired by these momentary glances into the internal abyss of madness, but there also is a danger that he too may step past the point of no return. One way of overcoming this fear is to study madness, distancing it by making it an object separate from oneself.

This basic concept, which lies at the heart of much psychoanalytic theory, may have been grasped intuitively by Hoffmann, who, perhaps because of his own severe emotional problems, was able to anticipate developments in psychoanalysis, such as a potentially disastrous maternal influence in the case of Werner.[218] Such attempts at control of

216. Segebrecht (Winkler), p. 1038, says that the book in question is *Die Elixiere des Teufels* and that this passage is one of those sections that proves that Hoffmann speaks with other voices than Theodor.

217. Cyprian regrets to some degree having published the *Elixiere* because of its dangerous aspects (pp. 28–29). The threatening element in madness appears again after the Krespel story, when Lothar remarks that Theodor's tale may be dangerous (p. 52). Numerous critics have noted in a general way the connection between the problems of the artist and madness in Hoffmann. See Mühlher, "Gedanken zum Humor bei E. T. A. Hoffmann," in *Gestalt und Wirklichkeit: Festschrift Ferdinand Weinhandl,* ed. Robert Mühlher and Johann Fischl (Berlin, 1967), pp. 505–19, p. 517; Motekat, "Vom Sehen," p. 22; Mühlher, *Deutsche Dichter,* pp. 275–76; Segebrecht, "Richteramt," pp. 136, 137, Marianne Thalmann, "Meisterschaft: Eine Studie zu E. T. A. Hoffmanns Genieproblem," in *Der Gesichtskreis: Festschrift Joseph Drexel,* (Munich, 1956), pp. 142–63, pp. 152–53, 158, 159; Margot Kuttner, *Die Gestaltung des Individualitätsproblems bei E. T. A. Hoffmann* (Hamburg, 1936), pp. 72–77. See also Reiner Matzker, *Der nützliche Idiot: Wahnsinn und Initiation bei Jean Paul und E. T. A. Hoffmann* (Frankfurt, 1984), pp. 103–30.

218. Jürgen Voerster, *160 Jahre E. T. A. Hoffmann-Forschung (1805–1965)* (Stuttgart, 1967), p. 16, says that Hoffmann's anticipation of the discoveries in psychiatry in the twentieth century certainly would merit additional study. In one of the few serious analyses of the entire frame of the first section, Auhuber, *Spiegel,* suggests that the telling of stories about those afflicted with madness is in itself therapeutic, though it may seem dangerous at first (p. 113).

madness are necessary if the artist is to integrate the knowledge of the inner mind gained from observation of these abnormal mental states. Serapion, though he cannot perceive the real world, does have the ability to experience a wide range of mental states, a capacity essential for the artist (53–54). This real experience comes from the perceptive ability of the inner eye, which must encounter as much as possible to express it in an individual way. Therein lies the importance of the abnormal: it gives us insight into experience we would not otherwise have had.

The artist, as a man immersed in the real world as well as his inner one, cannot escape the experience of *Duplizität*. Only two mental conditions make it possible for an individual to avoid this division: madness or philistinism. The madman lives in an inner world with no boundaries that touch on the outside; the philistine perceives no inner world.[219] In the beginning of the *Serapionsbrüder*, Hoffmann presents these two options in the frame in an extremely symmetrical manner, beginning with various ironic portrayals of philistinistic groups and ending with the story of Serapion.

Book I
Frame: "Der Einsiedler Serapion" and "Rat Krespel" (The Anchorite Serapion, Councillor Krespel)

When the friends meet to form what will become the *Serapions-brüder*, they confront the awkward situation of reunions of formerly close friends after a long separation. After a discomfiting beginning,

219. Wolfgang Preisendanz, "Eines matt geschliffenen Spiegels dunkler Widerschein; E. T. A. Hoffmanns Erzählkunst," reprinted in *Zu E. T. A. Hoffmann*, pp. 40–54, p. 45; originally appeared in *Festschrift für Jost Trier* (Köln, 1964), pp. 411–29. See Mühlher, *Deutsche Dichter*, pp. 292–301, for a discussion of the Philistine. Joachim Rosteutscher, *Das ästhetische Idol im Werke von Winckelmann, Novalis, Hoffmann, Goethe, Georg und Rilke* (Bern, 1956), notes that the Ritter Gluck, the Baron von B., Serapion, and, to some extent, Krespel have retreated from reality into a world that makes sense only to them (p. 164). In his recent book, *Sonne und Punsch*, p. 104, Manfred Momberger offers a perceptive analysis of the relation of the anecdote about the Kantians to Serapion by comparing the closed nature of each one's thought system. Pikulik, *Erzähler*, p. 20, says

Theodor confronts the situation honestly; they are forcing a false conviviality while privately thinking how much each has changed; therefore, they should make a new beginning and not try to revive the old
group (10-11). This speech enables the others to confess their inner
fears about the creeping philistinism of the encounter. Within this context, three different examples of bourgeois clubs surface that they had
known during their twelve years apart. Each of these groups illustrates
a different kind of preoccupation with externals to the exclusion of any
kind of inner spirit or experience, whether with law, gourmandise, or
banalities (12–15).

   The philistines surface again in the comments of Cyprian, the character who makes the transition from this group to madness. He first
tells the anecdote about the two philistines who were interrupted in
the middle of a violent philosophical argument in one city and who
pick it up again at the same juncture twenty years later. They do not
allow for the inner changes that intervening experience must have
brought to each of their lives, but persist in old forms of social intercourse (16–17). At this point, Cyprian, while warning that the story of
Serapion does not lend itself to the maintenance of a convivial atmosphere, begins his account of the mad nobleman.

   Hoffmann's choice of Serapion to appear at this juncture was necessary to justify the name of the group, but there is also a deeper symmetry involved in its position. It follows closely the various descriptions
of philistinism and forced conviviality, which, in its emphasis on externals, is deadly to the inner spirit. Cyprian now decisively turns the
group towards Serapion, in the direction of inner experience so extreme that it ignores the real world. Both the philistine Kantians and
Serapion cut themselves off from the real world, a theme that has major
implications in the *Serapionsbrüder* for the interpretation of Serapion's
significance and for many of the stories. The organization of the beginning part of the frame has introduced the two dangers that confront
the artist and that will pose constant threats in the frame and the inner
stories throughout the work.

   In this first section, Hoffmann not only introduces his major themes
but also includes an important structural element that recurs throughout the frame: the use of the anecdote as a device, relating the frame

---

that the philistine, a creature of habit in the extreme, has some of the characteristics of
the automat.

in several ways to the inner stories.[220] An anecdote may deal with themes that then receive artistic treatment in the stories, as will Vinzenz's account about the demented old man he meets in the woods (742-3), which comes directly before the story about the Baron von B. The anecdotes also serve to bring in technical information or objective confirmation of material presented in the stories, as they do in the frame section on magnetism. They may also impress a point in a manner less threatening than a direct statement. This function appears in the series of accounts about clubs, found in the first part of the frame. Giving examples of bourgeois behavior in the clubs to which various members have been exposed is just as effective and less disturbing than citing examples of such behavior among those assembled. In addition, the brevity of the anecdote keeps the point from becoming monotonous.

Alongside the anecdotes or short digressions in the frame are those stories that have no separate title in the text, such as "Serapion" and "Rat Krespel."[221] In comparison with anecdotes, these stories afford another sort of perspective, one that lies between that of the anecdote and the traditional inner story. Like the anecdotes, they generally fall within the range of direct personal experience.[222] The brothers who tell these stories dealing with madness or eccentricity have heard of or known the protagonist themselves. As with the anecdotes, this personal knowledge adds credibility to the points made through the stories. However, since they are longer than the anecdotes, they root themselves more firmly in the reader's consciousness, an effect their story form enhances greatly. At the same time, their fictional form distances them from the reader, a characteristic they share with the inner stories. All but two of these inserts deal with the theme of madness and strange unseen powers. Since these stories serve an intermediary role

220. Mühlher, *Deutsche Dichter*, p. 269, notes that Hoffmann was a master of the anecdote but does not mention its literary function in the frame. Pikulik, *Erzähler*, p. 19, makes only general remarks about the parallel direction of the themes on two planes, but does not mention specific examples or analyze its function.

221. These include: "Der Einsiedler Serapion," "Rat Krespel," "Eine Spukgeschichte," "Alte und Neue Kirchenmusik," "Nachricht aus dem Leben eines bekannten Mannes," "Der Baron von B," "Zacharias Werner," "Vampirismus," "Die ästhetische Teegesellschaft." The editors of both the Winkler and the Aufbau editions put them in brackets in their respective tables of contents. Georg Ellinger, *E. T. A. Hoffmanns Werke*, Part 5, *Die Serapionsbrüder* (Berlin, no date), p. 38, discusses in some detail characteristics of the narrative elements in the frame.

222. There is one exception, "Nachricht aus dem Leben eines bekannten Mannes," which comes from a chronicle. The essay on "Alte und neue Kirchenmusik" is divided up between Cyprian and Theodor; it is not a novella and no characters figure in it.

between the anecdote of the frame and the formal inner story, the significance of this theme becomes apparent once more, as does the need to confront personal knowledge of madness without being overwhelmed by it. For this reason the implications of the form of presentation are significant. As L. Pikulik points out in another context, an observer is necessary to register the existence of a departure from the norm.[223] The telling of these stories by the brothers, who, as sane and objective acquaintances, can ascertain the degree of deviation, forces them and the readers to confront the threats facing the artist on yet another level of perception.

The conversation regarding Serapion's mental condition leaves no doubt of the ambivalent attitude towards madness on the part of those assembled. Cyprian's remarks on the increased level of perception afforded to the insane call forth Theodor's warning that he who knows he can become dizzy should avoid such adventures (29). The unease felt by Theodor shows itself in Ottmar as well, who moves the conversation from the totally mad to those who were merely difficult in their behavior. With this move, he implicitly reintroduces the conflict between philistine and aesthete, which Theodor expands upon in preparation for his encounter with Rat Krespel: the incongruity of the inner mind with the external world often results in strange appearances and behavior on the part of affected individuals, which the philistine never notices (30). The uncomfortable reality of Serapion's condition can be distanced through another story, the one about Rat Krespel, which completes another transition, from splenetic madness to healthy good sense (30). This remark in the frame provides a clue to the way in which the reader is to understand the problematic councillor.

The Serapion-Krespel sequence also serves another function, since it leads ultimately to the formulation of the *Serapionsprinzip* and the introduction to the artist stories. Yet Krespel's relationship to Serapion has received little critical attention and offers a good example of how neglect of the frame has impeded understanding of the stories.[224] As

223. Lothar Pikulik, "Das Wunderliche bei E. T. A. Hoffmann: Zum romantischen Ungenügen an der Normalität," *Euphorion* 69 (1975), pp. 294–319, p. 308.
224. Werner, "Schriftsteller," pp. 84–85, compares the two briefly, in regard to their disturbed relationship to society, their approach to art, and their extra-rational experience. Wulf Segebrecht, "Heterogenität und Integration bei E. T. A. Hoffmann," originally in *Romantik heute* (Bonn, 1972), pp. 45–59, in Scher, pp. 10–21, pp. 11–12, compares Serapion and Krespel in their artistic shortcomings and comes to a more precise and useful distinction; both characters lack something that a real artist must possess.

Müller-Seidel has pointed out, there is great significance in the way one story points to another.[225] In the similarities and the contrasts between Serapion and Krespel, we learn much about Hoffmann's conception of the artistic personality that prepares us for the *Serapionsprinzip*. Both Serapion and Krespel were diplomats (19, 31) and both live, in different degrees, outside of the continuum of normal human relationships. Serapion is often described as an anchorite, as is Krespel, at least for a certain period of his life (30, 35). In the eyes of the world, the behavior of both men arouses reactions ranging from discomfort to revulsion. Serapion's extended relationships with people dead for hundreds of years as well as his manner of living draw ridicule from the Philistines in the area and attract concern from those both interested in and threatened by insanity, such as some of the *Serapionsbrüder*.

Krespel, like Serapion, has carefully regulated his life in a pattern that makes sense only to himself, refusing to see his daughter, his wife, or sometimes his friends, just as he has designed his house in an eccentrically unique manner. He determines the openings in the house—the windows and doors—just as he regulates his contacts and outlets to others. The major difference between them lies in Krespel's capacity to be influenced by personal contacts. Antonie begs him not to destroy a valuable old violin; he accedes to her request, although he normally dissected such instruments. The narrator asks for an account of her

In Krespel's case, his wrongheaded hunt for knowledge deprives him of much artistic experience (p. 12). In assessing Krespel's function, Segebrecht says that Serapion can only be interpreted with Krespel as a background (p. 11). Auhuber, *Spiegel*, pp. 142–55, analyzes Krespel's alleged madness, and, especially on p. 154, compares him to Serapion. See also Pikulik, *Erzähler*, p. 64, who sees Serapion as a unified personality and Krespel with the psychological split between the world of the spirit and the earthly one.

225. Müller-Seidel, p. 1014. A good example of the misunderstanding to which neglect of the frame can lead occurs in James M. McGlathery's article, "Der Himmel hängt ihm voller Geigen: E. T. A. Hoffmann's *Rat Krespel, Die Fermate* und *Der Baron von B*," *German Quarterly* 51 (1978), pp. 135–49, especially p. 142. Attention to the frame could have provided a number of elements in the area of thematic development that influenced Hoffmann. Neglect of the frame and its clues to interpretation also appear in John M. Ellis's book *Narration in the German Novelle: Theory and Interpretation* (Cambridge, England, 1974). Ellis, in his fertile analysis of "Rat Krespel," rests his negative opinion of Theodor, which influences his interpretation, solely on Theodor's appearance immediately before and after telling the story, instead of on Theodor as a frame character throughout the whole of the work. The arguments Ellis makes against Theodor about his lack of perception concern Theodor's first meeting with Krespel, when he can hardly be expected to see the inner consistency in Krespel's remarks, consistency that would be apparent only with a knowledge of Krespel's character. (Ellis, p. 97). Had he kept Theodor's role throughout the whole frame in mind, he might have revised this judgment.

death; Krespel gives it to him; he abandons violin building because of her loss. In all these ways, Krespel shows an awareness of, if not a conformity to, the milieu in which he lives, and, in this regard, maintains that contact with reality that Serapion lacks.

Krespel's function in the structure of the *Serapionsbrüder* does not lie merely in being a foil to Serapion; as the main character in a long series of inner stories, he represents themes and problems that recur frequently. Just as the unfortunate councillor drew the attention of his fellow citizens, so he has also drawn critics, who have pronounced rather contradictory verdicts over his extraordinary person. The two major areas of disagreement center around the nature of Krespel's artistic interests and his marriage to the Italian singer.[226] The answers to both of these questions, as articulated in the figure of Krespel, deserve attention, since both topics figure prominently in the inner stories of the *Serapionsbrüder*. A comparison of Krespel's comments in the story and comparison with other figures in the inner stories, such as Wolfram von Eschenbach in "Kampf," Salvator Rosa and Antonio Scacciati in "Signor Formica," make it difficult to consider him an artist. They were artists in regard to both profession and inner inspiration. Yet Krespel does not belong in the camp of the philistines, since he is aware of an inner life and has an abiding interest in art and applied arts—in this case, the building of violins.[227] Krespel's knowledge of this inner life and the contradiction between the ideal and reality lead to his bizarre behavior, which annoys those people who are too insensitive to notice the contradictions.[228] Because of his perception of the life of the mind and his interest in art, specifically music, the figure of Krespel serves as an introduction to many of the major themes and characters

226. Müller-Seidel considers Krespel an artist (p. 1019), while G. Vitt-Maucher, "Hoffmanns 'Rat Krespel' und der Schlafrock Gottes," *Monatshefte* 64, no. 1, (1972), confuses the issue, referring to him first as an amateur, then later as an artist (pp. 51–57). Müller-Seidel believes that Krespel has misused art in his success in marrying Angela (p. 1019). See also Segebrecht, *Autobiographie*, p. 134. Pikulik, *Erzähler*, p. 65, compares Krespel to a good magnetizer who wants to save Antonie.

227. Otto Nipperdey, "Wahnsinnsfiguren bei E. T. A. Hoffmann" (Diss., Köln, 1957), p. 120, points out that Krespel shows the blind spot in his artistic sensibility through his foolish belief that he can find the point where the soul of the sound is in the mechanism of the violin.

228. Herman Meyer, *Der Sonderling in der deutschen Dichtung* (1963), explains Krespel's bizarreness in a similar way (pp. 110–11). See also Wolfgang Nehring, "Gebärdensprache," pp. 220–21. In a discussion of Hoffmann eccentrics, Nipperdey, "Wahnsinnsfiguren," implies that their nonconformist character necessarily appears in behavior that seems abnormal to those individual unaffected by such conflicts (p. 111).

of the *Serapionsbrüder*. Even though Krespel has not devoted his life solely to art, he still experiences the contradiction between ideal and reality that leads to his bizarre behavior.

When the amateur violinist Krespel relates his life story to Theodor at the end of the novella, he describes his interest in violins as "die bis zur Leidenschaft gesteigerte Liebhaberei" ["the hobby that had intensified to a stage of passion"] (44). Krespel, who was a lawyer and diplomat by profession (31), built the best violins in Hoffmann's times (35). Therefore his marriage to Angela, the tempermental singer, should not be viewed as a betrayal of art or as a misguided attempt to reconcile art and a bourgeois relationship. Since the human voice and violins are often compared, Krespel's admiration for the voices of Angela and Antonie is consistent with the qualities of a connoisseur.[229] Krespel has been criticized because he misused art, playing the violin (45) to win Angela. It is precisely because Krespel is not a true artist that he makes such an attempt and does not see the folly of it.[230] The same misunderstanding of the function of art and the role of love occurs on another level in "Der Kampf der Sänger," where Heinrich von Ofterdingen allies himself with forces of the nether world in order to win Mathilde's love through his singing. Krespel is at fault because he misunderstands the function of art; Angela, because she did not accept the fact that she, like most of Hoffmann's artist figures, could not combine her art with a happy marriage.

Their relationship together culminates in Krespel's throwing her out of the window when she was pregnant. From this time on, i.e., after her physical separation from Krespel and from her marriage, she is a changed person, cooperative and agreeable. Krespel's defenestration of his wife occurred after she disturbed him with his Cremona violin. His action symbolizes his inability to resolve the demands of art and life. Neither of the partners feels able to function in both roles. Krespel fears a renewal of Angela's former temper tantrums if he returns, so the two of them exchange tender letters until her death, though they never see each other again.

The discord that characterizes their relationship is incarnate in their

229. See Ellis, 110–12; Mühlher, *Deutsche Dichter*, p. 280, says that, for Hoffmann, the human breast is the greatest instrument.

230. Krespel's successful attempts to convince Angela to marry him result from a false perception, whether or not one considers him an artist. This failure in perception links him to many other figures in the inner stories.

daughter Antonie, whose psychological and physical portrait reflects Hoffmann's reading of Reil and Schubert. There is a defect in her chest that gives her voice its extraordinary quality, but continued singing will cause a premature death (48).[231] Therefore she cannot marry a composer or anyone who loves music, because he and she would be unable to resist the pleasure of hearing the singing that would kill her. Her physical condition prevents her from combining dedication to art and a happy marriage. Her parents were unable to achieve this state because of character flaws. However, Antonie has not only her mother's charm but also the gentle personality that her mother lacked (47). Perhaps Antonie's disposition is the happy result of the psychological consequences of her pregnant mother's trip through the window, while her physical defect symbolizes the flaws in her parents' characters. Antonie resembles Julia Marc with her beauty, sweetness, purity, and her extraordinary voice.[232]

In many ways, she is a symbol for art, unfit for life in the real world, offering, in her weakened state, glimpses of an exalted kind of singing, in short, a Schubertian heroine. Her identification with the spirit and sound of the old violin adds to her unreal quality. In this context, it is perhaps significant that she appears to and leaves Krespel in a dream (47, 50–51). His last experience of her comes in the dream that the *Rat* has on the night she dies. In his dream, a sort of apotheosis takes place in which Antonie is united both with singing and with her fiancé, a union that cannot take place in this life. When Krespel finds her, she is dead, smiling happily, as if she had experienced Krespel's dream (50–51).

Antonie is now able to achieve a union that had eluded her and her parents in life, though for different reasons. The significance of dreams

231. The nature of the doctor's diagnosis has called forth contradictory opinions. Ellis (pp. 104–5) tries to discount the doctor's opinion, saying that the doctor did not really examine her. Antonie is, however, present when the diagnosis is made; one can hardly see the point of having the doctor make the diagnosis if it is to be discounted in the interpretation. Peter von Matt, *Augen*, finds it significant that Hoffmann puts the diagnosis in the mouth of a doctor, founding it on medical knowledge of the time about prenatal influence. See Matt, pp. 129–30. The discussions of Cardillac in "Scuderi" and Werner in the frame indicate that this subject was one of the many medical topics that interested Hoffmann.

232. Mistler, *Hoffmann*, notes that Julia Marc spat blood while singing, p. 199. Further clues that Antonie has very close ties with one of the most famous pupils in German literature are apparent in the letter accompanying the story that Hoffmann sent to Baron de la Motte Fouqué (p. 660, *Aufbau* 1, *Die Serapionsbrüder*). See also McGlathery, "Hoffmann's Krespel," p. 141.

lies in two areas; they arise from the innermost parts of one's being and they represent a journey into higher spiritual regions. The previous quotation about Krespel's vision of his daughter in a dream (47) reflects the first of these characteristics; Krespel's account of the apotheosis reflects the second one: "Plötzlich umgab ihn eine blendende Klarheit, . . ." (50–51). ["All at once he was surrounded by a dazzling brightness . . ."] (Bleiler, 235).[233] The world of the Schubertian dream is Antonie's proper sphere.[234] The physical limitations and conflicts that keep her from living a full artistic as well as private life on earth are gone.[235] As subsequent analyses will show, Schubert is often an important presence in both the inner stories and the frame.

Krespel, who remains behind, has failed with Antonie just as he failed with her mother. His solution to the problem of reconciling art and life is to give up his interest in violins. Perhaps Krespel has seen that the essence of tone, which he sought vainly in the structure of the violins, resides mainly in Antonie and cannot be achieved again. "Der Rat schien andern Tages ganz der vorige, nur erklärte er, daß er niemals mehr Violinen bauen, und auch auf keiner jemals mehr spielen wolle" (43). ["Next day the Councillor appeared to be just as he formerly was, only he averred that he would never make another violin, nor ever play on another"] (Bleiler, 227).

Krespel's attempts to find the secret of harmony in the old violins, especially those of Tartini's time, to which Hoffmann also alludes in "Baron von B." as a golden age of violin building, parallel other attempts in the inner stories of the *Serapionsbrüder*. In "Die Automate," the main characters attempt to find the *Urton* (original tone), another

233. Translations for "Rat Krespel" come from *The Best Tales of Hoffmann*, by E. T. A. Hoffmann, edited by E. F. Bleiler (New York, 1967); this one is found on p. 231. This collection is also the source of translations for the following stories: "The Mines of Falun," "Nutcracker and the King of Mice," "Tobias Martin, Master Cooper, and His Men," "Signor Formica," and "The King's Betrothed." Page numbers will be given in the text from now on, with the note "Bleiler, p.——." Passages from these stories with no accreditation have been translated by Beate Engel and the author.

234. Cramer, *Das Groteske*, p. 128, has remarked that Hoffmann used Schubert's work on dreams as one might a recipe book.

235. Inge Stegmann, "Deutung und Funktion des Traumes bei E. T. A. Hoffmann" (Diss., Bonn, 1973), pp. 257–58, says that through the dream, Krespel realized that he could no longer control Antonie's fate (p. 258). She interprets Krespel's enigmatic remark after Antonie's death (". . . aber es geschieht nur alles deshalb, weil ich mir vor einiger Zeit einen Schlafrock anfertigte, in dem ich aussehen wollte wie das Schicksal oder wie Gott!" [42–43]) as an indication that Krespel realized that his attempts to control destiny were futile. Momberger, *Sonne und Punsch*, p. 73, notes the ambivalent nature of music.

manifestation of Schubertian influence. In the essay, "Alte und neue Kirchenmusik" (Old and new church music), Hoffmann discusses how the highest harmony in music links us to the world of spirits and to the eternal (406–415). The discordant elements in Krespel's personality may reflect not only his bizarre outlook but also his inability to find the hidden secret of harmony in the violins.[236] In this regard, he differs from Serapion, who cannot perceive reality well enough to be influenced by it. Consequently, he serves as a bridge from Serapion to the world of the other inner stories and the frame. Krespel's eccentricity, which Lothar interprets as madness, helps to keep this theme present as a threat in the frame, where the story is embedded.

Although Krespel stands outside the world of the true artist, he is near enough to look in and understand. He experiences some of the same problems, although in a different key, as the subsequent characters do who struggle to reconcile art and life. His inability to sort out the demands of love for another person and love for his violins, reflected in his quick return to them after his marital failure, anticipates the problems that reappear in "Der Artushof," "Der Kampf der Sänger," "Meister Martin," and "Die Brautwahl," among other stories.

The tension in the story centers around music, which makes its thematic entrance and dominates many of the subsequent inner stories as it does in many of Hoffmann's other works, such as "Ritter Gluck" (Knight Gluck), the *Kreisleriana*, and *Kater Murr* (*Tomcat Murr*). Music, closely allied in several stories with hidden forces of nature, appears here linked with magnetism for the first time, a theme that will play such an important role in the preoccupation with mental states. As Krespel describes the violin that Antonie loves, he compares himself to the magnetizer: ". . . es war mir, da ich zum ersten Male darauf spielte, als wär ich nur der Magnetiseur, der die Somnambule zu erregen vermag, daß sie selbsttätig ihre innere Anschauung in Worten verkündet"

---

236. See the subsequent discussions of "Die Automate" and "Alte und Neue Kirchenmusik" in this analysis. Stegmann, *Deutung*, has some useful comments to make on sympathetic relationships in "Krespel," which run from the violin (artificial, but with a soul), to Antonie, to dreams, to suprasensuous recognition. He suggests that Krespel saw glimpses of the *Urton* (primeval tone) (pp. 258, 259). Wolfgang Wittkowski, "E. T. A. Hoffmanns musikalische Musikerdichtungen 'Ritter Gluck,' 'Don Juan,' 'Rat Krespel,' " *Aurora* 38 (1978), pp. 54–74, p. 74, notes that in Krespel's dream the music that continued while the couple embraced was from Nature. Pfotenhauer, "Exoterische und esoterische Poetik," p. 140, believes that Krespel wanted to be like God in his search for the secret of the tone of the old violins.

(38) ["The first time I played upon it I somehow fancied that I was only the magnetizer who has the power of moving his subject to reveal of his own accord in words the visions of his inner nature"] (Bleiler, 222).

The subsequent discussion of magnetism will show that the sleep-walker is in close touch with his inner being and will deal with the connection between these two psychic phenomena. Lothar refers to the hypnotic power that music has on Theodor in the frame discussion, an important reference, since it links music and magnetism (51–52).

Against the backdrop of the problematic Krespel, Antonie introduces major issues that revolve around the adjustment of art to life. Antonie is the incarnation of the perfect artist, but she cannot realize her art in this life, because that would kill her. Perhaps her mother's destruction of Krespel's Cremona violin just before he threw her out the window foreshadows Antonie's death. This interpretation seems plausible on the basis of the strong parallels made between Antonie and the one violin that Krespel does not tear apart. Antonie's life is a parable for the dangers of art, the ambiguity about it that Hoffmann himself seems to have felt. Within the story, Antonie's physical weakness is symbolic of her parents' flaw, but it also has a larger role for the entire work as a prefigurative element. The pursuit of art often brings misery, madness or death, and, at the very least, much mental anguish. Art is not possible without treading close to the limits of one's personal endurance, whether physical or psychological. Hoffmann's ideas on this point were probably influenced by Schubert and romantic medicine in general, which saw in physical weakness the opportunity to gain insight into hidden worlds.

The dangers that eccentricity bordering on madness represent to those assembled in the frame become immediately apparent when Lothar lashes out angrily for Theodor bringing up Krespel (52). The talk comes back to Serapion, and, at this point, the discussion ensues that leads to the formation of the *Serapionsprinzip*. The major requisite for a true artist is the ability to see beyond the surface (54).[237] Consequently, the only suitable stories are those that the writers have seen with the inner eye: "Jeder prüfe wohl, ob er auch wirklich das ge-

237. See Motekat, "Vom Sehen," pp. 21–22. He cites Cardillac and Fröbom as examples of figures whose ability to see into the depths doomed them. It is important to keep the disquieting aspect of a vocation for art in mind as the frame and inner stories progress, since it helps to explain the preoccupation with altered states of consciousness.

schaut, was er zu verkünden unternommen, ehe er es wagt, laut damit zu werden. ["Everyone should consider well whether he really beheld what he ventures to proclaim before he dares to voice it"]. (55)

While Serapion had such a faculty for seeing with the inner eye, his problem was that he did not perceive the real world and therefore misjudged its function in art and life. For this reason, he, too, like the philistine, was unaware of *Duplizität*.[238] In the philistine, it led to the renunciation of an inner life, as in the cases of the various clubs described at the outset. For the artist, this defect in perception leads to madness.

"Die Fermate"
(The Fermata)

After the intense discussions and the uncanny characters of Serapion and Krespel, the newly baptized *Serapionsbrüder* feel the need of a change of pace. Ottmar suggests that Theodor complete the transition to "gesunder Vernunft" (healthy good sense) with a light and cheerful story that will drive the dreadful things they have heard from their minds. Yet, in spite of the lighthearted tone accompanying its introduction, the theme of "Die Fermate" has much in common with that of "Rat Krespel": the conflict of art with life and love. "Fermate" certainly represents a break in mood with the accounts of Krespel and Serapion, but there is a *basso ostinato* going through all three stories that deals with the major preoccupation of the frame: the relationship between art and life.

The title of Theodor's second story fits in nicely with the members' expressed desire for a pause in the presentation of eccentric madmen. C. Schweizer, in his observations on the meaning of the title, observes that *fermate* means not only the trills of the Italian lady, but also the resting point and final note of a musical work. Figuratively speaking,

238. See Segebrecht, "Richteramt," p. 137. Also Mühlher, *Deutsche Dichter*, p. 357; he defines *Duplizität* as the primeval thought that every man has both physical parents and archetypes. See also Segebrecht, *Autobiographie*, pp. 185–86. Nipperdey, "Wahnsinnsfiguren," p. 212, notes that the philistine sees madness as a sickness with no redeeming possibilities.

the word also points to the conclusion of a stage of artistic development.[239] The pause that caused Theodor so much emotional pain occurred in the early stages of his development as a musician before he understood the appropriate relationship between art and life.

The continuing emphasis on music is only one of a number of obvious similarities between "Rat Krespel" and "Die Fermate." In each story, song plays the dominant role; in both, temperamental Italian singers make the lives of their German admirers miserable (Angela—Rat Krespel; Teresina, Lauretta—Theodor). In both cases, the singers' behavior causes the departure of their German suitors. In both stories, singers represent an embodiment of an artistic ideal. In Theodor's case, not only is Teresina for him art incarnate; she and her sister introduce him to a larger world of music from which life in his provincial hamlet has excluded him. In each case, the ideal disappears when its contact with life becomes too close. With Krespel, this change occurs after his marriage and, on still another level, with Antonie's demise. In "Fermate," Theodor's attempts to deepen the personal ties between himself and the sisters die painfully when he overhears their conversation with the Italian tenor. In this regard, these two stories have parallels with "Die Jesuitenkirche in G." (The Jesuit Church in G.), where the painter marries his ideal and loses his inspiration.

Symbolic of this doomed attempt to merge artistic inspiration with love is the physical attraction both Krespel and Theodor feel towards women who also embody artistic ideals for them. Both Angela's singing and her extraordinary beauty intoxicated Krespel (44). Theodor kisses Teresina's hand a thousand times and swears never to leave her (68). Lauretta, his earlier favorite, catches his eye when he first meets her because of her excellent figure (61).

Theodor's attempt to live on an intimate basis with the two women who inspired him was as predestined to failure as was Krespel's to live with either Angela or Antonie. While the two sisters are Theodor's passport out of the provincial village into the world of the professional musician and composer, living with them poses problems that eventually and inevitably break both personal and artistic ties. When he be-

239. Christoph E. Schweitzer, "Bild, Struktur und Bedeutung: E. T. A. Hoffmanns 'Die Fermate'," pp. 116–19 in Scher, *Zu E. T. A. Hoffmann*, p. 119. This article originally appeared in MHG, vol. 19 (1973), pp. 49–52.

comes aware of the copious measure of hypocrisy and deceit that permeate their characters, he breaks off both his personal and his professional relationship with them.

In the course of the next fourteen years, as Theodor's musical reputation grows, he far outdistances the achievements of his early mentors. The coincidental reunion with them shows him how sharply his memory contrasts with the reality of what he now hears. When Teresina sings for him some of the serious songs that had moved him so deeply, he notices that both her and Lauretta's singing now seems much different from what lives inside him as a memory (73). This disappointment even overshadows the disgust he felt at the hypocritically rapturous reception accorded him by the sisters.

The incompatibility of artistic inspiration and a shared life with that inspiration becomes apparent first in the frame of the inner story, when Edward, Theodor's friend, comments after hearing about the incident with the Italian tenor: ". . . der Teresina hätte ich solche Falschheit und Tücke nicht zugetraut" (70) ["I should not have dreamed Teresina capable of such artfulness and falsity"] (Lazare, 312).[240] Edward cannot reconcile the real Teresina with the picture of the vivacious artist playing her guitar and singing on the back of a horse as she puts it through rather intricate maneuvers. An even more telling indictment of the marriage of daily life and artistic inspiration comes at the end of the story in a passage significant for both "Rat Krespel" and "Fermate." It was a passage significant also for protagonists in "Der Artushof," "Der Kampf der Sänger," "Die Brautwahl," "Meister Martin," and others.[241] Remarking that he never should have seen the sisters again, Theodor says:

Jeder Komponist erinnert sich wohl eines mächtigen Eindrucks, den die Zeit nicht vernichtet. Der im Ton lebende Geist sprach und das war das Schöpfungswort, welches urplötzlich den ihm verwandten im Innern ruhenden Geist

240. Christopher Lazare, ed., *Tales of Hoffmann* (New York, 1946), pp. 315–16. Translations for "The Fermata" and "Mademoiselle de Scudery" come from this edition and will subsequently be indicated in the text as "Lazare, p. ——."

241. Karl Ludwig Schneider, "Künstlerliebe und Philistertum im Werk E. T. A. Hoffmanns" in *Die Deutsche Romantik*, ed. Hans Steffen, (Göttingen, 1978), pp. 200–218, interprets the love affairs of the artist as a test of the artist's dedication to his calling. The two stories from the *Serapionsbrüder* to which he devotes most attention are "Die Fermate" and "Der Artushof." See also Cronin, *Gestalt*, pp. 47–53, and Pikulik, *Erzähler*, p. 73.

weckte; . . . so angeregt, alle Melodien die aus dem Innern hervorgehen, uns nur der Sängerin zu gehören scheinen, die den ersten Funken in uns warf.

. . . Es ist aber das Erbteil von uns Schwachen, daß wir, an der Erdscholle klebend, so gern das Überirdische hinabziehen wollen in die irdische ärmliche Beengtheit. So wird die Sängerin unsere Geliebte—wohl gar unsere Frau! . . . die innere Melodie, sonst Herrliches verkündend, wird zur Klage über eine zerbrochene Suppenschüssel oder einen Tintenfleck in neuer Wäsche.— Glücklich ist der Komponist zu preisen, der niemals mehr im irdischen Leben *die* wiederschaut, die mit geheimnisvoller Kraft seine innere Musik zu entzünden wußte. (74)

Every composer . . . has experienced certain impressions that time does not obliterate. The spirit of music spoke, and the artist heard the creative word that suddenly awoke the answering spirit within himself . . . that when a melody has been called in this way from the depths of the composer's being, it seems to belong to the singer who fanned the artist's first inner spark. . . . But it is in the heritage of us weak mortals, . . . that we are all too prone to drag what is super-earthly down within the narrow enclosure of this earthly life where we, poor clods, dwell. And so it comes to pass that the singer becomes the lover, or even the wife. And all that melody of her nature, which was formerly the revelation of glorious things, is now voiced in complaints about broken soup plates or the ink stains on fresh linen. Happy is the composer who never again, as long as he lives, sets eyes upon the woman who by some mysterious power kindled the flame of music within him! (Lazare, 316–17)

The chance meeting fourteen years later helped form Theodor's convictions about the necessity to separate daily life from the sources of artistic inspiration.

In order to emphasize this central point for the reader, Hoffmann uses an artifact from another art form, the painting by Hummel of the two Italian singers in an inn. Schweitzer sees the painting as a device that enables Hoffmann to repeat on three levels a decisive experience in the artist's life. These recapitulations lead him to reach important conclusions about himself.[242] Such recurrences, as our introduction has pointed out, belong to the essential genius of the frame story, of which "Fermate" is a good example. The apparently coincidental events force the characters to confront the meaning of these experiences for their own lives, just as they force the reader to interpret the

---

242. Schweitzer, pp. 118–19. He comments also on the problem for the artist of the conflict between art and life, seeing the maturing process occur for the artist when he detaches himself from that which he formerly admired (p. 119).

significance as well. With the frame of the *Serapionsbrüder* that surrounds "Fermate," this confrontation occurs on yet another level, since the Theodor in "Fermate," the narrator, is the Theodor of the frame. He relates his artistic development to a larger group concerned with the same problems and uses this story as an integral piece of the complex problem of conflict between life and art that figures so prominently in the *Serapionsbrüder*.

In his eloquent and melancholy ending to "Fermate," Hoffmann strikes the chord that connects the story with "Krespel" and that points to many of the inner stories, a chord that, indeed, breaks into the middle of life's aria. In each story, the message is the same: art and artistic inspiration stand on uneasy footing with the real world. For this reason, Antonie must die, unable to be both wife and artist, and for this reason, Theodor should never have seen the two singers again.[243]

"Der Dichter und der Komponist"
(The Poet and the Composer)

At first glance, the dialogue, "Der Dichter und der Komponist" seems to be a filler, tossed in to round out an evening where the talk and stories have turned to music and the nature of art. The discussion in the frame of Theodor's musical development, which was the major topic in "Die Fermate," leads into one of the "dialogartige Erzählungen" (dialogue-like stories)[244] in the *Serapionsbrüder*. The brothers do not understand why Theodor cannot write the text as well as the music of an opera. In order to make his point, Theodor reads a story he

---

243. This analysis of "Fermate" in the context of the frame differs markedly from that of McGlathery in "Hoffmanns Krespel," who does not consider the context in which the story appears, nor its relationship to other inner stories. McGlathery offers the following interpretation: "Whereas there ['Rat Krespel'] Antonie's death saves Theodor from the dread prospect of being made a fool in love, in 'Die Fermate' he succumbs to the worst torment of lover's folly before taking refuge in the bachelor view that women are important to him only as inspiration for his musical compositions" (p. 142). Such an interpretation unnecessarily limits the significance of the story. Segebrecht, *Autobiographie*, sees this conflict arising from the 'Julia-Erlebnis' (p. 100).

244. Segebrecht (Winkler), p. 1045.

wrote years ago at the time of the Napoleonic wars, when he saw his work as an artist endangered. He identifies himself as "Ludwig," while Ferdinand is his "serapiontischer Freund" (serapiontic friend) (76).[245]

While the two previous stories, "Rat Krespel" and "Die Fermate" show the incompatibility of art with daily living, especially married life, this theoretical discussion offers what Hoffmann seems to consider sound connections between art and life.[246] Ferdinand, the soldier, relates the inspiration that writing poetry has given him in the battle "für Ehre und Freiheit" [for honor and freedom.] (79). The larger part of the dialogue deals with relating art to life in another way, in bringing music's consciousness-expanding role to others, especially through the Romantic opera. Hoffman said, in reference to "Der Dichter und der Komponist," that Romantic opera brings miraculous apparitions to life in such a manner that we find it easy to believe in them as the influence of higher natures displays itself to us.[247] Echoes of the discussion about the value of madness in expanding the range of conscious experience appear here and in remarks within the dialogue about this aspect of music: "Ist nicht die Musik die geheimnisvolle Sprache eines fernen Geisterreichs, deren wunderbare Akzente in unserm Innern widerklingen, und ein höheres intensives Leben erwecken?" "Is not music the mysterious language of a distant realm of spirits whose wonderful accents reverberate inside of us and inspire a higher intensive life?" (83). The reader has heard echoes of this transcendental world in the singing of Antonie and in Serapion's madness; in this dialogue, one receives a theoretical treatment of the concepts behind it, which lends the dialogue certain structural attributes of the frame.

The Romantic opera is the ideal medium to bring this infusion of the transcendental into everyday life, because its libretto is so intimately linked with the spirit of the music; through the union of works and action, the performance can have the desired effect on the listener. The

245. There is general agreement that this dialogue reflects the experiences Hoffmann had in Dresden in 1813 during the Napoleonic wars. See Segebrecht (Winkler), p. 1045; *Aufbau*, pp. 667–68; Pikulik, *Erzähler*, p. 74. During this time, Hoffmann unexpectedly met Hippel, who was in Dresden with von Hardenberg. See also Segebrecht, *Autobiographie*, pp. 21, 61, 109–10.

246. Segebrecht, *Autobiographie*, pp. 109–10, notes a number of such parallels, though he does not discuss the dialogues' relationship to the frame. Pikulik, *Erzähler*, pp. 74–75, suggests that Hoffmann's diaries show that he had an ambivalent attitude toward the effect war had on art.

247. Schnapp, *Dichter*, p. 88. It appeared in the *Allgemeine Musikalische Zeitung*, 1814, and was written in September/October, 1814.

conditions where this effect can be met are obtained in the Romantic opera, where fairies, spirits, and miracles are at home (83–84).[248] Hoffmann's insistence on the transcendental element causes him to inveigh heavily against these musical productions with scenes from daily life.[249] In order to demonstrate the kind of text that would fulfill the demands of the Romantic opera, Ludwig relates the plot of one of Carlo Graf Gozzi's fairy tales. The value of stories like these lies in their ability to bring us to the gates of the spirit world (87). The defense of fairy tales in the midst of this discussion of opera establishes connections to the fairy tales included in the *Serapionsbrüder* collection, "Nußknacker," "Das fremde Kind" (The strange child), and "Die Königsbraut," and gives them artistic currency.

In place of the Romantic world of fairies and magical transformations, the *opera buffa* offers the fantastic and the bizarrely coincendental. These forces tear the characters out of their daily routines and place them in the hands of a mad and whimsical spirit (90–91). Although its means are different, it has goals similar to those of the tragic and Romantic operas. Essential to Romantic opera, liturgical music helps to bring man in touch with divine power and with inexorable fate.[250] In all three kinds of opera, the dominant constant is the capacity of these works to lift one out of the miasma of daily life and to avoid philistinism.

In spite of the absence of narrative tension and character development, there is an underlying thematic unity in this dialogue that bears on the development of ideas discussed in the frame and illustrated in the stories: artistic experience bridges the gap between daily life and transcendent forces, between the Scylla and Charybdis of madness and philistinism. The unity of the first section, both in regard to frame and inner story, lies largely in the fact that it is an artistic biography of Theodor. This coherence has been overlooked, frequently leading, as

248. Mühlher, *Deutsche Dichter*, discusses musical background to "Dichter" on pp. 389–94. See also Wittkowski, "Hoffmann," pp. 54–56, for remarks on Romantic opera and the relationship of music to literature.

249. See also E. T. A. Hoffmann, *Schriften zur Musik, Aufsätze und Rezensionen*, Vol. 5 (Munich, 1977), ed. Friedrich Schnapp, p. 106. Hoffmann's review of "Der Augenarzt, Singspiel in zwey Aufzügen, von A. Gyrowetz," pp. 104–14, speaks to this point: "Was für Anregungen, in die geheimnisvolle Tiefe der Musik einzugehen, und ihre im Innersten verborgenen Geister zu wecken, kann denn ein solches bürgerliches Küchenstück geben?"

250. Hoffmann's love of liturgical music is a constant in his works, appearing in *Kater Murr*, among others. It will figure again in the frame discussions.

we have seen, to interpretations that are often one-sided. Theodor has dominated approximately two-thirds of the first book; his emotional and artistic biography fills not only the frame, but also the stories "Rat Krespel" and "Die Fermate" as well as "Der Dichter und der Komponist." It is he who tries to strike the balance between madness and the true artistic spirit through the relating of his own development. In so doing, he has brought the brothers a long way from the reluctant, doubting, and uncertain atmosphere at the beginning. Theodor, who has achieved the proper balance in his own life, serves to some extent as a bulwark in subsequent books of the *Serapionsbrüder*. At the end of the first book, they come to an exalted feeling of union (98–99).

Book I, Section 2
"Ein Fragment aus dem Leben dreier Freunde" (A Fragment from the Lives of Three Friends)

The exalted note on which the first section ends changes dramatically in the second part of the first book, which portrays the second meeting; it includes the stories "Ein Fragment aus dem Leben dreier Freunde," "Der Artushof," "Die Bergwerke zu Falun," and "Nußknacker und Mausekönig" (Nutcracker and king of the mice). The shift is immediately apparent in the frame preceding "Ein Fragment," where a light ironic tone predominates. It is often the case, both in the frame and in the inner stories of the *Serapionsbrüder*, that a serious theme, such as the influence of spirits on the everyday world, appears in a sort of capriccio, only to be transformed into more somber modes with the arrival of threatening events, as the frame and succession of stories in this section show. The ironic tone of the frame here, in which unserapiontic writers and writing projects, such as a group novel, are discussed, has a counterpart in the tone of the conversation in "Fragment," when three friends meet regularly to talk. The types of writing that the *Serapionsbrüder* mildly ridicule in the frame contrast with the inner story. Instead of the hodgepodge of unrelated events with no inner coherence arising out of group writing projects, Ottmar offers his story, which arose out of an incident seen by himself and Severin in the *Berliner Tiergarten* (Berlin zoological garden), where the friends observe a beautiful girl crying over a letter that has just been covertly handed to her (104). His tale is a closed-frame story, with three inner stories, told by each of the friends. It bears a superficial resemblance to the group writing project of the frame yet, because it is the product of one and not several artistic imaginations, it has an artistic unity that those projects mocked in the frame do not.

A fantasy, such as that among Ottmar and his friends, that interprets real events also is present among the friends in "Fragment" as they discuss the emotional motives of Alexander's eccentric old aunt, who leaves him her fortune. Deserted on her wedding day, she dressed herself every year on that day as a bride and waited for the truant bridegroom. Like Ottmar in his interpretation of the crying girl, so Marzell and Severin speculate on the effect of this disappointment in her life (106–7). This predilection to see inner reality, illuminated by fantasy, is an essential element of the *Serapionsprinzip*, yet it receives in this story an ironic treatment, in contrast to the serious mood that surrounded its formulation in the first night's collection of stories. Marzell and Severin misinterpret Pauline's distress in the *Tiergarten*, just as Alexander does. Marzell's worship of Pauline, nourished through frequent and intimate contact with the family, turns to contempt when he learns that her grief in the park was due to the shipping damage to a French hat she had ordered (134–5). Severin's experience with Pauline is a persiflage of delusionary states of mind, yet it has a serious undertone.

Like Cyprian in the frame, Severin notes that his mental state was at one time precarious (136). In a reflection whose content is related to magnetism (see fn. 131), Severin notes that this condition could have been brought about by his illness. According to Schubert, this illness made the individual more receptive to influences from the spirit world. During this period, Severin had a dream about a rose-scented heavenly creature.[251] His firm belief that Pauline is connected to the inner truth revealed in the dream leads to a painful and embarrassing

251. Pikulik, *Erzähler*, p. 83, notes that Severin's comment about the strange psychic stage into which one falls before going to sleep (p. 136) has parallels with Schubert's *Symbolik des Traumes*.

rout. While the power of dreams receives ironic treatment here, it appears elsewhere in the *Serapionsbrüder* as a force to be reckoned with seriously.

Varying the tone in which themes appear is one of the techniques that Hoffman uses to deepen the texture of this collection; in "Die Bergwerke zu Falun," "Artushof," and "Nußknacker," visions and dreams have singular powers that seem to break the usual boundaries of human existence. The influence of the spiritual world upon everyday life, in settings and moods that differ widely, is one of the unifying characteristics of the *Serapionsbrüder*, found in stories such as "Brautwahl" and "Königsbraut" vis-à-vis "Der unheimliche Gast" or "Bergwerke."

The same light approach seen in "Brautwahl" can be found in the portrayal of the aunt's ghost, a visitor from the spirit world. Unsettling, melancholy, she certainly is, but her nightly forays into the medicine cabinet to take stomach potions do not carry the same threat as the mysterious queen who lives in the mines in "Bergwerke." "Fragment" introduces the world of ghosts and spirits in a way calculated to disarm the sceptic before the unsettling material of subsequent stories appears. Alexander, the budding philistine, detests stories about the spirit realm (110) . Yet Alexander, a true son of the Enlightenment, is forced to accept the intrusion of the spirit world into everyday life. In the economy of the realm of ghosts, the disappointed aunt can only be paid back in kind: a marriage must take place in her house so that she can rest in peace.

Alexander wants to sell the house so that he and Pauline will not be haunted. But the *Geheimrat* (privy councillor), Pauline's father, suggesting that now is the time to keep the house and reach out to that other world, observes that the old way of seeing the world, recognizing a transcendent existence as well as the stupidity of our senses, gave way to the clarity of the Enlightenment, which was so clear that one could not see anything at all (143). In a metaphoric sense, the *Geheimrat*'s remark about grasping the transcendent world could serve as a motto for the entire work.

This tendency to present parallels in different contexts and degrees of intensity, which the preceding discussion has emphasized, is at work in the appearance of minor characters as well. Marzell's parallel to Ferdinand's first account of the haunting of his aunt's house deals with an apparition in his lodgings. It is not a ghost at all, but simply a nocturnal visitor, the former *Geheimsekretär* (privy secretary) Nettlemann, who now believes that he is the king of Amboina who was transformed into a kind of bird of paradise for awhile. Like Serapion, he is a victim of the *idée fixe:* ". . . worauf er in den jetzigen heitern beruhigten Zustand des fixen Wahnsinns überging" [". . . upon which he entered into his current happy state of fixated madness"] (117).

Although the story ends in a middle-class idyll, with Alexander and Pauline, the happily married couple, meeting in the *Tiergarten* with old jealousies and conflicts resolved, the tale serves a serious function among the inner stories in the *Serapionsbrüder*. The theme of madness recurs,[252] albeit in a harmless enough way, and the power of the spirit world receives its first strong contours. Severin, the figure in the story who parallels Cyprian most closely, brings material from Hoffmann's background reading in the literature of psychic phenomena and spirits.[253] The figure of Pauline also has some similarities with other light-headed girls whose minds are concentrated on their toilet or household. The ironic tone of the story contrasts sharply with the more serious one of "Artushof" and the frightening one of "Bergwerke," and shows how skilled Hoffmann, the musical artist, was at tone painting.

"Der Artushof"
(Arthur's Court)

Upon entering the world of the main characters of the "Artushof," where the figures in the paintings keep coming out of their frames,[254] the fantastic world seems nearer than when the elderly spin-

252. Nipperdey notes, p. 68 and footnotes, that Hoffmann's lovers always have a suggestion of madness in their makeup and that Hoffmann sometimes described these relationships in an ironic manner as a sort of self-criticism. This observation, seen in the light of our discussion of the frame-inner story relationship in the *Serapionsbrüder*, becomes a structural principle.
253. See especially p. 114, where Severin discusses these topics. *Aufbau* 1, pp. 679–80, comments that Hoffmann took the example of the sleepwalker who took the horse out of its stall from contemporary psychiatric literature. See also *Aufbau* 1, p. 681, which cites Severin's description of a psychic experience (p. 136) as being very similar to the opening statement in Schubert's *Symbolik des Traumes*.
254. Mühlher, *Deutsche Dichter*, pp. 402–3, discusses the Baroque background of figures in painting that come alive.

ster of "Fragment" went to the medicine cabinet during her haunting. Part of the reason for the increased emphasis on the supernatural lies in the artistic nature of the protagonist Traugott, who is consequently more open to such influences than the bourgeois characters in "Fragment" were. Traugott would have fled as quickly from the establishment in the *Grünstraße* and Pauline as from the Danzig stock exchange and Christina. However, as Conrad points out, the shock value of the fantastic is heightened by the fact that this intrusion of a man who says he is Godofredus Berklinger occurs in a tower of philistinism, the stock exchange.[255]

Like "Fragment," "Artushof" has a certain amount of local color;[256] in addition, it too arises from the experience of one of the *Serapionsbrüder*, in this case Cyprian. Its position in the series of stories of the second night is both paradigmatic and cautionary: paradigmatic because of the insight Traugott achieves at the end, and cautionary because of the ever-present danger of madness that surrounds the artist, as in the case of Berklinger.[257] Traugott's recognition of the role of Felizitas as inspiration forever separate from daily life is exemplary for Hoffmann's artists, as Theodor has already shown in his own autobiographical account in "Fermate." This similarity of theme ties the first and second sections together; in Theodor's case, life experience proved the necessity for such a separation. In "Artushof," the insight comes as the result of an inner vision on Traugott's part.[258] What has been overlooked is the importance of Berklinger in establishing connections that reach forward and backward. Karoli has noted his kinship with Zacharias Werner,[259] but his links with Serapion and to some extent with Fröbom, as well as with Cardillac, Heinrich von Ofterdingen, and the Baron von B., have not been noticed: he is the first serious artist in the work to fall victim to madness.

255. Conrad, *Angst*, p. 69, describes Hoffmann's tendency to integrate uncanny events into the everyday world.

256. Segebrecht, *Autobiographie*, p. 18.

257. Pikulik, *Erzähler*, says that Berklinger's madness has a more crippling effect on his art than Serapion's does on his, since Serapion is still able to write, whereas Berklinger can no longer paint. He sees parallels with Rat Krespel in two areas: the protection of a beautiful daughter and in his attempts to use his art as a key to understanding hidden secrets (pp. 84–85).

258. Segebrecht, *Autobiographie*, p. 151, comments on the necessary unity of a person with himself as a prerequisite for artistic achievement, a quality that Fröbom lacked; on pp. 151–53, he discusses the inner connections among "Artushof," "Bergwerke," and "Nußknacker" from the perspective of "Problematik der Erkenntis."

259. Karoli, "Hoffmann/Werner" p. 44.

Traugott is not only paradigm but also prototype: In "Die Braut-wahl," "Der Kampf der Sänger," and in "Meister Martin der Küfner" (Master Martin, the cooper), young artists who were inspired by beau-tiful women to great heights of artistic endeavor end by abandoning all desire or hope of living with that person. Traugott, like Theodor in "Fermate," realizes that inspiration in its incarnate form cannot live in an everyday world with the artist. At the end of "Artushof," as Traugott contemplates his loss of Felizitas, he realizes that he will always have her, since she is the spirit of creative art that lives in him (169). Like Theodor in "Fermate" (74), Traugott realizes that seeing women again who had inspired one originally is superfluous. Like Teresina, who started Theodor's "innere Melodie" (inner melody), Felizitas can exist only inside the artist if she is to continue to inspire.

The figure of Godefredus Berklinger, the mysterious painter of a much earlier age, is the first of several revenants, such as Torbern in "Berg-werke," and Meister Leonhard and the *Münzjude* in "Brautwahl." Per-haps Hoffmann's predilection for this type of character serves as an ele-ment symbolizing both the dangers and the absence of boundaries in the process of self-realization. Berklinger also introduces the "altdeutsch" (old German) motif into the work. For Hoffmann, as for Arnim, this pe-riod, by which they understood the fifteenth and sixteenth centuries, was a time of extraordinary artistic activity.[260] Both Hoffmann and Arnim harked back to it to inspire their characters and their readers, though both shaped and formed the material in different ways due in part to contrasting attitudes and differences in artistic capabilities.

This older German period inspires Traugott to leave the world of Aviso letters and become an artist. The murals in the stock market hall, a mute presence of art in the midst of so many Philistines, provide a tableau at the outset that symbolizes the background of the story. Traugott is an associate and the future son-in-law of Elis Roos. There is no understand-ing for art among Roos and his associates, nor in his estimable daughter, Christina, who never spoils a butter sauce; she is a spiritual cousin of Veronika Paulmann in "Der goldene Topf" (The golden pot).[261] Even

---

260. When Berklinger maintains that he is the painter whose work in the *Artushof* was completed more than two hundred years ago, he says of the period: "Überhaupt war es doch . . . eine herrliche, grünende, blühende Künstlerzeit, . . . " (156).

261. K. Schneider, "Künstlerliebe," p. 211, notes the reason why Christina and her ilk are such good cooks and such practical women is to emphasize their difference from the angelic female who inspires art, who seems to have shed all earthly preoccupations.

the businessmen who recognize Traugott's talents are otherwise limited in their vision: they see the artist as a sort of madman or art as a socially acceptable means of relaxation from business.

In this desert, the murals are the only presence of art for Traugott, most especially the beautiful youth in rich clothes. These figures draw him to the edge of the world of art, bring him to sketch their likenesses, and then address him in the middle of the exchange. The similarity of function of the murals in "Artushof" with the picture in "Fermate" offers yet another parallel between the stories.[262] In "Fermate," the picture occasioned the revelation of an inner story, which culminated in the scene represented in the picture. In "Artushof," the picture functions to bring the rest of the narrative into being, but it is a story that has not yet occurred; the mural is the catalyst.

Traugott is the first fictional representative in the *Serapionsbrüder* of the aspiring young artist, a recurrent figure in the *Serapionsbrüder* inner stories, as we have already seen in those dealing with Theodor's autobiography, and in the frame as well in the person of Zacharias Werner. Of this group of figures in the *Serapionsbrüder*, Traugott and Antonio in "Signor Formica" have the most trouble freeing themselves from the bourgeois world.

Traugott realizes only over a period of time that he does not belong in the stock market. One day he half-consciously begins to sketch the man and the beautiful young boy in the mural, when suddenly the two figures appear before his eyes in the middle of the Danzig stock exchange. Already the fateful combination of artistic inspiration and personal attraction are linked in the description of the boy (146). Only after this first attempt at drawing, which leads to his encounter with the art-collecting businessman and his nephew, does he remember that, even as a boy, these two figures riveted his attention through a force that seemed almost magical (153). The mention of the childhood occurrence serves two functions; first, it shows that Traugott is predestined to become an artist. The invocation of the childhood experience also adds a note of the irrational, since children are not capable of formulating an analytical response to situations in the manner of an adult.

262. See *Aufbau*, 1, pp. 681–82. The two stories were written together; he began "Artushof" the day after he finished "Fermate." One can use their different positions in the *Serapionsbrüder* collection as an added argument that Hoffmann had a definite thematic plan in mind when he arranged the stories in the collection.

This emotional aspect appears in the above description, in which the significant encounter takes place in the evening, when an irresistible force draws the young boy. Childhood functions in this passage as a symbol of the mysterious forces involved in the pursuit of art and self-knowledge.

In spite of the hostile environment in which he must work, Traugott achieves the essential serapiontic quality of the artist, even before Berklinger agrees to give him lessons: ". . . so vermag er, was sein inneres Auge geschaut, festzubannen, indem er es sinnlich darstellt" ["thus he was able to fix firmly what his inner eye saw by portraying it in a physical way"] (152). When he begins his lessons, Traugott has two goals: one, to learn from the old man and two, to find Felizitas. Her disguise symbolizes her unapproachability and prefigures Traugott's fate, as the narrator indicates at the beginning of Traugott's search for himself (153).

Traugott's adoration of Felizitas breaks out when he sees the portrait and slowly brings the portrait painting of a beautiful young woman and the youth in close connection (158–60). Berklinger's violent eviction of Traugott at the moment he falls at Felizitas' feet is necessary for the preservation of Traugott's artistic identity. Berklinger says Traugott's behavior will kill him and pulls a knife on him (169). Yet it is from Traugott's own death as an artist that Berklinger protects him. As soon as Traugott sees the real Felizitas, Berklinger leaves. For Berklinger, this precipitate departure is absolutely necessary, because he stands under a curse: he will die if Felizitas falls in love. However, Berklinger's withdrawal symbolizes, on another level, the impossibility of combining artistic inspiration and mundane daily life. Like Berklinger, Traugott, too, stands under a curse: if he wins Felizitas, he will die as an artist.

There are other parallels between Berklinger and Traugott, especially in regard to the *Artushof.* Berklinger recounts to Traugott his beginnings as an artist, telling of the period in which he painted the figures in the hall. At that time, King Arthur came before him, urging him to achieve perfection (156). Through Berklinger's picture, Traugott realizes his vocation; in a function similar to that of King Arthur, Berklinger appears to Traugott. As is the case with many of the artist figures in the *Serapionsbrüder*, there are doubts about Berklinger's sanity. When Berklinger tells Traugott who he is, Traugott wonders if the man is mad. When Berklinger describes a primed but empty canvas, which he says is his picture of paradise regained, he glides into a state in which his comments become less and less intelligible (157). His dream world, cut loose from reality, is very similar to that of Serapion.

Removed from Berklinger's lessons and the intoxicating presence of Felizitas, Traugott searches for them in Italy, mistakenly taking Sorrent for an Italian city. He internalizes her more and more and no longer sees her as a distinct person but paints her face when he portrays women. The intense desire to find her has transposed itself into a spiritualized longing (164). This process of spiritualization goes so far that he can no longer imagine Felizitas as his wife (166). In the meantime he has become fond of the daughter of an Italian painter. Dorina looks like Felizitas, but is not his muse.

The final physical ties with Felizitas break when he returns to Danzig to settle financial questions and learns that the Sorrent to which Berklinger and Felizitas withdrew is near Danzig. Felizitas has married *Kriminalrat* Mathesius and has several children. At this point, Traugott realizes that he already has the only Felizitas he needs (169). Traugott's insight enables him to combine the demands of art with his emotional needs as he prepares to marry Dorina. In contrast, Elis Fröbom in "Die Bergwerke zu Falun" has a split inner being. He is himself an ironic figure, in Hoffmann's terms, because irony reveals the contradictions in existence. The frame conversation about the differences between irony and humor relates to the characters in the next two stories, "Bergwerke" and "Nußknacker und Mausekönig." There is no humor in "Bergwerke," only irony, but humor in "Nußknacker" overcomes the discordant experiences.[263]

"Die Bergwerke zu Falun" (The Mines of Falun)

Clues to the interpretation of "Die Bergwerke zu Falun" and its role in the sequence of narratives lie in the frame conversation immediately following the story. Cyprian, who tends to be interested in abnor-

263. Segebrecht, *Autobiographie,* pp. 151–52.

mal states of consciousness, makes the following remarks, which seem to apply in particular to Elis Fröbom, the main character in "Bergwerke":

Wie oft stellten Dichter Menschen, welche auf irgendeine entsetzliche Weise untergehen, als im ganzen Leben mit sich entzweit, als von unbekannten finstren Mächten befangen dar. (197)

How often do poets depict people who go under in some horrible manner or other as having been at odds with themselves during their entire life and as mixed up with unknown sinister forces.

This remark implies that Fröbom lacked the necessary insight and understanding that would have enabled him to withstand the pressures of outside threatening forces.[264] Disregard of these remarks, which have, as will be shown, strong support in the text, has led to more than one misinterpretation of the story.[265]

To strengthen his point, Cyprian notes that he himself has known people who suddenly seemed pursued by evil forces, whose natures changed completely. Within a short time, some horrible event had torn them from their accustomed lives (198). This remark is reminiscent of a device that Hoffmann used in the beginning frame and that we find repeated throughout the work: personal experience corroborates material from poetic imagination. Cyprian's description of personal acquaintances could just as well apply to Fröbom. Another element that adds verisimilitude to the account of the unfortunate miner is the specific reference to an account of the recovery of a preserved body and the old woman who recognizes the corpse in Schubert's *Ansichten von der Nachtseite der Naturwissenschaften* (197).

Ottmar's reference to Schubert is the first specific one to him within the *Serapionsbrüder*.[266] While Schubert's account is often compared

264. Segebrecht, *Autobiographie,* p. 151.

265. See, for example, Albert H. Smith, "Variations on a Mythical Theme: Hoffmann, Gautier, Queneau and the Imagery of Mining," *Neophilologus* 63, (1979), pp. 179–86, where, in comparing mining themes, he disregards the framework of *Die Serapionsbrüder* and the context in which Hoffmann often places protagonists with difficulties in life. He also overlooks all of the negative references to the mine and the forces that inhabit it. See also Paul Sucher's introduction to *Le vase d'or, Les mines de Falun* (Paris, 1947), pp. 51–70, when he draws parallels to "Der goldene Topf" that overlook important differences between the two stories, such as the characters of the two deserted women.

266. Schubert, *Ansichten,* p. 215, reports on the strange incident, giving the outlines that Hoffmann used in his story: "Man fand diesen ehemaligen Bergmann in der schwedischen Eisengrube zu Falun, als zwischen zween Schachten ein Durchschlag ver-

with Hoffmann's interpretation of it, there has been little attention paid to more subtle influences of Schubert's thought in the interpretation of "Bergwerke". Schubert believed that dreams could be prophetic and that in altered states of consciousness one could learn a great deal about the future. However, not all these manifestations are healthy ones:

Der Blick in das Zukünftige, die Gabe der Vorahndungen, ist der menschlichen Natur nicht fremd. Doch giebt es eben sowohl eine von kranker und falscher als eine von gesunder und wahrhaft ächter Art, . . .[267]

The view into the future, the gift of premonitions, is not foreign to human nature. Yet there is a gift that is of a sick and wrong nature as well as a gift that is of a healthy and really honest kind.

These negative manifestations are connected with *Dämonismus* (demonism). Frequently an evil will exerts an extraordinary degree of control over the person afflicted with such visions:

Wie nun jene krankhaften Erscheinungen auch in ihrer äußeren Form einigen unter uns bekannten Nervenkrankheiten, und dem Zustand des künstlichen Somnambulismus ähnlich sind, kommen sie auch darin überein, daß über magnetisch Schlafende wie über Nervenkranke ein fremder fester Wille nicht selten eine bewundernswürdige Gewalt äußert.[268]

Just as these morbid manifestations, concerning their outer form, are similar to some nervous diseases known among us and to the state of artificial som-

---

sucht wurde. Der Leichnam, ganz mit Eisenvitriol durchdrungen, war anfangs weich, wurde aber, sobald man ihn an die Luft gebracht, so hart als Stein. Fünfzig Jahre hatte derselbe in einer Tiefe von dreihundert Ellen in . . . Vitriolwasser gelegen, und niemand hätte die noch unveränderten Gesichtszüge des verunglückten Jünglings erkannt, niemand die Zeit, seit welcher er in dem Schachte gelegen, gewußt . . . hätte nicht das Andenken der ehemals geliebten Züge eine alte treue Liebe bewahrt. Denn als um den kaum hervorgezogenen Leichnam das Volk, die unbekannten jugendlichen Gesichtszüge betrachtend, steht, da kömmt an Krücken und mit grauem Haar ein altes Mütterchen, mit Tränen über den geliebten Toten, der ihr verlobter Bräutigam gewesen, hinsinkend, die Stunde segnend, da ihr noch an den Pforten des Grabes ein solches Wiedersehen gegönnt war."

This frequently cited passage is not the only one in Schubert that would seem to have a direct bearing on "Falun." In his thirteenth lecture in the *Ansichten*, which deals with magnetism, Schubert, in discussing the effects of various metals on an individual in a magnetic state, ends his discussion of metals with the following remark: ". . . daß jenes Wohlgefallen, welches der Anblick und die Berührung der edlen Metalle, besonders des Goldes bey Vielen hervorbringt, vielleicht einen tieferen Grund in den Eigenschaften unsrer Natur hat als gewöhnlich geglaubt wird, und da der dunkle Trieb der die Menschen Metalle zu suchen, und ihren Werth bestimmen lehrte, ja selbst der sonst rätselhafte Geiz, hieraus begreiflich werden" (p. 337). Fröbom's problem lies in his response to this drive, which, like many hidden forces, can unhinge an individual.

267. Schubert, *Ansichten*, p. 90.
268. Schubert, *Ansichten*, p. 94.

nambulism, so do they agree with them regarding the fact that occasionally a strange firm will exerts a remarkable power over people suffering from nervous diseases as well as over individuals who are sleeping magnetically.

Although these passages point ahead to the ensuing discussion on magnetism, they also have relevance to the role of Torbern and the mysterious queen in the novella and relate closely to Cyprian's remarks about man in the grip of unhealthy dreams and strange outside forces. Subsequent stories in the *Serapionsbrüder* deal with this theme, particularly in regard to artists such as Heinrich von Ofterdingen in "Der Kampf der Sänger." Torbern-like characters, with mysterious powers over their victims, appear in "Der unheimliche Gast."

Another force that grips Fröbom is his fatal attraction to the riches of the mine. Not until he gives himself over to allegiance to the queen (191) does he become completely in thrall to the subterranean world. Then he can think and talk of little else but the splendors of the depths and the great treasures hidden there; it seems to him that his real self is with the queen and Falun was dark (193). Fascination with metals was a phenomenon that Schubert discussed in his chapter on animal magnetism in the *Ansichten* and on which C. A. Kluge commented as well:

Merkwürdig ist es hierbey, daß das Gold, wenn es rein angewendet wird, den magnetisch schlummernden immer ein angenehmes Gefühle macht, ohngefähr wie die Berührung des Magnetiseurs.[269]

In this context, it is remarkable that gold, if used in its pure form, always causes the person in a magnetic sleep a pleasant sensation more or less like the touch of the magnetizer.

Schubert believed that metals not only bewitched but also magnetized the susceptible. In an appendix to Chapter 13, he discusses those areas

---

269. Schubert, *Ansichten*, pp. 336, 337. See also *Ansichten*, pp. 335–36. Carl Alexander Friedrich Kluge, in his book, *Versuch einer Darstellung des animalischen Magnetismus, als Heilmittel* (Berlin, 1811), p. 447, notes that gold feels pleasant to some individuals in a magnetic state. Like Schubert, Kluge discusses the effect that metals have on such a person: "Bei stärkerer Wirkung erfolgen Unruhe, Angst, sehr heftige, sich durch den ganzen Körper verbreitende und oft in Convulsionen übergehende, höchst schmerzhafte Stöße, Lähmung oder Erstarrung des berühten Gliedes und endlich Bewußtlosigkeit" (p. 162). Kluge notes that metals in combination have a stronger effect (p. 164) and that experiments with extremely large amounts of metals and their effect on a person in a magnetic state cause first warmth, then anxiety, and finally convulsions or spasms (p. 166).

that show the greatest relationship with animal magnetism. One of these areas is that of precious metals:

Wenn es nähmlich unläugbar ist, daß die Metalle auf alle magnetisch Schlafenden, selbst aus einiger Entfernung, . . . heftig einwirken . . . daß diese selbst von ziemlich entfernt unter ihren Füßen, oder neben ihnen verborgenen Metallen einige deutliche Empfindungen haben.[270]

If it is undeniable that metals, even from some distance, have a strong effect on all people in magnetic sleep . . . that these people even have a clear sensation from metals that are rather far beneath their feet or that are hidden beside them.

These passages from Schubert seem to indicate that it is possible for a metal to act as a magnetizer. This quality of metals helps to explain why Elis, like Angelika and Moritz in "Der unheimliche Gast," seems sometimes not in his right mind. Just before his wedding, he appears, deathly pale, with dark fire flashing from his eyes (194). He speaks in a rather mad manner. At other times the dark influences seem to make him mute (192). Elis believes he alone knows where the richest veins are in the mine (193). This reflects Schubert's observation that only the magnetized person can sense the presence of metals.

The depths of the mines both fascinate and repel, and provide the story with a framework of imagery that dominates from beginning to end. They bewitch with their intimations of secret knowledge and hidden beauties. In his description of Torbern, the old miner says that legend had it that Torbern was in league with the secret power dwelling in the depths of the earth (188).[271] Yet, at the same time, Fröbom is regularly seized with feelings of dread and anxiety at the sight of the mysterious figure. His chest tightens, he feels under the sway of magical powers, and yet he is enthralled (177). Similar reactions on the part of Cyprian and the other members of the group surfaced when madness was the central theme of discussion, and this same ambivalent attitude appears in the preoccupation with magnetism. In this way, the major

270. Schubert, *Ansichten*, pp. 355–56.
271. Nipperdey, p. 102, in his discussion of madness caused by possession by other forces, says that the action of such individuals has a satanic quality about it. The strangeness of the figures of Torbern and the queen symbolize their inhuman function.
 In discussing Elis's wedding-day trip to the mine for the *Lebenstafel* on the *Almandin*, Negus (*Other World*) says that such knowledge is not available to humans (p. 112). Although Negus does not pursue the point, a comparison of Elis with Graf S in "Der unheimliche Gast" on this point seems useful. As the count indicates in his final letter to Marie (p. 637), such knowledge is dangerous. Both Elis and the count die because they are bewitched by the prospect of supernatural secrets.

themes of "Bergwerke" are intimately related to other inner stories and the frame. The path to secret knowledge is fraught with danger, especially for those whose inner beings are torn and despondent, as Elis was after learning of the death of his mother. Again and again in these stories, Hoffmann stresses the need for an inner core of self-knowledge and perception about the difference between good and evil as necessary components both to deeper knowledge and to self-preservation. Examples lie close at hand in the two subsequent stories—Marie in "Nußknacker" and Wolfram von Eschenbach in "Der Kampf der Sänger."

Elis Fröbom, in contrast, does not have such a firm inner core. In addition, he is a sensitive young man, unwilling to be satisfied with the crass and degenerate amusements of his fellow sailors. Consequently, he is an easy prey for outside forces that seem predestined to take over his soul after the death of his mother. Foreshadowings appear even before he meets Torbern: one of Elis's comrades on board ship curses when Elis refuses to join in the carousing. The friend calls down the fury of the sea devil Näcken, the god who leads his victims into the depths.[272] Shortly thereafter, Elis wishes that he might be buried at the bottom of the sea because his mother is gone (173). These scenes parallel his final capitulation to the forces of darkness when he thinks Ulla will marry another man. Torbern appears after his death wish, the queen after his desperate descent into the mines.

The absence of a central core of belief that can guide his actions becomes especially apparent when he pledges himself to the queen: "Unten liegt mein Schatz, mein Leben, mein alles!" (190) ["My treasure, my life, everything for me, is down below"] (Bleiler, 302). After his promise to the nether world, he is torn from one allegiance to the other. Above ground, with Ulla, he sometimes can forget what occurred below. At other times, he is distraught and somewhat incoherent. The final symbol of his indecisiveness is his decision to bring Ulla the "kirschrot funkelnden Almandin" (194) ["the cherry-colored sparkling amandine"] (Bleiler, 305). His reason for doing so is that they will see, as they gaze into it, how intimately connected they are with the heart of the queen (194).[273] Elis still does not realize that the

272. Winkler, p. 1052, note to p. 172.
273. See Klaus J. Heinisch, in his book, *Deutsche Romantik: Interpretationen* (Paderborn, 1966), p. 139. See also Lee B. Jennings, whose recent provocative article, "The Downward Transcendence: Hoffmann's *Bergwerke Zu Falun*," in *Deutsche Vierteljahrs-*

forces of darkness consider his relationship with Ulla an infidelity. He has been warned repeatedly both by Torbern (187) and the *Obersteiger* (chief mining deputy) that disaster will come if Torbern helps an individual who does not have total dedication to mining. The first such catastrophe, on St. John's Day in 1687, occurred when the miners ignored Torbern's warning that a tragedy would follow if they lost their love of the ores; lust for profit drove them to enlarge the excavations more and more, until there was a collapse (188–89). A similar disaster happens on Elis's wedding day, St. John's Day: as Ulla and the wedding party wait, a terrible landslide occurs in Dahlsjö's mine area.

The figure of Ulla is problematic: surely she can make butter sauces as well as Christina Roos, yet there is nowhere an overtone of the invective Hoffmann usually reserves for such daughters. In contrast, her willingness to help and her loving devotion are continually remarked upon by the narrator (184, 186, 192). Peter noticed the striking difference and attributes it to Hoffmann's changing ideas towards women.[274] Another possibility suggests itself, given the repetitive light-dark imagery in the works.[275] If one contrasts the world of the Dahlsjös, the whole and healthy one above ground, with the alluring yet evil one below the earth—Elis refers to the mine as a *Höllenschlunde* (pit of hell) (180)—one can see why Hoffmann does not present Ulla as just another pretty bourgeois face.[276] Again the parallels with Marie in

---

schrift 59 (1985), pp. 278–89, views the descent into the nether reaches of the mine as an actual transcendence.

274. Peters, "Conciliatory Satirist," p. 64: "Here the housewife type . . . is not only sympathetically portrayed, but juxtaposed to a muse figure . . . who ultimately destroys both art and life." Pikulik, *Erzähler*, p. 94, attributes the sympathetic treatment of Ulla to the fact that she is a reincarnation of his mother, a view the text seems to support.

275. See Mühlher, p. 446.

276. Heinisch, *Deutsche Romantik*, p. 142, compares Ulla to Kriemhild, who unwittingly sent Siegfried to his death. Although it is true that Elis wants to be successful in the mines to win Ulla, two other considerations need to be examined. There are many miners who work in the mines yet are not affected by Torbern or the mountain queen. Heinisch later notes that Elis is more susceptible than the other miners, due to his lack of human contact, his inherited tendencies, his sensitivity and imagination (148). The miners are the happy, friendly fellows whom we first see at the celebration when Elis arrives in Falun, and contrast favorably with the sailors who celebrate in a degenerate manner.

The other point is that Torbern has already gotten control of Elis before he comes to Falun because Elis's mental state is such that he is an easy prey to dark forces. Heinisch's observation also overlooks the positive imagery connected with Ulla. Although it is true that Elis only gives himself completely to the *Bergkönigin* after he thinks he has lost Ulla to Eric Olawsen, (and, in this regard, one could say that she unwittingly sent him to his destruction), the text points out that the fault clearly was that of Elis. Dahlsjö tells him that no mine owner in Falun would turn him away as a prospective son-in-law and Elis

"Nußknacker" and with Wolfram von Eschenbach in "Kampf" come to mind. Secret, mysterious forces from outside are best resisted with a pure and unscarred heart.[277] A paradigmatic example for the differences between the two choices that lie before Elis comes in the dream he has directly after meeting Torbern. In this dream a succession of women appear who foreshadow the options open to him. As he gazes at the Queen of Metals, he feels the delight in his heart changed into crushing fear (178). As Torbern warns him that he may still look up, Elis sees the stars and believed he hears the voice of his mother and thinks he sees her. But it is a beautiful young girl who stretches out her hand and calls his name (178). The beneficent presence of his mother was sufficient to give him an emotional anchor; Ulla should take her place.

But Elis is not whole enough to grasp this hand and so must perish. This dream turns out to be prophetic;[278] Torbern captures his victim with his insistence on a strange oath of fealty to the queen, whose counterforces are his mother and Ulla.

"Nußknacker und Mausekönig" (Nutcracker and the King of Mice)

Another female figure with the potential to redeem others, Marie Stahlbaum, appears in "Nußknacker und Mausekönig." Drosselmeier recognizes this capacity in her when he hears her description of the

---

says nothing. He knows that he should tell Dahlsjö how much he loves his daughter then, but he remains silent (p. 187). Because he will not speak, Dahlsjö, not Ulla, decides on the ruse with Olawsen, as he explains afterwards to Elis (p. 191). Once again, it is Elis's inner disintegration that leads him to destruction, unable to grasp the hints given him by others who want to help. Hoffmann shows once again how intuitively he grasped much of what is known today about personality development.

277. See Mühlher, *Deutsche Dichter*, p. 446.

278. Segebrecht (Winkler, p. 1130) says that Hoffmann used Heinrich Nudow's book, *Versuch einer Theorie des Schlafs* (Königsberg, 1791) for the conversations of the *Serapionsbrüder*. There is a discussion of dreams in this book, in which a passage occurs that might have some interest in the context of Elis's dream and the statement Hoffmann seems to be making about Elis's weakened mental state: "Es gibt gesunde und krankhafte Träume. Beide stehen mit der individuellen Gesundheit und Krankheit des beseelten Menschen in genauer Verbindung. Sehr lebhaft und beunruhigende Träume sind immer als etwas Krankhaftes anzusehen" (p. 118).

fierce battle between Nußknacker and the mice. Instead of mocking her, he tells her that she has been given more than he and the others have, but that she will have to suffer very much if she intends to befriend the bewitched Nutcracker (234). Marie, like Ulla, represents a harmonious alternative to the realm of evil forces. A major reason why both Ulla and Marie offer a redemptive possibility is their childlike nature, which remains more open to unseen harmonies; when Hoffmann describes Ulla, he frequently does so with terms relating to childhood (see 183, 193). Marie, the youngest in the Stahlbaum family, is also the one who grasps the true nature of the nutcracker and the battle in which he is engaged. As Reimann points out, Fritz, who is a little older, has already lost some of the capacity that Marie still has to comprehend this other realm;[279] the others do not understand at all. In that they try to talk her out of what they perceive as quixotic and irrational fantasies, they are unwitting allies of the forces of evil.[280] "Nußknacker" presents on yet another level—a fairy tale taking place within the intimate circle of the family—the conflict between philistine and poetic natures. Marie is related to many characters who preceded her and who will come after her: Ulla in "Bergwerke" Wolfram in "Kampf der Sänger," Felix und Christlieb in "Das fremde Kind."[281]

Although Marie is able to withstand the assaults of the "feindlichen Prinzips" (hostile forces), she must rid herself of her initial doubt that the *Nußknacker* really could feel (208). Her pangs of doubt change abruptly to certainty when the toys come alive. At this point she wounds herself as she falls into the glass cabinet. However, in spite of the pain, she feels relieved (210), since she hopes her fall has scared the

279. Olga Reimann, "Das Märchen bei E. T. A. Hoffmann" (Diss., Munich, 1926), p. 34. See also Mühlher, *Deutsche Dichter*, p. 335f. Schubert frequently idealized the state of childhood, because he saw it as standing closer to the original unity in existence: "Wir wissen nicht, welcher tiefe Reiz über der ersten Kindheit ruhet. Sey es daß ein Nachklang jenes unbekannten Traumes, aus welchem wir kamen, oder daß jener Abglanz des Göttlichen sie verherrlicht, welcher am reinsten über den Stillen und Kindlichen schwebet" (p. 303, *Ansichten*). Ellinger recognizes the value of a childlike spirit, pp. 18–19. Nino Erné, in his afterword to a volume of Hoffmann's *Märchen* 2 (Hamburg, 1965), misunderstands the function of a childlike nature and sees it as a limitation for Hoffmann (p. 763).

280. In regard to the parents' behavior, Reimann, *Märchen*, notes the influence of Hoffmann's ideas about the lost paradise, p. 35.

281. Hans von Müller, in his "Nachwort zu den Märchen der *Serapionsbrüder*," in *Gesammelte Aufsätze*, pp. 91–145, notes that "Nußknacker" and "Das fremde Kind" are closely related, because in both the child can see the realm of dream, fantasy, and illusion (p. 93).

mice back to where they came from. This small incident foreshadows Marie's future bravery and constancy: although she has hurt herself, she is happy because she believes that she has helped the situation.

The wound is also the cause of the fever that befalls her and that forces her to bed for a number of days. In this state, she dreams of Nußknacker, who keeps telling her that she could do more to help him (217).[282] During her convalescence, when she is too weak to read, Drosselmeier tells her the story of how Nußknacker came to have his bizarre shape. During the installments of the story, Marie, who has no other diversion, begins to have her own thoughts about correspondences in her world to this fairy tale (223). When she recuperates and goes to the glass case to see the *Nußknacker,* she realizes the extent of the parallels. Since Marie's period of illness enables her to learn the background of the strange scene she has witnessed and helps to strengthen her resolve to aid Nußknacker, it serves a positive purpose within the context of the story. While sickness in Hoffmann can be a crisis period, as in "Der unheimliche Gast," it can also be a time when hidden truths are made manifest.[283] The subsection "Onkel und Neffe" (Uncle and nephew) comes directly after the end of the inner fairy tale and the recovery of Marie; in this section, Marie not only sees the real identities and relationships in her mind but has her perception confirmed for her by Drosselmeier. He tells her that she has been given much but that much will be demanded of her. Like Anselmus in "Der goldene Topf," she must withstand the assaults of evil. Because she has heard the story and is convinced of its truth, she has much stronger motivation for her steadfastness. The content of the fairy tale, in which the princess Pirlipat is physically attacked by the queen, prepares Marie for the horrible visits of Mauserinks's son to her bedside.[284]

282. Cf. the dream Moritz has in "Der unheimliche Gast" during the time in which he is held prisoner in the chevalier's estate (p. 633).

283. See Müller-Seidel, in his *Nachwort* to the Winkler edition, on this point (p. 1010). See also Ellinger, p. 19.

Nipperdey, p. 38, notes that Ottmar's subsequent remark in the frame conversation that Marie is nothing but a little somnambulist (p. 274) shows that Marie is especially receptive to dreams and that she has a very sensitive soul. To this connection between the dream state and magnetism, see Schubert, *Ansichten,* p. 352: ". . . so muß auch das dunkle Gebiet der Vorahndungen hierdurch einiges Licht erhalten. Meistens empfängt sie die Seele im Traume oder in einem dem Traum ähnlichen Zustand, und es gleicht dieser Zustand auch durch die Erhöhung aller geistigen Kräfte . . . dem magnetischen Schlaf."

284. Christa-Maria Beardsley, *E. T. A. Hoffmanns Tierfiguren im Kontext der Romantik* (Bonn, 1985), p. 61.

The "Onkel und Neffe" section firmly embeds the "Märchen von der harten Nuß" in the frame story of the fairy tale, but only in the figures of Marie and Drosselmeier.[285] The other adults in the frame fairy tale never understand, even when Marie shows them the mouse crowns. Like the Pharisees, they see and do not see; their reason tells them it cannot be so.

The role of the mice in "Nußknacker" has connections with other *Serapionsbrüder* stories, most notably with "Das fremde Kind" and "Die Königsbraut" and of course "Bergwerke." The mice, Pepser/Tinte, and the world of Daucus Carota all belong to the negative, dark side of human existence. The mice, for example, come out of a hole in the floor, apparently driven by a subterranean power (210). The gnome Pepser, who appears as Tinte (501), keeps the pheasants and the children close to the earth; he also covers everything with a black juice (495–96) and appears as a fly. When Fräulein Ännchen looks inside the silken tent of Daucus Carota, she sees the true nature of his kingdom, which contains both worms and insects (983–84). The mice perform another function similar to that of Pepser and his minions: they try to take all of Marie's toys, the inhabitants of her fantasy world, while Pepser tries in various ways to ruin nature, which is where the children's fantasy world exists.[286]

The structural function of the mice within "Nußknacker" lies in their embodiment of the negative aspects, the dangerous side, of the fantastic world. Their grotesqueness, their greed, and their desire for revenge, as well as the violence that they are prepared to commit to achieve their ends, reveal the dangers of exposure to this world, dangers that have become real with the curse on Nußknacker and the destruction of Marie's toys. The young Drosselmeier, however, reveals to Marie the positive side of this fantastic world in showing her his kingdom and in his decision to marry Marie.

Like the *Medizinalrat* (senior medical officer) and *Rätin* (his wife), many of Hoffmann's contemporary critics dismissed the world of dolls,

285. Matt, *Augen,* ascribes a more limited role to the inner story, simply to give the *Nußknacker* a history and to make Marie accept a second "künstliches Werk" after she had shown a lack of interest in his palace (p. 91).

Beardsley, *Tiere,* recognizes the importance of the inner story as a motivational factor when she writes that only insofar as Marie takes the inner story seriously will she make the connection between it and the outer story (p. 169). See also Dämmrich, *Shattered Self,* p. 57.

286. Beardsley, *Tiere,* p. 171.

seven-headed mice, and unbreakable nuts. Von Müller notes that Hoffmann used the opportunity of including *Nußknacker* in the *Serapionsbrüder* to answer some of the critical reviews of the fairy tale in the *Morgenblatt* and the *Jenasche Allgemeine Literatur-Zeitung* in the frame discussion.[287] The *Morgenblatt* attacked the bizarre nature of the story and referred to Marie and Drosselmeier as puppets.[288] The *Jenasche Allgemeine Literatur-zeitung* referred to the "eingestreuten Späße" (interspersed jokes), which left the reader in doubt as to what sort of audience he was seeking.[289] The discussion of *Märchen* (fairy tale) theory in the *Serapionsbrüder* frame (252–55) takes up these points, which appear in the remarks of Theodor and Ottmar to Lothar. Theodor's objection that children could not understand the fine threads of the story receives short shrift from Lothar, who explains that children are the only competent judges, because they rightly and vividly comprehend many things that learned fathers miss (252–53).

The ability of children to grasp the essence of the story, and see it in the mind's eye, and appreciate it, rests to a high degree in Marie as well, as the earlier discussion has shown. Hoffmann responds to his attackers by suggesting that they were never children (253) and brings in some points about the role of reality made in the earlier discussion about Serapion after the Krespel story. Only when a rational mind goes through this fantastic potpourri and spins the threads can such material be valuable. Once again, Hoffmann insists on both the sense of fantasy as well as the necessity to see the real world, just as he did at the beginning of the work (54).

The mixing on various levels of the everyday and the fairy tale world attracts the comments of the *Serapionsbrüder*. Cyprian, the most inclined towards the spirit world of the group, notes the tendency in this fairy tale, as in the "Goldene Topf", for the fantastic world to intrude into everyday life by throwing magic hats on ordinary people (254). Such a practice leads to irony, which Ottmar and Theodor both perceive as dangerous. Lothar, while admitting that, in this respect, his

287. See Müller, "Nachwort," *Gesammelte Aufsätze*, pp. 107–12, who cites the reviews in *Morgenblatt*, March 25, 1817, Jahrgang 11, probably Therese Huber; April, 1817, *Jenaische Allgemeine Literatur-Zeitung*, Jahrgang 14, no. 65, 2 (Cols. 46–48). See also Müller, "Nachwort, *Gesammelte Aufsätze*, pp. 103–4, 102–12.

288. See Müller, "Nachwort," in *Gesammelte Aufsätze*, p. 104, who cites the *Morgenblatt* review.

289. Müller, "Nachwort," in *Gesammelte Aufsätze*, pp. 104–5.

172   E. T. A. Hoffmann

fairy tale differs from the description made by Tieck in *Phantasus*, defends his approach (254). Hoffmann, as Müller-Seidel points out, cannot stay away from reality, even in his fairy tales, just as he cannot clench reality in his literary fist without snatching a bit of fantasy to mix in.[290]

This kind of rational analysis and perception, which differs sharply from the unexamined real world of the Philistine, appears on several levels in Nußknacker. Perhaps its most striking embodiment lies in the figure of Drosselmeier whose role is that of a mentor for his godchild Marie.[291] Because Drosselmeier is an adult and because he has more knowledge about the true nature of the nutcracker than Marie, he is in a position to use both reason and perception to lead her to the point where she can serve as a redemptive figure. Drosselmeier brings the realm of the fantastic into the bourgeois Stahlbaum household, where he slowly leads Marie to see into this world, first through the mechanical toys and then through his stories.[292] Drosselmeier is both an *Arkanist* (specialist in secret things) and an *Obergerichtsrat* (senior judge): his real nephew has been wounded in his contacts with the fantastic world and Drosselmeier must bring Marie into the fairy-tale realm in order to bring his nephew back into the real world. To keep his reputation as a professional figure intact, Drosselmeier must often maintain an anti-fantastical stance, such as when he sides with Fritz regarding Nußknacker, or when he says he gave Marie the crowns (205, 250). However, in each instance his apparent duplicity or rudeness forces Marie to remain true to Nußknacker and to defend him, thereby enabling Marie to take Nußknacker's part and break the spell.[293] Drossel-

290. Müller-Seidel, "Nachwort," pp. 1010–11.
291. Ochsner, *Dichter des Unbewußten*, p. 51. Matt, *Augen*, says that the mentors in Hoffmann's stories must be seen in the context of what they effect in the heroes (p. 95). Matt suggests that this explanation provides an answer to the apparent contradictions in and among such characters. See also von Müller, "Nachwort," pp. 96–97. See also Pikulik, *Erzähler*, pp. 100–101, who says that Drosselmeier's strength is his knowledge of the supernatural, his weakness, that he can produce only mechanical things.
292. Christa-Maria Beardsley, *E. T. A. Hoffmann: Die Gestalt des Meisters in seinen Märchen* (Bonn, 1975), pp. 160–61.
293. In an unpublished paper, "E. T. A. Hoffmann's 'Nußknacker und Mäusekönig': Thematic Threads in Divided Worlds," Linda Slocum offers a consistent interpretation of Drosselmeier that reconciles many contradictions in his portrayal. She notes that the black patch over his eye shows that one eye is focused on the inner world (p. 10) and suggests that the negative remarks of Drosselmeier about Nußknacker's appearance are designed to make Marie take his part (p. 14), and interprets Drosselmeier's false assertion that the crowns were a present from him to Marie as a test of Marie's "allegiance to her inner reality" (p. 17). Marie, who must retreat into a dream world to avoid being

meier himself has told Marie she must remain steadfast (234); without convincing proof of her loyalty and willingness to love the nutcracker, he cannot be freed. Throughout the story, Pate Drosselmeier carefully brings Marie into his world in such a way that she does not become frightened, but becomes a person open to all levels of human existence.[294]

Drosselmeier also provides another point of comparison with the story immediately preceding this one, "Bergwerke." Like Drosselmeier, Torbern is also a master, possessing knowledge that his young follower does not have. But instead of trying to help Elis achieve a balance between the real world and the fantastic, which was Hoffmann's goal and was what Serapion lacked, Torbern draws Elis into a nether world: Drosselmeier functions as a proper godfather, aiding the child in areas where her parents could not, making it possible for her to reconcile both worlds. Drosselmeier also stands in sharp contrast to Klingsohr in the subsequent story, "Der Kampf der Sänger," and to Magister Tinte in the related fairy tale, "Das fremde Kind."

Both Drosselmeier and his nephew, the *Nußknacker*, figure in the frame as well as the inner fairy story. While they are real in the world of the frame, reality functions on another level in the "Märchen von der harten Nuß," where Hoffmann indulged himself with a satire on court life. While children would enjoy the sight of a king stirring soup with his scepter (220), the numerous shots that Hoffmann fired at a vapid social class would have been overlooked in the nursery. This kind of reality mixes with the fantastic in other inner frame stories in the *Serapionsbrüder*. In "Brautwahl," Hoffmann mixes the strange world of the revenant Leonhard with an uproarious portrait of the amorous pedant Tusmann; in "Das fremde Kind," in the figure of Magister Tinte he attacks the wrong kind of learning. While some of Hoffmann's critics thought such irony was out of place in a fairy tale, their own philistine tendencies prevented them from seeing that the fantastic is always present in the everyday world and is an integral part of it. As a consequence fantasy has both the ability and the right to criticize the real world.

---

scolded (p. 251), now speaks the words to Nußknacker that break the spell and enable him to appear in the Stahlbaum's apartment to the family.

294. DeLoecker, *Atlantis,* notes a number of parallel motifs between the inner "Märchen von der harten Nuß" and the outer story (p. 74).

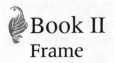

Book II
Frame

In the second book of the series, which appeared in 1819, Hoffmann's extensive discussion of magnetism picks up the theme that dominated the frame of Book I, especially at the beginning: the inner knowledge of the mind and its value for the artist. The potential of magnetism for expanding perception and consciousness plays an important role in the brothers' discussion (see especially 263–65). Consequently, one cannot be totally opposed to magnetism, since it, like madness, can serve as a vault into the realm of mysterious forces (274). Magnetism, as part of the outer world of reality, can reveal the existence of hidden forces at work in the mind and enhance the inner vision. This potential in magnetism was very attractive to the Romantics, since it was generally believed that the subconscious was a basis for knowledge of the whole man.[295] Magnetism's capacity to open new roads into the inner world attracted Hoffmann strongly, though at the same time he feared the loss of control over the individual self, just as he did when confronting madness.

The large amount of clinical detail about magnetism that Hoffmann presented in this section reflects the extraordinary interest of the laity in medicine in the early Romantic period. Doctors let themselves be influenced in their thinking by laymen to a point scarcely credible today.[296] Hoffmann himself, as we have seen earlier, was an avid reader of current medical and quasi-medical material. Magnetism and its potential for good and evil was a major topic of conversation in the literate circles in which Hoffmann moved. Maasen notes that even though Mesmer's discovery was made years before Hoffmann was writing, the intensive work of German doctors kept the concept in the public's mind. Information about new miracle psychic cures was constantly

---

295. Conrad, *Angst*, p. 97, notes that a major reason why mesmerism continued to be important in Hoffmann's works was that Berlin was the only place in Europe at the time where it had academic recognition. See also Ochsner, *Dichter des Unbewußten* p. 51.

296. Paul Diepgen, *Geschichte der Medizin: Die historische Entwicklung der Heilkunde und des ärztlichen Lebens*. Bd. 2, 1. Hälfte (Berlin, 1959), p. 83.

forthcoming, not only in the medical journals, but also in newspapers.[297]

The magnetic state resembled what we would call hypnotism today,[298] but Mesmer himself did not use it; if his patients went into that state, it was coincidental. Mesmer was primarily interested in the attributes of the magnet and the magnetic fluid. Magnets, because of their mysterious ability to attract iron, seemed to possess extraordinary powers. Mesmer's work exploited two assumptions: the idea that some individuals were gifted with healing powers; and the classical concepts, formulated by the Greeks, that Paracelsus and others such as William Maxwell (1577–1644) revived, that all things stood in a sympathetic secret relationship held together by a fluid.[299] Mesmer tried to capitalize on these two commonly held beliefs, especially while he lived in Paris. Dressed in a dramatic costume, he would enter the treatment room, where soft music was being played and fragrant orange blossoms filled the air. The process of healing was full of deceptive showmanship, designed to make his patients believe they were in contact with the magnetic fluid. They believed that they would do whatever Mesmer said they should. Although suggestive patients were probably hypnotized in such conditions, Mesmer was not interested in this side effect. If there were a number of patients, they stood around a *baquet*, in which were water, magnets, and iron shavings. Each patient grasped a protruding iron rod. To transmit the fluid, Mesmer would make passes in the air with his hands. This invasion of the magnetic fluid was supposed to induce a crisis with curative powers: when patients woke up, they felt better. Crucial to the success of this undertaking was the power of mass suggestion, the existence of which was unknown to Mesmer.[300]

297. G. von Maasen, *E. T. A. Hoffmanns Sämtliche Werke* 6 (Munich-Leipzig, 1912), pp. 10–11.

298. The reader will already have noticed that Hoffmann does not mention hypnotism, but magnetism. Magnetism and mesmerism, a term coined by Mesmer's friend Karl Wolfhart, were the names most commonly given to the phenomenon before a Scottish doctor, James Braid, made important strides toward a scientific approach to mesmerism and renamed it hypnotism. See Alexander and Selesnick, *History of Psychiatry*, pp. 131–32, and H. B. Gibson, *Hypnosis: Its Nature and Therapeutic Uses* (London, 1977), pp. 35–36.

299. Ochsner, *Dichter des Unbewußten*, p. 42; Alexander and Selesnick, p. 126. See also Peter Schmidt, "Gesundheit und Krankheit in romantischer Medizin und Erzählkunst," *Jahrbuch des freien deutschen Hochstifts* (1966), pp. 197–228, 207–8 for explanation of fluid.

300. See Gibson, *Hypnosis*, pp. 36–37; Alexander and Selesnick, p. 128.

Hysterical states were probably most receptive to this procedure; the length of the cure was more dependent on the patient's emotional health than on anything else. Mesmer's followers dropped many of the theatrical trappings from their techniques, but they did not yet realize that psychological mechanisms rather than the fluid might be at work. The first detailed account of induced hypnosis was that of Comte de Puységur's treatment of a servant on his estate. He described the state through which the boy passed with the characteristic details, such as lucidity, suggestibility, and lack of memory of the event when reawakened.[301] Puységur came to the conclusion that those who had been put into a "magnetic sleepwalking" state had a supernormal capacity.[302] Although Puységur believed in the existence of a magnetic fluid, he dropped the sensational aspects of Mesmer's treatment. He used instead a tree magnetized with a fluid believed to contain electricity. What Puységur seems to have done was to hypnotize through suggestion.[303]

The exaggerated powers falsely attributed to the magnetizer in Hoffmann's day were a source of both fascination and concern.[304] It was clear already in the late eighteenth century that the person in a magnetized state was indeed in a condition of enhanced receptivity and responsiveness to suggestion and stimuli.[305] In addition to these beliefs, confirmed in our time by modern research, it was commonly believed in the early nineteenth century that the magnetizer could control the subject by thought alone.[306] This is a state of affairs that has awful con-

301. Gibson, *Hypnosis*, pp. 36–38.

302. Diepgen, *Geschichte*, pp. 82–83. Reil, *Rhapsodien*, deals with the interconnection among sleep, dream, and madness (p. 87): "Sie [sleep and dream] stehen mit dem Bewußtseyn, dessen verschiedenen Zuständen und mit dem Wahnsinn in einer so nahen Verwandtschaft, . . . " (p. 87).

303. Alexander and Selesnick, *History of Psychiatry*, p. 130.

304. Kluge, *Versuch*, repeatedly emphasizes the powerful influence of the magnetizer over the patient. Some of the most powerful descriptions of this relationship are as follows, "Vorzüglich wohl fühlen sie sich in der Nähe ihres Magnetiseurs, der gleichsam ein zweites Ich ihres magnetischen Lebens ist, . . . " (p. 207); ". . . tritt er jetzt . . . auch unter die Herrschaft des Willens seines Magnetiseurs . . . " (p. 228). Kluge states (p. 230) that the person who is magnetized cannot resist the power of the magnetizer even if he would have done so while awake. With such direct statements by the physicians of the time, it is no wonder that Hoffmann saw the great potential for evil in this treatment.

305. Schubert, *Ansichten*, pp. 334–37, 340. Franz Anton Mesmer, *Mesmerismus: oder System der Wechselwirkungen, Theorie und Anwendung des thierischen Magnetismus als die allgemeine Heilkunde zur Erhaltung des Menschen*, ed. Karl Christian Wolfart (Berlin, 1814) (reprinted Amsterdam, 1966), pp. 199–209.

306. Gibson, *Hypnosis*, p. 38. Auhuber, *Spiegel* says that it was the fear of misuse of magnetism that scared Hoffmann the most (p. 76).

sequences in "Der unheimliche Gast" and "Der Magnetiseur." Psychiatrists now know that a person under hypnosis cannot be made to do anything against his will. However, because of the false powers imputed to the hypnotizer, the belief became widespread in the early nineteenth century that only someone who practiced with an uncalculating heart could cure most effectively and safely.[307]

The exciting expectations and grave fears that discussion of magnetism often provoked dominate the discussion of the topic among the *Serapionsbrüder*. The first part of their conversation (262–66) deals with the description of magnetism, as well as various attitudes, favorable as well as critical, toward the phenomenon. This dialogue serves a structural purpose as well, since it prefaces the series of case histories about magnetism that follow and anticipates many of the issues raised in those histories and in the inner stories.[308] Even the introduction of magnetism into their conversation shows the ambivalence characteristic of the entire section. Lothar, suffering from a severe headache, let his physician friend Vinzenz magnetize him. Although Vinzenz had promised an immediate cure, the headache persisted for days, destroying Lothar's faith in the healing powers of magnetism, which he debunks. Ottmar, having seen Lothar in the recent grip of a nervous illness, reveals to the brothers that Lothar did indeed let himself be magnetized again (262). Lothar excuses his behavior with the weakness and desperation sick people often feel, a weakness that leads to temporary madness (262). In the story, "Das öde Haus" (The desolate house) (1817), Theodor receives help from his physician, a magnetizer, in a serious mental crisis. The altered state of consciousness that sickness brings about was generally recognized by writers dealing with magnetism and plays a significant role in Hoffmann's treatment of the subject.[309] The connection between sickness and altered emotional states has already surfaced in "Nußknacker," during Marie's illness, where she goes into the Nutcracker's world of mice and marzipan.

307. Diepgen, *Geschichte*, p. 83.
308. Kruse, *Aufbau (Serapionsbrüder* 1), pp. 627–28, notes that Hoffmann moves skillfully to the inner stories, but he does not analyze how.
309. Mesmer, pp. 199–200, Schubert, *Ansichten*, p. 333, "Die Kranken beantworteten nun alle ihnen vorgelegten Fragen mit einer Klarheit und Lebhaftigkeit des Geistes, die man sonst nie an ihnen bemerkte." Schmidt, "Romantische Medizin," p. 211, says: "Magnetisieren kann deshalb immer nur jemand, dessen positiver Pol stärker ist als der des Magnetisierten, d.h. ein völlig Gesunder kann nicht magnetisiert werden, ein Kranker nicht magnetisieren."

Cyprian, who introduces Serapion and is a member of the group most interested in the subconscious, begins the serious theoretical discussion of magnetism with a statement that resembles closely some of Mesmer's descriptions of its potential: "Was ist der Magnetismus, als Heilmittel gedacht, anders als die potenziierte Kraft des psychischen Prinzips, die nun vermag das physische ganz zu beherrschen" ["Seen as a cure, what is magnetism but the intensified power of the psychic principle, a power that now is able to control the physical principle completely"] (262–63). This quotation reflects the belief of Mesmer and his disciples that the sick person in a somnambulistic state was able to recognize the symptoms of his illness and divine what was necessary to cure it.[310]

Another positive aspect of magnetism for Cyprian is its connection with music, since magnetism helps us understand the psychic principle that deals with the secret harmonies that we otherwise cannot perceive. This remark of Cyprian's in the frame anticipates a longer discussion in the subsequent inner story, "Die Automate", of the same theme that Hoffmann takes directly from Schubert.[311] Mesmer believed deeply in a universal harmony and was himself a talented musician,

---

310. Mesmer, *Mesmerismus*, p. 200, in discussing the somnambulistic state and its potential, writes: "Indessen sind diese Eigenschaften nach der Beschaffenheit eines jeden Individuums verschieden; die gewöhnliche Erscheinung ist, in das Innere ihrer und selbst anderer Körper zu sehen, und mit der größten Genauigkeit die Krankheiten, den Gang derselben, die nötigen Mittel dafür und ihre Wirkungen angeben zu können."

See also Schubert, *Ansichten*, p. 340: "Nicht minder wunderbar als diese Eigenschaft des Nach-innen Sehens, ist jene merkwürdige des Vorhersagens aller körperlichen Veränderungen, welche auf die Krankheit Beziehung haben, und das Selberverordnen der Arzneyen."

Leibbrand, *Romantische Medizin*, notes that this opinion was extremely significant among the beliefs held about magnetism p. 133. See also *Der Magnetiseur*, p. 165. *Fantasie und Nachtstücke*, ed. W. Müller-Seidel and W. Kron (Winkler). Schmidt, "Romantische Medizin," describes the fifth level of magnetic sleep, in which the sick individual is able to prescribe the cures for his ailment (p. 211). Kluge, *Versuch*, discusses the ability of the magnetized individual in the fifth level to see the interior of his body, diagnose the disease, and prescribe medicine (pp. 192, 196, 197).

311. See Schubert, *Ansichten*, p. 63: ". . . ob nicht die alten Sagen von der Harmonie der Weltkörper, von den Tönen des Universums, wirklich einige Wahrheit enthielten?" Pages 64–65 of Schubert's *Ansichten* appear in a somewhat revised form on p. 349 in the *Serapionsbrüder;* see discussion of "Die Automate." See Paul Sucher, *Les Sources du Merveilleux chez E. T. A. Hoffmann* (Paris, 1912), pp. 26–27, who indicates that the sympathy with the magnetizer can bring about a state of harmony with the entire universe, or as much of it as is present in the soul of the magnetizer. For the connection between music and magnetism, see also Karl Olbrich, "E. T. A. Hoffmann und der deutsche Volksglaube," in *E. T. A. Hoffmann, Wege der Forschung*, (Darmstadt, 1976) pp. 56–88, ed. Helmut Prang, p. 61. Mühlher, *Deutsche Dichter*, notes "Wie der Magnetiseur zur Somnambule verhält sich der Musiker zur Natur" (p. 379).

often expressing his theories with the vocabulary of music.[312] Because magnetism offers a view into hidden harmonies, it can be of great value to the artist, who can expand his consciousness with it.[313]

The excitement caused by magnetism's potential attracts even someone as skeptical as Lothar, who admits that magnetism's reach into the realm of the spiritual holds an irresistible charm for anyone of a poetic nature, like himself (263). Lothar, like Cyprian, links magnetism to the spirit world. However, he also connects it with artistic perception as well, underscoring its importance for the artist in regard to opportunity as well as danger, a connection with some significance for "Kampf der Sänger." Lothar's choice of the adjective *dunkel* (dark) begins his agitated and eloquent attack on magnetism (263–64). His objections are worth considering in some detail, because they resurface in the inner stories. Lothar's deep mistrust of magnetism comes from a fear of meddling with the secret bond between soul and body. Yet magnetism, whose authority rests on whatever dim and possibly incorrect knowledge one has about these matters, resembles the fumbling of a blind man (263). Lothar's anxiety takes artistic shape in stories that have magnetism or magnetic influences as a major theme, especially in "Der unheimliche Gast." There are other narratives, such as "Der Kampf der Sänger" or "Nußknacker" or "Bergwerke," where a strong hypnotic role played by Klingsor, the mice, or Torbern have an evil influence on sensitive individuals such as Heinrich, Marie, and Fröbom.[314]

Lothar fears magnetism, not because it is an illusion that hurts people, but because he believes it is true and contains the potential for great harm. The connection between mind and body and the mysterious bond between them, important in the Serapion discussion, appears here in another context: that of the sick but still sane individual subjected to the interfering treatment of a magnetizer and exposed to great

312. Mesmer, *Mesmerismus*, p. 47; see also Leibbrand, *Romantische Medizin*, p. 127: ". . . seine ganze Lehre konnte der Musik nicht entraten . . . ".

313. Kluge, *Versuch*, describes the higher level of consciousness that magnetism offers; in the state of magnetic sleep, the individual stands ". . . an der dunklen Pforte zum Übergange in ein höheres, besseres Seyn" (p. 110). At another point, he adds that magnetism provides ". . . höhere, erweckte Kräfte, die zuvor ungekannt und ungeahnet in dem Inneren des Menschen schlummerten" (p. 373).

314. Kruse, in *Aufbau*, *Serapionsbrüder I*, notes that Hoffmann grew more and more distrustful of magnetism in the course of his life (p. 695). In "Der Magnetiseur" the painter Bickert already voices reservations. See pp. 150–52, *Fantasie und Nachtstücke* (Winkler).

potential danger to his mind. The following passage of Lothar's speech uses current medical knowledge to form the basis for Hoffmann's literary treatment of magnetism:

Es ist gewiß, daß es erhöhte Zustände gibt, in denen der Geist den Körper beherrschend, seine Tätigkeit hemmend, mächtig wirkt und in dieser Wirkung die seltsamsten Phänomene erzeugt. Ahnungen, dunkle Vorgefühle gestalten sich deutlich und wir erschauen das mit aller Kraft unseres vollen Fassungsvermögens, was tief in unserer Seele regungslos schlummerte; der Traum, gewiß die wunderbarste Erscheinung im menschlichen Organismus, dessen höchste Potenz meines Bedünkens eben der sogenannte Somnambulismus sein dürfte, gehört ganz hieher. Aber gewiß ist es auch, *daß solch ein Zustand irgendeine Abnormität in dem Verhältnis des psychischen und physischen Prinzips voraussetzt.* Die lebhaftesten stärksten Träume kommen, wenn irgendein krankhaftes Gefühl den Körper angreift. *Der Geist nutzt die Ohnmacht seines Mitherrschers und macht ihn, den Thron allein einnehmend, zum dienenden Vasallen.* So soll ja auch der Magnetismus nur durch irgendeinen krankhaften Zustand des Körpers indiziert werden (emphasis mine). (263–64)

It is certain that there are heightened states in which the mind, ruling the body and impeding its activity, has a powerful effect and with this effect creates the most peculiar phenomena. Presentiments, dark premonitions take a clear shape and we behold with all the power of our faculty for comprehension that which lay dormant and slumbered motionlessly deep in our soul. The dream, which is certainly the most wonderful manifestation in the human organism and whose highest potency must be the so-called somnambulism, certainly belongs in this category. Yet it is also certain *that such a state presupposes some abnormality or other in the relation of the psychological and the physical principle.* The most vivid and the strongest dreams occur when some pathological feeling or other attacks the body. *The mind takes advantage of the helplessness of its co-ruler and, taking the throne for itself, makes him a serving vassal.* Thus even magnetism is said to be induced only by some pathological state or other of the body.

The belief that the sick person was in an exalted state of consciousness appears often in contemporary medical writings.[315] Lothar, in his elaboration of this tenet, turns it around, saying that expanded consciousness always presupposed an abnormality in the relationship between soul and body. This interpretation leads in many directions for Hoff-

315. Mesmer, *Mesmerismus*, pp. 199–200; Schubert, *Ansichten*, pp. 340–60; See also Leibbrand, *Romantische Medizin*, p. 136; Schmidt, "Romantische Medizin," pp. 210–11. Segebrecht, "Krankheit," in regard to Hoffmann's medical background material in his writing, says that Hoffmann wanted to make his portrayal medically irreproachable (p. 276).

mann, since it links artistic creativity with illness and since any exalted state in his characters indicates an imbalance, a dangerous situation that, if the characters are basically sound, like Marie in "Nußknacker" and Wolfram von Eschenbach in "Kampf," they can survive. If they are torn in their inner beings, like Elis Fröbom, they cannot. Therefore, the individual in an exalted state is in a precarious position: capable of sublime understanding, but never far from the reef of madness or total destruction.[316]

Since, in Hoffmann's eyes, the magnetizer could represent a force that took advantage of the individual's weakened state to further his own ends, regardless of the other person's welfare, he feared the practitioner's power.[317] Lothar admits the validity of the magnetizer's command over his patients (264), but dreads its effects, fearing that it could destroy him (264, 265). Given the degree of power of the magnetizer, he could easily mold the subject so completely to his desires that the weaker personality would disappear. This fear dominates Lothar's opinion about physicians who treat the magnetized individuals in a despotic manner and experiment with them as though they were machines (265). This problem foreshadows the thematic complex of the automaton, which figures prominently in a number of the subsequent stories and is closely related to magnetism. Like madness, it represents the fear of losing control of one's identity.

Lothar's dread of coming into the grip of an evil magnetizer has striking parallels to the fears of madness appearing in the discussions in the frame of the first book, when consideration of Serapion's condition causes anxiety that too much contact with mad individuals could create madness in a healthy person (29). The figure of Alban in "Der Magnetiseur" and the count in "Der unheimliche Gast" provide literary

316. Olga Randl, in an unjustly neglected dissertation, "Das Dämonische als Stilform in den literarischen Werken E. T. A. Hoffmanns" (Munich, 1912), notes the connection between magnetic states and madness (p. 21). See also Natalie Reber, *Studien zum Motiv des Doppelgängers bei E. T. A. Hoffmann* (Giessen, 1964), p. 209.

317. Leibbrand, *Romantische Medizin*, p. 134, "Ferner schien die eigene Individualität in die des Magnetiseurs einzugehen . . .". Schubert, *Ansichten*, pp. 344–45: "Es bleibt nun vorzüglich nur noch eine Erscheinung des magnetischen Schlafs übrig, die ohnstreitig zu den merkwürdigsten unter allen gehört, jene tiefe Sympathie der Somnambule mit dem Magnetiseur und andern mit ihr und ihm im Rapport stehenden Personen," p. 344. Heinz Otto Burger, "Arzt und Kranker in der deutschen schönen Literatur des 19. Jahrhunderts," in *Der Arzt und der Kranke in der Gesellschaft des 19. Jahrhunderts* (Stuttgart, 1967), pp. 98–106, connects the portrayal of the magnetiseur as an evil doctor with the negative literary tradition of the portrayal of physicians, p. 102. See also Schmidt, "Romantische Medizin" (p. 223), and Mühlher, *Deutsche Dichter*, p. 361.

portraits of the kind of magnetizer described by Lothar. Like madness, the exalted state of a sick person can provide glimpses of hidden worlds, but it can also destroy. The parallel positions of madness and magnetism in the frames of the first and second books of the *Serapions-brüder* show Hoffmann discussing, in an apparently nonfictional setting, ideas about these two topics that were of vital significance to the artistic consciousness before the brothers told stories that revealed in a serapiontic way what the conversation was about.[318] According to Conrad, Hoffmann used scientific knowledge to create strong feelings of anxiety in his readers. Conrad connects that with magnetism, but it could also relate to the clinical discussion of madness in the frame of Book 1.[319] In each situation, the scientific information in the frame, which both distances and disquiets the hearers, appears before the stories that contain some of the medical information transformed into the safer world of fiction.

Following Lothar's searing criticism of magnetism, Theodor brings two case histories full of medical detail. Theodor performs a function here similar to the one he exercised in Book I when the conversation about madness had taken an emotional turn. In both cases he relates incidents that happened to him and that have the effect of putting what has been said previously in perspective or that serve as a bridge to future discussion or to inner stories. In Book I, his personal experience involves Rat Krespel and appears as a novella; in Book II, the information he reveals comes from two experiments with magnetism that he has witnessed. Here, the descriptive discursive form of the anecdote suits the scientific material better than the form of the novella would. The inclusion of this clinical information serves several functions in regard both to the frame and to the inner stories. The narrative takes up a number of points that punctuated Lothar's denunciation of magnetism, such as the control of the hypnotizer over the patient, and the exalted consciousness of the person being treated. Theodor sees his anecdotes as illustrative examples (265).

318. Segebrecht, "Krankheit," in discussion of the subsequent account of Theodor about the peasant girl, implies that there is a connection between magnetism and madness, citing Serapion as an exemplary figure for the object of the director's medical art and poetic principle (p. 274).

319. Conrad, *Angst*, p. 97: "Die Magie- und Naturangst des Schauerromans wird verdrängt durch die Angst vor dem Mesmerischen Magnetismus, der Hypnose und der Automatenmechanik."

The two direct experiences that Theodor has of magnetism differ greatly in every respect. In the first, a woman supposedly in the highest magnetic state repeatedly amazes onlookers with her clairvoyant abilities. This demonstration of magnetism does not cure but entertains. Much of the setting seems reminiscent of Mesmer's demonstrations; it takes place among an aristocratic group, in a room luxuriously appointed (266). The hypnotized person lies on the sofa "in ein sehr reizendes Negligé gekleidet" ["dressed in a very attractive negligee"]. Instead of healing her, the magnetizer, whom Theodor knows as an extremely honest man, wants to show the psychic powers released by this new technique. Description of objects that she knew nothing about, and revelation of personal details in Theodor's life all show a connection with hidden psychic powers. Yet Theodor is never entirely free of the suspicion that the lady is a fake, fooling even the doctor. His mistrust is confirmed when an older physician, well known as a sceptic in matters magnetic, applies a hot iron to the lady at a time when the audience has been assured that her soul is out of her body (269–70). Theodor's tone as he relates the story of the hypnotized impostor is ironic and mocking. This first anecdote distances the threat of magnetism by debunking it, just as Lothar did. However, the second anecdote, which is a sober and unsettling account of a magnetic cure that worked, carried out under irreproachable scientific conditions,[320] sets the reader on tenterhooks again, just as the end of Lothar's speech does. After Theodor's account of the peasant girl who flourished after a magnetic cure, the reader must accept the fact that there are hidden reserves of psychic power that all sorts of men, both good and bad, may tap. This disquieting information figures prominently in the subsequent two stories, "Der Kampf der Sänger" and "Die Automate" and contributes to their effect on the reader.

The second account takes place in a Bamberg hospital and seems to be autobiographical, giving a description of the magnetic cure that Hoffmann witnessed with his good friend, Dr. Marcus. In quoting the

320. Segebrecht's notes (Winkler) and Kruse's (*Aufbau*) in the respective editions contain copious notes on Hoffmann's sources for the discussion and the clinical cases. See Segebrecht, pp. 1055–57, and Kruse, pp. 694–700. See also Segebrecht, "Krankheit", esp. pp. 268–76, where Segebrecht discusses in considerable detail Hoffmann's relationship with Marcus as well as Friedrich Speyer, whose advice Hoffmann relied on in "Der Magnetiseur." There is general agreement that the account of the experiment on the peasant girl reflects an actual experience that Hoffmann had at the Sankt Getreu hospital in Bamberg. See *Aufbau I*, p. 700.

unimpeachably professional doctor, Hoffmann repeats some of the warnings about magnetism that Lothar and Theodor have made, thereby assuring the reader of their veracity and making the subsequent stories more frightening. The physician considers the awakening of magnetism the most dangerous experiment that there is; it can only be done by a calm and rational individual (271).

The peasant girl who undergoes a magnetic cure was suffering from a kind of nervous fever that left her progressively weaker. The description of the girl before the magnetic treatment (272) serves to heighten the dramatic changes that took place when she was under hypnosis and thereby to prepare the readers of the inner stories for similar overwhelming metamorphoses. Her apparently low intelligence and dreadful dialect vanish during the treatment, when she speaks in the eloquent and educated phrases of her doctor. In addition, her facial features seem ennobled and lively (272–73). As the girl takes on the personality of her doctor, showing herself capable of intellectual power far beyond her grasp when she is not hypnotized, her own personality disappears. This loss of control, a major concern in the sections on madness, figures at the heart of "Der Kampf der Sänger" and "Der unheimliche Gast," as well as in "Die Automate." In this story, the person who makes use of these secret psychic forces no longer even pretends to rationalize his activity with the prospect of improved health for the patient, but uses psychic principles as a means of power and scientific experiment.

"Der Kampf der Sänger" (The Fight of the Singers)

The transformation of the peasant girl's personality finds a parallel in the experience of Heinrich von Ofterdingen in "Der Kampf der Sänger." Therefore, the narrative of this clinical incident, coming directly before the inner story, reveals in neutral territory the kind of control and change that can occur. It also prepares the reader for the terror that the intervention of demonic figures instead of humane doctors can induce. At the same time these forces offer to Heinrich glimpses of a bewitching world and alluring secrets. The alternating attraction and repulsion of this secret knowledge forms a definitive thread throughout "Kampf," just as it has in the discussion of magnetism by the *Serapionsbrüder*. Like the forces lurking behind the manifestations of madness, the powers of magnetism cannot be completely banished from consideration and examination, since it can set mysterious powers in motion (274). The secret forces mentioned by Ottmar affect all characters in "Der Kampf der Sänger" to one degree or another and put in sharp relief the dangers that can afflict an artistic temperament. To combat these dangers yet remain open to the inner harmonies of nature demands a heart at once pure and aware, like that of Marie in "Nußknacker." Her counterpoint in "Kampf" is Wolfram von Eschenbach. Both must overcome the forces of evil in a fierce contest of will. These two inner stories that come at the end of the first book and the beginning of the second present similar solutions to the problem of combating potentially destructive powers; the first victory occurs in a fairy tale, the next in a story allegedly from a medieval chronicle and therefore remote in time.

"Der Kampf der Sänger" repeats the central problem of "Bergwerke" but transposes it into another key, from the world of the artisan to that of the artist. Like Elis Fröbom and Torbern, Heinrich von Ofterdingen and Klingsohr stand in a relationship of pupil and master. Both of the students feel the same sort of attraction and repulsion in the presence of their apparent mentors (cf. 177, 286–87). Both practice their craft for the sake of a woman's love, although Ulla has a rival in the subterranean queen, whereas Mathilde does not. Elis perishes and Ofterdingen survives, but only through Wolfram's intercession for him; Wolfram's art, because of its essential purity, can vanquish demonic forces. Both Elis and Ofterdingen seem possessed by the powers into whose hands they have placed themselves. Both men make an easy mark for their evil teachers because of their inner turmoil. Unlike Elis, however, a melancholy Neriker by birth (172), Heinrich's agitation seems a more temporary state, like that of the magnetized individual in the frame immediately preceding "Kampf."[321]

The way in which Hoffmann started this story bears strong resemblances to the beginnings of previous tales: "Die Fermate," "Frag-

---

321. At the beginning of the frame tableau and the narrative of the story itself, the six *Minnesänger* live in harmony, pp. 275, 279.

ment," and "Artushof." In each case, a picture or a tableau inspires or is the occasion for a story.[322] While the source for "Kampf" is Wagenseil's chronicle,[323] the description of the scene with the main characters gives the plot in a nutshell before the actual story starts (275–78). This strong visual element helps tie the stories closely to the *Serapionsprinzip* (see 55).

The narrator speaks of the beginning frame as a dream (275) and of the subsequent story as "der erzählte Traum" (the narrated dream) (279). Hoffmann's description of the frame dream at the beginning of the story and the frame's structure have a lot in common with the beginning of Schubert's *Symbolik des Traumes*. The description of the frame dream includes a reference to the inner eye that can catch glimpses of a higher life (275). The pictures one sees in a dream are, according to Schubert, the dream's special hieroglyphic language, expressing major events in a sort of visual shorthand:

Im Traume . . . scheint die Seele eine ganz andre Sprache zu sprechen als gewöhnlich. Gewisse Naturgegenstände oder Eigenschaften der Dinge, bedeuten jetzt auf einmal Personen und umgekehrt stellen sich uns gewisse Eigenschaften oder Handlungen, unter dem Bilde von Personen dar.[324]

In a dream . . . the soul seems to be speaking a quite different language than usual. Now certain objects of nature or properties of things suddenly stand for people and vice versa, certain characteristics or actions appear to us in the guise of people.

This beginning tableau of "Kampf" fits Schubert's description of dream language and its function very closely. The long description of bird song and the music of the hunt (275) foreshadows the emphasis on music, while the major figures of the story are described in such a way that the main plot outlines become visible; Heinrich von Ofterdingen, who first rode happily with his colleagues, is now pale with flaming eyes, tortured by invisible spirits. Immediately after this description of Heinrich comes a longer one of Wolfram, full of knightly grace and virtue (277). Only Heinrich and Wolfram figure prominently at this point in the dream. This fact, and the juxtaposition of these two passages, hint at the importance of these two figures. The shorthand

322. Segebrecht (Winkler), p. 1050.
323. Kruse, *Aufbau*, pp. 701–2. Segebrecht (Winkler), pp. 1057.
324. Schubert, *Symbolik des Traumes*, p. 1.

descriptions also give the outlines of the plot: Heinrich in the grip of mental despair and Wolfram, the model of courtly rectitude, in love with and loved by Mathilde.

Dreams figure significantly in the frame discussion preceding "Kampf," where they are linked with somnambulism and thereby implicitly with magnetism (263). The value of dreams, as with the potential of magnetism and madness, lies in their ability to touch the inner soul and raise it to a higher level. With its sharpened inner eye, the dream with which the story begins is necessary to penetrate the world of the *Minnesänger*. This was a period of great artistic inspiration, as was the late medieval world from which the picture in "Artushof" came.

In "Kampf der Sänger," the problems of the artist receive a somewhat different emphasis than they did in the earlier stories in the first book. "Krespel," "Fermate," and "Artushof" all deal with the physical renunciation of artistic inspiration to preserve the artist. While Heinrich must give up Mathilde, the focus here is different. With ulterior motives, Heinrich seeks the wrong sources of artistic inspiration: he wants to win the love of Mathilde through magic, since he cannot obtain it on his own. Because he is willing to give himself to evil forces to fulfill this desire, he comes close to suffering the same fate as Count S in "Der unheimliche Gast," and he foreshadows Cardillac's problem in "Scuderi."

The manner in which Hoffmann builds up the portrait of an artist in thrall to demonic powers gives us important clues about subsequent protagonists in inner stories in the *Serapionsbrüder*. Heinrich's songs call forth melancholy in the soul. More alarming are the discordant notes: ". . . die mochten wohl aus dem wunden zerrissenen Gemüt kommen, in dem sich böser Hohn angesiedelt, bohrend und zehrend wie ein giftiges Insekt" [". . . they probably came from the sore and torn spirit, in which an evil scorn had settled, boring and consuming like a poisonous insect" (280).[325] Pale and nervous, he feels suspended between heaven and earth, held there by a hellish monster who separates him from the one and keeps him out of the other (281).

325. Hoffmann used the metaphors of poison and noxious vermin in describing the condition of Zacharias Werner at the end of the *Serapionsbrüder*: ". . . wie mit dem Keim der schönsten Blüte der Wurm mitgeboren werden kann, der sie zum Tode vergiftet." See also ". . . ich habe vielmehr jenen abnormen Seelenzustand im Sinn, in dem das psychische Prinzip durch das Glühfeuer überreizter Fantasie, zum Sublimat verflüchtigt, ein Gift worden, das die Lebensgeister angreift, so daß sie zum Tode erkranken" p. 856 (Winkler). Evil insects flourish in "Das fremde Kind" and "Die Königsbraut" as well.

In such a state, Heinrich falls easy prey to Klingsohr's advances. As he sits outside the *Wartburg*, watching the happiness of Wolfram and Mathilde, Klingsohr or his emissary interrupts with "ein gellendes schneidendes Gelächter" [shrill screeching laughter] (285). The frame tableau already indicated Heinrich's subservience to demonic spirits when it described the song he sang in the contest: "einige seltsam gellende Laute" ["some peculiar piercing sounds"] (278). As he speaks with the mysterious figure, he tries to fight off feelings of fear, sensing that he is on the edge of the abyss.[326] As the stranger talks to him about music, the characteristic ambivalence towards madness and magnetism that we find in the frame comes out clearly in the effect the stranger and his comments have on Heinrich. They awaken a new world of sensuality in him, changing his initially unfavorable impression (287).[327] Like the devil figure in "Nachricht aus dem Leben eines bekannten Mannes" (News about the life of a well-known man) and Count S, Klingsohr and the figures around him have an attractive side. Klingsohr has much in common with these two characters as well as with the *Münzjude* in "Brautwahl." While there are important differences among these figures, they all serve to illuminate the nature of evil and its particular threat to the sensitive, striving personality. Like Count S and the *Münzjude*, the stranger in "Kampf" appears mysteriously, causing feelings of attraction and repulsion for Heinrich (286–87). Like the count, he seems to be in league with the Devil (288). This association with the devil appears several times throughout the story; Wolfram recognizes Klingsohr as an ally of Satan, the source of his talent, and Klingsohr admits it after Wolfram beats him in a singing contest (300, 303). The end of the singing match also underscores this connection, as the bailiffs were thwarted in their attempts to seize the loser by a cloud of black smoke (313). The ending of "Nachricht" has

326. Imagery dealing with heights and depths occurs frequently in these inner stories whenever the artist tries to enlarge his range of perception. These attempts place him at risk, whether of madness or of possession by strange spirits or forces that lead to the loss of self-identity. Passages in the frame dealing with madness, magnetism, or in "Bergwerke" provide good examples (pp. 29, 180, 182, 273) as do other passages (pp. 294, 314, 315).

327. In his dissertation, "Die Gestalt der Geliebten in den poetischen Werken E. T. A. Hoffmanns" (Bonn, 1967), John Cronin deals with this story. He says that Heinrich's love for Mathilde is really self-love, since he is primarily concerned with his own feelings and not with her. Cronin implies that it is this self-love that leads Heinrich to disassociate himself from the others around him at the court and seek a connection with darker powers (p. 86).

a similar black cloud, as the burning woman calls on Satan (525). An intimacy with Satan traditionally brings other benefits; Klingsohr seems to have an extraordinary grasp of secret knowledge.

Klingsohr has many of the traits customarily associated with evil in Hoffmann's characters, yet his personality is not the only way in which the reader is supposed to understand his true nature. The second major means of characterization is the effect he has on those whom he successfully seduces or on those able to resist. Hoffmann's descriptions in both cases are quite consistent, paralleling similar characters throughout the *Serapionsbrüder*, and focus on a fairly narrow range of reactions. Heinrich's feeling of impending danger, a nameless sense of dread in Klingsohr's presence, is apparent from the first, just as it was with Elis Fröbom in the presence of Torbern. The inability of certain sensitive persons to flee from evil though they sense the danger is a common motif in the stories in the *Serapionsbrüder*, including "Bergwerke," "Gast," "Automate," and "Vampirismus."

As the evil outside influences gain on figures like Heinrich, they change internally and reflect this change in their outward appearance and manner. At several points in the story, the degree of possession of Heinrich by his teacher becomes clear, a control recognized by Heinrich as well as Wolfram (see 296, 312). These changes show the similarity between the state into which Heinrich has fallen and that of the magnetized person, such as the peasant girl in the frame, who spoke in the cultivated accents of her physician. The difference here is in the nature of the person who has the power; Klingsohr, Nasias, and others are aligned with the forces of evil while the physician wants only to heal the girl and functions with good intent. The fears of some of the *Serapionsbrüder* about possession leading to madness become real in this story, as they do in subsequent ones as well.

The reach of evil in this story extends beyond Heinrich to Mathilde and to Count Hermann. Mathilde, described previously in idealized terms as the incarnation of womanly virtue (289, 290), now succumbs to the siren song of Klingsohr, losing her charm and beauty and becoming an object of ridicule (295). Mysterious forces of the spirit have a similar effect on Marguerite in "Der unheimliche Gast" as she comes under the magnetic spell of the count (623).[328] Although Count Her-

---

328. This fear of madness spreading like an infection comes out frequently in the frame; see, for example, pp. 29, 271. Ellinger notes that Mathilde's condition resembles

mann, described as a great friend of the arts and protector of those at his court (279, 281, 291), realizes the source of the alluring force of Heinrich's songs, he too subsequently forgets his own insights (295). As is often the case with Hoffmann characters who fall prey to the advances of evil, Count Hermann succumbs to the temptation of secret knowledge, in this case astrology (309–10).

Over against the fascinating figure of Klingsohr with his Jupiter-like countenance, his arcane and exotic knowledge,[329] bewitching music and connections to strange forces, only the character of Wolfram can stand. Wolfram illuminates for the reader not only the extent of Klingsohr's evil but also the power of harmony and goodness. Wolfram's exceptional art arises from his natural as well as his spiritual gifts, and makes him, in contrast to Serapion or Zacharias Werner, a real artist. Hoffmann's picture of Wolfram in the story stands in counterpoint to those of Heinrich and Klingsohr. Instead of the mysterious Siebenbürgen home of vampires and their ilk, Wolfram is a native of Switzerland: "Seine Lieder voller süßer Anmut und Klarheit glichen dem reinen blauen Himmel seiner Heimat" ["His songs full of sweet charm and clarity resembled the pure blue sky of his homeland"] (280). Klingsohr mocks this source of strength in Wolfram (301), which gives added weight to its importance for Wolfram's character. Wolfram's apprenticeship with Master Fridebrand stands also in contrast to Heinrich's with Klingsohr. Instead of dark and hidden forces, Fridebrand's songs brought light into his pupils' souls (280). Further recognition of Wolfram's stature lies in the general feeling among the other singers that he is the first among equals and in Mathilde's acceptance of his suit. Wolfram's songs contrast sharply with those of Heinrich. Instead of "gewaltigen Tönen an die dunklen Pforten eines

---

the state in which women were in "Gast" and notes another parallel of Mathilde's condition with that of magnetism: ". . . daß die Gräfin nach dem Erwachen aus der Bezauberung sich deutlich der auf sie geübten und sie ihrem eigentlichen Sein entfremdenden Macht bewußt ist" (p. 28). Ellinger does not connect the figures in the stories with the discussion of magnetism in the frame.

Although Pikulik, *Erzähler*, pp. 109 and 112, dismisses Mathilde's character change as crass, it might be more understandable if she is indeed under a kind of hypnotic influence.

329. Another example of Klingsohr's alliance with dark forces is his knowledge about metal, with which he has enriched Andreas II (p. 310). In "Bergwerke," such knowledge is in the possession of Torbern and the queen. See also "Der Magnetiseur" (Winkler), p. 168.

fremden verhängnisvollen Reichs" ["powerful tones at the dark gate of a strange and fateful sphere"] (292), Wolfram's song is one in which "in den herrlichsten, gewaltigsten Tönen die Himmelsseligkeit der reinen Liebe des frommen Sängers pries" ["praised the heavenly bliss of the pious singer's pure love in the most magnificent and powerful melodies"] (307).

Unlike Heinrich, Wolfram is healthy and strong, with none of the inner contradictions that destroy Heinrich's health and make him susceptible to Klingsohr. His generosity of spirit shows itself repeatedly in his kindness towards Heinrich, from his lack of enmity when Heinrich reveals he loves Mathlide (284) to his forgiveness of Heinrich's supercilious behavior towards him upon his return from Siebenburgen. Wolfram prophetically offers to hold his arms around Heinrich should he ever be close to the abyss (294). This passage foreshadows Wolfram's role as the savior of both Heinrich and Mathilde and stands in contrast to the fate of Fröbom.

In order to keep his friend as well as his beloved from the grasp of demonic forces, Wolfram must use both his skills as an artist and his strength of character. For Wolfram, these two realms are related. He tells Klingsohr that even the best efforts of the greatest masters of song would not have helped him had he not kept evil from his heart (301).[330] Wolfram needs all of this strength in the contest with Nasias, whose song tempts even him (306). Both Klingsohr and Nasias have the power to change a potential victim's perception; Klingsohr takes a stone from a capsule that makes his exotic study seem bright and changes Wolfram's impressions (302). These reactions are similar to those of someone who is magnetized, at least for the moment. The power of both the devil and the evil magnetizer rests on weakness or abnormality of spirit in his victims, but Wolfram is able to resist because of his inner harmony and strength. Klingsohr recognizes this when he says, "über finstre Mächte gebietet meine Wissenschaft, unser inneres Wesen muß uns entzweien" ["my knowledge rules over dark powers; our inner beings must divide us"] (303).

Further evidence that Wolfram's character lay at the heart of his

---

330. This passage would seem to belie Kruse's position that trust in the unconquerable spirit of poetry was the reason for Wolfram's victory, p. 702. Hoffmann also continually refers to Klingsohr and his art as heathen, and Wolfram banishes the devil in Christ's name (p. 307).

victory over the forces ensnarling the lives of Heinrich and Mathilde comes in the final section of the story, when Mathilde explains what freed her from the spell. During the night of Wolfram's contest with Nasias, both sides struggled for her soul in a dream, while Wolfram fell into a dream-like state (307). In each case, forces of good gained the upper hand. Wolfram heard beautiful music and saw the forces of evil disappear (306–7). Mathilde's dream seems to resemble the kind of spell cast by an evil magnetizer. In the dream an irresistible force compels her to write a song in the manner of her uncanny master (314–15).[331] Mathilde's urge to create a song like that of Klingsohr resembles the situation of Angelika and Moritz in "Der unheimliche Gast," where psychic forces are used by the magnetizers in an attempt to change behavior as well as the clinical experiment with the peasant girl in the frame. All of these situations have as a common element the loss of self-identity in the victim.

Mathilda's dream has certain other elements in common with subsequent dream-like states in the *Serapionsbrüder;* these conditions seem to show some influence of Schubert. In a chapter in *Symbolik des Traumes* entitled "Der versteckte Poet" (the hidden poet), he discusses the good and bad demons in our inner spirits, which either protect us from or lead us into evil:

Jenes geistige Organ im Menschen, in seiner Doppelseitigkeit, ist der gute und böse Dämon, welcher den Menschen durchs Leben begleitet, und, je nachdem er der einen oder anderen Stimme mehr Gehör gegeben, ihn zu einem glücklichen oder unglücklichen Ziele führet. . . . Dieser Dämon [the good one] ist prophetisch, und jeder der mit den Führungen des inneren Lebens bekannt ist, wird erfahren haben, wie oft uns derselbe schon vor jenen Veranlassungen und Gelegenheiten warnt, und mit höherer Gewalt bewahrt.[332]

That spiritual organ in man, in its ambiguity, is the good and the bad demon that accompanies him through life and that leads him to a happy or an unhappy end, depending on whether he heeded the one or the other voice more. . . . This demon (the good one) is prophetic, and everyone who is familiar with the direction of the inner life will have already experienced how often it has warned us in advance about those causes and occasions and has saved us with a higher power.

331. See "Der Magnetiseur" (Winkler), pp. 167–68.
332. Schubert, *Symbolik des Traumes*, p. 80.

Mathilde's dream seems to reflect the workings of her good demon, as Wolfram's song comes to save her.

"Kampf der Sänger" shows, as does "Nußknacker," the triumph of the good, but not without a desperate battle with the forces of evil. This sequence of inner stories, beginning with the portrayal in "Bergwerke" of an existence destroyed through inner disharmony and possession by evil forces, and followed by a fairy tale and a medieval narrative in which unity and strength of character win out over the spirits of darkness, sets up a backdrop for the subsequent inner stories dealing with madness and demonic possession. Schubert, in describing the effect of the bad demon, delineates a state of mind that has affinities with that of Heinrich, Cardillac, and Count S:

In ähnlicher Manier, nur mit ganz entgegengesetzter Absicht und zu entgegengesetztem Zwecke, wirkt auch der böse Dämon. Er erregt in der Seele die Neigung zum Bösen, weckt die Lust durch Vorspiegelung vergangenen oder zukünftigen Genusses, und treibt uns, anfangs leiser, je mehr wir ihm aber Gehör geben, desto gewältiger von Gedanken und Worten bis zur schlimmen That, widerspricht der besseren Stimme in uns.[333]

In a similar manner, only with diametrically opposed intent and for the opposite purpose, the bad demon works: he awakens the inclination towards evil in the soul; he arouses lust through the illusion of past and future pleasures; he drives us, more quietly at the beginning, but the more we listen to him, the more vigorously from the thought and the word to the evil deed; he contradicts the better voice in us.

In the struggle with mysterious forces, "Bergwerke" and "Nußknacker" show two possible outcomes in an inner story narrative; then the clinical discussion in the frame at the beginning of the second volume goes into the scientific phenomena of the time that can help explain how individuals react in such bouts with the spirit world. "Kampf der Sänger" gives the reader an example of possession and exorcism; however, it is set in the Middle Ages so that it seems more remote. Marie, in "Nußknacker," and Wolfram both stand as guiding stars for those who want to keep from falling into the abyss; they contrast sharply with characters in "Spukgeschichte" and "Automate."

333. Schubert, *Symbolik*, p. 62.

"Eine Spukgeschichte"
(A Ghost Story)

The short frame after "Kampf der Sänger" and before "Spuk-geschichte" is a mixture of ironic comments about psychic forces and literature, mixed in with serious discussion and anecdotal material about magnetism. The fragmentary scraps of conversation and the gently disparaging remarks underscore the seriousness of the central topics at the same time that they help to distance the threat of poorly understood psychic forces. Magnetism once again occupies center stage, with Cyprian championing its diagnostic potential and maintaining that the poets, as the favorites of nature, should naturally learn her secrets (318–19). Its fascination for the *Serapionsbrüder* is evident in Ottmar's comment that he finds magnetism fatiguing, yet he proceeds immediately to tell a story that deals with magnetic powers (319–20).[334]

The two anecdotes, Ottmar's and Theodor's, both deal with objects that seemed to move independently but were brought in motion by the concentration of someone nearby. The psychokinetic forces at work here rest on the strength of will of the person trying to move the inanimate object. These anecdotes foreshadow a similar one in "Spuk-geschichte." The fact that an inanimate object as well as individuals receive the force of the magnetizer's personality would seem to have clear connections with the concerns expressed in the frame at the beginning of the book and with "Kampf der Sänger" as well as with the subsequent stories "Spukgeschichte" and "Automate." In all cases, the major female characters in the story seem to be under the control of an extraordinarily strong will. In contrast to "Nußknacker" and "Kampf der Sänger," the source of these psychic powers in "Spukgeschichte" and "Automate" is never explained. In "Nußknacker" and "Kampf der Sänger," the resolution of the story cleared up many of the questions surrounding the mysteries. "Spukgeschichte" and "Automate" leave

334. See Kruse, *Aufbau* 1, pp. 708–9 and G. Wittkop-Ménardeau, *Hoffmans Leben und Werk in Daten und Bildern* (Frankfurt, 1968), pp. 103. Safranski, *Hoffman*, p. 305, notes that Hoffman feared the effects of magnetism on the passive victim as well as the will to power on the part of the magnetizer.

their readers with things that are not explained and implicitly cannot be.

Like so many of the narrative accounts in the frame, "Spuk-geschichte" serves several functions, some within the context of the frame itself, others within the overall theme, and others vis-à-vis the inner stories. Written in connection with the frame, it serves to bring home the reality of the spirit world, reinforcing the stories. Stories such as "Spukgeschichte," which illustrate the workings of this "fremden psychischen Prinzips" (320–21), help to convince the artists in the cir-cle of the *Serapionsbrüder* that it is very real danger they face when they expand perception to the fringes of consciousness. "Spukgeschichte" makes the threatening figures of "Kampf der Sänger" more real and points ahead as well to the intervention of strange psychic powers into daily life, as in the case of Ferdinand and Ludwig in "Automate," whom the reader already knows from "Dichter und Komponist."[335]

Cyprian brings the nearness of this threat home when he blames his own uneasy frame of mind on these events, assures the assembled group of the story's veracity, and situates it in the context of recent events (321). In order to make his friends feel the full horror of what happens to the family, Cyprian spends the first part of the story describ-ing their personalities in some detail. The colonel was good-tempered and jovial, his wife quiet and uncomplicated, the older of the two daughters extraordinarily animated as well as beautiful (321–22). In this kind and lively group, there is only one disturbing person, the at-tractive younger daughter, Adelgunde, who seems haunted (322). Ad-elgunde's symptoms are easily recognizable as those of a person under the nefarious influence of a destructive external force. Cyprian has just learned that her condition arose as a result of an apparently childish attempt to imitate the ghost of the *weiße Frau* (white lady)[336] at her

335. See Kruse, *Aufbau* 1, p. 709. Kruse also notes that this story helped to add to the tension created by the discussion of magnetism and belief in strange occurrences (p. 709).

Auhuber, *Spiegel*, pp. 23–27, sees the deceptive method of treatment chosen for Adel-gunde as a criticism of Reil's methods, just as the description of Serapion was (pp. 32–33).

336. Kruse notes that this figure appears in numerous ghost stories and always brings unhappiness. The source of the figure is supposedly a countess, Agnes von Orlau-münde, who killed both her children. As atonement for this sin, she had to appear after her death in white, in order to warn the Hohenzollerns of impending family troubles (p. 709). See also Pikulik, *Erzähler*, p. 114–15, who suggests as the source Countess Rosenberg of Bohemia who, after a life spent in the arduous exercise of difficult duties, dedicated herself to further such work after her death, appearing to forecast death.

birthday party. Although the children have been playing in the woods for some time, they do not notice the approaching dark; the "magische Dämmerung" [magical twilight (323)] leads them to play at elves and spirits. Adelgunde, with a white shawl wrapped around her, stares in horror, because she, and she alone, sees the white lady. In spite of repeated attempts by her family to talk her out of it or even to trick her out of seeing it, Adelgunde sees the white lady every night at nine.

The white lady has pushed Adelgunde to the brink of madness, but when Adelgunde tries to throw a plate at her, the dish is stopped, then carried by an unseen hand and set on the table. This manifestation drives the rest of the family to destruction. The mother dies soon after, the father is killed at Waterloo under mysterious circumstances, and the older sister goes mad. Adelgunde, however, who has been healed by this mysterious encounter, now cares for her broken sister. The proximity of the threat to the members of the circle is emphasized by the reference to Dr. R, whose arrival for consultation is imminent.

The *Serapionsbrüder* react to Cyprian's story with audible unease. Ottmar retells its main points, which makes these events even more real to the reader and applies rational perspective to it with the result that he cannot explain such occurrences. To add to their disquiet, Ottmar remarks that he has heard from officer friends that the Obrist's last battle was peculiar; ". . . der Obrist sei beim Angriff plötzlich wie von Furien getrieben ins feindliche Feuer hineingesprengt" (326–27) ["that he suddenly dashed into the thick of the enemy's fire as if impelled by the furies"] (Bleiler, 77).

The lack of an explanation as well as the plausibility of the story add to its unsettling effects. Ottmar provides an important clue to the function of these frame reports when he says, ". . . und das Ganze so ungesucht, so einfach, daß gerade in der Wahrscheinlichkeit die das Unwahrscheinlichste dadurch erhält, für mich das Grauenhafte liegt" ["the entire event so natural, so simple that I see the gruesome exactly in the probability that the improbable acquires by this naturalness and simplicity"] (327). The events that occur in the lives of people known to the *Serapionsbrüder* are not only more frightening because they happen to acquaintances but precisely because they take place in a way and in a milieu that is very real.

"Spukgeschichte," like the magnetic anecdotes, depicts possession of the will by outside forces. Theodor sums up the horror he feels towards them: "Es ist das Gefühl der gänzlichen hülflosesten Ohnmacht, das den Geist zermalmen müßte" (327) ["The sense of the most utter, most helpless powerlessness must grind the spirit to dust"] (Bleiler, 78). He reinforces his words with a brief anecdote about a childhood memory. The participation of several of the group in this discussion leads Lothar to complain that he cannot stand the proliferation of such stories (327), which underscores the attraction and repulsion that the circle, like the characters in the stories, feel towards psychic forces. As at the end of the discussion of Serapion, the need for relief from threatening topics becomes evident. Theodor, as in the first book, takes charge to lead the group back to an allegedly more comfortable reality with the fragment of a story (326; cf. 30).

"Die Automate"
(The Automaton)

The opening scene of "Die Automate" takes place in the present time in a realistic situation. A new, talking automat has appeared in the city, causing a great amount of investigation and speculation, because of both its mechanical skills and its apparent intellectual sophistication. Even though the beginning of the story has something of the carnival about it in its description of the automatic talking Turk, the story is yet another variation on the theme of inexplicable forces that burst into everyday lives. The fascination of Hoffmann for these strange machines is apparent in his description of the Turk, who seems dead and alive at the same time, mechanical, yet apparently able to answer each question (328–29). The subsequent analysis of the Turk's capabilities is a strange mixture of technical explanation, hypothesis and bafflement (329). Hoffmann's fascination with such figures lay in part in the mixture of technical aspects that could be explained and other qualities that could not.[337] Yet in the measure of the inexplicable that

337. Nipperdey, "Wahnsinnsfiguren," p. 40. In his article, "Das Automatenmotiv und die Technik der Motivschichtung im Erzählwerk E. T. A. Hoffmanns," MHG, vol. 30 (1984), pp. 25–33, Silvio Vietta provides background information about automats in the late eighteenth century (p. 28), where he notes that *Orakelautomaten* (oracle automata) were fashionable in the late eighteenth and at the beginning of the nineteenth cen-

rested in the behavior of the mechanical Turk, such as his knowledge of Ferdinand's secret, lies the degree of evil that lurked for Hoffmann in every psychic force that he could not explain, including magnetism. The depressing and horrifying effect that automatic figures have lies in their capacity to destroy the soul. These creatures with dead, vacantly staring, eyes (330) can foreshadow the fate of a person who falls under their power, as the related story, "Der Sandmann," shows.

At times the automat seems to function like the magnetizer,[338] setting the subject in touch with his innermost spirit, which is otherwise inaccessible. Ludwig wonders if, in answering their questions, this being can acquire a psychic influence over them, with knowledge of their inner beings. He suggests that because of this rapport, the automat evokes an ecstasy in which everything one sees with the eyes of the soul is brightly illuminated (343). Though Ludwig tries to minimize the effect of the Turk by comparing it unfavorably to the nutcracker he had as a child (339), the machine's potential clearly unsettles them.[339]

It is through psychic connections that the automat comes by knowledge that only one other creature possesses, as in Ferdinand's case with the mysterious singer.[340] Just as in a dream, the person understands things otherwise hidden, and the automat is able to tap this knowledge (343). Though this state of affairs clearly connects the story with the previous one as well as with the frame discussions, its linkage of the automat with the powers of the magnetizer shows why Hoffmann was both scared by and fascinated with the machines. Mechanical music-

---

tury, a fact that may have led Hoffmann to fuse the theme of the automat with that of prophecy and determination of one's fate. See also Pikulik, *Erzähler*, pp. 117–18. See also Dieter Müller, "Zeit der Automate: Zum Automatenproblem bei Hoffmann," MHG, vol. 12 (1966), pp. 1–8, p. 1. The truth of Müller's comment about the automaton as the counterpart of a human being is apparent in Ferdinand and Ludwig's reaction to it (see pp. 331, 333, 337, 346).

338. Vietta, "Das Automatenmotiv," seems to share this view. See p. 29. See also Sucher, *Sources*, pp. 40–41, for remarks on Hoffmann's linkage of magnetism and the automat theme. Pikulik, *Erzähler*, mentions it briefly, p. 121.

339. See Segebrecht (Winkler), pp. 1063–64. While there are obvious connections here to "Nußknacker," the more subtle ones, which point back to "Nußknacker" and ahead to "Das fremde Kind," have been ignored. The nutcracker that Ludwig has as a child, like Marie's, seemed to warm to life when lovingly caressed. This quality made it superior to all other marionettes and infinitely better than mechanical toys, both in "Nußknacker" and in "Das fremde Kind," where the children reject such artificiality.

340. In a letter to the singer Johanna R., Hoffmann describes a similar mystical experience with a voice that he hears at Warmbrunn. Intensive questioning does not clarify the matter and he concludes it must have been Johanna herself (p. 95 in E. T. A. Hoffmann's *Nachlese*, edited by Friedrich Schnapp [Winkler, Munich].

making machines also belong in the realm of the automat and have connections as well to the magnetizer.[341] When Ludwig and Ferdinand visit Professor X, he shows the human automats playing musical instruments (345–46). Ludwig describes their effect on him with phrases similar to those used for the Turk (346–47; see also 348).

Yet even though Ludwig damns the attempts of technicians to imitate or replace the human voice (347), he does not reject "die höhere musikalische Mechanik" (347–48).[342] These efforts Ludwig and Ferdinand commend because they aid in penetrating the secrets of nature and the music of the spheres (348). Since Ferdinand does not completely understand Ludwig's hopes for these endeavors, Ludwig uses material from Schubert's *Ansichten,* which Hoffmann cites almost verbatim (349–50).[343] This section of Schubert deals with man in the first Golden Age, when he was still in harmony with nature. At that time, Nature surrounded man with sacred music, which "verkündete[n] die Geheimnisse ihres ewigen Treibens" (349). ["spoke of the mysteries of her unceasing activity"], (Bleiler, 97). Remnants of this lost music still remain, in the *Sphärenmusik,* in the *Luftmusik,* or *Teufelsstimme* in Ceylon, and in other isolated cases in East Prussia (Music of the spheres, music of the air, and voice of the Devil, respectively). The modern instrument closest to this earlier perfection is the *Glocken-* or *Glasharmonika* (glass harmonica).[344] There are several reasons that could explain why Hoffmann uses this passage in this story at this point. By putting Schubert on the side of the "höhere musikalische Mechanik" (higher musical mechanics), he justifies this search for new knowledge in the

341. Numerous commentators have noted the proliferation of mechanical musical instruments at this time. See Kruse, *Aufbau* 1, 717–18; Segebrecht (Winkler), p. 1064. See also Müller, pp. 5–6, who notes that the eighteenth century was very fond of such experiments and that the professor in "Automate" is a representative of the mechanistic, automatic, enlightened world view (p. 6).

342. In *Lebens-Ansichten des Katers Murr,* E. T. A. Hoffmann, ed. Wolfgang Kron (Winkler, Munich), Hoffmann makes a similar connection between mechanics and the secrets of nature, p. 439.

343. See Schubert, *Ansichten,* p. 64. Sucher, *Sources,* p. 59, notes the connection of a sense of déja vu with the impressions of a dream, which for Hoffmann was one of the symptoms of rapport with the occult, a theme that he treated in "Automate." Sucher also suggests Novalis as a source of information on the reappearance of figures of whom one has a dim memory. See Kluge, *Versuch,* p. 346.

344. See Kruse, *Aufbau* 1, pp. 718–19, for a description of the *Glasharmonika.* In a passage from "Ritter Glück," *Fantasie und Nachtstücke* (Winkler), p. 39, Hoffmann describes this connection between nature and music. Although the passage is intended to be ironical (see text notes, p. 780), the remarks reflect Hoffmann's own views, similar to ones expressed in "Die Automate" and "Der unheimliche Gast."

hopes that it will reveal hidden harmonies in new levels of perception.[345] Through music, as in a dream or under magnetic influence,[346] the *Gemüt* (spirit) can rediscover what lies in its innermost parts and bring it to conscious life:

Ist es nicht vielmehr das Gemüt, welches sich nur jener physischen Organe bedient, um das, was in seiner tiefsten Tiefe erklungen, in das rege Leben zu bringen, daß es andern vernehmbar ertönt und die gleichen Anklänge im Innern erweckt, welche dann im harmonischen Widerhall dem Geist das wundervolle Reich erschließen, . . . (347)

Is it not, rather, the mind, the soul, the heart, that merely employ those bodily organs to give forth into our external life what we feel in our inner depths, so that it can be communicated to others, and awaken kindred chords in them, opening, in harmonious echoes, that marvelous kingdom, . . . (Bleiler, 95)

Such a state of affairs makes it possible to communicate this experience to others. Other comments on *Gemüt*, such as in "Kampf der Sänger," make its importance clear. Wolfram's strong and pure inner spirit attunes him to the original harmonies of nature, while Heinrich's flirtation with the nether world opens his soul to dreadful secrets and bars him from more valuable perceptions.

This earlier harmony that one should recapture finds its closest approximation in the *Glocken-* or *Glasharmonika*.[347] Immediately after praising the *Glockenharmonika*, the two friends hear the mysterious song in a garden outside of the city. It is the same aria that Ferdinand heard earlier and that had so transformed his inner experience. Hoffmann describes it: "ein seltsamer Klang durch die Luft, der im stärkern Anschwellen dem Ton einer Harmonika ähnlich wurde" ["a peculiar sound in the air, that in its stronger crescendos resembled the sound of a harmonica"] (351). The similarity of the girl's voice with this instrument explains the unique effect she had on Ferdinand.[348] Why does

345. Klaus Dobat, *Musik als romantische Illusion*, (Tübingen, 1984), in his analysis of Hoffmann's music theories in connection with this story, comes to conclusions agreeing with mine, though in a different context. See pp. 189–94, especially 190–92. Meyer, *Sonderling*, p. 117, notes that mechanical devices offered, to the Romantics, a means of penetrating into the innermost secrets of nature. D. Müller, "Zeit," misses the distinction between the two types of mechanical efforts that Dobat sees.

346. In the following frame, Theodor refers to Ferdinand's relationship with the girl as "der somnambulen Liebschaft" (p. 354).

347. See Kruse, p. 718, for a description and Matt, *Augen*, p. 28.

348. Vietta, "Das Automatenmotiv," sees her song as ". . . die klanggewordene Erinnerung an den harmonischen Urzustand der Natur" (p. 30). His observation would seem to confirm the hint that Hoffmann gives in the text, that her voice is like the *Har-*

this girl, whose voice embodies such perfection, appear in the company of Professor X and apparently marry him in a faraway city, though Professor X has allegedly never left town? The answer could well lie in the belief, expressed so often in Hoffmann's stories, especially in those of Book I, that the source of poetic inspiration can never be possessed by the artist whom she inspired, as well as in the ambivalent attitude of Hoffmann towards an expanding of consciousness. The sublime beauty of the girl's voice, symbolizing this hidden harmony, seems to be accessible only in the company of Professor X, who seems to represent hidden knowledge and dangerous shoals on the one hand and heavenly transfiguration on the other. The hazardous potential she offers is confirmed through Theodor's frame reference to Ferdinand's "somnambulen Liebschaft" (somnambulistic romance) (354). When the professor shows Ferdinand and Ludwig his musical machines, his voice has a dissonant and unappealing quality, his mouth has a sarcastic expression, and his tiny eyes blink in a piercing way (345). Yet, when the two friends find him again in the garden outside the city with the girl, he seems to reveal a completely different side. Gone is his repugnant ironic expression and in its place they see a deep melancholy seriousness as he gazes at the sky, as if he had been transformed and was seeing into the world beyond (351). As Ferdinand and Ludwig learn more about the professor, they find that the musical machines are merely a hobby and that his real interest lies in penetrating the secrets of natural sciences (352). Professor X and the girl represent, on another plane, the promise and the danger of expanding perception.

Since there are no definite answers to the questions posed in this story, questions symbolized by the figure of the talking Turk, it must, as Theodor says, remain a fragment (354). But seeing it in the context of the frame has made a coherent interpretation of the story possible. It is not, as Klaus Dobat has recently maintained, a contradictory story with vague plot levels. Ferdinand's love story forms an integral part of Hoffmann's basic thematic complex dealing with the problems of

---

monika (351). Significant as well is the fact that the aria in the garden comes immediately after the praise of the *Glockenharmonika* and the discussion of Schubert.

Matt, *Augen*, pp. 129–130, sees a parallel between Elis Fröbom's relationship to the carbuncle and Antonie's to the violin, connecting this relationship with the musical automat theme.

artistic perception and inspiration.[349] The figure of Professor X is, as Dobat says, contradictory, but the reasons for these inner contradictions lie in the ambivalent nature of Hoffmann's beliefs about the pursuit of hidden knowledge. These inner relationships in "Die Automate" become clear when we look at its themes in comparison with the discussion on magnetism, the inexplicable events surrounding "Spukgeschichte," and the contrasting figures of the sound artist and the doomed artist in "Der Kampf der Sänger."

The problem of perception and understanding that preoccupies Ludwig at the end of the story points ahead to the perilous situation in which those who skirt the boundaries of the psyche find themselves. Ludwig wonders if these events could result from the clash of various psychic relations among a few people, in situations where outside independent events were pulled in as well, yet included in such a way that the deluded inner spirit believes that they came only from within himself (354). This possibility, that the inner mind misinterprets certain events, was apparent at the end of "Spukgeschichte," when the narrator mentions that Adelgunde's delusion could have influenced her family. "Bergwerke," "Der unheimliche Gast," "Vampirismus," "Der Zusammenhang der Dinge," "Doge und Dogaresse," and "Fräulein von Scuderi" all contain telling examples of characters whose souls fall under the influence of strange forces and who sometimes misinterpret these messages to bring about misery and destruction.

After the ending of "Automate," Ottmar expresses a certain amount of irritation that the story has not tied up all the loose ends. Theodor justifies his approach with a defense of fragments that leads into a brief comment on fantasy and history. Theodor attacks stories and novels that do not leave any place for the reader's imagination:

Nichts ist mir mehr zuwider als wenn in einer Erzählung, in einem Roman der Boden, auf dem sich die fantastische Welt bewegt hat, zuletzt mit dem historischen Besen so rein gekehrt wird, daß auch kein Körnchen, kein

---

349. Dobat, *Musik*, p. 193. Matt, pp. 176–78, criticizes the story severely, missing the connections it has to the frame and other inner stories, as well as its inner unity. Pikulik, *Erzähler*, pp. 121–22, sees a connection between Traugott in "Artushof" and Ferdinand in the theme of the inspirational love of the artist, which can never be possessed.

For related material on the effect of such stories on the reader, see Jürgen Walter, "Das Unheimliche als Wirkungsfunktion: Eine rezeptionsästhetische Analyse von E. T. A. Hoffmanns Erzählung "Der Sandmann," MHG, vol. 30, (1984), pp. 15–33, p. 23.

Stäubchen bleibt, wenn man so ganz abgefunden nach Hause geht, daß man gar keine Sehnsucht empfindet noch einmal hinter die Gardinen zu kucken. (355)

Nothing is so distasteful to me as when, in a story or novel, the stage on which the imaginary world has been in action is swept so clean by the historic broom that not the smallest grain or particle of dust is left on it; when you go home so completely sated and satisfied that you have not the faintest desire left to have another peep behind the curtain. (Bleiler, 102)

The "historische Besen" (historic broom) is probably a metaphor for the Enlightenment's approach to history, which attempted to view it as a logical and inevitable sequence of events. Since such an approach deadens speculation, it does not allow for exploration at the edges of perception, for expansion of one's understanding of what goes on behind the scenes. Caspar sees perception as a necessary element in Hoffmann's understanding of history, without which the event would have had no meaning or cannot even be said to have occurred at all.[350]

"Doge und Dogaresse"
(Doge and Dogaressa)

The value that a perceptive fantasy can bring to historical events comes strongly in evidence in the next story, "Doge und Dogaresse." Hoffmann takes the historical events surrounding the election and execution of the fourteenth-century Venetian Doge Marino Falieri and invents a love story connected with them, as well as the figure of the prophetic old nursemaid, Margaretha.[351] The apparent inspiration for this story was a picture by Karl Kolbe that depicted an aged Doge, a very young, beautiful and sad Dogaressa, an old woman behind them, and a young man blowing a horn shaped like a seashell (355). Although the picture attracts the attention of many visitors to the gallery, it also causes a number of pointless arguments about whether it portrays an historical event or is simply a picture of an aged ruler who

350. Bernhard Casper, "Der historische Besen," pp. 492, 493.
351. See Ellinger, pp. 22–25; Kruse, *Aufbau* 2, pp. 720–21; Segebrecht (Winkler), pp. 1065–66.

cannot satisfy his beautiful young wife. Some would like to match it to a specific historical event without an understanding of what really happened behind the scenes and how the characters in the picture might be related. They are like the people in the *Serapionsbrüder* frame who want to tidy everything with an historical broom without leaving room for fantasy. The old painter in the outer frame of "Doge" takes a different approach; he believes that within the soul of the artist images often unfold whose shapes transform themselves into life, tying in with the past and perhaps the future, so that the painter can depict what really happened or what will happen (357).[352] A painter who is capable of such a picture is one who is in touch with hidden forces, since prophecy is common to those in an exalted or a magnetic state. Further evidence that the painter who can portray real history is in touch with psychic revelations from an earlier time lies in the old painter's remark that historians like himself are a kind of talking ghost from the *Vorzeit* (past ages) (357).[353]

In its minute as well as lyrical description of an event far back in time, "Doge" has definite formal and thematic similarities with the story that began section three, "Der Kampf der Sänger." Both stories also examine the workings of forces just on the edge of consciousness in the context of the remote past. In both stories, there are descriptions of a paradisiacal Golden Age, of the harmony among the singers, of Wolfram's childhood in "Kampf," and of Antonio's earlier life in "Doge."[354] These two stories, which begin and end section three, frame two inner stories, "Die Automate" and "Spukgeschichte," which dealt with the presence of mysterious principles and spirits in the immediate present among people known to members of the *Serapionsbrüder*. By once again locating the fictional description of these secret forces in the Middle Ages, the narrator relieves some of the anxiety and tension that builds up in the *Serapionsbrüder* circle as well as in the readers.

The major narrative vehicle Hoffmann uses to describe the role of

352. Casper, "Der historische Besen," p. 492, says that events are not already there just for their own sakes, but that they must arrive.

353. Schubert maintains that glimpses of the former union between man and nature can occur in the soul of the student in a sort of *Begeisterung* (pp. 84–85).

354. The opening lines of the inner story are very similar in both "Kampf" and "Doge." Kampf: "Es mochte wohl ums Jahr eintausendzweihundertundacht sein" (279). Doge: "Vor gar langer Zeit und, irr ich nicht, so war's im Monat August des Jahres eintausendddreihundertundvierundfünfzig, . . . " (357). See Pikulik, *Erzähler*, pp. 128–29, for an analysis of the theme of the Golden Age in "Doge."

dreams and prophecy in "Doge" is the plot he added about the love story between Antonio (Anton Dahlberger) and the Dogaressa. This inner story, which is intimately intertwined with the figures of the outer story represented in the picture, represents on a literary level the psychic revelation that the old painter described in the above quotation. In addition, the story is full of motifs and characters that link it to the frame and to other stories.

The old nursemaid, Margaretha, plays a key role in this narrative, for it is she who is aligned most closely with psychic forces. Hoffmann's description of her foreshadows her role, since it contains elements that make her seem eccentric and slightly insane, particularly her strange giggle and her twitching face (361, 368–69). Margaretha knows who Antonio really is, but she cannot make him believe her until she explains that torture gave her such a wretched appearance and repugnant gestures (375–77). After the murder of Antonio's father, her gifts of healing, by which she supported herself, aroused the envy of the established medical profession. They accused her of being in league with the Devil and condemned her to the hellish torture that so disfigured her. This explanation is important both to the reader and to Antonio, because it lessens fears that the old woman is in the Devil's power (see 369, 375).[355] Although Margaretha is not mad, her strange appearance reminds the reader once again how closely madness and psychic powers are linked in Hoffmann's works.

Among the mysterious gifts Margaretha has is that of prophecy, given to her by a mysterious force she cannot resist (376). She foretells Antonio's rescue of the Doge, which leads to his wealth, and she warns him of future dangers. Margaretha shares this suggestibility to semi-conscious suggestion with Antonio, who is drawn to the woman for reasons he cannot explain before he finally realizes that she is indeed his former nursemaid (369). Margaretha's sympathy with the subcon-

355. In a passage that could be related to Margarethe's psychic powers, Schubert, in *Ansichten*, says: "Endlich werden wir in mannigfaltigen Erscheinungen, das Eingreifen eines künftigen höheren Daseyns, in das jetzige minder vollkommene anerkennen, und wie der tief im innern unsers Wesens schlummernde Keim eines neuen Lebens, in gewißen Momenten, wo die Kräfte des jetzigen ruhen, deutlich hervorblickt. Hier ist es vorzüglich, wo alle die Erscheinungen, welche jenen Tatsachen eigentlich ihren Namen gegeben haben, die des thierischen Magnetismus, der Vorahndungen, Träume, Sympathien und dergleichen, zusammen eintreten werden" (p. 22). Pikulik, *Erzähler*, pp. 128–29, sees Margarethe's condition as a reflection of the distortion that comes when mankind despoils the Golden Age.

scious powers of the soul also allows her to diagnose Antonio's disease of the spirit: he has lost his identity during his illness, an identity that Margaretha helps him to find. In this regard, Antonio's search parallels Hoffmann the narrator's hunt for the real story behind the picture. It satisfies as well the desire of the present to recapture the lost harmonious identity of the past.

Much of Antonio's earlier life has a dream-like quality that makes him unsure of who he is and leaves him with the longing and frustrated feeling that he is missing something. Infected with the plague, he forgets much of his childhood. However, it comes back to him repeatedly in a dream, moments of extreme happiness that he refers to as "jenes unbekannte Eden" ["that unknown Eden"] (373). This characterization of childhood is also found in "Das fremde Kind," where the Golden Age theme is also prevalent.[356] During their childhood, Annunziata, now the Dogaressa, saved Antonio from a poisonous snake. Antonio realizes who it was only after he sees Annunziata during one of her rare public appearances. Up until this time, the memory of that incident was gone, and only the feeling of longing remained (383–84). When Antonio is fully aware of his own history, he involves himself very quickly in the main story, which is a chronicle of political events in Venice.[357] Antonio and his background help to make the reader understand historical events or figures; for example, why the Doge is executed or why the Dogaressa in the picture frame looked sad and full of longing. The plot to kill the Signorie, which ends in the execution of the Doge, arose because of ambition on the part of the plotters and abuse of power on the part of the Signorie, such as the framing and murder of Antonio's father. Antonio's past, his earlier meeting with Annunziata, also explains the reason for the Dogaressa's longing.

While the preceding analysis has pointed out ways in which "Doge" is connected with earlier stories and with discussions in the frame, there is one element that appeared in the picture that has a connection with "Bergwerke": the sea, which seems to symbolize the same sort of demonic might that the earth's interior did in "Bergwerke." Just as the sea appears at its most glorious in the October sunset, a monstrous storm arises that threatens the Doge's life (363). The demonic power

356. See Schubert, *Symbolik*, p. 12.
357. Ellinger, p. 24: ". . . die eindringliche Wirkung der chronikartigen Tatsachen wird durch die sie einschließenden Partien hervorgehoben."

of the sea is also apparent in its grip on Falieri, who feels himself married to the sea both before and after his marriage to Annunziata (365, 392). Falieri says that his watery bride keeps the ring he threw her deep in her bosom (392). Annunziata rightly recognizes the evil of the sea that, as the end of the story says, was jealous of her and destroyed her and Antonio (399). The points of comparison with "Bergwerke" are the attraction that both Fröbom and Falieri feel for the cold destructive forces of the deep (which in both cases are personifications of females), and the capacity of these natural forces to destroy humans who cross them in one way or another.[358]

The picture from the frame reappears near the end of the story (393); the reader now knows how to interpret it. Hoffmann's use of the picture motif at widely separated points in the story binds the frame more tightly to the inner story, but it also underscores in a dramatic way the importance of the subplot. When the reader first sees the picture, he cannot give the reasons for the facial expressions of the Doge and Dogaressa. Nor does he know if the two gondoliers, one of whom was the disguised Antonio, are of any significance. Like his characters (the painter and Margaretha) who can see past and future in their innermost souls, Hoffmann has in his terms glimpsed the reality behind the picture. This approach is a variation on the themes of "Fermate," "Artushof," and "Meister Martin" in regard to paintings, on the meaning of the grandmother's prophecy in "Meister Martin," and, in a lighter key, the real events behind the tableau in the park in "Fragment."

"Alte und neue Kirchenmusik"
(Old and New Church Music)

The distancing of threatening forces from the world of spirits that has been apparent in the insertion of "Doge," a story remote in time, continues in the frame of the fourth section, but in a different key.

---

358. Pikulik, *Erzähler*, pp. 127, 129–30, sees a parallel with "Falun," but also believes that the sea makes it possible for Antonio to be united with Annunziata, though it ultimately kills them. He cites numerous passages from Schubert's *Ansichten* about the connection between love and death.

The irrepressible Vinzenz, a physician who interests himself keenly in magnetism, and who is known for his wit, makes his first appearance. While there is much reference to various medical theories and their advocates,[359] the literate and witty conversation resembles that around a table in an inn more than it does a serious discussion, yet the presence of the hidden psychic world is never far away. Sylvester brings it to general discussion again when he mentions a performance he has just heard of a Beethoven mass. At this point, Hoffmann takes two earlier essays on music and divides them among the friends,[360] with different individuals representing various points of view discussed in the essays. This procedure supports the argument that the characters in the frame simply represent different aspects of a question or different ways of looking at the world that existed in Hoffmann's own mind.

The discussions in the frame about music are reminiscent of the earlier ones regarding opera texts and music that preceded "Dichter und Komponist" as well as those in that story itself. There are stylistic and thematic similarities among these three groups of theoretical discussions, two in the frame and those in "Dichter und Komponist." Just as Hoffmann considered the Romantic opera the best possible form because it gave the imagination the greatest freedom, so he also believes that Romantic church music, in which category he includes Mozart's Requiem, can also come from the soul (408). The value of music lies in its ability to bring the innermost being of the composer and listener in touch with infinity. Since this potential is important for all artists, Hoffmann's discussion of music contains significant material touching on inspiration and the nature of true art that have a bearing on various characters in the stories. One of the most telling sections in regard to the *Serapionsbrüder* is that dealing with Palestrina and liturgical music, since Palestrina has certain qualities in common with some of Hoffmann's characters and serves as a counterpoint to others. Music as we know it only became possible with the advent of Christianity, when it could open previously hidden worlds (410–11). During this great period of Christianity, when composers had the inner capacity

359. See Kruse, *Aufbau* 1, pp. 729–30; Segebrecht (Winkler), pp. 1069–70.
360. The two essays in question are Hoffmann's review of Beethoven's C Major Mass in Schnapp, *Schriften zur Musik*, E. T. A. Hoffmann (Winkler, Munich), pp. 154–69; published in 1813, and the essay "Alte und Neue Kirchenmusik," in Schnapp, *Schriften*, pp. 209–35, published in 1814. Kruse, *Aufbau* 1, gives the references for which essay appears in which part of the *Serapionsbrüder* version on pp. 731–32.

to grasp these secrets, there was a unique opportunity for a man like Palestrina, whose *frommes Gemüt* (devout soul) made it possible for him to be receptive to the harmonic love espoused by Christianity and to communicate this inner harmony in his music:

Die Liebe, der Einklang alles Geistigen in der Natur, wie er dem Christen verheißen, spricht sich aus im Akkord, . . . und so wird der Akkord, die Harmonie, Bild und Ausdruck der Geistergemeinschaft, der Vereinigung mit dem Ewigen, dem Idealen, das über uns thront und doch uns einschließt. (412)

The love, the harmony of everything spiritual in nature, as it is promised to the Christian, expresses itself in the chord, . . . and thus the chord, the harmony becomes the image and expression of the community of spirits, of the union with the eternal, the ideal that is enthroned above us and yet includes us.

The description of Palestrina and his music has strong affinities with that of Wolfram von Eschenbach in "Kampf der Sänger." Wolfram too had a devout nature (307) and the music that arose from his inner soul was in harmony with the remembered scenes of childhood in Switzerland. Because of this concord, Wolfram makes a music full of love that is so strong that it can besiege and overcome the Devil and all his works. Heinrich von Ofterdingen, Cardillac, and Count S in "Der unheimliche Gast" are out of harmony with nature, as the use of adjectives like *gellend* (shrill) and *zerrissen* (inwardly torn) to describe them indicates.

Palestrina's music hints at the presence of a Golden Age during this period. The childlike simplicity of composers at that time cannot be imitated again, but their visions appear in the works of Hayden, Mozart and Beethoven (414–15).[361] Hoffmann's stirring defense of modern music, which incorporates some of the visions of the past, offers a model for the *Serapionsbrüder* as well as for the characters in the stories (414). This communion with kindred spirits of the past, present and future is available to the characters in Hoffmann's stories, such as in "Artushof" and "Brautwahl," where revenants come to aid, and in some cases, hurt the heroes. The above quotation can also refer to those stories like "Kampf" and "Doge," where the past is made to come alive

---

361. Ernst Lichtenhahn, "Zur Idee des goldenen Zeitalters in der Musikanschauung E. T. A. Hoffmanns," in *Romantik in Deutschland,* ed. Richard Brinkmann (Stuttgart, 1978), pp. 502–12, p. 510. See also Dobat, *Musik,* pp. 78–89, for a discussion of the topic and the essay on church music.

before the audience in the frame. An artist, because of his striving, can become part of this *Geistergemeinschaft*.

Although the essays from which Hoffmann took this material were written well before he began the *Serapionsbrüder*, its inclusion at this point in the frame serves a valuable function. Since the beginning of Book 2, various forms of madness caused by outside forces have dominated the discussion. The power of liturgical music to set the soul in harmony with nature and with God is an effective defense against those other powers of the supernatural. Wolfram's music proves the strength of a composition that reflects this harmony of creation and a transcending love, just as Palestrina's does. The essays incorporated here offer also a sort of exemplary model in that they describe composers not only of the past but also the present whose art also shows glimpses of earlier harmonies. Against the backdrop of Palestrina and Mozart, the figures of Count S, Cardillac, and Magister Tinte appear in a sharpened relief of evil.

"Meister Martin der Küfner und seine Gesellen" (Tobias Martin, Master Cooper, and His Men)

The emphasis in Book 2 on past eras where art and life seemed in harmony continues with the story of "Meister Martin der Küfner und seine Gesellen," which takes place in an artisan's workshop and home in sixteenth-century Nürnberg. For Hoffmann, as for most Romantics, the sixteenth century was a part of that period that was more reflective of a Golden Age, conducive to the development of profound and good art, as we have seen in the previous remarks about Palestrina. "Meister Martin" depicts on the bourgeois level what Hoffmann described for Palestrina at the highest levels of artistic and religious expression. The narrator remarks on this harmony at the beginning of "Meister Martin," when even the artisans were not without a sense of the aesthetic (416–17).

In the permeation of one's life with art and a sense of unity in life, the world of Meister Martin, which is also filled with *Meistergesang*, is not unlike that of Wolfram von Eschenbach in "Kampf der Sänger."[362] Like "Kampf," "Meister Martin" opens with a preface to the reader, in which a tableau appears; but this scene, in contrast to that of the Wartburg, is a good burgher's house.[363] Hoffmann further underscores the connection between art and the artisan in this preface when he refers to Dürer, who reappears in the story, and mentions various artistic monuments in the city, some of which have a connection with Friedrich. Portraying a world in which "Kunst und Handwerk sich in wackerm Treiben die Hände boten" ["art and craft offered each other their hands in honest activity"] (417), Hoffmann holds up yet another model for the contemporary artist.

In addition to the direct links with "Alte und neue Kirchenmusik" and "Kampf der Sänger," "Meister Martin" also has direct ties with some of the stories of the first book including "Krespel," "Fermate," and "Artushof," where the relationship between artistic inspiration and human relationships was examined from different perspectives. The treatment of this theme in "Meister Martin" shows its domination of Hoffmann's thinking as well as his versatility in presenting a bourgeois context in which to view it. The source of this inspiration is Meister Martin's only child, Rosa. Three apprentices apparently devoted to perfecting their craft are actually serving time for Rosa. The unsuccessful dissembling of the apprentices in regard to their true vocation or position in life comes about as a result of Meister Martin's obstinacy in interpreting a mysterious song that Rosa's grandmother sang on her deathbed; Martin takes it to mean that he is to marry his daughter to no one but another master cooper.

Friedrich and Reinhold, the bronze caster and the artist masquerading as cooper's apprentices, offer two solutions to the problem of

362. Ellinger says that Nürnberg provided the opportunity both to include poetry of the mastersingers and to furnish a bourgeois counterpoint to "Kampf" (p. 30). Pikulik, *Erzähler*, sees the union between art and the bourgeois in the early sixteenth century as standing in sharp contrast to the situation in Hoffmann's own time (pp. 133–36).

363. Kruse, *Aufbau* 1, p. 737, describes the painting, now lost, that stirred Hoffmann's imagination—one of the workshop of a cooper with his beautiful daughter and two artisans.

The three stories that are set in earlier time periods, "Kampf," "Doge," and "Meister Martin," were all written in 1817–18. All three of them share as well a strong pictorial or tableau-like effect at the beginning. Painting as a source of inspiration for the story is discussed in the frame at the end (p. 471), where its tableau-like quality comes in for severe criticism.

whether one can marry the source of artistic inspiration and remain true to one's calling as an artist. The description of Friedrich and Reinhold as they meet on the outside of Nürnberg foreshadows the resolution of the story.[364] Friedrich is returning home to start his campaign to win Rosa's hand. He is "von stattlichem Ansehen" (of dignified appearance) and his eyes are full of longing as he gazes into the valley where Nürnberg lies (431). His singing voice, like that of Wolfram von Eschenbach, is *hell* and *lieblich* (bright, lovely) (432). This description contrasts sharply with that of Reinhold, whose eyes are friendly but dark and who wears a costume completely unsuited to a cooper's apprentice: a jerkin trimmed in velvet, a delicate ruff, a sword and a hat with a large feather. Reinhold's extraordinary bearing matches his costume (433). Demonic traces in his character betray his artistic calling to Hoffmann's reader: "widrig gellender Stimme, . . . fielen die tiefen Nachtschatten auf sein verblaßtes Antlitz und verzerrten die milden Züge des Jünglings auf recht häßliche Weise" (435) ["such an unpleasant, yelling tone, . . . the evening shadows fell on his pale face, and distorted his gentle features in such an unpleasant way"] (Bleiler, 252).[365] In Reinhold this mood is a temporary one but is still reminiscent of Heinrich von Ofterdingen, especially as it comes about, as Heinrich's moods did, as a result of his fear of losing the woman he loves from a distance.

The figure of Rosa, daughter of a well-to-do artisan and herself adept at running a home, might seem at first to be the sort of woman whom Hoffmann mocks, as he does Christiane Roos in "Artushof." But Rosa receives the imprimatur of the narrator when he first introduces her into the story, since he compares her with Dürer's madonnas (420–21). According to Hoffmann, Dürer's pictures come from a world where art and daily life can exist together in harmony. Rosa lives in this time and therefore she partakes of this harmony. The comparison with Dürer's work functions on another level as well: Dürer's art has brought Reinhold back to his native country and to Rosa as the incarnation of Dürer's art. Although his infatuation with Rosa made even his art seem worth something only as it enabled him to conjure her

364. Ellinger, p. 31, notes that the aristocrat disguised as an artisan who becomes an apprentice to win the master's daughter is an old motif from earlier comedies.

365. Cronin, *Gestalt* (pp. 90–91), makes an extended comparison between Reinhold in "Meister Martin" and Heinrich in "Der Kampf der Sänger."

image before him, he finally realized that he could never possess her in this life (462). This insight is similar to the end of "Fermate" and that of "Artushof." Reinhold wants Rosa only in his soul, where she can generate works of art. The hateful service in Martin's workshop, for which Reinhold was both too talented and not talented enough, symbolized the unsuitability of his desires to his calling: Reinhold realizes that painting is incompatible with domestic existence (471).

Yet, in an age where "Kunst und Handwerk sich in wackerm Treiben die Hände boten" ["art and craft offered each other their hands in honest activity"] (417), art may still marry inspiration. Therefore, Friedrich may finally marry Rosa. Though he has shown himself incapable of sacrificing his art for his long-standing love for Rosa (464), in an ironic twist of fate, through the art-bronze casting that has caused him to be cast out by Meister Martin, he is able to obtain Rosa. The chalice he makes for her as a parting gift fulfills the conditions of the prophetic song of Rosa's grandmother (467). Reinhold recognizes the possibility of the union of domestic bliss and certain art forms when he tells Friedrich on his wedding day, "Halt nur fest an deiner Kunst, die auch wohl mehr Hauswesen und dergleichen leiden mag, als die meinige" (471) ["stick to your own art; very probably it is better suited to domesticity and the like than mine"] (Bleiler, 284).[366] Like the musician Theodor in "Fermate" and the painter Traugott in "Artushof," Reinhold must keep the picture of his artistic inspiration within him and deny himself daily contact with her.

"Das fremde Kind"
(The Strange Child)

Like "Meister Martin" and many of the other stories in Book 2, "Das fremde Kind," written in 1817, takes place in a remote setting. But while "Kampf," "Doge," and "Meister Martin" occur at a specific

---

366. Feldges and Stadler, *Hoffmann*, note that artisans in sixteenth-century Augsburg and Nürnberg often had the status of artists, especially gold and silversmiths (pp. 176–177). Cronin, *Gestalt*, believes that Hoffmann's attitude toward fulfilled love for the artist shows signs of change in this story, amplifying the themes of "Der Kampf der Sänger." He cites the passage on pp. 467–68, which describes Friedrich's feelings of

period in history, the allegorical nature of "Das fremde Kind" lends it a timeless quality. Coming as it does in the collection's middle, this densely symbolic fairy tale includes several major themes of the *Serapionsbrüder*, such as the struggle between good and evil spiritual principles. Within the context of this large theme, which dominates the second and third volumes and appears in the first and fourth, there appear related motifs, such as that of the automat and of the Golden Age.

As in "Nußknacker," the drama unfolds in the world of the child, a world inaccessible in varying degrees to adults. The child's sensibility is closest to that of the artists, since a capacity for fantasy is common to both. In addition, the child is nearest to the innocence and harmony that the Romantics believed characterized the Golden Age in earlier civilizations.[367] The forces of light and harmony, represented by the strange child and his allies in the woods and air, struggle with the evil spirits of the gnome Pepser and his henchmen, Magister Tinte and the mechanical toys.

The inner division of the story, with three sections and five parts in each, reflects this struggle.[368] In the first section (472–84), the paradise-like existence of Thaddeus Brakel and the ominous visit of his grand relative sound the major themes in a muted key. Brakelheim is not the paradise of the Golden Age described in the second section, but it is as close as one can be now. The visit of the cousin from court seems merely disquieting and not the fatal threat which it is. In the second section (484–97), the strange child and his mother's world dominate. The child, for brief moments, opens the children's eyes to the harmony between man and nature in an earlier time. Felix and Christlieb can hear flowers and trees talking and feel at one with their beloved

---

being in harmony with nature after he has won Rosa. Although Cronin does not mention it, this passage describing Friedrich is very reminiscent of Schubert's ideas about the hidden unity of nature. If Cronin's supposition is correct, a changing attitude toward love in Hoffmann could have come about because of his interest in Schubert. Wittkop-Ménardeau's verdict on "Meister Martin," *Hoffmann* (p. 129), seems a little severe if one looks at the story from the perspective of the frame and its position in the sequence of stories. See Pikulik, *Erzähler*, p. 136.

367. See Urs Orland von Planta, *E. T. A. Hoffmanns Märchen "Das fremde Kind"* (Bern, 1958), p. 76. See also Müller "Nachwort," p. 114, who discusses the figure of the child. Marianne Thalmann, *Das Märchen und die Moderne* (Stuttgart, 1961), p. 88, dismisses the story as a refugee from ". . . den überwärmten Bürgerstuben."

368. Both Planta, *Märchen*, p. 113, and Hans von Müller, "Nachwort zu den Märchen der Serapionsbrüder," *Gesammelte Aufsätze*, p. 120, note the tripartite division.

woods.[369] The child also tells them of his mother's world wrecked by an evil spirit (see esp. 492–93), the gnome Pepser. He ruined the work of the good spirits, poured a black liquid over all of the natural beauties of his mother's kingdom and changed into a monstrous fly when he planned to assume his rule over her realm.

Immediately following the middle section, which portrayed the spirit world at its height in the Golden Age and the subsequent invasion, comes the arrival of Magister Tinte to begin the third and final section where the confrontation between good and evil takes place in individual lives (497–510). The battle described in the second part continues for the Brakels, just as it does for individuals in "Bergwerke," "Nußknacker," "Kampf," "Nachricht," "Scuderi," "Königsbraut," "Spukgeschichte," "Vampirismus," and "Der unheimliche Gast." The invasion of one's life by forces from the spirit world, which disrupts so many lives in the other inner stories, occurs here and in "Nußknacker" in a fairy tale; this invasion defuses the threat on one level and yet, particularly in the case of "Das fremde Kind," makes the struggle between fantasy and evil forces a possibility for each sensitive individual.

A closer examination of symbolic elements in the story will establish more specific ties to other parts of the *Serapionsbrüder*. As we have seen, there are two major groups in the story, the strange child and his companions versus Pepser and his allies. Each group has its own landscape and its own accoutrements that are suited to its mission. The idyllic Brakelheim and the realm of the strange child differ in the degree of harmony and number of spirits and fairies present but they are closely related.[370] In the beginning of the story "Der Herr von Brakel auf Brakelheim" (The Lord Brakel at Brakelheim), the description of the Brakels and their estate already sets them apart from the life at a court and, as such, has a foreshadowing function. The friendly atmosphere, established by luxuriant welcoming foliage and voices that seemed to call from the crystal-clear windows, beckoned to the stranger (473). This unassuming little house surrounded by talking trees and grape-

---

369. Planta, *Märchen*, notes (p. 73) that the appearance of the child accompanied by music is similar to that of the *Wetterharfe*, which figured prominently in "Automate" (p. 485).

370. Planta, *Märchen* (pp. 76–77). Pikulik, *Erzähler*, pp. 145–46, says that the realm of the fairy queen can only be considered a limited portrayal of the Golden Age, since there is pain there as well.

vines, as well as a well-satisfied resident stork, shows a deep harmony with nature; it stands in sharp contrast to a palace where one feels stared at by the dead eyes in stone figures as he feels the ice-cold air coming from within (473). This description of the palace foreshadows the imminent arrival of Count Brakel and his family, who inject a false atmosphere into a previously happy world. Felix and Christlieb, Thaddeus's children, are much like their unpretentious father was as a child and are happiest outside in their beloved woods (474–75). Their innocence and love of nature contrast sharply with the character of Cyprianus von Brakel's children, Hermann and Adelgunde. Like the palace's statues with dead eyes and like the toys they bring as gifts, they are mechanical and lifeless (". . . mit . . . den trüben schläfrigen Augen blöd und scheu hervorkuckte . . . " [". . . peeked stupidly and fearfully from his dull and sleepy eyes . . . "] (476), with a great fear of living creatures, including Felix, Christlieb, and Sultan (476, 479).

The toys that Hermann and Adelgunde present to their country cousins are much like they are, overcivilized and incapable of surviving in the woods or having any relationship with living creatures there. Their incongruence becomes immediately apparent when the noises they make sound so ugly and dead in comparison with the birds in the forest. The hunter can only shoot at his target, not at anything else. Felix sees the similarity of the toys with their donors when he says the *Harfenmännlein* is like Cousin Plus Fours (482). Even though the toys seem ugly and are useless in the woods, like Pepser and Magister Tinte, they are powerful when their overlords are in control.[371] Like the automaton, even with their dead eyes they can attack the children (506). The similarities between the toys in this story and the musical machines and the talking Turk in "Automate" are quite striking, since in both cases the creatures are apparently lifeless; yet, as the toys themselves say, they are in contact with a higher power, ". . . wir sind die gehorsa-

371. Melanie Archangeli, in an unpublished paper, "Magister Tinte: The Evil Force in 'Das Fremde Kind,' " says: "The toys . . . destroy the beauty and serenity of the woods in much the same way that the gnome Pepser will attempt to destroy the fairy kingdom and Magister Tinte will continue to try to bend the minds and wills of the children in the direction of reason and order and away from imagination and nature." (p. 8). See pp. 481–85 of text. In this sense, the toys function as a prefiguration of the negative effects of Pepser and Tinte. Feldges and Stadler, *Hoffmann*, (p. 98), say that the revenge of the toys shows that at that time, no citizen could withdraw from the grasp of temporal powers without suffering for it.

men Zöglinge des Herrn Magister Tinte . . . " ["we are Magister Tinte's obedient pupils"] (506) and as such, they can endanger the lives of those connected with the good spirits.

The threat to the innocent paradise in which the less noble Brakels live appears in a series of similar characters: Cyprianus von Brakel, a thin, over-enlightened man, the gnome Pepser, and Magister Tinte, each dominating the respective sections of the story in which they appear. Pepser, who is the key figure among the three, is one of the *Elementargeister* (elemental spirits), one of the gnomes who live in the earth.[372] All of the other three, the spirits of air, fire, and water, serve the mother of the strange child (495) and open the beauties of nature to childlike hearts. Pepser, alias Pepasilio, alias Magister Tinte, has the opposite effect on the realm of fantasy. Like Magister Tinte, he calls himself a scholar, treats the children sadistically,[373] drags the tail of the magic pheasant down, and covers all the realm with a disgusting black liquid that kills all of its creatures (495–96).

Pepser, like all spirits, can change his shape easily;[374] as he prepares to snatch leadership from the fairy queen, he becomes a monstrous fly with "abscheulichem Summen und Brausen" ["an abominable buzzing and raging"] (496). Hoffmann builds in much more detail in regard to insect imagery in the description of Magister Tinte;

Der Mann mochte kaun mehr als einen halben Kopf höher sein als Felix, dabei war er aber untersetzt; nur stachen gegen den sehr starken breiten Leib die kleinen ganz dünnen Spinnenbeinchen seltsam ab. Der unförmliche Kopf war beinahe viereckig zu nennen, und das Gesicht fast gar zu häßlich, denn außerdem, daß zu den dicken braunroten Backen und dem breiten Maule die viel

372. Kruse, *Aufbau* 1, pp. 745–46; Planta, *Märchen*, p. 630.

373. Planta, *Märchen*, p. 61, notes an incident in *Symbolik des Traumes* (p. 118) that he believes stood behind the incident in the story in which Magister Tinte stabs the children with a hidden needle when they shake hands with him (p. 498): "Ein sonst stiller, gleichgültiger Junge, den ich in den ersten Monaten meiner Praxis an einer Art von Veitstanz zu behandeln hatte, war, sobald der Anfall kam, wie von einem boshaften Teufel besessen. Die Augen blickten wild und tückisch, . . . Jetzt mußten alle Messer u. dgl. entfernt werden, auf die hinterlistigste Weise suchte er die Umstehenden zu verletzen, und wenn er nichts anders haben konnte, versteckte er wenigstens eine Nadel unter eine Blume, womit er seinen kleinen Bruder, als wenn er ihn wollte an die Blume riechen lassen, listig tückisch stach" (pp. 118–19, Schubert, *Symbolik*). It is worth noting that Schubert includes this incident in a discussion of the dark side of human nature, including madness.

374. Planta, *Märchen*, p. 64, notes the characteristic common to all spirits, that of being able to change form.

zu lange spitze Nase gar nicht passen wollte, . . . Übrigens hatte der Mann eine pechschwarze Perücke auf den viereckichten Kopf gestülpt, war auch von Kopf bis Fuß pechschwarz gekleidet . . . (497)

The man could hardly have been more than half a head taller than Felix, and, on top of that, he was stocky. Only his small, and altogether very thin, spider legs contrasted strangely with his rather broad, strong body. His unshapely head could best be described as nearly square and his face almost too ugly; not only did the pointed nose that was much too long not match the chubby brownish-red cheeks and the broad mouth . . . Furthermore, the man had a jet-black wig clapped on his square head and he was also dressed black as pitch from head to foot.

This description, coming as it does directly after the story of Pepser's depredations, lets the reader know that Pepser has invaded Brakelheim, a fact the strange child confirms (501). Subsequent descriptions of Tinte, as he comes back from the fateful excursion into the woods with the children, show the same insect parallels with Pepser (502, 504). The choice of a fly as the creature to represent the essential nature of an evil spirit probably has several sources.[375] According to Schubert in *Symbolik des Traumes*, the destructive evil principle manifests itself in the insect world:

Die Klasse der Insecten und zum Theil die der Würmer, sind schon von Mehreren als später entstanden, als jünger denn die übrige Natur betrachtet worden. In der That gründet sich das Daseyn dieser Thiere größtenteils auf den Tod, auf die Verwesung und Zerstörung der früheren Natur . . . [376]

The class of the insects and to some extent, that of the worms, has been regarded by many as having developed later, as being younger than the rest of nature. Indeed, for the most part, the existence of these animals has its foundation in death, in the decay and destruction of earlier nature.

In Schubertian terms, Hoffmann's choice of an insect as the destroyer of an ideal landscape is entirely appropriate.[377]

The embodiment of the evil principle found in the insect-like Pepser-Tinte shows parallels with characters in other stories: Torbern,

375. Kruse, *Aufbau* 1, p. 746, notes that many cultures commonly believe that an evil spirit takes the form of a fly. Planta thinks that Hoffmann was influenced by Schubert's beliefs about insects and their inferior and destructive natures. See note 165. See also Pikulik, *Erzähler*, p. 142, for other sources.

376. Schubert, *Symbolik*, p. 41.

377. Planta, *Märchen*, p. 69.

Cardillac, Count S, Mauserinks, Professor X, and Nasias.[378] All of these figures in varying degrees represent destructive forces that can only be vanquished by the pure in heart. That is why Lothar says in advance that his fairy tale is "fromm" (pious, 472). In both fairy tales, though the struggles against evil seem to have cosmic implications, there are also ironic touches in the portrayal of each battle—the mice's addiction to bacon and the chasing of Magister Tinte with a fly swatter. In the other stories mentioned above, which are not fairy tales and where the conflict seems more local, these humorous touches are absent. They seem to help give the fairy tales an additional touch of irreality.

Another link with the frame and the inner stories is Magister Tinte and Cyprianus von Brakel's roles as the embodiment of Philistinism and the deleterious effects of too much reason. The threatening presence of the Philistine appeared in the frame of the first book and the "Artushof" story, as well as in the "Fragment aus dem Leben." The descriptions of the dead and useless knowledge, a specialty of the city children and Tinte as well as the black liquid they pour on fantasy, show the destructive effects of the philistine and the Enlightenment on the world of the child and the Golden Age.[379]

As in "Bergwerke," the struggle with the forces of the earth ends in death for one and hardship for the survivors. Planta has suggested that Thaddeus Brakel died ultimately as a result of being tempted away from a paradisiacal state by court sophistries.[380] Thaddeus and his wife, overcome in their admiration of the mechanical erudition of Hermann and Adelgunde (478–79), allow Cyprianus to engage a teacher, thereby introducing the destructive principle into their family circle. Such behavior is typical of the *Obrist* in "Der unheimliche Gast" and

378. Planta, *Märchen*, pp. 56–60, lists a number of qualities he believes Tinte, Cardillac, and Hoffmann share. The textual comparisons between Cardillac and Tinte are more convincing than the ones he cites, which place Hoffmann in the same category. Planta notices a similarity between Drosselmeier and Tinte, pp. 52ff., but he overlooks the fact that Drosselmeier is on Marie's side in the final analysis and is not a supporter of evil.

Ellinger, pp. 20–21, sees Drosselmeier in a much more positive light, comparing him with Thaddeus von Brakel. Both older men know how to recognize the longing for fantasy in children.

379. See Ellinger, p. 20; Planta, p. 40; Hans von Müller, "Nachwort," p. 119; Archangeli, pp. 6–7. Pikulik, *Erzähler*, p. 146, believes that the ink symbolizes the Enlightenment's urge to describe things in a manner that destroys their essence.

380. Planta, *Märchen*, p. 66.

Ottmar in "Der Magnetiseur." If that is so, there is a certain parallel with Elis Fröbom, who dies because he, too, was lured by a false vision.

The ending of the story, with the death of Thaddeus, the destruction of Brakelheim and the impoverishment of the family is quite different from that of "Nußknacker". These two fairy tales are in many ways mirror images of each other. In "Nußknacker," the light and dark sides of the fantastic world both appear but evil is vanquished by good to the advantage of life in the real world. In "Das fremde Kind," the children experience both the sublime and the ghastly aspects of the fantastic realm. However, the evil side predominates in the disastrous effects the dark side has on the country Brakels. This mirror image quality shows itself most clearly in the figures of Drosselmeier and Tinte. Drosselmeier wants to deepen and enrich Marie's perception through her contact with the fantastic realm, a bond that looks as if it will bring her happiness with Drosselmeier's nephew. Tinte wants to destroy the children's world and use the fantastic realm as a place where horrors so paralyse the children that their life in the real world is made melancholy and difficult.[381] Like Leonard in "Die Brautwahl," Drosselmeier is ultimately a force for good, while Pepser/Tinte spreads death and destruction.

The conclusion of "Das fremde Kind" is appropriate to the position of the fairy tale in the narrative sequence of the *Serapionsbrüder*. Seen in the context of inner story sequence, "Das fremde Kind" appears just before the third book, which contains an uninterrupted series of stories showing various aspects of the evil destructive principle. The ending of this fairy tale serves as both a warning and a foreshadowing of the power of this principle, which Lothar himself describes at the beginning of the third volume (515).

While the friends praise Lothar's second fairy tale as "ein reineres Kindermärchen" (a fairy tale more suitable for children) than the first, Sylvester also comments that Lothar has a little devil that sits on his shoulder and whispers the strangest things into his ear (510–11). This mention of the devil, although in a lighthearted manner, foreshadows the preoccupation with the devil that characterizes the frame and stories of the first part of the third book, just as it harks back to the representatives of the evil principle in "Das fremde Kind."

381. See Beardsley, *Meister*, pp. 163–67.

Book III
Frame: "Nachricht aus dem Leben eines bekannten Mannes" (Information about the Life of a Well-Known Man)

The sad and discontented tone in the beginning of the third book arises from the fact that the *Serapionsbrüder* have gone their separate ways; Theodor lies barely recovered from a serious illness, and Lothar, who has tended him, seems to be in a rather severe state of depression. This mood accurately foreshadows the theme of the subsequent inner stories; the major subject of conversation, the Devil, whose minions Pepser and Tinte have just left the stage, also points to those narratives.

Although Theodor suffered greatly from his illness, he remained in a much more optimistic frame of mind than Lothar. Theodor's good spirits helped him to overcome his sickness[382] while Lothar, in the sloughs of despond, read stories about the Devil in old chronicles. Lothar's preoccupation with earlier history may have more significance than a facile justification for the "Nachricht aus dem Leben eines bekannten Mannes": his interest may also be due to his perilous emotional state. In times when the established order of existence seems threatened for Hoffmann's characters, the demons become stronger.[383] Lothar's depressed state led him to scorn existence (515); he notes that when his depression was bad, the Devil appeared to him during sleepless nights (519). The same mixture of irony and fear we find in "Nachricht" is also apparent in Lothar's remarks that he feels horror at the Devil's presence yet is ready to use him as an assistant in his writing.[384]

The lighter tones in this story and in "Brautwahl" leaven some of the seriousness that usually surrounds treatment of this theme, espe-

---

382. Theodor's mental attitude during his sickness seems to show some Schubertian influences, since the insight he reached during his illness was in itself a kind of medicine provided by the eternal power (p. 517). See Schubert, *Ansichten*, p. 340.

383. Mühlher, *Deutsche Dichter*, p. 436. Mühlher also notes that the more corrupt or desperate a man is, the less he is able to tell whether it is an angel or a devil that confronts him (pp. 438–39).

384. Kruse, *Aufbau* 2, p. 602.

cially in later sections of Book III.[385] The combination of the dreadful and the ironic titillates the reader, as Lothar observes in the frame after the story is finished (526). This reaction, occasioned by brushes with the supernatural, has similarities with the pleasant shivering to which Dagobert refers at the beginning of "Der unheimliche Gast" (601). In "Nachricht" and "Brautwahl," either the period or characters from the remote past distance the threat, a technique used effectively in "Kampf der Sänger" and "Doge und Dogaresse." The exact date of the reference to the Hafftitz chronicle at the beginning of "Nachricht" adds verisimilitude (519, 520). The first part of the account seems to disarm in that the reader sees the Devil as an essentially harmless old gentleman, who comes to weddings, gives presents, and dances in spite of his lame foot. In the second part of the story, he is the main character, revealing his true nature.[386] Barbara Roloffin's behavior when she sees the stranger at the Lütkens's house is strikingly similar to that of Marguerite, Angelika's French companion in "Der unheimliche Gast." In both cases, a striking change is apparent in their appearance and behavior (522–23, 613). Marguerite, like Barbara, is under the influence or control of evil forces, as are Count S and Cardillac. The full extent of the relationship between Roloffin and the Devil becomes clear only at the end. At that point, she has confessed to witchcraft and been rescued by the stranger, who turns himself into a bat for the occasion. This terrifying scene is all the more effective because of the slightly ridiculous nature of the stranger at the beginning. In its treatment of inexplicable phenomena, "Nachricht" harks back to "Bergwerke" and "Spukgeschichte" and ahead to "Erscheinungen." The Devil-like figures have parallels in "Brautwahl," "Der unheimliche Gast," "Fräulein Scuderi," and "Vampirismus."

385. Kenneth Negus, in *E. T. A. Hoffmann's Other World* (Philadelphia, 1965), compares Hoffmann's Devil figures in *Elixiere des Teufels* and Lothar's comments at this point in the frame and sees a consistent development of Hoffmann's Devil figures from the wholly sinister to the agreeably threatening (pp. 92–94). Whether or not there was, as Negus maintains, a "decrease in Hoffmann's obsession with satanic figures" (p. 94), consideration of the frame as a whole in Book Three does seem to indicate that Hoffmann used the figure of the Devil as part of his constellation of evil in this book and that the distancing techniques afforded by the use of a sixteenth-century chronicle (noted also by Negus, pp. 92–93) are similar to those used elsewhere in the *Serapionsbrüder*.

386. Olbrich, "E. T. A. Hoffmann und der deutsche Volksglaube," pp. 73–75, notes that Hoffmann often embodies this evil principle in a human figure, who appears suddenly in the family circle. This unexpected appearance is characteristic of the Devil in "Nachricht" as well as Count S in "Der unheimliche Gast."

The *Serapionsbrüder* continue their discussion of supernatural forces in the frame. As has been the case in the sections on magnetism and madness, the characters in the frame like to include personal anecdotes about the people they have known, such as the second account here of individuals in league with the Devil (528–29). As in the stories about madness and magnetism, it is Theodor who provides the personal experience.[387] This story, like the preceding one, has an old woman who consorts with the Devil; she lures the nobleman (on whose estate the black arts were to flourish) into her power by promising him success in love (529). As in the first story, the full horror of what has taken place comes at the end, as they go into the room where the face of a child in red outline appears. Theodor's eyewitness account, like that of Cyprian in "Spukgeschichte," increases its effect on the *Serapionsbrüder*; it makes the ensuing stories that deal with heinous crimes committed by maddened or bewitched people more credible.

The connection of madness with those who make pacts with the Devil (527) relates this part of the frame to earlier sections, such as in "Kampf." The lure of a bargain with the Devil, whether for material gain or supernatural power or knowledge, places an individual at risk for both madness and criminal acts. While Elis Fröbom and Heinrich von Ofterdingen fell under the power of satanic creatures, neither was guilty of crime. In Book III, many of the stories deal with this additional aspect of madness, for which Hoffmann's own background in the law and his extensive reading in medical literature set the stage.

Theodor's anecdote has an unshakeable quality of the uncanny about it, which the brothers are glad to shake off as they again return to the theme of a rather agreeable German devil. At this point Hoffmann begins a literary evaluation of the best of the recent devil stories: Fouqué's "Galgenmännlein" (Mandrake). This literary discussion serves several functions, one of them being transition from the unease brought on by Theodor's recounting of his experience to the sunnier atmosphere of the "Brautwahl." The frame conversation about the Devil in novellas immediately precedes Hoffmann's own story about one of Satan's minions and a good spirit. It also continues the emphasis

---

387. Kruse, *Aufbau* 2, pp. 603–4, and Segebrecht, pp. 1078–79, cite a letter Hoffmann wrote to Hippel in May 14, 1804, in which he speaks of a visit to Lazienki, the palace of the last Polish king, Stanislas II, who had to abdicate during the third division of Poland. Kruse relates the reference to "verworrene Schicksale" to this king (p. 604).

from Book II on the value of reworking old chronicles, using Kleist's "Michael Kohlhaas" as an example, and foreshadowing Hoffmann's continued use of Hafftitz. As in the preceding discussion of Satan and his role as a literary aide-de-camp, Hoffmann again holds the combination of amusement with a slight shiver up for admiration, a combination that picks up the tone of the earlier frame discussion of the Devil and foreshadows the content of "Brautwahl".

"Die Brautwahl" (Choosing a Bride)

The clash of good and evil forces, depicted in "Das fremde Kind" with the child and Tinte-Pepser, here takes place, not in a symbolic paradisiacal atmosphere, but in the real world of Berlin. *Münzjude* Lippold, a Satanic figure, confronts Meister Leonhard, who seems able to defang him. The major difference between these revenants and figures from the spirit world, such as Pepser, is that the revenants are historical figures, not creatures of fantasy. The relationship between their recorded deaths and their reappearance in the present is never explained.[388]

Meister Leonhard, who is firmly in control of events in the story, immediately offers several clues about whose side he is on. Although his eyes flash, often a sign of evil in Hoffmann, his forehead is free and open; some of his clothes date from the sixteenth century (which previous stories in the work have shown as a time when art and artisan were in total harmony) and he announces that he is an artist (535–36). Throughout the story, the reader is never quite sure what to expect from him, since the range of his capacities is never totally clear. It is difficult also to know who he really is, as he himself admits (589).[389]

388. Kuttner, *Individualitätsprobleme*, p. 66.

389. Kruse, *Aufbau* 2, p. 611, notes that Hoffmann presents the Swiss goldsmith Leonhard Thurneysser zum Thurn in a different light than did Hafftitz, who portrayed him as a charlatan. Leonhard was a physician, chemist, alchemist, astrologer, printer, and collector of plants and minerals. As the personal physician of Johann Georg von Brandenburg in the late sixteenth century, he soon became well known among the crowned heads of Europe. See Hans von Müller, "Nachwort zu Hoffmanns 'Brautwahl,' " pp. 257–58, who reprints the section from Hafftitz's chronicle.

This unknown aspect of his character helps heighten narrative tension; whether Leonhard is telling stories about sixteenth-century events in Berlin (540, 542), outwitting the *Münzjude* (544), or removing the green from Tusmann's face (581), he is confronting Edmund, Tusmann, Albertine and the privy councillor with worlds whose existence they only barely suspect or of which they are totally ignorant. Leonhard wants what is best for the figures whose lives he influences; he even helps them towards goals that he himself thinks are poor ones, such as Edmund's proposed engagement to Albertine. His goal is not personal gain or wealth, but the advancement of art. In contrast to Leonhard, who was in the sixteenth century an accomplished goldsmith so admired at court in Berlin that he had to leave, *Münzjude* Lippold has aligned himself with Satanic forces in order to obtain money and control (542).[390] All his efforts in magic are to gain gold and influence and still continue in that direction (544, 594–96).

The revenants raise in a particularly striking way the question of what remains from the past, since the revenant is a historical figure that the poet who sees with the inner eye can reinterpret. He belongs in his period, yet wears some modern clothes just as Leonhard does (535).[391] Not only his dress, but also his memory, mark him as an intermediary figure. What for other men is history is for Leonhard personal reminiscence; for that reason, he can talk about Edmund's childhood in much the same manner as he talks about the history of the city hall tower.[392] Precisely because figures like Leonhard are anchored in history, they show some of the unsuspected potential in human existence,[393] which as we have seen, is a major theme in the *Serapionsbrüder*. For this reason the narrator insists on their historical illusions and their interaction with the characters, such as Leonhard with Edmund in the latter's early childhood. The unknown dimensions of human existence that the reader glimpses in Leonhard and Lippold foreshadow the strange powers that Count S and Cardillac have. Lippold is the first cousin of those two men, while Leonhard (who, like

---

390. See Müller, "Nachwort zu Hoffmanns 'Brautwahl,' " pp. 253–54; Kruse, *Aufbau* 2, p. 608.

391. Kuttner, *Individualitätsprobleme*, pp. 68 and 69.

392. Kuttner, *Individualitätsprobleme*, p. 69. She adds that one reason Leonhard can make changes in the lives of Edmund and Tusmann is that both are interested in the past (p. 69).

393. Kuttner, *Individualitätsprobleme*, p. 69.

Cardillac, is a goldsmith) stands in sharp contrast to him. Neither his art nor his traffic with higher powers has destroyed his inner spirit.

In order to achieve their goals, both of the revenants have a large stock of magic powers.[394] These efforts leave no character untouched; Tusmann, the prototype of a Prussian pedant and bureaucrat, suffers the most, though his old school friend, Melchior Voßwinkel, has terrified moments as well. If the fantastic can impinge on even such tightly laced lives as theirs, then it can affect anyone. While a Tusmann may never be weaned enough from his pedantry to wander in the realm of fantasy, an Edmund can be. Hoffmann, speaking through Theodor, justifies the intrusion of fantasy, the most magnificent part of life because it is accessible to everyone if firmly grounded in day-to-day existence (599). Since the Tusmanns and Voßwinkels of this world, like the philistine in the frame and in "Artushof," may have too little fantasy, they seldom climb this ladder into the fantastical realm without external pressure being applied, such as that by Leonhard.

This anchoring in life, in day-to-day existence, which was apparent in the historical references (540, 542) in the biographies of the revenants, shows up in the characters as well, all of whom have some tangible connection with Berlin. In this regard, "Brautwahl" has more in common with "Nußknacker" (where the Stahlbaums seem to be part of the everyday world) than it does with the symbolic characters of "Das fremde Kind." The profusion of prosaic elements, which characters like Leonhard and the *Münzjude* encounter, figures in Lothar's remarks in the frame about including fairy tale elements in a contemporary story (599). Many of the characters who confront the fantastic in everyday life have counterparts in other stories, such as the young painter Edmund Lohsen,[395] who resembles Theodor in "Die Fermate" und Traugott in "Artushof." Like them, he ultimately does not marry the source of his inspiration, Albertine Voßwinkel, an above-average representative of upper-middle-class young ladies in Berlin, who

394. Kuttner, *Individualitätsprobleme,* p. 66 notes that generally these figures were seen as typical of Hoffmann's mixing of fairy-tale elements with prosaic ones, but she sees a deeper significance in the questions they raise about what is permanent in the transitoriness of life (pp. 66–69). For discussion of the mixing of fairy-tale and everyday scenes, see Hans von Müller, "Nachwort zu Hoffmanns 'Brautwahl,' " pp. 223–29. See also Pikulik, *Erzähler,* p. 154.

395. Hans von Müller, "Nachwort zu Hoffmanns 'Brautwahl,' " pp. 239–44, discusses the painter, Wilhelm Hensel, whose name appears in an anagram in "Brautwahl" as Lehsen. See also Kruse, *Aufbau* 2, p. 608.

shines at *Teegesellschaften* (social teas) and loves clothes (553). Like Christine Roos and Pauline Asling in "Artushof" and "Fragment," she comes from a bourgeois family with a decidedly philistine father. However, Hoffmann does not describe her with the same kind of scathing prose he reserved for Christine Roos. This gentler treatment may be due to her capacity to appreciate art (550–51), which leads her to admire Edmund's paintings and be somewhat knowledgeable about poetry.[396]

In its mixing of supernatural and prosaic elements, "Brautwahl" has much in common with another Berlin story, "Fragment," which appears in the first book of this work. In that story, the spirit was the spinster aunt who had been deserted on her wedding day. In both instances, the involvement of the supernatural world with the day-to-day ultimately has no bad effects. Both stories come at the beginning of a short series of threatening tales; "Fragment" appears before "Artushof" and "Bergwerke," and "Brautwahl" comes before "Der unheimliche Gast" and "Fräulein Scuderi." As we have seen in the discussion of "Fragment," Hoffmann is able to vary the tone and the level at which he conveys his ideas and fears about the unseen subconscious world. He also seems to like to place a relatively happy story directly before stories of a more threatening nature.

"Der unheimliche Gast"
(The Uncanny Guest)

The advent of late evening in the frame sets the scene for "Der unheimliche Gast" as the *Serapionsbrüder* go inside for warmth and a restorative cup of tea. Signs that the ensuing story will be one dealing with dark forces appear in the first paragraph, with the description of the late autumn storm.[397] The immediate connection with the frame

---

396. Müller, "Nachwort zu Hoffmanns 'Brautwahl,' " sees Albertine as a mixture of Christina Roos and Felizitas, p. 225.

397. Conrad, *Angst*, pp. 80–81, sees these elements—tea kettle, storm, fire, discussion of ghost stories, pleasant shivers—as literary furniture borrowed from the Gothic novel. Conrad misinterprets the end of the story when he says that the pleasant shudders of horror are the subject of conversation so that he can substantiate his claim that the end represents philistine blindness to the existential threat. The reference to horror made

and previous inner stories are the discussion of spirits, ghost tales, and the "angenehme Frösteln" (pleasant shivering), (601) one feels upon hearing them. These conversation topics pick up on the discussion in the frame of the beginning and repeat on an inner story level the real situation of the *Serapionsbrüder* at the beginning of Book V (350). However, this apparently innocent enjoyment is not as harmless as it may seem. Dagobert notes it may be a lure that brings them into the uncanny spirit world (606). From the spirit world it is not far to the power of foreign psychic influences, especially magnetism, to which Dagobert alludes in discussing Angelika's dreams (608). At this point, the larger connection among spirits, magnetism, dreams, and evil forces begins to emerge and gradually dominate the story, involving the ensuing madness that can come as a result of preoccupation with these strange forces. This interrelationship affects the count, Moritz, Bogislav, Marguerite, and Angelika to varying degrees, depending on whether they are active practitioners or passive victims.

The previous discussion of magnetism in the *Serapionsbrüder* frame showed that Hoffmann's attitude towards it was ambivalent: he valued it as a means to probe the outer reaches of consciousness, but feared its potential for evil in the hands of an unscrupulous manipulator.[398] "Der unheimliche Gast," the various sections of the *Serapionsbrüder* frame, and the earlier story "Der Magnetiseur" provide important information on the development of Hoffmann's feeling on the subject. In the frame at the end of "Der unheimliche Gast," Theodor notes the similarity between the two stories, saying that the strange count resembles Alban in "Magnetiseur" (640).[399] An examination of the structure of both stories helps clarify the function of "Der unheimliche Gast" within the *Serapionsbrüder* frame. This analysis also clarifies the role of the frame anecdotes and discussions, which bear some resemblance to the conversations in "Magnetiseur."

As we have often seen, the frame provides anecdotes from real life, anecdotes that function as parallels or counterpoint to the novellas. The case histories in the frame depict the phenomenon of magnetism either as the happy hunting ground of charlatans or as an effective but

---

at the end of the story occurs in Angelika and Moritz remembering the events that led to their dreadful experiences (p. 639).

398. Kruse, *Aufbau* 2, notes the connection between the frame conversations at the beginning of the third part of the *Serapionsbrüder*, p. 621.

399. Kruse, *Aufbau* 2, pp. 620–21; Conrad, p. 90.

unsettling tool in the hands of an intelligent and virtuous doctor. "Der Magnetiseur" and "Der unheimliche Gast" show by contrast the evil that Faust-like figures who have sold their souls to the black powers can wreak through those powers over the souls of men. Hoffmann's choice of the novella rather than the frame anecdote to portray the darker side of magnetism affords certain artistic advantages. The dangers inherent in this "fremden geistigen Prinzip" can be portrayed most dramatically in fiction, where the reader can identify with the victim without feeling immediately threatened himself.

Unlike "Der unheimliche Gast," "Der Magnetiseur" offers long theoretical discussions of magnetism and shows, as do the anecdotes in the *Serapionsbrüder* frame, its potential for good.[400] The three major points of view that the discussion of magnetism in the *Serapionsbrüder* frame adumbrated are all present in the minds of the characters of "Der Magnetiseur." Because this novella depends for its effect on the differing views the baron, Ottmar, and Bickert hold with great consistency, there is less of the objective discussion found in the *Serapionsbrüder* description. The baron is against all manifestations of magnetism because it reminds him of an incident during his military career in which a Danish major, one of his professors at the military academy, was supposed to be in league with the Devil. This major tries to get the baron into his power by appearing at his bedside in what the baron believed was a dream. Events occurring after he awakens indicate that it was probably not a dream, that the major did indeed sit beside him as he slept in the hopes of gaining power over his soul (146–47). Like Count S in "Der unheimliche Gast," the major dies a violent death, when he planned to be in control of his victim. The baron's dream comes early in the story and foreshadows the events with Alban, who may be the major (176–77). It also motivates the baron's attempts to defend himself from further attack by men connected with psychic forces.

Ottmar, the baron's son, must be an unequivocal defender of magnetism, since, without his zeal, Alban would never have made his way into the baron's house. Ottmar's exuberant, uncritical espousal of magnetism at the story's beginning introduces aspects of the new knowledge that Hoffmann found attractive and that also come under

---

400. E. T. A. Hoffmann, *Fantasie- und Nachtstücke*, pp. 146–47. Subsequent references to passages in "Der Magnetiseur," found in the text, come from this edition.

discussion in the *Serapionsbrüder* frame; Ottmar sees dreams as the passport to a higher spiritual principle (142). Ottmar sees in his father's dream a chance to verify the claims of magnetism (143). The dream did this but in a way that foreshadows the terrible fate of the family. Marie dies as she is about to marry Hypolit, with the implication that Alban killed her.

Bickert, the painter and old family friend, does not react with the terrified rejection of the old baron nor with the uncritical acceptance of Ottmar. He sees the interrelatedness of nature with our psychic and physical beings, but feels that danger attends any human attempt to meddle with this relationship. He distances himself with humorous and ironic accounts in an attempt to banish the threat (150). Like the young lawyer Dagobert in "Der unheimliche Gast," Bickert helps make the threat credible to the reader: both men are able to react rationally and critically. In this regard, they serve a function similar to that of several of the *Serapionsbrüder* in the frame, such as Theodor, who view magnetism from a similar viewpoint.[401]

Long discussions about the nature of magnetism, its promise and its perils, do not appear in the "unheimliche Gast" for several reasons. The most obvious is that the frame, at the beginning of Book II, has already dealt with these questions on a theoretical level. The second, less obvious, reason is that "Der unheimliche Gast" has a definite function to fulfill in the sequence of frame and inner stories. Book III, Section Five, contains the following series of narratives: "Nachricht aus dem Leben eines bekannten Mannes," "Die Brautwahl," and "Der unheimliche Gast." In each of these stories, different as they are, is a figure with a great potential for evil: The Devil in the first, with whom *Münzjude* Lippold in the second, and Count S in the third are both in league. In Book III, Section Six, major characters are also in the grip of evil forces: Cardillac, under a fateful star from birth; the Chevalier, possessed by gambling; and the baron, who nearly falls victim to a similar nemesis.

In the middle of this scurvy crew stand Count S and Cardillac, the two most vivid illustrations of evil incarnate and possession by secret

401. See Pikulik, "Das Wunderliche," p. 308, on the role of the observant bystander. See also Wolfgang Trautwein, *Erlesene Angst-Schauerliteratur im 18. und 19. Jahrhundert. Systematischer Aufriß; Untersuchungen zu Bürger, Maturin, Hoffmann, Poe und Maupassant* (Munich, 1980), p. 158.

forces in the entire collection. Because of its position in this series of tales, "Der unheimliche Gast" cannot dilute the effect of a parade of rogues with theoretical discussions but must get on with the portrayal of a character who tries to learn secrets of nature that are not appropriate for mortals to discover (637). Lifting of this veil of nature, as Count S implies in this excerpt from his letter to Marguerite, leads to destruction of the individual soul. The magnetizer opens himself to secret forces and succumbs to the temptation to use them, which leads to a welter of contradictory stresses.[402]

While "Magnetiseur" and "Der unheimliche Gast" have structural differences, there are also striking similarities. Both begin with a scene in which old friends gather round a fire on a stormy autumn night and talk about threats that lie just beyond the reach of the hearth and the comfortable rooms. In both instances, the themes of mysterious forces in nature, dreams, and magnetism appear. Both Angelika and Maria come under the influence of the magnetizers before they meet them, through the medium of dreams.[403] Both magnetizers, Alban and the count, gain entrance to the house through bonds of friendship that one family member does not wish to rupture. Alban tolerates Ottmar's youthful enthusiasms, while Count S has saved the Obrist from personal ruin. In each story, the magnetizer is given an early opportunity to heal someone: Maria, who faints, and Marguerite, who takes opium at the news of Moritz's and Angelika's engagement. The narrative function of these apparent acts of mercy is to establish the impression of power, of secret knowledge, and to create the illusion of kindness so as to soften the feelings of fear that the manifestations of such power causes in the onlookers. In both stories, Alban and Count S are quite prepared to remove whoever is standing in their respective paths. Both men try to win over the daughters in the same manner, through acts of apparent kindness and by standing by their beds while the girls are asleep.[404]

Artistically speaking, "Der unheimliche Gast" is a much better story than "Der Magnetiseur." In order to make his points about magnetism, Hoffmann used an extraordinarily complex structure in "Gast," which

402. Nipperdey, "Wahnsinnsfiguren," p. 97.
403. Nipperdey, "Wahnsinnsfiguren," p. 45; Kruse, *Aufbau* 2, p. 622.
404. Nipperdey, "Wahnsinnsfiguren," notes that the influence of magnetizers was believed to be greatest on women because of the greater degree of passivity often found in their natures (p. 43).

has not yet received sufficient attention. The profusion of parallel events and characters involves even one of the *Serapionsbrüder*, Cyprian, who bursts into the assembled company listening to the story just as the count does within the story itself. The importance of the parallel structure in "Gast" becomes quickly apparent when one looks at the story's divisions:

600–611, Prelude: ghost stories, talk about magnetism, dreams, Bogislav, Marguerite's first eccentric behavior.

611–12   Cyprian's entrance, before that of the count.

612–32   The arrival of the count, Angelika's engagement to Moritz, her approaching marriage to the count, his death, Moritz's return.

632–39   Explanation of Moritz's absence and plot to trap him; final scene.

From the above outline, it is clear that approximately one half of the story consists of prelude and explanation, sections that include the subplots. The middle part, devoted to the count, is intimately related to the themes in the prelude and in the explanation of the strange events occurring in the middle section. One of these events is Angelika's decision to marry the count. Hoffmann's structure allows for a subtle building of suspense before the count arrives, as well as an opportunity to introduce the theme of magnetism in an apparently offhand way. The conversation about magnetism and other hidden forces, while it does not involve the lengthy theoretical digressions in the frame, is reminiscent of the frame discussions, in that intelligent contemporaries in the story have reactions of fear similar to those of the *Serapionsbrüder*. Moritz, Angelika, Dagobert, and the Obristin become involved with and threatened by these forces, a fate which, since it happened to people whose backgrounds and class have some similarity to the *Serapionsbrüder*, could also happen to them.[405] This first, apparently innocuous, introduction to magnetism is followed by the middle section, as Moritz and Dagobert are discomfited by the count's strange powers. In the

---

405. Sucher, *Sources*, p. 22, makes too sweeping a statement when he says that the magnetized individuals in Hoffmann are all neurotic, unhealthy hyphochondriacs. The fact that Angelika, Moritz, and Bogislav—all healthy, well-adjusted individuals—could fall under the spell of an evil hypnotizer demonstrates the danger of it even more vividly than the destruction of a hysterical or nervous woman.

explanation at the end, the full extent of the count's involvement with evil forces becomes clear, but only after he is safely dead and can no longer threaten anyone.

Hoffmann made excellent use of the opportunities his structure offered. He built two subplots into the story with intimate connections to the main one, those dealing with Bogislav and Marguerite.[406] Both the main plot and the subplots have a romantic interest at the center; however, each of the subplots serves a different function. Bogislav's situation is very similar to that of Moritz and foreshadows the difficulties Moritz will have; the subplot with Marguerite has parallels with the situation between the count and Angelika. Bogislav, the brave Baltic officer who was engaged to a Neapolitan, has to leave the city under a cloud because of the machinations of a Sicilian count who tries to win the Slav's fiancée for himself. Bogislav challenges the count, stabs him and goes to his fiancée who rejects him, saying he has killed her beloved. Unable to explain their daughter's change of heart, her parents hide Bogislav, who now is followed by strange noises that resemble the voice of the count whom he assumes is dead. Bogislav tries to stave off madness, takes foolhardy risks in battle, unable to free himself from the count's spell until a shot destroys the miniature of his fiancée that he carries over his heart.

Bogislav's story, much of which Moritz relates immediately prior to the arrival of the Sicilian count, foreshadows the control the count will exercise over Angelika. Like the Neapolitan girl who suddenly fell in love with him, Angelika decides all at once to marry him. As for Bogislav, the presence of the count signifies grave dangers for Moritz. When, at the end of the story, the nefarious influence of the fiancée's miniature of Bogislav becomes apparent, another parallel between Bogislav's story and that of Moritz appears. Just as the miniature of his former fiancée maintained the count's power over Bogislav, so the picture of Marguerite that the chevalier places in Moritz's room while he is a prisoner keeps his attention fixed on Marguerite. This element in the Bogislav story links it to the other subplot, that between Marguerite and the count.

This second subplot also figures in the beginning section in the scene

406. Nipperdey, "Wahnsinnsfiguren," p. 96, notes Bogislav's and Moritz's susceptibility to magnetic influence because they are in love. See Trautwein, *Erlesene Angst*, pp. 171–72 for comments on the story's structure.

in which Marguerite behaves oddly as Moritz gives Angelika a dropped shawl. Dagobert later explains to Moritz that he has unwittingly awakened Marguerite's interest while trying to court Angelika through her. The reader's attention again fastens on Marguerite when the count arrives. She seems to be in an exalted, fluttery state, like that of the old Barbara Rolofin in the presence of the devil (see discussion of "Nachricht").[407] Another event that shows her connection to the count and her love for Moritz occurs when she tries to kill herself after Moritz and Angelika announce their engagement. Only the count can save her, further evidence that he exercises strange power over her.[408] The full extent of the unholy alliance between Marguerite and the count and its consequences comes to light only in the final section, where the relationship between Marguerite and the count and its effect on Moritz dominates—just as the Bogislav subplot was most prominent in the prelude. The complete explanation of the connection comes in a letter from the count, which Marguerite, in an extreme stage of madness, gives to Dagobert. Like the count, the secret knowledge she wishes to use to achieve her ends has proved her undoing.

In addition to the parallelism of the subplots, Hoffmann fills the story with recurrent motifs, including dreams, pictures, and strange noises. The sound motif, which begins the story in the form of the tea kettle and the autumn storms, soon moves over into the mysterious noises in nature, including the *Teufelsstimme* (devil's voice) of Ceylon, a frequent motif in the *Serapionsbrüder*, and the groans that haunt Bogislav.[409] In a lengthy passage, (601–2), Dagobert suggests that the reasons these sounds in nature discomfit us is because nature wishes to punish us for our falling away from the universal harmony that reigned in the Golden Age (602); then, no terror or horror disturbed us, whereas now sounds of nature may fill us with dread (602–3).[410] Not only Dagobert, but also the count allude to the angry forces of nature, which punish those who try to use the secrets of nature for their own

---

407. Nipperdey, "Wahnsinnsfiguren," notes that Marguerite shows traces of hysteria, often an early development on the ultimate road to madness (p. 27). Auhuber, *Spiegel,* pp. 81–82), discusses the connection between dancing and madness.

408. See Nipperdey, pp. 44–45.

409. See Kruse, *Aufbau* 2, p. 622, and the preceding discussion of this passage from Schubert in "Automate."

410. See Schubert, *Ansichten* (pp. 4, 7ff.). These parallels are noted by Carl G. Von Maassen, in *Die Serapionsbrüder* 3 and 7; in *E. T. A. Hoffmanns Sämtliche Werke,* p. 351. See also the previous discussion of "Die Automate," pp. 197–203.

ends (637). The connection between Dagobert's remarks and the count's insight is that the magnetizer, who in one way tries to get himself in touch with the hidden secrets of nature, runs afoul of these forces, since his goal is not so much to reestablish original harmonies but to use these forces for his personal benefit; he therefore becomes the enemy.

As the progression of sounds that cause frightened reactions within one intensifies—beginning with the sounds of the tea kettle and storm, and going to Ceylonese *Luftmusik* (music of the air), the atmospheric noise in Spain, and the terrifying ghost sounds in an inn—the conversation comes to the limits of conscious knowledge of hidden forces.[411] Just at this point, Angelika mentions her strange dreams that paralyze her with fear; they are like the one on her fourteenth birthday, which terrified her for several days (608).[412] As the reader later learns, this dream was the result of the count's first attempt to set himself in magnetic rapport with her.[413]

While Angelika's remarks may seem to reflect the normal twists and turns of polite conversation, they skillfully link dreams, strange forces, and the mystery of odd noises in the reader's mind. Moritz reinforces this connection and unwittingly brings in the count with his account of Bogislav's haunting by the strange noise that sounds like the count in pain from the stab wound that Bogislav gave him. The brush with this strange force makes Bogislav irrational, which is characteristic of Moritz and Angelika as well when they fall under the count's spell. In thrall to forces that seem to direct their thoughts and actions, they resemble sleepwalkers. Moritz relates that during his detention with

411. Von Maassen, *Serapionsbrüder* 7, citing p. 60, notes that Schubert wrote about this phenomenon and that Hoffmann cites a similar experience in "Die Automate" (Von Maassen, pp. 351–52). See p. 349 of Winkler and pp. 1064–65.

412. See Kluge, *Versuch,* pp. 186 and 109. Von Maassen, vol. 7, p. 352, suggested these references. Schubert, *Symbolik,* p. 180: "In einem gewissen Falle begann der innere Kampf beym plötzlichen Aufschrecken aus einem bedeutungsvollen Traume, dessen eigentlichen Inhalt der Erwachsene nicht mehr wußte, der aber eine tiefe innere Wirkung zurückgelassen." This passage describes Angelika's feelings as she awoke after the count had tried to magnetize her in a dream.

In a later phase of her relationship with the count, Angelika had pleasant dreams of him, which was how he eventually came to insinuate himself into her mind as her husband. The Obristin relates this circumstance at the end of the story (p. 638, Von Maassen, vol. 3, *Serapionsbrüder,* p. 354).

413. Paul Sucher, *Sources* (72), notes that control of the subject from a distance was "la forme la plus frappante de la sympathie qui unit le magnetisé au magnetiseur" (p. 21).

the chevalier, he seemed dissociated from himself, possessed by a strange power and unable to leave Marguerite (634). When Angelika prepares to marry the count, she says she cannot love him as she loved Moritz and yet she feels that she could not live without him, that she can only feel and think through him. A spectral voice keeps telling her she must marry him or perish (628).[414] Both Angelika and Moritz fall into this state of mind through the effect of magnetizing them while they sleep. This state comes about through the presence of the count himself, in Angelika's case, or through Marguerite's picture, as in Moritz's (638, 634–35).

The motif of the picture figures prominently in these attempts, since the count first decides to win Angelika when he sees a miniature of her.[415] Angelika's account of her dream contains several motifs typical of magnetism for Hoffmann: the *Holunder* (elder) tree under which the count finally dies, the fixed gaze of human eyes that comes from the tree, the hand making circles as well as the *Klagelaut* (plaintive sound), similar to the one that haunts Bogislav (619).[416] The description of dreams during which magnetic influences took place harkens back to earlier discussions in the *Serapionsbrüder* frame.

Repetition of the scene from the beginning of the story occurs at the end, where Moritz, Angelika, and the family sit around a fire on a November evening, much like the one on which the count arrived and disturbing noises made themselves heard. Now, however, the sounds of nature seem happy rather than threatening, as they did at that time (639). The present happy setting is reminiscent of the Golden Age that Dagobert described at the beginning of the story (602). Now that the threat from individuals who upset nature's harmony is past, the voices of nature seem as welcoming as they must have been in past times.[417]

414. See *Aufbau II*, (pp. 622 and 624). In vol. 7, *Serapionsbrüder*, Von Maassen cites a passage from Kluge (p. 354). See Kluge, *Versuch*, p. 110.
415. See Olbrich, "Hoffmann und der deutsche Volksglaube," who ties Hoffmann's use of pictures in this story with the widespread superstition that there was a connection between the picture and the person (pp. 68–69).
416. See *Aufbau* 2, pp. 622–23. Stegmann, *Deutung*, discusses Angelika's dream, p. 262, and the role of the staring eye, basing her interpretation on Schubert, *Symbolik*, pp. 80–81, where he says: "Auf diese Weise wird auch das erkennende Auge (der Brunnen des Lichts, das Wort) auf der einen Seite zur bauenden, schaffenden Hand, auf der andern, zugleich mit der Hand, gleichbedeutend mit dem Organ der körperlichen Erzeugung. Das belebende Auge wird nun zugleich tödtend, die Wahrheit zeugende, schwörende Hand, wird die täuschende, Lügen verkündende, zaubernde."
417. Conrad, *Angst*, overlooks the comments of the assembled characters at the end of "Der unheimliche Gast" that the sounds of nature are now friendly and not threaten-

"Das Fräulein von Scuderi"
(Mademoiselle von Scuderi)

In the frame that immediately precedes "Fräulein Scuderi," there is an animated conversation about the fate of plays that are performed and the various effects public reaction has on the author. How much does the production determine the significance of the play? Can a good actor reveal levels of meaning hitherto hidden from the author? Or is the playwright inevitably sentenced to disappointment and misinterpretation when he allows his innermost soul to be reworked by others? At first, this discussion would seem to have little to do with the mad artisan Cardillac. However, there is a parallel between the reluctance of a poet to let his vision of art be degraded and misunderstood by others and Cardillac's unwillingness to let his masterworks of the goldsmith's art become the possession of courtesans and actresses. Sylvester's remarks about the playwright's dilemma highlight the connection: the playwright has conceived each character in his soul and expects from an actor the same understanding that he himself has (643–44). Just as the playwright sees his work distorted and misunderstood when another interprets it, so Cardillac cannot bear the lack of appreciation he felt a courtesan or opera dancer must bring to his work.[418] The lack of appreciation on the part of the philistine public that upsets any artist reaches monstrous proportions in Cardillac; not only is he the only one capable of understanding and appreciating his work, but for their inability to comprehend, others deserve to die (693).[419] Cardillac relates how the thought that a member of the court

ing, as well as Dagobert's description of the harmony between nature and man in the golden age (p. 81).

418. Mühlher, *Deutsche Dichter*, p. 302, relates the problems connected with the separation of an artist from his work to Cardillac. See also Nipperdey, p. 107, and Helmut Himmel, "Schuld und Sühne der Scuderi," MHG 7 (1960), pp. 1–15, pp. 9–10, where Himmel compares Cardillac to Ritter Gluck.

See also Gisela Gorski, *E. T. A. Hoffmann: Fräulein von Scuderi* (Stuttgart, 1980), pp. 64–66, where she compares Krespel with Cardillac saying that both do not use the projects they produce but do not want others to have them.

419. Both Meyer, *Sonderling*, p. 112, and Edgar Marsch, *Die Kriminalerzählung: Theorie, Geschichte, Analyse* (Munich, 1972), p. 148, analyze the problems of a one-sided artistic mania.

was going to give one of his creations to an opera dancer drove him to his first murder (693–94). In the note to Scuderi that accompanies the jewels, Cardillac says, "und uns Schätze zueignen, die auf unwürdige Weise vergeudet werden sollten" (663) ["in order to possess ourselves of treasures that would otherwise be disgracefully squandered on unworthy objects"] (Lazare, 53). He thus justifies his larceny and murder to repossess his work. Coupled with this perversion of artistic consciousness is the lust for jewels which becomes a mania in Cardillac. This *idée fixe* ultimately destroys Cardillac just as it did Zacharias Werner. Cardillac's insatiable desire for precious stones is the reason for his becoming a goldsmith, not his love of art (692). His extraordinary skill only masks the basic perversion of art that his *"böser Stern"* (evil star) causes.[420]

In Cardillac's account of his life which Olivier relates, Cardillac reveals the source of his obsession with jewels and precious metals, the experience his pregnant mother had with a knight who wore a chain of diamonds and gold (692). In earliest childhood, Cardillac remembers being fascinated by diamonds and gold above all else, even resorting to stealing them when he could (692). Cardillac, like Elis Fröbom, is fascinated with precious metals and jewels. While several critics have noticed similarities between the two characters, none have explored the deeper connection with Schubert that our earlier analysis of "Bergwerke" examined.[421] According to Schubert, gold has a powerful influence on people in a magnetic state that may explain their greed for it.[422] This attraction led Fröbom to his destruction, just as it does Cardillac.

A major difference between the two men is that Fröbom committed no crimes while under the influence of the queen of metals and Torbern, while Cardillac did. With the question of crime, a further issue

420. See Müller-Seidel, *Nachwort*, p. 1016, who notes that he used his own art to selfish ends.

421. Klaus D. Post, "Kriminalgeschichte als Heilsgeschichte," *Zeitschrift für deutsche Philologie* 95 (1976), pp. 132–56, p. 133, notes that Cardillac, like Torbern, has fallen prey to the telluric powers. Himmel, "Schuld," notes the similarity between the two stories on pages 7, 9, and 10, but does not touch on magnetism and metals. See also Peter von Matt, *Automate*, pp. 127ff. Negus, *Other World*, compares the two stories and notes that "the symbolic materials of both dark underworlds are the same stone and metal" (p. 109), but does not mention magnetism.

422. See previous discussion of "Bergwerke," pp. 160–67, and of magnetism, pp. 174–84. See also the thirteenth chapter of Schubert's *Ansichten*, especially pp. 336–37 and 355–56. Himmel "Schuld," p. 2, notes the connection but does not analyze it.

related to Hoffmann's view of magnetism enters into the picture, that of personal responsibility for one's actions. As the previous discussion of magnetism indicated, Hoffmann, like many of his contemporaries, believed that a magnetized individual had no control over his actions. If Cardillac is magnetized by the metals, then this state decreases his personal responsibility. The voices that haunt Cardillac, urging him onto murder (695), are reminiscent of the subliminal suggestions of the count in "Der unheimliche Gast" and the urgings of Torbern in "Bergwerke."

Magnetism, with its domination of the mind of the subject and the attendant decrease in individual accountability, has ties to another major theme in Cardillac's autobiography: the role of prenatal influences.[423] During her pregnancy, Cardillac's mother saw a knight in a stunning, bejeweled Spanish costume at a court festival. This particular gentleman, who had pursued her in vain before her marriage, seems, because of his jewelry, to be an extraterrestrial creature. The cavalier, who hoped to be more fortunate now than he was earlier, approached and embraced her and, as she reached for the necklace, fell dead to the ground. The gold and jewels in the chain had clearly mesmerized the pregnant woman;[424] but her prospective seducer, like Count S in "Der

423. Critical material on prenatal influences and the role of the knight includes the following: Nipperdey, "Wahnsinnsfiguren," p. 108; J. M. Ellis, "E. T. A. Hoffmann's 'Fräulein von Scuderi,' " *Modern Language Notes* 64 (1969), pp. 340–50; Hermann F. Weiss, "The Labyrinth of Crime: a Reinterpretation of E. T. A. Hoffmann's 'Das Fräulein von Scuderi,' " *Germanic Review* 51 (1976), pp. 180–89, especially pp. 182–83; Post, "Kriminalgeschichte," p. 148.

424. In his discussion of Kluge, McGlathery, p. 158, intimates that magnetism was at work between the knight and Cardillac's mother, but does not follow up on it nor connect it with Schubert, p. 158. Gorski, *Scuderi*, notes that the magnetic gaze has been transferred to the jewels (p. 151). See also Marianne Thalmann, *Der Trivialroman des 18. Jahrhunderts* (Liechtenstein, 1967), p. 203.

The question of prenatal influences on the fetus was hotly debated in the eighteenth century and in Hoffmann's era, with ardent defenders of both positions. A book debunking prenatal influences, Christian Rickmann's *Von der Unwahrheit des Versehens,* appeared in Jena in 1770, while an equally passionate defense of the theory appeared in 1809, published in Rostock, and entitled *Versuch über die Einbildungskraft der Schwangeren in Bezug auf ihre Leibesfrüchte zur Beantwortung der Frage: "Können Schwangere sich wirklich versehen?"* by D. H. G. Wüstnei. Wüstnei offers as one of the supports of his belief the argument that soul and body stand in such an intimate relationship that such transfers must take place. Although no one knows if Hoffmann saw this contemporary medical opinion, it does present the position in a way that would have attracted Hoffmann and quite likely reflects current medical thinking of those who believed in prenatal influences. Wüstnei says: "Daß der menschliche Geist mit seinem Körper in der genauesten Verbindung stehe, ist ein Axiom, das wohl keines Beweises bedarf; regt sich denn je eine Hand, ein Fuß oder irgend ein Glied des menschlichen Körpers, wenn keine Vorstellung voraufgegangen, wenn der Wille dazu nicht den Befehl

unheimliche Gast," falls dead before he can enjoy the advantage of her magnetic state. The knight looks like Count S in death, staring at her with sunken, glinting eyes that seemed without vision (692; see for comparison, 629). The effect of this incident sends the expectant mother to her bed. Reflecting a common lay belief shared by some of Hoffmann's contemporaries who were physicians (see note 424), Cardillac claims that the horrors of this incident were visited upon him in his mother's womb and refers to his evil star (692).

One of the significant aspects of both magnetic and prenatal influences is their emphasis on fate, on the individual as victim. Cardillac himself points out that he struggled against the inner voices and that his murderous instincts did not constitute the whole of his personality (696). The outside forces at work on Cardillac have infected his mental condition, producing a sort of *idée fixe*. In his account of his life, which Olivier relates, he tells of the combination of instinct and an inner voice that kept telling him to get the jewelry back. Even theft does not satisfy this inner voice; murder is the only deed that stills it (692–94). In "Der unheimliche Gast", inner voices told Moritz and Angelika what they should do against their will (628, 634). If Cardillac is under the magnetic influence of the jewels and metals, it would not be surprising for him to hear inner voices, as Fröbom does. Further evidence that he does not consider his murderous desires his real self (just as Moritz and Angelika knew they did not totally want to do what the voice was telling them to) lies in his admission to Olivier that there were times when he felt that "das, was der böse Stern begonnen durch mich, meiner unsterblichen Seele, die daran keinen Teil hat, zugerechnet werden könne" (696) ["the crimes I commit as the blind instrument of my ill-starred birth may be charged upon my immortal soul, which has no share in them"] (Lazare, 89).

Since Hoffmann limns Cardillac's portrait with prenatal and magnetic influences, his purpose may well lie in his attempt to show the degree to which unseen forces can fasten onto a mind, as he has with Fröbom, Heinrich von Ofterdingen, Count S, and Zacharias Werner. All the stories in the third volume deal with possession of one kind or

gegeben?" (p. 20). Wüstnei sees also magnetic and electrical connections between the mother and the unborn child (pp. 23–24).

Kluge, *Versuch*, also deals with this matter, saying that the doctors disagreed, though he himself believed in prenatal influences, and thought that they were especially likely to occur when magnetism was in evidence during a pregnancy. See pp. 352–54, p. 473.

another. In Cardillac, Hoffmann presents the most destructive character of the lot, doomed by the double circumstances of prenatal influence as well as magnetic forces.[425]

In addition to the above characters, there are other important connections between "Scuderi" and the frame. The anecdotal parallel in
the frame, which we have seen repeatedly throughout the *Serapionsbrüder*, appears here as well. In answer to Lothar's protest that
Cardillac cannot be real, Ottmar cites the true story of a Venetian cobbler, known as a pious, hard-working sort, who killed the rich with a
single masterful dagger stroke as they slept so that he could rob them.
When the cobbler was locked up, the murders stopped; when he was
released, they began again. To vouch for the veracity of the existence
of such figures, Sylvester says that Scuderi's *bon mot* about fearful lovers
as well as other elements in the story came from the Nürnberg chronicle (709–10).

Although Cardillac has many similarities with other mad figures in
the frame and the inner stories, Hoffmann has provided a vivid coun-
terexample, whose importance has been overlooked.[426] Friedrich, the
goldsmith in "Meister Martin der Küfner und seine Gesellen," appears
at the end of the second book, just before the fairy tale, "Das fremde
Kind," and immediately preceded the series of evil characters in Book
III. Unlike the turbulent setting of Paris in the late seventeenth century,
where murder was the order of the day and family relationships lay in

425. See also Schubert, *Symbolik*, p. 110, regarding the double personality that
seems to afflict madmen. In a recent study, Georg Reuchlin, *Das Problem der Zurechnungsfähigkeit bei E. T. A. Hoffmann und Georg Büchner. Zum Verhältnis von Literatur, Psychiatrie
und Justiz im frühen neunzehnten Jahrhundert* (Frankfurt, 1985), gives extensive background material on *Zurechnungsfähigkeit* in the late eighteenth and early nineteenth centuries, pp. 10–19, and discusses accountability in Hoffmann's works, chiefly in *Die Elixiere des Teufels* and "Fräulein von Scuderi" (pp. 20–44). In his opinion, Cardillac did not
suffer from an *idée fixe*, but from strong passion (pp. 27–30). Of particular interest to
readers of "Scuderi" is his conclusion that Hoffmann was more interested in the criminal
psychology of Cardillac than in how the legal system dealt with the question of accountability. Reuchlin bases this observation in part on the fact that Cardillac dies before coming to trial (see pp. 24, 32–33). Reuchlin, p. 41, explains why Hoffmann in his legal
briefs showed little inclination to accept insanity as a plea for Schmolling, yet was ready
in his novella to portray Cardillac as a figure who deserved some understanding. The
Schmolling murder case that Reuchlin refers to figures prominently in Wulf Segebrecht's
article, "E. T. A. Hoffmanns Auffassung vom Richteramt"; see especially pp. 97–128,
which contain the documents pertinent to the event, especially Hoffmann's essay, "Über
die Zurechnungsfähigkeit." See also pp. 66, 110, 111.

426. Weiss, "Labyrinth," p. 183, alludes briefly to the social atmosphere in "Meister
Martin," as compared with that in "Scuderi," but does not mention the contrasts between Friedrich and Cardillac.

shambles, Friedrich lives and works in the context of a family setting in a community of artisans in a sixteenth-century milieu favored by Hoffmann. In such a context, art and life stand in a close relationship to each other, making it a period with overtones of a golden age. In Cardillac's Paris, wave after wave of murders terrorizes the population; the cause and the source of the attacks seems almost demonic (655). Not only does this turbulent setting imply that unseen forces hover just beyond the hearth, but it also orders Cardillac's crime in this series by describing the jewel theft-murders (657).[427] The disappearance of the killer into the wall soon gives rise to the rumor that the Devil is at work (659), underscoring the connection between Cardillac and the other figures of Book III. The context of evil within which Cardillac lives and works, and of which he is a part, contrasts sharply with that of Friedrich.

Unlike Cardillac, Friedrich becomes a goldsmith because he loves the beauty of the craft, not out of a lust for precious metals and stones. When he has to serve a cooper to win Rosa, he frequently steals away to Sankt Sebald to admire Peter Vischer's work (464). As a farewell gift for Rosa, he fashions a beautiful chalice to show how much he loves her (467). His art testifies to his skill; his relationship to it, his generosity. In contrast, Cardillac cannot really sell, let alone give away, the fruit of his artistic labors. The one time he does try, with Fräulein Scuderi, ominous signs show that he will have to get the jewels back again. He wants his work locked deep in his vault. Cardillac's murder of those who admire his art enough to buy it symbolizes his killing of the inspirational power of art to expand man's consciousness. Friedrich, in contrast, lets himself be inspired by others' art and gives his work for the same purpose.

427. Weiss, "Labyrinth," offers a perceptive analysis of the function of the historic milieu, especially pp. 181–82. See also Conrad, *Angst*, pp. 107; Post, "Kriminalgeschichte," pp. 135–37, 140–46; Ellis, "Scuderi," pp. 348–49.

Winfried Freund, in his book, *Die deutsche Kriminalnovelle von Schiller bis Hauptmann* (Paderborn, 1980), pp. 43–46, discusses the relationship of the seventeenth-century Parisian milieu to the tension between liberal tendencies and the Prussian state at the time in which Hoffmann wrote the story. A somewhat superficial discussion of the Parisian milieu appears in Thomas A. Kovach, "Mythic Structure in E. T. A. Hoffmann's 'Das Fräulein von Scuderi': A Case-Study in 'Romantic Realism,' " pp. 121–28, pp. 123–24, in *Sprache und Literatur: Festschrift für Arval L. Streadbach zum 65. Geburtstag*, ed. Gerhard P. Knopp et al. (Bern, 1981). Hoffmann's obvious interest in the historical setting and the combination of historical fact with individual lives appears again and again in the *Serapionsbrüder*.

Another significant difference between Friedrich and Cardillac is that Friedrich marries Rosa (who is very like Madelon, Cardillac's daughter), but Cardillac is never shown as being in love. Madelon's presence is, of course, testimony to a marriage, but the only love for which there is space in Cardillac's tormented mind is that of jewels and precious metals. Cardillac, like the other evil characters in the inner stories of the *Serapionsbrüder*, is incapable of real love; when they do direct their considerable energies towards a woman, it is not to offer love but to possess that person, as in the case of Count S.

Over against Cardillac, Hoffmann's most dastardly victim of possession by outside forces, stands the figure of Fräulein Scuderi. Unique in the *Serapionsbrüder*, she is both an artist and a female redeemer,[428] a combination that would be more startling for Hoffmann if she were a really first-rate writer, which, by her own description, she is not (662). She is capable, however, of great eloquence and wit, as the king's reception of her poem about Cardillac shows (670). But for these gifts to reach their highest development, they must be put in the service of virtue, to which Scuderi has remained faithful her entire life (681). Hoffmann contrasts the situation at the beginning of the story, where her *bon mot*, "un amant qui craint les voleurs, n'est point digne d'amour" [a lover who fears thieves is scarcely worthy of love], is for Cardillac an invitation for him to continue in his murderous ways, with her rhetorical skills at the end of the story. There she wins the king over to pardon Brusson (708). Scuderi can recognize truth and virtue in others, because she represents it herself. When she puts her articulateness to work for a righteous cause, she is invincible, as the king recognizes.

In addition to Scuderi's references to her own attempts to live virtuously, the story conveys a sense of her goodness in other ways. Individual characters testify to it, directly or indirectly, and Hoffmann compares her to the Virgin Mary. Both Cardillac and Olivier Brusson see her in this light.[429] Cardillac, in the torments caused by his black deeds,

428. For the historical background on the figure of Scuderi, see Segebrecht, p. 1090, (Winkler); Kruse, *Aufbau* 2, p. 629. See also Hans Ulrich Lindken, *E. T. A. Hoffmann: Das Fräulein von Scuderi, Erläuterungen und Dokumente* (Stuttgart, 1979), pp. 33–34; Müller-Seidel, "Nachwort" (Winkler), p. 1017; Post, "Kriminalgeschichte," p. 139; Weiss, "Labyrinth," p. 189; Himmel, "Schuld," p. 11; Yvonne Holbeche, "The Relationship of the Artist to Power: E. T. A. Hoffmann's 'Das Fräulein von Scuderi,'" *Seminar* 16 (1981), pp. 1–11, 1, pp. 9–10.

429. See Post, "Kriminalgeschichte," pp. 153–54.

decided to make a diamond crown for the Virgin in the church of St. Eustache, but he cannot finish it.[430] In his mind he substitutes Scuderi for the Virgin, as he decides to give her the jewelry (696). Brusson, too, thinks of Scuderi in the same terms as he does of the Virgin Mary, saying he had as much faith that Scuderi would help him as he did in Mary's help (696). The absence of any love interest in Scuderi's past reinforces this parallel. She is shown in a mothering role, both with Anne Guiot, Olivier's mother, and with him, but not as a wife or mistress (683–84, 671).

Scuderi's role as a mother figure with the gift of salvation aligns her with other women in the cycle.[431] As we have seen, she has similarities with Marie in "Nußknacker" and with Ulla in "Bergwerke," but she also points ahead to a major theme of "Spielerglück," the subsequent story. (Angela, the saving female figure of "Spielerglück" is destroyed by the man she wanted to help.) Of this group of redemptive or potentially redemptive female figures, Marie and Scuderi have the most in common. In each case, the chosen person must go through painful experiences that demand courage and self-sacrifice in order to make redemption possible. However, redemption, as in the Church, depends as well on the individual's receptiveness to being saved. Neither Ulla nor Scuderi can help Fröbom or Cardillac: they have passed the point of no return in their connection with the unseen world of mysterious forces. In contrast, Nußknacker and Olivier have a healthy sense of right and goodness, which makes their rescue possible.

"Spielerglück"
(Gamblers' Luck)

"Spielerglück," the story that follows "Scuderi," contains a cast of characters with many similarities to those of its predecessor: no bloodthirsty murderers, but a series of men who are either possessed

430. See Feldges and Stadler, *Hoffmann*, p. 167, for material on Eustachius.
431. Himmel, "Schuld," p. 8. Pikulik, *Erzähler*, pp. 169, 170, compares Scuderi to a mother figure, similar to Margarethe in "Doge," and contrasts the redemptive relationship between Olivier and Scuderi with the destructive one between Cardillac and his mother.

by Satanic forces or in danger of it. There is no influential poet-aristo-
crat who functions as a lifeline, but there are women who through
their own sacrifice try to save the men they love from ruin.

Within this novella, which is a frame story, there are three narrative
levels that contain the stories of, or reference to, five men who are
compulsive gamblers:[432]

Level One: Baron Siegfried, a promising, talented man, becomes
              infatuated with his luck. In order to save him, an old
              man tells him the story of Chevalier Menars, without
              revealing that he himself is the chevalier.

Level Two: Menars relates his own rise and fall. In his story is
              that of Vertua, who begs Menars to show mercy, just
              as Menars begs the French officer not to destroy him
              at the table.

Level Three: Vertua tells his story to Menars, in which he relates
              the story of a young Roman on the edge of ruin who
              begs Vertua for mercy and stabs Vertua when he is
              rejected.

In addition to the dramatic series of men with ruined lives in the story,
Theodor offers a corroborative autobiographical anecdote in the frame.
Tempted by the luck at cards that brought him a large sum of money,
he was saved by the warning of an older man.[433]

The striking similarities among the gamblers in the inner story and
the frame of the novella, as well as in the *Serapionsbrüder* frame, serve
several functions. Not only does the repeated description of promising
young men in ruin serve as an emphatic warning made weighty
through repetition, but it also implies the machinations of an unseen,
unforgiving power. The narrators refer to this power again and again
in the various descriptions of their careers; generally they describe this
force as satanic (721, 729).[434] The Devil's power over his victims in

432. I am indebted to the perceptive analysis of Margot Kuttner, *Individualitätsprobleme*, pp. 60–61, for much of the material in this discussion of the structure. She
sees in repetition, in apparent coincidence, the working of unseen forces in our lives;
gambling is the most obvious manifestation of this power. For more material on coincidence in Hoffmann, see Pikulik, *Erzähler*, pp. 177–78.

433. Kruse, *Aufbau* 2, gives background information on biographical influences in
this story (pp. 655–56).

434. See also pp. 726, 732, 736, 740, 741. The quotation in the text mentions the
Höllenabgrund. The abyss as symbol functions in much the same way here as it did in

such cases receives further emphasis when Vertua, Menars's father-in-law, after giving up gambling twice, dies in his lust for the dice, rejecting confession and absolution from the priest (731–32). Vertua's daughter Angela, Menars's wife, fears, correctly as it turns out, that her husband may relapse into his old ways (732).

Like Angelika in "Der unheimliche Gast," Angela in "Spielerglück" is a pure and noble, self-sacrificing girl; she resembles many of the redemptive female figures such as Marie and Ulla in the *Serapionsbrüder*. Angela's first appearance in a white nightdress (727) and her speech to her despairing father, in which she praises the value of love over material goods (727), underscore her redemptive qualities. Vertua has already suggested such an interpretation to the reader, because he has just related to the chevalier the manner in which Angela's mother saved him from a certain death. Because of Vertua's mistreatment of his faithful wife, whom he learned to appreciate only shortly before her death, he gives up gambling. This parallel between Angela and her mother receives added strength when Vertua remarks that Angela is the picture of her mother (726).

After begging her husband to quit gambling, Angela dies, but she is yet able to save him, even in death. When he finds her dead in her bed, after he has gambled her away to her former admirer,[435] he gives up gambling forever. From there on, he tries to save others, like Baron Siegfried. In her purity of spirit, Angela resembles not only the other female heroines in the *Serapionsbrüder* but also Wolfram von Eschenbach, who is able to wrest Heinrich von Ofterdingen and Mathilde from the control of satanic forces through his strength of character.

There are two types of gamblers in the story: the one for whom the play of coincidence in the game itself, its apparent communion with extrasensory sources of power, is the attractive aspect;[436] and the type of player who lusts after gold (720). Although the sources are different,

---

"Bergwerke." It appears first in the warning to the young baron (p. 717), and then, in the moment in which the chevalier realizes he loves Angela, in the preceding quotation.

435. Both Vertua and Chevalier Menars made their final disastrous bets with the Dame, losing in both cases (pp. 729–35), which in Vertua's case was a symbolic reconfirmation of events in his life and in the chevalier's, foreshadowing.

436. In *Die Elixiere des Teufels*, edited by Wolfgang Kron (Munich), the prince describes his fascination with gambling (in this case, *Faro*), because it allows one to see the strange entanglements that the secret power of chance designs (p. 125).

the result, emotional and financial ruin, is the same. Menars has seen this in himself and in Vertua. Gambling destroys finer human emotions (721, 725). The addicted gambler bears certain resemblances to Cardillac[437] and Count S, who cannot feel the measure of the wrong they do to others. The possession by a higher power, consciously chosen or not, leads to a dehumanizing of the individual. Anesthesis of normal human feelings makes possible a complete triumph of evil. The assumption that such complete control over another human being was possible, whether through magnetism, automats, or gambling, frightened Hoffmann and his contemporaries.

The corroborating anecdote in the *Serapionsbrüder* frame mirrors closely the frame incident in "Spielerglück," in which Chevalier Menars succeeds in attracting the attention of Siegfried in order to warn him. Theodor is stopped by an old officer who warns he is in danger of coming under the power of the Devil, who lurks in wait for him. It seems to Theodor that a poisonous worm is gnawing at his soul (740–41);[438] this phrase appears also in the discussion of Zacharias Werner and Werner's madness, providing further evidence that Hoffmann saw an interrelatedness between the unseen forces of magnetism, the spirit world, and destructive desires.

"Der Baron von B."
(The Baron of B.)

The succession of odd, older men, ranging from the satanic to the eccentric, which dominates the stories of Volume III, ends with the Baron von B., the wealthy expert on violins who plays in a manner beyond abomination.[439] The preceding five stories all contained satanic

437. Another similarity between Cardillac and the gamblers is that all speak of themselves as being under the influence of the stars and outside powers (pp. 694, 712, 732, 739).

438. A different kind of gold, that of the morning sun, pulls Theodor out of his desperate mood (p. 741).

439. The historic figure of Baron von Bagge stands behind this narrative. See Kruse, *Aufbau* 2, pp. 638–39; Segebrecht (Winkler), pp. 1094–95.

figures or men possessed by demonic forces, sometimes to the point of madness. Baron von B., like them, is also possessed and definitely somewhat mad, but he is not evil. His obvious knowledge of violin technique seems incommensurate with his accurate ear for weaknesses in the playing of his pupils.

The baron's bizarre personality instantly brings to mind two earlier characters, Serapion and Rat Krespel. Like Serapion, the baron has a skewed perception of reality; like him, he is an *artiste manqué* because of this failure.[440] Like Krespel, the baron has a passionate love affair with the violin, but Krespel cannot give himself completely to the inner mystery of music; he continually tries to tear apart violins to find out what produces their tone.

The character of the baron also points forward to Zacharias Werner. Like the baron, Werner does not have too firm a grip on reality. In one of his descriptions of Werner's madness, Hoffmann says Werner took the vision of another existence for real life in his delirium (856). The baron, in his belief that he and one other old man are the sole heirs to Tartini's skills, lives in a dream that he too takes for reality. In spite of his eccentricity, Baron von B. appears as a real artist. Hoffmann describes him in terms reminiscent of his portrayals of other artists in the collection (745, 748). The baron's particular madness should not obscure his real value for the music, just as Werner's insanity has not precluded his creation of works of literary merit.

Cyprian bases his account of the Baron von B. on material given him by a famous virtuoso, but he tells the story as if he himself were that musician. This technique differs sharply from the one employed for Theodor's long anecdote about his gambling experiences. In that narrative, Theodor related his own brush with the dangerous allure of the dice, resulting in a convincing immediacy that underscored the message of "Spielerglück." Here, Cyprian gives artistic form to an anecdote related to him. Cyprian's approach makes the anecdote he relates more remote from immediate experience than Theodor's story. However, Cyprian's account is less removed from the real world than an inner story with its own proper title.

---

440. Dobat, *Musik,* no. 65, pp. 193; see also p. 229, where Dobat says that both Serapion and Baron von B. believe that what they hear in spirit is real. See also Pikulik, *Erzähler,* p. 184.

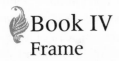# Book IV
Frame

The frame that begins the fourth volume of stories deals with various disturbers of the peace in polite society, those people who kill a party. Hoffmann introduces this topic with the most banal example of social intercourse, a conversation about the weather. The discussion of various types of intellectual women, the anecdote from Theodor about his uncle's method of ridding himself of bores both point ahead to characters in "Der Zusammenhang der Dinge" and the "Ästhetische Teegesellschaft." Talk of bores naturally leads Cyprian to think of fools and therefore of madness, which one can study in one's daily life without the necessity of visiting an asylum (764). Some of these people cannot rid themselves of an idea or a concept that has taken hold, and repeat it continuously, regardless of the circumstances. Cyprian asks if it is not so that "liegt in solchen Leuten nicht der Keim . . . des fixen Wahns" ["in such people the sprout of fixated madness lies"] (765). This observation could apply to Zacharias Werner, who figures prominently in this book. It also picks up the frequent references to the *idée fixe* that have appeared throughout the work.

"Signor Formica"

Before the brothers fall into a potentially upsetting discussion about madness, Ottmar prepares to tell his "Signor Formica." Like "Brautwahl" in the third volume, this story furnishes relief through the use of irony, satire, and a happy ending. Both stories contain stock elements of European comedy.[441] A clue to the essentially bright notes

---

441. Pikulik, *Erzähler*, pp. 152–54, 185–91, gives interesting background material from the Viennese theater for "Brautwahl" and on the commedia dell'arte for "Formica."

of "Signor Formica" lies in Ottmar's remark that he tried to write in Boccaccio's style (766). Just as "Brautwahl" appeared before the series of Hoffmann's most depraved characters, Sabatini and Cardillac, so the Italian atmosphere of "Signor Formica," with its series of intrigues to save true love, its ridiculous old fool and his supporting cast of familiars, helps to lighten the atmosphere. This witty portrayal of the artist's confrontation with the bourgeoisie comes before the conversation of the assembled company turns to the darker side of the artistic temperament as embodied in Zacharias Werner.

The two stories contain parallels in theme as well as in function, like the *Märchen*, which also serve to relieve tension and depression by placing struggles in a fairy-tale setting. In both "Brautwahl" and "Formica," dashing young artists pursue beautiful young women, both of whom are also besieged by suitors (Tusmann in "Brautwahl" and Capuzzi in "Formica") whose age and disposition render them ludicrously unsuitable. In both cases, the artists, Eduard and Antonio, received assistance from an older artist, wise in the ways of the world, who enables them to defeat the old fools. In "Brautwahl" the presence of the supernatural is much stronger than in "Formica." In those instances where the supernatural seems to appear in "Formica," such as the midnight attack on Capuzzi and his companions, the apparent visitation from the spirit world turns out to be a ruse. Where Leonhard in "Brautwahl" would have used white magic, Salvator Rosa uses his clever mind. Physical attacks in both stories serve to educate the old fools, not to kill them, as mysterious forces do in "Bergwerke." The attack on Splendiano, when he is terrified by the accusing spirits of dead patients whom he has prematurely brought to their final rewards, results in his decision to give up his administration of deadly elixirs.

"Formica" also stands in a special relationship with the story immediately preceding it. Capuzzi, like the Baron von B., is devoted to music and also cannot produce it, though he himself, like the baron, greatly enjoys his own productions (787). Both men delude themselves about their own musical abilities, but the madness of the baron is more tolerable than that of Capuzzi, primarily because the baron, in spite of his inability to judge his own work, is still able to help others understand music better, showing some traits of character that the reader finds admirable. By contrast, Capuzzi is a totally selfish individual during much of the story.[442] The juxtaposition of the two men in successive stories helps to maintain continuity between the third and fourth sections.

The absence of menace to sanity helps to maintain the generally lighthearted tone of the story.[443] The only threats in the story come from the comic figures, Splendiano and Capuzzi, though the danger in which they occasionally place the main characters is very real. Splendiano almost kills Salvator with his potions, since he believes the sick artist has a chest full of paintings. Capuzzi is determined to ruin Marianne's life and nearly succeeds in doing so. Both men, though, are clearly ridiculous in many ways. The exaggeration and self-delusion in their sense of reality undo both of them when faced with Salvator Rosa, whose perception of reality includes a deep understanding of the foibles of human nature combined with the readiness of the Bohemian to dare the unusual.[444]

As Sylvester notes in the frame (841), the darker, more serious side of Salvator's character is not emphasized in this story. The narrator sees Salvator as a perceptive man of contrasts, exuberant and fiery, yet noble, loyal, and wise (768). This description foreshadows not only the discussions between Antonio and Salvator about art, where the significance of proper perception is important, but also Salvator's balanced, spirited perception of life. In Salvator's painting, Antonio senses the presence of an artist who knows how to unlock the hidden secrets of nature in order to portray it in an exalted harmony (778, 779). Salvator can depict nature in the kind of union it must originally have possessed. The concord of all nature revealed, as Antonio says, through the hieroglyphs of stones and trees to the perceptive individual, gives testimony to Salvator's artistic vision.[445]

442. Meyer, *Sonderling*, pp. 103–4, correctly sees the close relationship between the Baron von B. and Capuzzi, but he does not mention the *Serapionsbrüder* or the fact that the stories stand in sequence in that work.

443. A clue to the essentially bright notes of the story lies in Ottmar's remark that he tried to write in Boccaccio's style (p. 766).

444. See McGlathery, *Mysticism*, p. 95. For background material on Salvator Rosa and his attraction for Hoffmann, see Gerd Hemmerich, "Verteidigung des Signor Formica: Zu E. T. A. Hoffmanns Novelle," *Jahrbuch der Jean-Paul-Gesellschaft*, 17 (1982), pp. 113–28, especially pp. 113–16.

445. Hoffmann's description of Rosa seems to reflect the influence of Schubert, as the following passage from p. 29 of the *Symbolik des Traumes* makes clear: "Die uns umgebende Natur in allen ihren mannigfaltigen Elementen und Gestalten, erscheint hiernach als ein Wort, eine Offenbarung Gottes an den Menschen, deren Buchstaben (wie denn in dieser Region alles Leben und Wirklichkeit hat) lebendige Gestalten und sich

Salvator's ability to interpret the latent harmonies of nature and bring the viewers of his pictures in tune with a lost time in which this harmony existed has considerable significance for the novella's outcome. He can establish harmony in individual lives as well: he frees Marianne from the unwelcome attentions of her guardian, arranges for her to marry Antonio, and, in the end, restores to Capuzzi a kind of happiness appropriate to his age and station.

Salvator bears some similarity with other artists in the *Serapionsbrüder*, particularly Wolfram von Eschenbach, who appeared at the beginning of the second volume of stories. Both men, though quite different in temperament, are at one with themselves and are therefore capable of helping others, as well as being superior artists (779). While the dangers from which Salvator saves Antonio are in a lighter key here than the difficulties in "Kampf der Sänger," the inner strength necessary to see the right relationship and bring it about is common to both men.

As far as Antonio and Marianne are concerned, Rosa is a savior in fact as well as in name. The *Salvator* theme appears in the frame immediately after the story. One of Rosa's sonnets is cited in which he compares himself to the betrayed and crucified Christ because of critics who claim he took his poetry from other writers (841–42). The character of Rosa as well as the inclusion of the sonnet seem to indicate that Hoffmann was setting up a definite contrast between the integrated artistic personality of Rosa and the fragmented one of Werner. The points of comparison between the two, placed in immediate juxtaposition, are very striking. Rosa, gifted with an ironic sense of humor totally lacking in the mad Werner, establishes harmony in his paintings as well as among his friends. He sees things in their proper perspective; if he compares himself to Christ, it is simply an image for a sonnet and not an *ideé fixe*, which determines his mode of behavior and eventually drives him mad, as with Werner.

Since "Formica" itself resembles a comedy with its rapid shift of scene, stock characters, and traditional plot, it is not surprising that the conversation turns to the theater and its problems.[446] After criticizing

---

bewegende Kräfte sind. Auf diese Weise wird dann die Natur das Original jener Naturbildersprache."

446. Hemmerich, "Verteidigung," pp. 119–20 and 123, discusses the connection between the frame conversation on pp. 842–44 and the novella. Pikulik, *Erzähler*, p.

Ottmar's story for being a disconnected series of pictures, the brothers' conversation makes the same judgment of comedy in the contemporary theatrical scene. In earlier times, there was an underlying continuity that gave meaning to the plays (842). The contemporary malaise of the theater finds expression in the long anecdote about a talented actor who, in deep despair about the current theater, continued to play hack roles in provincial theaters.

"Zacharias Werner"

Dealing as it does with the theater and with one of life's unfortunate creatures who can still be mordant in his misery, this anecdote also has some parallels with Zacharias Werner. He, like the actor, started his career with great success but came into troubled times without completely losing his gift of observation.[447] Cyprian compares the gifted actor's descent with that of Werner, who vanished as if drawn into a maelstrom (848–49). With the introduction of Werner into the discussion, Hoffmann begins one of the most significant sections of the frame. This consideration of Werner's *ideé fixe*, the madness of his mother, and the precarious position of the artist vis-à-vis the nether side of consciousness resume many themes on which Hoffmann has expanded often throughout the work. However, instead of adumbrating his ideas through fictional characters or through an individual like Serapion known only to Cyprian, Hoffmann incorporates these themes into an analysis of a living artist familiar to all present. This application of the nonfictional anecdote, which has been so prevalent in the frame, achieves a unique intensity because of Werner's fame. In addition, the parallel position of Serapion, in the first part of the first book, and Werner, at the beginning of the fourth and final book, presents a formal symmetry with a deeper significance. Both men, like some of the characters in the inner stories, are failed artists whose flaws can be charged to their mental confusion.

190, treats the close relationship between the comic and the serious on the one hand and life and theater on the other.

447. Christa Karoli, "E. T. A. Hoffmann und Zacharias Werner: Ein Beitrag zum romantischen Genieproblem" MHG 16 (1970), pp. 43–61, pp. 59–60, note 48.

While the parallel between Serapion and Werner has been noted briefly,[448] no one has analyzed in detail the striking similarities between them. Both men are highly gifted artists with a keen sense of humor. Both fancy themselves important religious figures: Serapion, the early Christian martyr of the same name; Werner, Jesus Christ or a prophet. For both, madness offers a safe harbor that blocks their realistic understanding of the exterior world; they take their dream state to be the only true one (see 55, 856). Serapion and Werner believe they are superior to other men, that they penetrate truths not seen or perceived by the average person. When this process goes to the extreme, then the madness cannot be healed: the "grauenvolle Hypermystik" ["ghastly hypermysticism"] (858), in which a large capacity for sin can be proof of one's divine nature, seems to have influenced Werner, whose psyche was a curious mixture of religious ecstasy and extreme eroticism.

The religious hysteria dominating Werner is a knot in which the major themes of this excursus—madness, the nature of genius, the influence of heredity and environment on an individual—converge. Werner's belief in himself as a sort of Christ figure came about from his mother, an intelligent, sensitive woman who was also quite mad. The Werners lived in the same house Hoffmann did as a child; Hoffmann used to hear Mrs. Werner screaming when she was in a particularly bad way. Mrs. Werner believed she was the Virgin Mary and that Zacharias was the Messiah.[449] This tendency seemed to run in the family, as Mrs. Werner's brother showed similar traits.

After the death of her husband in 1782, when Zacharias was almost fourteen, Mrs. Werner came to the frequent attention of the authorities because of her delight in legal action regarding her husband's will. From the depositions of her son's guardians, as well as from various doctors who examined her, comes most of the information about her mental state and much about the young Zacharias. Her illness seems to have begun in earnest about 1780; it came in acute stages, then lifted

448. Karoli, "Hoffmann/Werner," MHG 16 (1970) pp. 45, 47.

449. Mühlpfordt, "Vererbung," pp. 119–20; Erich Jenisch, "Zacharias Werners Mutter," *Euphorion* 31 (1930), pp. 95–119; see also Peter Lomas, "The Significance of Post-partum Breakdown," in *The Predicament of the Family* (London, 1967), pp. 126–39, ed. Peter Lomas: "In puerperal breakdown a characteristic fantasy of the mother is either that of the immaculate conception of a Christ-child or the production of an ugly and evil creature resulting from intercourse with the Devil. In the former case, the mother becomes consumed by a dread of envy . . . "(p. 137).

for a time.[450] Some of the guardians lamented the mother's influence on her son, while another noted that Werner's mother loved him to the point of indecency. Zacharias therefore seems to have been congenitally predisposed to mental illness through his mother; in addition, they shared certain obsessions, such as a deranged approach to religion. With Zacharias it took the form of a quasi-prophetic, mystical preoccupation.[451]

Hoffmann's early, personal knowledge of Mrs. Werner would have later interested him in the family, but his keen and passionate discussion of Werner's problems long after Werner's prominence had faded had other roots. Among these was Hoffmann's fervent desire to succeed as an artist, which Werner thwarted through selfishness and treachery. Werner, eight years Hoffmann's senior, achieved what success he did early in his career, beginning with "Die Söhne des Tales" (1803/4) (the sons of the valley)", when Hoffmann was unknown and sometimes out of work. In 1804, Hoffmann met Werner again when he was sent to Warsaw, where Werner was also working as a Prussian official. Werner, who was writing "Das Kreuz an der Ostsee" (The cross at the Baltic Sea) chose Hoffmann as the composer for the stage music for the first part, "Die Brautnacht" (The wedding night). Werner forced Hoffmann to work long hours on it; this greatly deepened Hoffmann's disappointment when the dramatist and theater director Iffland refused to produce the play.[452] In a letter to his friend Hippel, Hoffmann noted that he would have long since been famous if his music to the play could have been heard.[453] Alluding to his work on the music for Werner's play, Hoffmann vainly tried to get Werner to support his musical arrangement of the "Kanonikus von Mailand" (The canon of Milan).[454]

450. Jenisch, "Zacharias," pp. 111, 118: he notes on pp. 97–98 that there was a tendency in Mrs. Werner's family toward a pathological emotional life prone to excitement over religious ideas.
451. Jenisch, "Zacharias," p. 119.
452. Karoli, "Hoffmann/Werner," MHG 16 (1970), p. 50. See also Werner's letter to Iffland in Berlin, from Warsaw, March 10, 1805, in Friedrich Schnapp's book, *Der Musiker E. T. A. Hoffmann: Ein Dokumentband* (Hildesheim, 1981), pp. 44–45. In this letter Werner relates in an almost apologetic manner his engagement of Hoffmann. Werner was always concerned about the maximum benefit to himself; even in this first collaboration with Hoffmann, his letter shows that he was ready to dump Hoffmann if Iffland made any objections to the music (p. 45).
453. Vol. 1, *E. T. A. Hoffmanns Briefwechsel, Königsberg bis Leipzig 1794–1814*, ed. Hans von Müller and Friedrich Schnapp (Munich, 1967), p. 230.
454. Karoli, "Hoffmann/Werner," MHG 16 (1970), pp. 50–51; *Briefwechsel* 1, pp. 201–2.

Upon the loss of his position at the collapse of the Prussian government, Hoffmann went to Berlin. Out of work, separated from his wife, still unknown as an artist, and frequently very hungry, he seized any opportunity. Hearing that Werner planned to bring a new drama to the Berlin stage, Hoffmann asked in December 1807 that he be allowed to compose the music. Werner, who at the time was prospering, told Hoffmann, "Denken Sie auch ein bißchen an Gott" ["Do think of God a little, too"].[455] In the spring of 1808, Werner gave Hoffmann the job of illustrating the edition of his play *Attila*. Hoffmann worked long hours living on bread and water. When he had the sketches ready, Werner informed him that he had given the job to a better-known artist.[456]

Werner's willful cancellation of his agreement with Hoffmann caused the break in their relations. Although Hoffmann remained objective about Werner's work even immediately after this event, his critical assessment of Werner's personality that appears in "Nachricht von den neuesten Schicksalen des Hundes Berganza" (News of the dog Berganza's latest fortunes) and in the *Serapionsbrüder* frame had its beginnings during their time in Warsaw. In 1805, Hoffmann could already see some of Werner's negative qualities; in a letter to Hippel, he says that Werner is living and depressing truth of how the greatest talents can be ruined by unfortunate parents.[457] In "Berganza," Hoffmann gives an ironic description of the home life of Werner and his mother, in which he alludes to the problems of heredity and upbringing:

Die Frau bildete sich ein, sie sei die Jungfrau Maria und ihr Sohn der verkannte Christus, der auf Erden wandle, Kaffee trinke und Billiard spiele, aber bald werde die Zeit kommen, wo er seine Gemeine sammeln und sie geradesweges in den Himmel führen würde. Des Sohnes rege Fantasie fand in der Mutter Wahnsinn die Andeutung seines höheren Berufs.[458]

---

455. *Briefwechsel* 1, p. 232. See p. 228 for an account of Hoffmann's plea to Werner. In note 5, p. 233, the editor notes that Werner, in a letter of March 21st to Iffland, never mentions Hoffmann's name, although in his letter to Hoffmann (p. 232) he pretended not to be undecided between Hoffmann and Weber. See also Safranski, *Hoffmann*, 180–187; Karoli, "Hoffmann/Werner," MHG 16 (1970), p. 51.

456. Karoli, "Hoffmann/Werner," MHG 16 (1970) p. 50; *Briefwechsel* 1, pp. 242–43, contains one of Hoffmann's most desperate letters, that to Hippel on May 7, 1808, where he says he has had nothing but bread to eat for five days and works morning and night on scenes for Werner's *Attila*, which will soon be published. In a calmer letter a few days later to Hippel (pp. 244–45), he writes that Werner preferred another artist.

457. *Briefwechsel* 1, p. 196; Karoli, "Hoffmann/Werner," MHG 16 (1970), p. 50.

458. "Nachricht von den neuesten Schicksalen des Hundes Berganza," p. 139, *Fantasiestücke*.

The woman imagined that she was the Virgin Mary and her son the unrecognized Christ, who was walking on earth, drinking coffee and playing billiards, but soon the time would come when he would collect his flock and lead them straight into Heaven. The son's vivid imagination found in his mother's madness the intimation of his higher calling.

The effect of a mother on a child's upbringing was closer to Hoffmann even than Mrs. Werner when he was growing up. His own mother, shattered by the disgrace of divorce, regressed to her childhood when she moved back to the Doerffer house with her younger son. She tended to be both hysterical and afraid of people.[459] While Hoffmann apparently had considerably less contact with his mother than most children, it cannot have escaped him that she had emotional problems; as an adult, the memory of his mother's condition might well have added to his own fears of madness. This fear could account for the personal engagement one feels in reading the discussion of Werner's personality in the *Serapionsbrüder;* it seems to be reflected in the following quotation:

Man sagt daß der Hysterismus der Mütter sich zwar nicht auf die Söhne vererbe in ihnen aber eine vorzüglich lebendige ja ganz exzentrische Fantasie erzeuge (856)

People say that although the mothers' hysteria is not inherited by their sons, it creates in them an especially lively, indeed, a quite eccentric imagination.

Hoffmann uses the plural for mothers and sons, which reinforces the interpretation that he was thinking of himself as well as Werner. This eccentric fantasy can bring that individual to ruin, just as the incident with the necklace before Cardillac's birth left a dangerous fascination in him.[460]

When Theodor ends his apparently theoretical description of the disastrous end of a person so afflicted, he brings out a bust of Werner, whose facial expression belies madness. Theodor describes the Werner Hoffmann knew, as a man of humor and irony (801). In an implicit comparison between the earlier Werner and the Werner Hoffmann described, Theodor exclaims that it is not possible that this promise should have withered, poisoned by delusion; he hopes that true

459. See Safranski, *Hoffmann,* pp. 21–22; Mühlpfordt, "Vererbung," p. 89.
460. Karoli, "Hoffmann/Werner," MHG 16 (1970), pp. 54–56. See also Eva R. Möllers, *Ernst Theodor Amadeus Hoffmann als Darsteller aktueller rechtlicher Fragen* (Vienna, 1934), pp. 22–25.

knowledge may yet break through (861). This hope is not just for Werner but for Hoffmann himself. As Karoli points out, Hoffmann was working at this time on the second and third parts of *Kater Murr*. In this, he was deeply immersed in the problems of genius and the potential for mental illness that comes with it.[461]

Because Werner is a person known to the brothers, the dangers seem especially real, more so than with Serapion. It was perhaps even more so than in the discussion of magnetism, where the charlatan-like character of some of its practitioners affords an easy means of distancing the phenomenon. In all of Hoffmann's mad heroes in the *Serapionsbrüder*, one senses an innate sympathy, born out of fear that the narrator could fall into the same abyss. In each case, such as that of Fröbom and Ofterdingen and here with Werner as well as Serapion, a fatal flaw in their perception poses major threats. Hoffmann's reason for portraying Werner in the way he did most probably lies behind this sympathetic treatment of his mad fictional characters. Such empathy appears near the end of the Werner excursus, when Theodor warns against negative talk about a person who succumbs to oppressive forces that they themselves might not have been able to resist (860–61).

"Erscheinungen" (Apparitions)

The sketch, "Erscheinungen," which appears as an inner story after Zacharias Werner, is, like the Werner essay, highly autobiographical. It takes place in Dresden on November 5–6, 1813, as the city lay under siege of the Prussian-Russian troops. The historical incident behind the story, which Hoffmann himself witnessed and then wrote about, was the decision of Graf von der Lobau to lead a rally by French troops out of Dresden to attack the allied positions around the city, a rally that was repelled.[462] The obvious autobiographical parallels can

461. Karoli, "Hoffmann/Werner," MHG 16 (1970), pp. 56–57; Segebrecht, *Autobiographie*, pp. 84–85.
462. See Kruse, *Aufbau* 2, pp. 672, 673. Safranski, *Hoffmann*, pp. 282–83; Segebrecht (Winkler), p. 1109.

be found in Hoffmann's letters, diary entries, and in other accounts, such as "Der Dichter und der Komponist," and in "Drey verhängniß- volle Monathe!" (Three fateful months!)[463]

While attention will be paid to specifically autobiographical paral- lels in the ensuing discussion, the autobiographical nature of the sketch has definite connections with the preceding excursus about Werner. The main character in "Erscheinungen" is the Anselmus of "Der gol- dene Topf," who has certain similarities with Werner. In the subse- quent frame discussion, Cyprian explains that everything he read to them was literally true (870). Cyprian admits here that he is Anselmus, just as Theodor recounts his personal knowledge of Werner (861) after talking about mental illness in the case of an apparently theoretical example. As the subsequent discussion will show, the material in Cyp- rian's frame account of the material in "Erscheinungen" has striking parallels to Hoffmann's letters, allowing the conclusion that Anselmus reflects to some degree aspects of Hoffmann's personality, just as he has parallels with Werner.

These correspondences touch important thematic complexes in the context of the work, such as madness and the *Serapionsprinzip*. Ansel- mus, like Werner, has problems with mental stability, as his behavior among his friends indicates (863). The nature of reality and the mean- ing of individual experience are also points of comparison between the two narratives. Werner, because of his distorted perceptions, arrogates to himself a quasi-divine role and views life experiences through it. Anselmus/Cyprian cannot distinguish which interpretation most ac- curately fits the strange sequence of events that occur on the night of November 5–6, 1813. Who is Dorothee/Agafiz? What is her connec- tion with the Russians? Why is she ready to kill Anselmus one mi- nute and save him the next? The reader is even more confused than Anselmus/Cyprian, because in the frame following the story, Cypri- anus says he was the one who received the wedding cake that Dor- othee/Agafiz made (868, 873). In the figure of Agafiz and the close correspondence between Hoffmann's letters and the account of the

---

463. Schnapp, *Tagebücher*, pp. 201–35, especially 223–35, 407–38, esp. 427–38; "Drey verhängnisvolle Monathe!," pp. 296–77, 474–77; Müller and Schnapp, *E. T. A. Hoffmanns Briefwechsel*, 1, pp. 377–425. The letter to Hitzig on December 1, 1813, is particularly valuable, since Hoffmann mentions the departure of Lobau (p. 423). For background information on the battle of Leipzig, see Freiherr von Aretin, "Vom deutschen Reich zum deutschen Bund," in *Deutsche Geschichte* 2, pp. 515–672, 642–44.

siege of Dresden in "Erscheinungen" lie examples of the strangeness that leaks into everyday life.[464] Agafiz is a major character in Werner's *Das Kreuz an der Ostsee;* an estimable woman of great personal courage, she remains steadfast in the midst of attack as her namesake in "Erscheinungen" does. In Dorothee/Agafiz's contradictory behavior, she resembles another shadowy female figure, Ferdinand's beloved in "Die Automate."

The intimate relationship between autobiography and literature that Cyprian demonstrates through an example of story and fact provides another basic point of comparison with the Werner excursus, where there is sustained discussion on the relationship of Werner's personality to his literary work (cf. previous Werner section and 849, 852, 858). Werner's literary production falters, because of his life experience, while Cyprian uses life to produce literature. This positive example of the interaction of life and literature that closely follows the Werner excursus reveals on yet another level how closely Hoffmann felt his own life related to that of Werner.

With the emphasis on personal experience forming an integral part of literature, the *Serapionsprinzip* reappears; two references in the frame make the specific connection between Cyprian and Serapion (872, 873).[465] The analysis of the Werner excursus showed how closely related he was to Serapion; Hoffmann finds another way here to adumbrate the principle in his account of Anselmus/Cyprian's experiences during the war.

Seen in the context of Zacharias Werner and the frame dealing with autobiography and literature, "Erscheinungen" takes on an added significance that cannot be appreciated unless one sees the story where Hoffmann placed it. Segebrecht, in commenting on the work, says that hardly any one of the stories that make up the cycle can be removed from its context without losing in substance. Isolation of the story from the frame leads to a changed image of the story and therefore to a different interpretation.[466]

---

464. Segebrecht, *Autobiographie,* p. 112.
465. Segebrecht, *Autobiographie,* p. 110.
466. Segebrecht, *Autobiographie,* p. 112. A good example of what can be missed when these stories are not seen in both the context of the frame and their relationship to each other appears in Negus (*Other World;* pp. 71–72) when he discusses the stories dealing with musicians.

"Der Zusammenhang der Dinge"
(The Interdependence of Things)

The connections to which Segebrecht alludes in a general way are apparent between the end of section seven, with "Erscheinungen," and the beginning of section eight, with "Der Zusammenhang der Dinge." Both narratives occur during the period of the Napoleonic wars, the latter during the Spanish Revolution of 1808–14. However, in "Zusammenhang" Hoffmann moved away from personal experience of the war to fictional evocations of a period of history that explain his interest in the frame in the novels of Sir Walter Scott (924).[467] This interest helps explain some of Hoffmann's goals in "Zusammenhang" and relates to the remark in the frame that dexterous use of historically accurate customs of a people lends life to a poetic work (924). The atmosphere of the desperate struggle of the Spanish revolutionaries, the clandestine operations, and the passionate Spanish nature in this story all reflect Hoffmann's intentions in this area.

Numerous other novellas in the *Serapionsbrüder*, such as "Der Kampf der Sänger," "Doge und Dogaresse," "Meister Martin," "Die Brautwahl," "Fräulein von Scuderi," and "Signor Formica" share with "Zusammenhang" an attention to period or regional detail. However, history figures on yet another level in "Zusammenhang": Hoffmann juxtaposes two characters representing two different philosophical approaches to history: Ludwig's, the mechanistic, Enlightenment attitude, and Euchar's, an anti-Enlightenment world view. This conflict also affords an opportunity to explore the themes of the automat and philistinism in their relationship to the Enlightenment interpretation of history. Ludwig, whose philistinism is highly developed, speaks a lot and understands very little. His inner emptiness symbolizes his inability to comprehend beauty (886).[468] Ludwig's fatal superficiality

---

467. Segebrecht, Winkler, p. 1115; Kruse, *Aufbau*, 2, pp. 682–83, p. 677.
468. The translation for "The Interdependence of Things" comes either from *Tales of Hoffmann* (no translator given) (London, 1932) or from the author and her translators.

and his equally destructive laziness lead him to embrace the doctrine of "Zusammenhang der Dinge," a concept he finds in an old book.[469] This teaching explains and excuses Ludwig's laziness and lack of commitment, since it emphasizes the mechanistic interdependence of things (886). Ludwig can in good conscience ascribe his inactive life to the ineluctable course of fate. This doctrine also makes it possible for him to avoid understanding of what is going on, whether it be the situation between Emanuela and her father's trusted servant Cubas, or between himself and Viktorine, who shows repeatedly that she loathes him (890, 891, 917, 918, 919).

This deterministic world view ties in closely with the theme of the *Automate*, a figure that has no will of its own.[470] Ludwig tends to speak of petty events in which he is a player in mechanistic images appropriate to a larger stage (887–88, 889). No decisions are necessary for Ludwig because everything that is going to happen must happen.

In Ludwig's relationship with others, he shows a predetermined, rigid approach in refusing to let reality shape his perceptions. Like Tusmann in "Brautwahl" and Capuzzi in "Formica," he stays with a preconceived opinion, whether or not it fits the situation. Emanuela (880) is Mignon; fiction, not reality, determines Ludwig's view of her. Through mechanistic, meaningless signs, Ludwig is convinced that Emanuela loves him. Sure that Euchar is cold and immune to the joys of love (891), Ludwig persists in his misinterpretation of Viktorine and Emanuela's real love interest, which is not directed towards him but towards Euchar. Because all events are predetermined, he stands outside them and never takes part; in this regard as well he resembles the *Automate*. For that reason, he never acts himself nor does he influence the outcome of events as Euchar does through his intervention.

Euchar's life stands in direct opposition to that of Ludwig, since even as a child, he talked little, but did a lot (864). Euchar knows he can influence the course of events through his personality and does not draw back from putting all of his strength and intelligence on the line.[471] In Hoffmann's account of Euchar, he incorporated many of his

---

Page references will appear in the text with Hoffmann plus the page number; this translation can be found on p. 24.

469. Kruse, *Aufbau* 2, p. 679, believes that the book in question probably was P. T. d'Holbach's *Système de la nature ou des lois du monde physique et du monde moral* (1770).

470. See Casper, "Der historische Besen," p. 494, who notes that for Hoffmann the automata became a symbol for the person with a mechanistic outlook.

471. Segebrecht, *Autobiographie*, p. 195.

beliefs about history: the predominance of the unexpected, the necessity of interpreting it, and the imperative of individual action.[472] Euchar let himself be open to events, just as Anselmus does in the previous narrative, "Erscheinungen," and Felix and Christlieb in "Das fremde Kind." The two country Brakels react against the representative of the enlightened urban world and its mechanistic forms by embracing nature and nature's strange child.

Just as the mechanical toys and the figure of Magister Tinte exercise a constricting influence on the Brakel children, so does Ludwig on Viktorine, further proof of the deadliness of his world view. When Ludwig comes in to ask for Viktorine's hand in marriage, her reaction is similar to that of Hoffmann's other *Automaten:* "Sie ließ das geschehen, aber es wurde mir in der Tat seltsam zumute, als ihr ernster, starrer Blick mir wie ohne Sehkraft, als sei sie ein lebloses Bild, schien!" ["She let it happen, but I had a strange feeling indeed when her rigid glance struck me as if she had no vision, as if she were a lifeless picture!"] (918). Viktorine, who has married Ludwig probably out of despair at having lost Euchar, comes to an insight about the real relationship of things that runs counter to that of her husband: for her, life's cohesion is made of the foolish things one does and repents of, and repeats, a frenzied succession of events that wears us down (920). Although this analysis is resigned and melancholy, it implies that the individual acts freely. Had Viktorine been capable of the kind of dramatic action characteristic of Euchar and Emanuela, she might have avoided an unhappy marriage. We never see her truly apart from her aristocratic world. She is capable of tiny revolts against convention, such as foxing Ludwig with a look-alike cousin, but she never really breaks away (889–90).

The complex framework of "Zusammenhang" divides into four parts of unequal length, which provide a contrastive pattern for the two opposing characters:

I.   876–84   Ludwig's fall; introduction of Emanuela

II.   884–93   Description of Euchar and Ludwig; Ludwig in society; Viktorine

III.   884–914   Euchar's story at the aesthetic tea; reappearance of Emanuela and Viktorine at the end

---

472. Casper, "Der historische Besen," p. 492.

IV.   914–23   Euchar's return, flashback of Ludwig's courtship and marriage of Viktorine; her insight; introduction of Emanuela as Euchar's wife

Whenever Ludwig and the other German aristocrats appear, the ironic tone of the narrator describes a superficial society prone to attach great importance to dancing, cards, and empty literature. When the passage of Euchar/Edgar's adventures in Spain and the scenes with Emanuela dominate, the narrator's mocking tone vanishes. The story begins with an apparent coincidence, an occurrence impossible in Ludwig's world view. He trips over a tree root, necessitating a stop in an inn, where Euchar sees Emanuela dancing. At his request, she sings "Laur L'immortal," celebrating General Palafox, who defended Saragossa against Napoleon.[473] As Euchar rewards her with a generous purse, she sees a strange ring on his finger, kisses his hand repeatedly, and leaves. Euchar later notices that the ring is gone. His passionate interest in all things Spanish and the theft of the ring hint at deeper connections, but Euchar remains silent. Ludwig, however, who has no experience with Spain, rattles on, misinterpreting and insulting as he goes. The beginning incident, though an extremely unlikely coincidence, is for Hoffmann the essence of history, since such events are both unforeseen and full of meaning.[474]

The interlude at the inn also functions as an introduction to the characters of Ludwig and Euchar, forming impressions in the readers' minds that are confirmed in the next chapter when the actual deceptions appear (884–87). The remainder of the second section (887–93), an account of Ludwig's misadventure at the ball, serves to highlight Ludwig's superficiality. It appears immediately before the long inner story, the third section dealing with Euchar's experiences in Spain. The ending of the third section, with its repetition of motifs in a different context, serves once more to point up the lack of understanding of Ludwig and his cohorts. It offers a pointed contrast to Euchar's passionate involvement in Spain.

The final section shows the fruits of the two different philosophies

473. Segebrecht (Winkler), p. 1113.
474. Casper, "Der historische Besen," p. 492. Pikulik, *Erzähler,* pp. 198–99, analyzes the higher power that stands behind apparent coincidences and gives coherence to the story.

of Ludwig and Euchar. Ludwig, oblivious to the meaning of life, since all events are predetermined, has aged ten years in the two that have elapsed since Euchar left (915). His paleness and dull demeanor reflect the miserable life he has with Viktorine, who is moody and irritable while Ludwig pretends she is a model of charm and sweetness. Euchar, happily married, with the fortune and reputations of his in-laws restored through his efforts, is able to see the true meaning behind Ludwig's story; yet Ludwig himself is totally unaware that Viktorine was hopelessly in love with Euchar. At the end, everyone is reconciled except Ludwig, who still holds stubbornly to the view that "Das alles lag im Zusammenhang der Dinge" ["all this was supposed to happen"] (923).

"Vampirismus"
(Vampirism)

The connection of the untitled narrative of *Vampirismus* with the preceding inner story and with the frame provides a clear example of Hoffmann's use of contrasts within the mechanism of the frame-inner story structure. In "Zusammenhang der Dinge," the hero, Euchar, shapes his destiny by the force of his own virtues, against the backdrop of a heroic struggle by a courageous people. Evil is punished, good rewarded; metaphorically speaking, whatever abysses there might have been have undergone land reclamation projects. "Vampirismus" presents the opposite kind of world: one in which good is destroyed by evil forces, no matter how much generosity and bravery virtue can muster. Graf Hyppolit (who behaved graciously to a relative his father had apparently wronged) marries her beautiful but disturbed daughter. He tries to help in the dreadful problems she faces, but for his pains is driven mad. This progressive disintegration of his personality occurs on the family estate, in the midst of familiar surroundings carefully tended. The story helps bring home, as so many in the collection have done, the nearness of demonic forces to everyday life.[475] Aurelie tries

475. Reil's *Rhapsodien* contain a detailed and highly provocative section entitled "Tobsucht, Raserey, Furor, Mania," pp. 364–95, which contains accounts of people af-

valiantly to struggle against the fate her mother seems to have foreordained for her (937–38) and continues to meet the dreadful crises of her life with kindness and bravery—until the last one.

The transition to this chamber of horrors appears in the frame discussion between the two narratives. "Zusammenhang" reminds the brothers of Scott and his wonderful world of lively historical characters; yet, talented as he is, they miss an inner quickening spirit, which is certainly present in Scott's contemporary, Lord Byron: "Vorherrschend soll sein Hang zum Düstern, ja Grauenhaften und Entsetzlichen sein, und seinen Vampir hab ich gar nicht lesen mögen" ["His proclivity towards the ominous, even the ghastly and the horrid, is said to be predominant; I have never cared to read his Vampire" (925–26). Following this observation, a somewhat detailed discussion of actual vampires takes place. Once again, Hoffmann used the technique of taking factual accounts from Ranft's book and elsewhere (926–27). In order to give these descriptions verisimilitude, he names names. Just as in the section on magnetism, factual descriptions appear before a longer narrative. "Vampirismus," like many of these stories without titles that appear in the frame, was apparently told to Cyprian by someone who knew the family (929).

The previous discussion has indicated that "Vampirismus" is typical of other untitled narratives in the frame in regard to the factual accounts that precede it and to its connection with one of the brothers' personal experience. It contains many of the same leitmotifs used elsewhere, both in the frame and in inner stories, to indicate the presence of evil in a given individual—the intensive, searing gaze of the *Baronesse*, the cold shudders the count feels in her presence, the laming of the power of speech, eyes that stare without seeing. All of these manifestations indicate that a higher power makes its presence felt; we have seen similar descriptions in "Der Unheimliche Gast," "Der Kampf der Sänger," "Die Automate," and "Nachricht aus dem Leben eines bekannten Mannes." There are numerous hints in the story's flashbacks that the old *Baronesse* is in the power of the Devil (935, 937); when her mother describes how Satan gained ascendancy over her

---

flicted in a manner similar to Hyppolit's wife. Reil says: "Die Raserey charakterisiert sich also durch abnorme Handlungen (365)." "Die Sitten des Kranken sind aufs sonderbarste verändert; das züchtige Weib stößt Zoten aus, entblößt sich, die sanfte Schöne wird eine wütende Megäre (373)."

during Aurelie's birth, Aurelie cannot continue (937–38). Like the Count in "Der unheimliche Gast," Aurelie's mother is found dead on the morning of the wedding (932). But, while the power of the count disappears upon his death, the curse of the *Baronesse* survives her and visits itself upon her daughter; the daughter shows herself to be totally in the grip of ghoulish forces, finally sinking her teeth in her husband's breast.[476] In its emphasis on the impossibility of escape from mysterious forces, "Vampirismus" has much in common with "Die Bergwerke zu Falun," "Der Kampf der Sänger," and "Fräulein von Scuderi." As with madness and magnetism, terror can also serve as a lever that expands the artist's consciousness (927), providing yet another example of the interrelatedness of Hoffmann's themes of madness, magnetism, and the spirit world in providing inspiration for the artist as long as he can keep a safe distance.

"Die ästhetische Teegesellschaft" (The Aesthetic Society Tea) "Die Königsbraut" (The King's Betrothed)

The last narratives, the "Ästhetische Teegesellschaft" and "Die Königsbraut," mark an abrupt change from the horrors of "Vampirismus" and hark back to the sections of "Der Zusammenhang der Dinge" where Ludwig figures prominently. In all three narratives, there are satirical elements that merge into caricature and verge on the burlesque. The aesthetic gathering in the "Zusammenhang der Dinge," where a dreadful poet read his pathetic tragedy, only to collapse in a fit of coughing, corresponds to the group in which Ottmar reads his deliberately inane verses. It has parallels as well with the literary efforts of Amandus von Nebelstern, Ännchen's fiancé, in "Die Königsbraut." The emphasis on such pseudo-writers reflects yet another instance of

476. Pikulik, *Erzähler*, p. 202, cites a pertinent passage from Reil's *Rhapsodien*, pp. 394ff. , which could have influenced Hoffmann. A pregnant woman lusted after the flesh of her husband so much that she killed him and salted his flesh so that she could enjoy it for a long time.

Hoffmann's criticism of the philistine, which appeared at the beginning of the *Serapionsbrüder* in the account of the bourgeois clubs and that echoes throughout the work.[477] In making the philistines an object of ridicule, Hoffmann decreases their threat.

Another point of comparison between the two stories that begin and end the eighth section is that they hold up for ironic amusement subjects that are treated with gravity elsewhere. Ludwig's superficial attempts to find relationships where none exist mock ideas that Hoffmann elsewhere takes seriously. A similar process is at work in "Die Königsbraut" in regard to magic and the occult world.

Hoffmann makes fun of it through the figure of Lord Dapsul, who has ridiculous rather than frightening characteristics, particularly since he is so ineffectual at casting spells. Although his daughter stands in awe of him, he still is powerless to convince her not to marry Daucus Carota, nor is he successful in keeping Corduanspitz in the pot. Dapsul, a parody of the figure of the wise magician, the Drosselmeiers, and the Leonhards who appear in other *Serapionsbrüder* stories, is never so truly lost in the contemplation of the other world that the smell of lunch cannot lure him down from the tower.[478]

In his role as burlesque magician, Dapsul parallels Daucus Carota, who, though he is representative of the worst of the *Elementargeister*, below even the king of the metals (982), does not excite the terror that such figures usually do in Hoffmann's works. Part of the reason for the absence of threat in his presence lies in the appearance of the gnomes in the form of vegetables from a kitchen garden.[479] Even susceptible Romantics could not be transfixed by a carrot.

Hoffmann mentions one of his sources in the frame, an anecdote about a lady whose workers found a ring grown into a *Mohrrübe*

---

477. See Müller, "Nachwort," *Aufsätze*, p. 129, who also noted this similarity.

478. Müller, "Nachwort," *Aufsätze*, p. 126, notes a parallel between the ludicrousness of the gnome figure in "Das fremde Kind" and the comic elements in "Die Königsbraut," with the difference that the burlesque qualities of the situation could be fully exploited in a fairy tale like "Die Königsbraut," whereas they could not in a serious story such as "Das fremde Kind." See also Marianne Thalmann, *Märchen*, pp. 91–94, for a discussion of Hoffmann's satire in "Die Königsbraut." DeLoecker, in *Atlantis*, pp. 201–2, in an analysis of the narrative, says that "Königsbraut" differs significantly from the other *Märchen* in the amount of text devoted to reporting and to monologues. Because of the large percentage of the text given over to these two types of narrative, there is little opportunity for dialogue or introspection.

479. See DeLoecker, *Atlantis*, p. 203.

[carrot] they dug up (994). She notes, "das müsse ja einen herrlichen Stoff geben zu einem Märchen" ["that must be wonderful material for a fairy tale"] (994). Shortly before Hoffmann wrote "Die Königsbraut," he mentions in one of the "Briefe aus den Bergen" (Schnapp dates it November 1820)[480] that Rübezahl was speaking to him as he sat under a tree—always a dangerous place in Hoffmann's stories.[481]

Rübezahl, as the reader of Musäus will remember, received his name because of the trick the beautiful girl he loved played on him to gain time to escape: he was to count the carrots. Carrots had been the major means the spirit had to keep her from being lonely. He changed them into her friends and companions who, however, withered with the passage of seasons.[482] Hoffmann makes several important changes in the Rübezahl material that suit the extended persiflage he seems to have had in mind.

Rübezahl is not a carrot, but a rather threatening spirit, who can make or destroy the fortune of humans. In Hoffmann's story, Daucus Carota is the spirit, but he is also a carrot, which decreases his threatening aspect. Hoffmann may have taken the changing of carrots into human beings who then wither like old carrots and applied it to his story to the grotesque shape of Daucus and the saffron-like color that Ännchen takes on.[483] Superficially at least, the form of Daucus has certain similarities with Nußknacker, since the head is oversized in both cases (204, 963). Yet, Nußknacker's similarity in shape to Daucus is only a result of his being under a spell; he does not have the character of a destructive spirit like Daucus.

The blackness of the garden and the deadening effect that Daucus has on it are reminiscent of the effect of Magister Tinte on the woods in "Das fremde Kind." But Daucus destroys a kitchen garden; this deed produces a symbolic effect different from the destruction of a woods. The wondrous world that Daucus shows Ännchen and that tempts her to make an alliance with him has a parallel in "Die Bergwerke zu Fa-

---

480. E. T. A. Hoffmann, *Nachlese*, ed. Friedrich Schnapp, p. 82.
481. *Nachlese*, pp. 88–89.
482. J. K. A. Musäus, *Volksmärchen der Deutschen* (Munich, no year), "Legenden von Rübezahl," esp. pp. 178–96. See also Von Müller, "Nachwort," *Aufsätze*, pp. 135–37.
483. Negus, *Other World*, compares Ännchen's changed appearance after her association with Daucus to Fröbom's "stone-like rigidity" (p. 115) when Dahlsjö brings him back from the mine.

lun." Here Elis is first attracted to the world of the inner earth by the vision of it in a dream (178).[484] Dapsul's two references to magnetism show other parallels as well. When Ännchen is unable to remove the ring from her finger, her father wants to find out the secret of the ring, and starts to magnetize his daughter: "nahm Herr Dapsul von Zabelthau ein kleines Eisen zur Hand, berührte damit Ännchens Stirne und bestrich dann einigemal ihren rechten Arm von der Achsel bis in die Spitze des kleinen Ringefingers herab" (956–57) ["Herr Dapsul von Zabelthau took a small tool of iron in his hand, touched Ännchen's forehead with it, and then stroked it along her right arm several times, from the armpit to the tip of the little finger"] (Bleiler, 387). Dapsul's efforts come to naught since he falls in the middle of them. In the second reference, Dapsul relates how much the *Elementargeister* love human scientific experiments, which Kruse sees as a sardonic reference to magnetism on Hoffmann's part.[485]

The appearance of Daucus Carota in Ännchen's very mundane world has parallels with other stories and also with the other two fairy tales in the *Serapionsbrüder*. In "Die Brautwahl," "Der Artushof," "Fragment aus dem Leben dreier Freunde," "Nußknacker und Mausekönig," and "Das fremde Kind," representatives from another world upset the everyday order of life and threaten it in varying degrees for other characters. Yet the elements of burlesque in "Die Königsbraut" enable it to resume these themes in a capriccio mood rather than one that seems really threatening.

Hoffmann's most telling sally against the spirit world is also a sublimely funny parting shot at the pseudo-poets. Dapsul, with his *Geheimniskrämerei* (947), his many books and his years of study, cannot outwit Daucus; changed into an inedible mushroom, he awaits the certain fate of decapitation by his daughter who gets rid of such fungi. What saves Dapsul is the abominable poetry and music of Amandus, who, bedazzled by the fact that he is to be a court poet for Daucus, sings some of his work, driving Daucus back to the netherworld. The

484. Negus, *Other World*, pp. 113–17, offers an excellent analysis of "Die Königsbraut," which he sees as a parody of "Die Bergwerke zu Falun." Momberger, *Sonne und Punsch*, notes that even though the miraculous seems to be present in Daucus, it is a deceptive facade. He interprets Daucus as a representation of the collapse of romantic symbolism (p. 118).

485. Kruse, *Aufbau* 2, p. 690.

poetic muse of Amandus produces such appalling symptoms in Daucus's digestive tract that even the prospect of Ännchen cannot hold him (991).

The obvious persiflage in "Die Königsbraut" has, until recently, blinded many critics to the serious aspects of the story. Gisela Vitt-Maucher's recent analysis of the novella in terms of Schubert's teachings shows how Hoffmann adumbrated Schubertian concepts in the use of the ring motif, the metamorphosis of plants into human-like creatures, and the theme of fertility. The ring connects Anna with the magic world, the dark side of nature: when she takes it off, the spell is over, just as it is for the person who awakens out of a magnetic sleep.[486] There are parallels here with Mathilde in "Der Kampf der Sänger," with the Nutcracker in "Nußknacker und Mausekönig," and with Bogislav, Moritz, and Angelika in "Der unheimliche Gast." The anthropomorphizing of the plant world here is similar to the figure of the queen in "Die Bergwerke zu Falun," where there is also a contest between the subterranean and the earthly lover.

This interaction between man and the forces lying in his surroundings receives a compressed, highly symbolic, and ironic treatment that does suit it as the final story in the *Serapionsbrüder*. The themes of magic, magnetism, spirits from the nether world, and the problems of the artist receive here a satirical treatment that makes them less threatening. The story functions as frame in this regard. Just as we have seen parts of the frame serve as a distancing mechanism through the means of anecdotes, intellectual discussions, persiflage, so we see the story "Die Königsbraut" performing this function at the end of the work. Since "Die Königsbraut" combines elements from the two major thematic concerns—the subterranean world of madness and evil spirits, and the figure of the Romantic artist—it is ideally suited not only in its satirical tone, but also in its content, to end the work. The genie is put back into the bottle so everyone can get a good night's sleep.

486. See Gisela Vitt-Maucher, "E. T. A. Hoffmanns 'Die Königsbraut': ein nach der Natur entworfenes Märchen," *MHG*, vol. 30 (1984), pp. 42–58, especially pp. 45, 48–50, 53. Vitt-Maucher also has a useful analysis of previous criticism, pp. 42–43.

Conclusion

This study's consideration of *Die Serapionsbrüder* as a whole has demonstrated that the sequence of stories, far from being the haphazard, slapdash arrangement that some critics have suggested, possesses an overall aesthetic unity. Even at the outset, the juxtaposition of Serapion and Krespel gives us important clues to the understanding of both figures. The sequence of narratives beginning with "Rat Krespel" and ending with "Der Dichter und der Komponist" constitutes an artistic biography of Theodor, one of the frame characters. This context is significant not only for the interpretation of those inner stories, but also for the placement of this biography at the beginning of the cycle, which foreshadows on yet another level the major theme of the work. The positioning of the Serapion story, at the very beginning of the entire work, balances the appearance of his real-life counterpart, Zacharias Werner, near the end and shows the importance of the relationship between artistic creativity and madness that dominates both the inner stories and the frame.

The theme of madness, often connected with the nether side of consciousness, that manifests itself only in the individual in the first section moves into areas that transcend the individual in the second part of the first book. Introduced in a lighthearted way in "Ein Fragment aus dem Leben dreier Freunde," the supernatural world erupts into daily life as a source of inspiration in the revenant Berklinger of "Der Artushof" and as a threat to sanity in "Die Bergwerke zu Falun," where the mysterious forces that take hold of an individual and drive him to destruction start to reveal their more threatening aspects. While such forces dominate "Nußknacker und Mausekönig," the fairy tale atmosphere so at odds with the bourgeois setting in which the story takes place distances them from the reader.

The supernatural world that figured so prominently in the inner stories of the second part of Book I now dominates the beginning frame of Book II. Here a protracted discussion of magnetism with many clinical details gives scientific explanations for the mysterious forces such as the talking Turk in "Die Automate", which seem to influence the lives of some inner-story characters, such as Heinrich von Ofterdingen in "Der Kampf der Sänger". Klingsohr in "Der Kampf der Sänger", the ghost in "Spukgeschichte", the mysterious characters in "Die Automate", the stunning series of coincidence and revelation in "Doge und Dogaresse", as well as the threatening role of the sea, all reflect the workings of forces that unsettle because they cannot be completely understood.

The second part of Book II, as if to give some relief from these difficult people and situations, deals with various representations of the Golden Age in music, art, and nature. In "Alte und neue Kirchenmusik," the narrator looks back to the time of Palestrina, whose Christian sensibility combined with great musical gifts made it possible to write music revealing unsuspected harmonies in nature and man. "Meister Martin der Küfner und seine Gesellen" depicts a period in which art, craft, and marriage could coexist productively. "Das fremde Kind" portrays a natural setting with paradisiacal elements, but under attack from vicious external forces, foreshadowing the ominous stories of the third book.

Though Book III begins with a rather witty conversation about the Devil, "Nachricht aus dem Leben eines bekannten Mannes" shows enough of his dark side to add unsettling notes. "Die Brautwahl," like "Ein Fragment aus dem Leben dreier Freunde" in regard to ghosts, treats the themes of evil and external possession in an ironic and entertaining way before they break through in two of the most powerful stories in the collection, "Der unheimliche Gast" and "Das Fräulein von Scuderi." The full force and danger of magnetism appears in these stories, first for the powerful individual, Count S, and then for the artist, Cardillac. The degenerate atmosphere of the Paris of Fräulein Scuderi stands in sharp contrast to the idyllic parts of the second section of Book II. "Spielerglück" and "Der Baron von B." deal with possession and madness, respectively, but in contexts that are less extensive and somewhat, particularly in the case of the baron, less threatening.

In Book IV, Hoffmann contrasts the ideal artist, Signor Formica, a man of the highest artistic gifts who has such a firm grasp on reality that he can help both himself and others, with Zacharias Werner, a dramatist who never really fulfilled his promise because of his madness and who has parallels with Serapion. "Erscheinungen" continues in the autobiographical vein of the Werner excursus, dealing with the nature of reality and the meaning of individual experience in the eccentric Anselmus. Much of Part II, Book IV contrasts the bourgeois world of the philistine with either an anti-Enlightenment approach, as in the case of Euchar in "Der Zusammenhang der Dinge," or with threatening forces from outside, as in "Die Königsbraut." The terror inspired by "Vampirismus" can, as the frame indicates, serve as a lever to expand the artist's consciousness, just as madness and magnetism do, though each has its attendant dangers. By picking up the themes of the juxtaposition of the philistine world in its confrontation with forces it does not understand, as well as with its links with Serapion, Hoffmann has brought the work full circle.

This interpretation has shown that, far from being the random, jerry-built structure older critics said it was, the frame is an integral part of the work. It elucidates the stories through intellectual discussion and anecdote, offering important clues to their interpretation, not only because of the frame's content but also because of the superstructure and sequence it provides for the inner narratives. Finished shortly before Hoffmann's death in 1822, the *Serapionsbrüder* takes on special importance for Hoffmann research, since it is, in many ways, his most complete literary treatment, combining his opinions on many of the major themes of his poetry with some of his best short narratives, in a sequence and context that seemed to him significant.

Afterword

Der Wintergarten and *Die Serapionsbrüder*, published just ten to twelve years apart, seem in many ways as different as their creators' personalities were. Yet there are areas in which the Prussian patrician and the impecunious imbiber from Königsberg had similar approaches, especially in relation to the past. Both men seemed to be influenced by the general interest in the German Middle Ages and the sixteenth century that was so characteristic of the intellectual climate of the period. This fascination with the German past coalesced with speculations about the Golden Age, making this somewhat remote period a fruitful source of narrative topics. Two of Arnim's nine evenings, the third and the sixth, come from the medieval period; Hoffmann's "Der Kampf der Sänger," "Doge und Dogaresse," "Nachricht aus dem Leben eines bekannten Mannes," and "Meister Martin der Küfner und seine Gesellen" take place completely in the Middle Ages or the sixteenth century, and other stories, such as "Der Artushof" and "Die Brautwahl," have characters from those times.

While each writer used the material from old chronicles as sources, for example, for different purposes, both had in common the need to explain what the events described in them meant. Arnim, in the frame of the fourth evening, has the envoy scold the invalid for not writing down the significant events behind the Napoleonic conflicts as a participant would have seen them: only through memoirs, from the individual's point of view, can one know what actually took place and what was significant. Hoffmann, reacting against the Enlightenment approach to history, which made the past into a logical and inevitable sequence of events, preferred to use his inner eye to look behind the scenes and understand the psychological forces at work.

Because both men wanted to explore the hidden elements of the

275

past, they used similar methods of uncovering them, using the material from chronicles and other historical or quasi-historical narratives. Both interpreted what they found with frequent additions or transformations from their own viewpoints. Arnim's version of the Battle of Trafalgar is as unlikely an explanation of that event as Hoffmann's fantasy about the historical reality behind the painting of the Doge. Yet for both men such explanations influenced their own understanding of their times and themselves. The setting of material in a historical period either remote from one's own time or, as in the Nelson and Meduse poem, in a genre not usually reserved for historical writing, serves several narrative purposes. For Arnim, it made it possible to try to educate his hearers, either with material from another age, when individuals could act selflessly and courageously, or with material from recent events transposed into a quasi-mythic context. The distance afforded by either time or genre gave him the latitude he needed to explore difficult or sensitive topics. Hoffmann, though generally uninterested in current events, also used the past to provide a safe distance, just as he did in the fairy tales. Hoffmann's stories set in remoter periods gave him the opportunity to explore material that threatens one's psychological balance. Through a skillful alternation between material from the past as well as more contemporary sources, Hoffmann provided his readers his own peculiar perspective on the pervasive aspects of supernatural powers as well as giving them, like Arnim, a picture of times which were not out of joint. For Arnim, the forays into the past aided the didactic and moral purposes that he espoused in the hope of transforming his country; for Hoffmann, preoccupation with the past was one of several springboards he made use of to dive into the mysteries of the subconscious and supernatural forces.

There are also important similarities in their adaptations of the frame genre to their own ends. Arnim's *Wintergarten* frame, more extensive than in his other novella collections, *Die Novellensammlung von 1812* and *Landhausleben* (1826), suited his didactic tendencies well. It afforded him the opportunity to pull in material from the most disparate of sources in attempting to invigorate the apathetic Germans of his day. The adaptability of the frame also must have appealed to Hoffmann, who used it to advocate the Serapiontic principle that the inner stories were supposed to illustrate. Through this mechanism, he was able to unite novellas, fairy tales, and anecdotes, which at first might seem to have little in common, into a sequence that itself afforded clues to their interpretation. In contrast with Boccaccio and, to some extent, with Goethe, both men used the frame not primarily as a means to escape, but as a way to accomplish a goal, whether one of reeducating others, as in Arnim, or exploring artistic sensibilities and consciousness, as with Hoffmann.

Because they ignored the option of treating the frame as a solely mechanical device to present the stories, both men expanded its role greatly, following the precedent Goethe established with *Unterhaltungen*. In Arnim's work, the characters are individuals who represent various personality and social types. They are not, as they are in Hoffmann, primarily refractions of his own complex personality. Arnim carefully avoided giving them names, since he did not want to individualize them so much that the readers will not identify with them. Since his goals were to a large extent political, it is no accident that two of his characters, the invalid and the envoy, have experience in this sphere and serve, in part, as preceptors to the group.

Hoffmann's constellation of alter egos contains characters with some traits or interests of his friends, yet these men do not develop as much as human beings as some of Arnim's characters do. While they seem more like individuals, since they have names, in reality they serve generally to advocate certain positions. Cyprian is the character most susceptible to supernatural influences, while Vinzenz, the physician, is the most sardonic of the group. In many cases, they seem interchangeable, which is not the case with Arnim's characters. Hoffmann uses this similarity among them to good effect when he constructs the frame conversations, which owe much to Tieck's *Phantasus*. Hoffmann's lively interest in medical science's advances on the psychological front, personal experiences, and his own sometimes contradictory opinions on topics such as magnetism, madness, automatic machines, different types of music and composition, fill the frame with discussions that cover a variety of aspects of each issue. He presents this material in a way that keeps it from being dull; individual recollection and anecdotal experience adumbrate the theoretical positions and serve to make more credible the inner stories in the frame. When Theodor follows Lothar's critical theoretical exposition of magnetism with his own more balanced description of clinical experiments, the reader is more inclined to take seriously the potential and the threat of this new approach and to find believable and therefore unsettling the inner stories, which have magnetism as a theme. The discussion of Zacharias Werner near the end of the work resumes many of the ideas about madness discussed in the frame in a dramatic way: the description of the disintegration of a gifted artistic psyche. The plunge into the abyss of insanity by a prominent writer known to the assembled company validates the concerns addressed throughout the frame.

Arnim's frame characters build up their own novella within the frame; it centers on the relationship between the lady of the house and the invalid. Although it soon becomes clear he adores her, the nature and extent of their relationship is only revealed at the last, when the lady has undergone changes in her attitude that make her ready to entertain a renewed suit on the part of the invalid. In this way, Arnim shows the effectiveness of the reeducation program that the stay in the country house has provided. The lady, who represents the defeated, disoriented German nation, has realized the wrongness and the futility of her choice of the Frenchman. She married Winter out of resignation and desperation; with his death, she is ready for a new spring. The ending of the frame novella, with the lady and the assembled company setting off on new ventures, proves that the inner stories have had the desired effect.

Because of the novella contained in it, the nature of Arnim's frame differs significantly from that of Hoffmann. Arnim's is often more elliptical and symbolic; its meaning reveals itself only through careful reading. Events that transpire in the frame have significance on several levels for an understanding of the work; for example, both the arrival of Winter as a passenger with the narrator in the introduction and the fire that breaks out in the stable in the frame of the second evening are interpreted in the light of the current political situation. Part of the difficulty in coming to terms with Arnim's elusive allusive style lies in his retention of a stock element in the frame genre: nothing may be said about the upsetting events that brought the disparate group together. This situation makes it impossible to talk about the very issue that weighs on everyone's mind: Napoleon's crushing defeat of the Germans. Arnim probably retained this convention because it was useful to his purposes; neither his group of characters (many of whom were defensive about their own meager contribution to their nation's cause) nor his potential readers would have responded in the manner

Arnim wished had he begun a frontal assault on their behavior. He chooses instead a more indirect method to achieve his ends; while current events cannot be discussed directly, he finds a hundred ways to keep the debacle before everyone's eyes. You may not mention Napoleon, but you may talk about the lady of the house's misplaced affections for a French officer; you avoid direct criticism of individuals who were less valorous than they might have been, but you offer an idealized account of the Scottish Rebellion of 1745 and of Admiral Nelson at Trafalgar. The envoy, in the frame of the third evening, discusses the selfishness of Germans he has known abroad and their willingness to follow foreign masters; he scarcely touched on the recent disaster, but the significance is clear: the weak inner fibre of the Germans has contributed to their defeat. In the very center of the work, the poem "Träume" contains oblique references to the French as it describes the abduction of the statue on the Brandenburg Gate and the destruction of Prussia.

Although Arnim's characteristically different prose and his symbolic use of events make his frame generally more difficult to understand than Hoffmann's, he, too, uses material in the frame in order to point up or accentuate the inner story. For example, at the end of the fourth evening, the assembled company decides to imitate Philander and bivouac in the snow. They cannot even endure it for half an hour, which points up the contrast between their soft lives, untouched by war, on the one hand, and the experiences of Philander in the inner story and the invalid in the frame on the other. When action occurs in Hoffmann's frame, it comes through the account of one of the brothers, not as an event that takes place in the frame. Arnim, like Hoffmann, also uses discussions to frame the stories, as in the third and eighth evenings. Unlike Hoffmann, he occasionally elects to delete a closing frame after a story or, as in the case of the ninth evening, to begin a story without a frame. Perhaps a hint as to why Arnim occasionally omitted the frame lies in the closing section of *Landhausleben* (Country house life); in the only section that functions as a frame, the *Schlußbericht* (Closing report), Arnim writes,

"Also ist hier noch nichts gesagt von den Erzählern und von unsrer Gesellschaft", fragte der Marchese . . . , "das ist gegen die Manier, welche im 'Wintergarten' beobachtet wurde, Sie hätten jeder Erzählung ihren geselligen Rahmen und die dabei gewonnene Kritik lassen sollen." "Die Erfahrung hat mich belehrt," entgegenete ich, "daß diese Zwischenreden der Gesellschaft von den meisten Lesern, eben weil sie nur Bruchstücke einer fortlaufenden Geschichte sind, überschlagen oder überlaufen werden." (Migge, III, 518–19)

"But is there nothing said here about the narrators and about our group?" asked the Marchese . . . , "that differs from the way in which things were done in 'Wintergarten,' you should have given every story its frame within the group and included the criticism that arose from it." "Experience has taught me," I replied, "that these verbal interludes by members of the group are skipped or overlooked by most people, precisely because they are only fragments of a continuing story."

Whatever the source of the disillusionment with the frame apparent in this quotation, the fact remains that *Wintergarten* represents Arnim's first and most extensive effort to create a frame that bore a great deal of interpretative weight.

The organization of the frame in the two works centers around what is told in an evening, though the "evenings" are appreciably longer with Hoffmann. Common to both works is the tendency to make the frame that begins the session longer than that which follows it or which follows the individual inner story. Hoffmann's organization does change somewhat at the end of the third book and in parts of the fourth book, where he sometimes includes longer frame passages between the stories. Both works contain a group that is supposed to interact with the stories. However, the very different nature of the two cycles influences not only the types of characters, as we have seen, but also the content of the frame. Because Hoffmann's frame consists of writers who meet to hear each other's stories and comment on them, there are extensive passages devoted to literary criticism, both of the stories and other contemporary works. At the end of "Die Brautwahl," for example, the brothers discuss the nature of the fairy tale and how much real or everyday life should be mixed in with it; after "Fräulein von Scuderi," contemporary drama. Arnim's work contains few remarks about literary merit, because his concerns lie elsewhere. A clue to Arnim's aversion to literary criticism in the frame, which is so important to Hoffmann, may lie in his remarks in the report at the end of *Landhausleben*:

Kritisches Urteil über die Geschichten scheint aber außerdem ein gänzlicher Mißgriff, weil jeder Leser, wenn er nun einmal diese unselige Richtung zur Kritik hat, sich lieber selbst seinen Weg schafft, gegen einen fremden Stangen-

zaun aufbäumt: wenn er aber von diesem Unheil noch frei geblieben, dieses
Beurteilen von Dingen, die ihm leben, als Eingriff in die Rechte des freien Da-
seins verabscheuen muß. (Migge, III, 519)

A critical verdict about the stories seems moreover a real mistake, since
every reader, even if he has this unfortunate tendency to criticism, would prefer
to make his own way and rebels against a foreign rail fence; if, however, he is
still free from such an affliction, then he must detest this evaluation of things
that are meaningful for him as an assault on the rights of independent existence.

Although Arnim seemed to think that remarks about literary values
detract from a work, he had every intent of letting the reader know
what he was about with the inner stories that he either adapted or
created. The frame that precedes the story of the evening gives some
direction about how the assembled company is to understand it. When
there are sections of the frame that close the story, they may contain
action scenes, such as in the fourth evening with the camp-out. These
scenes then introduce subsequent figures and insertions, such as Ariel
and the poem "Träume." The eighth evening closes with the grief of
the invalid over the upcoming marriage of the lady of the house to
Winter. Like Hoffmann, Arnim did use discussion to move to the next
insertion, as he did after "Mistris Lee" in the fifth evening.

The collections of inner stories in both *Wintergarten* and *Die Serapionsbrüder* contain some narratives that were not originally intended to be
part of a frame. With the exception of "Mistris Lee" and most of the
poems, Arnim adapted all of his material from other sources and
shaped it to fit his didactic purposes, giving it a consistency of intent
that is only apparent after the original sources have been examined;
this effort has previously not been made. Partly because of Arnim's skill
in imitating the tone and style of his sources, critics have underesti-
mated his contribution. Arnim's approach towards his sources was
consistent with that of *Wunderhorn:* he wanted to make the past accessible to the present. Since this desire continued to shape Arnim's writing, the examples that *Wintergarten* provides at the beginning of his
career are especially helpful in understanding some of his later work.
Information in the Hoffmann chapter has already indicated which stories Hoffmann had already written before he started collecting work
for a cyclical narrative. Hoffmann's attitude towards sources and the
frame-inner story relationship was both similar to and different from

that of Arnim. As we have seen, both men wanted to explain what really happened, but Hoffmann either greatly expanded the source, as in "Die Bergwerke zu Falun," or simply used it in a fairly rudimentary way to get his imagination going, as in the case of "Rat Krespel." Nor did Hoffmann have an overriding ethical or didactic goal in mind that could have aided him in the shaping of frame and inner story. The connections between the frame and inner story in *Die Serapionsbrüder* lie in the overriding thematic concerns, not in advocating moral or political responses. While Arnim used his singleminded purpose, his vision for a new Germany, to unite the most heterogeneous sources, Hoffmann maintained an underlying consistency with his own preoccupation with the mysteries and malaises of the artistic consciousness. This interest, which sometimes bordered on an obsession, shaped the frame, the arrangement of stories, and, with the later narratives, probably the kind of story he wrote.

Arnim wrote *Wintergarten* early in his career; Hoffmann finished the *Serapionsbrüder* near the end of his life. Arnim's work is valuable to us, not only for its reflection of German sensibilities after the defeat by the French, but also as an early example of tendencies that became important in his later works, such as the manner in which he adapted the past for the present. In contrast, Hoffmann's cyclical narrative represents a sort of *summa;* in the frame conversations, he set down some of what were to be his final commentaries on major issues in German Romanticism. The topics under consideration here figure in all his major works; consequently, the frame is an important interpretative resource, not only for the inner stories, but also for his earlier writing.

As this critical cycle closes, the writer hopes that this study has shown that bending the frame leads, not to obfuscating distortion, but to unsuspected vistas.

Appendix

"Das Lied von der Jugend," from Achim von Arnim, *Der Wintergarten,* in *Sämtliche Romane und Erzählungen,* edited by Walther Migge. Volume II (Munich, 1963), 412–21.

"The War of Inis-Thona," from *The Poems of Ossian,* translated by James MacPherson (New York, no date given), 280–84.

[Reflections on the poet's youth. An apostrophe to Selma. Oscar obtains leave to go to Inis-Thona, an island of Scandinavia. The mournful story of Argon and Ruro, the two sons of the king of Inis-Thona. Oscar revenges their death, and returns in triumph to Selma. A soliloquy by the poet himself.]

O Jugend, wie gleichst du dem schimmernden
    Traume des Jägers,
Den wärmende Sonne entschläfert am Hügel;
Da weckt ihn der Sturm und die jagenden
    Schloßen,

Our youth is like the dream of the hunter on the hill of the heath. He sleeps in the mild beams of the sun: he awakes amidst a storm; the red lightning flies around: trees shake their heads to the wind! He looks back with joy on the days of the sun, and the pleasant dreams of his rest!

Da fühlt sich beben, er sieht sich allein;
Da beugen sich Blume ins wallende Grün,
Da stürzen die schwebenden Wolken hernieder,
Da weichet die Röte vom rastlosen Himmel,
Da stehet er frierend und wischt sich die Augen
Und schauet hinüber zum Aufgang der Sonne,
Die ging ihm schon unter, verflogener Traum!
O kehre mir wieder O Jugend im Traum nur!
O klinget mir wieder ihr Waffen im Ohre!
Wann ziehe ich weiter im strahlenden Stahle?

When shall Ossian's youth return? When his ear delight in the sound of arms? When shall I, like Oscar, travel in the light of my steel?
Come with your streams, ye hills of Cona! Listen to the voice of Ossian,

The song rises, like the sun, in my soul. I feel the joys of other times.

Dann trete ich nieder die trotzenden Feinde!
Es gehet der Seele die Sonn des Gesanges
Wohl auf und wohl unter, ich fühle die Wonne,
Die Schmerzen entstrahlender, blendender Zeit.
Ich schau die getürmten Schlösser der Väter,
Die schattigen Eichen dort hinter dem Walle,
Am Tore die Ströme erschwellen, umrauschen,

I behold thy towers, O Selma! the oaks of thy shaded wall: thy streams sound in my ear;

283

Die Vögel in Lüften, sie ziehen schon wieder,
Es hallen die Tritte der Meinen im Hause,
Sie sammeln sich rings an der gastlichen
Schwelle,
Steht Fingal nicht mitten gelehnt auf dem
Schilde?
Sein Speer ist gestützet dem Walle entgegen,
Er horchet Gesängen der wandernden Sänger,
Getanene Taten, als Jugend sein Arm.

Sein Oscar, heim kehrend vom Jagen, auch
horchet
Dem Loblied des Helden und sieht ihn mit
Staunen,
Wie Großes der tat, den er täglich so schauet,
Da reißet er heftig sein Schild von dem Walle,
Daß schreckend emporspringt sein Leibhund und
anschlägt,
Der müde vom Jagen ihm lag zu den Füßen;
Die Spitze des Speeres erblinket geduldlos,
Der Degenknopf blitzt in den mächtigen Händen
Mit leichtem Erzittern, voll Tränen das Auge
Die Röte der Jugend in pochenden Wangen,
So spricht er zu Fingal und kniet vor ihm nieder:
»O Fingal, du König der Helden und Ossian,
Nächster im Kriege, ihr fochtet in Jugend,
Ihr lebet im Sange die ewigen Tage,
Doch Oskar erscheinet, verschwindet wie Nebel,

Kein Sänger mich kennet, kein Mädchen mich
nennet,
Kein Jäger einst suchet mein Grab auf der Heide;
O lasset mich fechten in Inisthona,
Und sollte ich fallen in Inisthona,
Ihr hört nicht mein Fallen im Lande so ferne,

Die Tochter der Fremde soll sehen mein Grab,
Und klagen die Jugend, die fern aus der Fremde,
Ihr nahte in Taten, des Todes erfreut;
Dann kommt einst ein Sänger zu dir aus der
Fremde,
Und rufet beim Feste: ›O höret die Taten,
Von Oskar aus fernem umfluteten Land‹.«
»Mein Oskar«, erwidert der König der Helden,
»Du Erbe des Ruhmes lautschallender Hallen,
Auch du sollst nun fechten, weil Fechten dein
Sinn,
Bereite den Schoß dir des dunkelen Schiffes,
Der Ferne gebär es der Unseren Ruhm;
So stehe denn auf und so beug dich vor keinem;
Auf führe die Helden nach Inisthona,
Doch denke des Ruhmes von Vater zu Vater,

thy heroes gather round.

Fingal sits in the midst. He leans on the
shield of Trenmor;
his spear stands against the wall;
he listens to the songs of his bards.
The deeds of his arm are heard; the actions
of the king in his youth!
Oscar had returned from the chase, and
heard the hero's praise.

He took the shield of Branno[1] from the wall;

his eyes were filled with tears. Red was the
cheek of youth. His voice was trembling
low.
My spear shook its bright head in his hand:
he spoke to Morven's king.

"Fingal! thou king of heroes! Ossian, next to
him in war! ye have fought in your youth;
your names are renowned in song. Oscar is
like the mist of Cona; I appear and I vanish
away.
The bard will not know my name.

The hunter will not search in the heath for
my tomb. Let me fight, O heroes, in the
battles of Inis-Thona. Distant is the land of
my war! ye shall not hear of Oscar's fall:
some bard may find me there; some bard
may give my name to song.
The daughter of the stranger shall see my
tomb, and weep over the youth, that came
from afar.

The bard shall say, at the feast, Hear the
song of Oscar from the distant land!"
"Oscar," replied the king of Morven,

"thou shalt fight, son of my fame! Prepare
my dark bosomed ship to carry my hero to
Inis-Thona.
Son of my son, regard our fame; thou art of
the race of renown: Let not the children of
strangers say, Feeble are the sons of
Morven! Be thou, in battle, a roaring storm:

---

1. The father of Everallin, and grandfather to Oscar.

Des ewigen Glanzes in unserm Geschlechte,
Daß Kinder der Ferne, nicht spotten und sagen,
Die Kinder des Fingal, die sind nicht von ihm.
Sei kriegend ein Sturmwind, im Frieden wie
    Sonne,
Sag Annir, dem König von Inisthona,
Ich denke mit Liebe der Jugend, wir stritten
Zusammen in Tagen von Agandeka.«
Es eilet so ruhlos die Jugend zu Taten,
Als wollte einfrieren das wegsame Meer,
Bald zogen die Segel glückahnend zur Ferne,
Es wispern die Winde durch Leinen des Mastes,
Es rauschen die Fluten
am grimmigen Kiele,
Es zeichnet die Bahn sich weit hinter dem Schiffe,

Bald schaut er die Klippe, gepeitschet vom
    Meere,
Erkennet am wallenden Lustwald das Land,
Er wendet zum stilleren Busen des Meeres,
Er tritt auf den schwankenden Boden des
    Ruhmes
Und ziehet das Schiff zu dem trockenen Lande,
Dann bringt er das Schwert des vielherrlichen
    Vaters
Zu Annir, der saß auf dem eisernen Thron.
Der Held in dem Grauhaar rief auf als er sahe
Von Fingal das blinkende, schmetternde Schwert.
Er dachte der Schlachten, der Jugend mit Tränen,
Sie stritten zusammen in Glanz Agandekens,

Sie stritten der Lieblichen Erbe zu schützen.
Die Helden rings standen, als ob in den Wettern
Wetteifern zwei Geister beim kreuzenden Lichte,
Dann sagte der König:» Veraltet mir ruhet
So nutzlos das Schwert schon und rostet im
    Saale,

Das oftmals geblinket durch kreuzende Speere;
Verwittert, verbleichet ich gleiche der Eiche,
Verdorrend auf Felsen, die Wurzeln zerhauen.
Ich habe nicht Söhne mit dir sich zu freuen,
Umher dich zu führen in Hallen der Väter!
Ach Argon und Ruro, ihr ruhet verblichen,

Wie kann ich euch rächen, die heimlich
    ermordet;
Die Tochter im Hause des feindlichen Mörders,
Sie sehnt sich zu sehen mein Grab bei dem euren!
Ihr Gatte, ihr Cormalo schüttelt zehntausend
Der Speere entgegen wie Wolken des Todes,
Mein Schwert ist verrostet!

mild as the evening sun in peace! Tell,
Oscar, to Inis-Thona's king, that Fingal
remembers his youth; when we strove in the
combat togther, in the days of Agandecca."

They lifted up the sounding sail: the wind
whistled through the thongs[2] of their masts.
Waves lashed

the oozy rocks; the strength of ocean roars.
My son beheld, from the wave, the land of
groves.

He rushed into Runa's sounding bay, and
sent his sword to Annir of spears.

The gray-headed hero rose, when he saw
the sword of Fingal. His eyes were full of
tears; he remembered his battles in youth.
Twice had they lifted the spear before the
lovely Agandecca:

heroes stood far distant, as if two spirits
were striving in winds.
"But now," began the king, "I am old; the
sword lies useless in my hall.

Thou who art of Morven's race!

Annir has seen the battle of spears; but now
he is pale and withered, like the oak of
Lano. I have no son to meet thee with joy,
to bring thee to the halls of his fathers.
Argon is pale in the tomb, and Ruro is no
more.

My daughter is in the hall of strangers: she
longs to behold my tomb. Her spouse shakes
ten thousand spears; he comes a cloud of
death from Lano.

---

2. Among the Celtic nations, leather
thongs were used instead of ropes.

Auf nun zum Feste
Du Erbe des Ruhmes, dann will ich erzählen.«
Drei Tage vergingen in Festen, am vierten,
Da hörte der König den Namen des Gastes,
Sie lebten gar herrlich, sie jagten die Eber,
Sie weilten bei Steinen, die groß und bemooset;
Die Quellen da rieseln, da weinte der König,
Er hebet die Augen,

sie leuchten wie Sterne
Durch finstere Wolken; so bricht er die Stille:
»Hier ruhet, was blieben von Kindern der
    Jugend;
Der Stein ist das Grabmal von Ruro, *die* Esche
Umwurzelt nun Argon im Grabe.—Ach hört ihr
Im klemmenden Hause, auch sprecht ihr im
    Laube
Wie rauschende Winde,

ihr rauschet so traurig«
Die Winde durchstreifen die Loden von Oskar,
Wie Winters sie eisen die stürmischen Seen,
Die eilenden Wellen erstarren im Laufe.
Er fragte: »Wie fielen die Söhne der Jugend,
Daß Eber des Forstes die Gräber umstreifen,

Und stören ihr Ruhbett; hier müssen sie's leiden!
Doch droben da jagen die Geister der Helden
Die flüchtigen Wolken, umgarnen mit Bogen
Der Lüfte vielfarbig das ruchlose Wild.
O tröste dich König, es leben die Starken,
Wir hören die eilenden Sohlen im Winde,
Wir hören die bellenden Hunde in Nächten,
Sie lieben noch immer das Jagen der Jugend,
Besteigen mit Freuden schnellfüßige Stürme.«
Der König erwidert, nachdem er gestillt
Die stickenden Tränen, den nagenden Kummer:
»Zehntausend der Speere beherrschte Cormalo,
Er hauset beim Wasser, das hauchet den Tod,
Gekommen zu meiner hellschallenden Halle
Er focht um die Ehre des Sieges mit Speeren,
Die Jugend war herrlich, doch konnte sich keiner
Mehr messen mit ihm, sie gaben den Kranz ihm
Die Tochter ihm Liebe. Da kamen die Söhne
Vom Jagen zurücke, kam Argon und Ruro
Verbissene Schmerzen des Stolzes im Auge,

Come, to share the feast of Annir, son of
echoing Morven."
Three days they feasted together; on the
fourth, Annir heard the name of Oscar. They
rejoiced in the shell.[3] They pursued the
boars of Runa. Beside the fount of mossy
stones the weary heroes rest. The tear steals
in secret from Annir:
he broke the rising sigh.

"Here darkly rest," the hero said, "the
children of my youth. This stone is the tomb
of Ruro; that tree sounds over the grave of
Argon. Do ye hear my voice, O my sons,
within your narrow house? Or do ye speak
in these rustling leaves,

when the wind of the desert rises?"

"King of Inis-Thona," said Oscar, "how fell
the children of youth? The wild boar rushes
over their tombs,
but he does not disturb their repose.

They pursue deer formed of clouds, and
bend their airy bow.

They still love the sport of their youth; and
mount the wind with joy."

"Cormalo," replied the king, "is a chief of
ten thousand spears. He dwells at the waters
of Lano,[4] which sends forth the vapor of
death. He came to Runa's echoing halls, and
sought the honor of the spear.[5] The youth
was lovely as the first beam of the sun; few
were they who could meet him in fight! My
heroes yielded to Cormalo; my daughter
was seized in his love. Argon and Ruro

---

3. To "rejoice in the shell" is a phrase for
feasting sumptuously and drinking freely.

4. Lano was a lake of Scandinavia, remarkable in the days of Ossian for emitting a
pestilential vapor in autumn.

5. By "the honor of the spear" is meant
the tournament practised among the ancient
northern nations.

Sie sahen den Kranz auf dem Haupte des
    Fremdlings,
Die Helden, die ihren bezwungen im Lustkampf.
Drei Tage sie festen, am vierten focht Argon
Mit Cormalo freudig, wer konnt ihn bestehen!
Besieget ward Cormalo von ihm, auch von Ruro;
Da schwoll ihm sein Herz gar von gräulichem
    Ärger,
Er trachtet zu sehen das Blut von den Söhnen,
Verschließet im Herzen die kochende Wut.
Sie gingen in Eintracht zu jagen am Hügel
    Die bräunliche Hirschin, die häufig hier trank;
Da flogen die Pfeile von Cormalo heimlich,
So heimlich, so schrecklich, es fielen die Söhne
Im Blut, gezeuget im Blute des tobenden Krieges,
Die Sonne ging auf und ging unter in Blut;
Gleich eilet der Frevler
zur Tochter nach Hause,
Sie strählte die langen, die goldenen Haare,

Er greifet die Flechten und zieht sie mit sich.
Ich blieb da allein, nichts ahndend von allem,
Erwartend die Jäger. Der Tag war versunken,
Ein neuer erschien, nicht Argon, nicht Ruro;
Am dritten da sah ich den spürenden Leibhund,
Er kam in die Halle und heulte und schien mich
Zu locken zur Stelle des Falles; ich folgte,
Und fand sie - begrub sie an selbiger Stelle,
Die stattlichen Leiber, mit eigenen Händen.
Hier wohn ich immer, wenn's Jagen geschlossen.
Ich leg mich hinüber auf kühlenden Boden,
Den Augen entströmt wie gebrochenen Ästen
Der Frühlingssaft, wehe mein Herz ist
    gebrochen.«
»Ihr Geister auf Wolken«, rief Oskar und eilte

»O ruft mir zur Seite die Heldenvertrauten,
Noch heute wir eilen zum tödlichen Wasser,
Ich räche euch heilig ihr herrlichen Brüder,
Nicht länger soll Cormalo lebend sich freuen;
Auf dring in die Spitze des Schwertes, o Tod!«
Es schwellen die Segel, er eilt mit den Seinen,
Es hob sich der bleiche, der kühlende Mond,
Es schläfert der Jugend, die bläulichen Helme
Erflimmerten helle, es sinken die Feurigen
Die Augen der Helden, die Sterne verschwinden,
Nur Oskar der Führer, er schläft nicht, er steuert,
Und stehet am Ruder und schauet zur Ferne,
Und schauet die wolkigen Küsten des Feindes.
Es naht sich ein Windstoß, weitspannend die
    Schwingen,
Der stärkste der Geister, er schüttelt sein duftig
Gehaar und den Speer und Augen, sie funkeln,
    Wie glühendes Eisen, die Stimme ein Donner,
Verhallend so spricht er: »O Oskar zurück!«
Doch Oskar streckt vorwärts den Speer und
    erhebet

returned from the chase; the tears of their
pride descend: they roll their silent eyes on
Runa's heroes, who had yielded to a
stranger. Three days they feasted with
Cormalo; on the fourth young Argon
fought. But who could fight with Argon?
Cormalo is overcome. His heart swelled with
the grief of pride; he resolved in secret to
behold the death of my sons.

They went to the hills of Runa; they pursued
the dark-brown hinds. The arrow of
Cormalo flew in secret; my children fell in
blood.

He came to the maid of his love; to Inis-
Thona's long-haired maid.
They fled over the desert.

Annir remained alone. Night came on, and
day appeared; nor Argon's voice nor Ruro's
came. At length their much loved dog was
seen; the fleet and bounding Runa. He came
into the hall and howled; and seemed to
look towards the place of their fall. We
followed him; we found them here: we laid
them by this mossy stream. This is the haunt
of Annir, when the chase of the hinds is
past. I bend like the trunk of an aged oak;
my tears for ever flow!"

"O Ronnan!" said the rising Oscar, "Ogar,
king of spears!
call my heroes to my side, the sons of
streamy Morven. To-day we go to Lano's
water, that sends forth the vapor of death.
Cormalo will not long rejoice: death is often
at the point of our swords!"

Die Stimme zur Höhe und redet entgeistert:
»Entfliehe du Nachtbild mit Stürmen, den
   Deinen,
Wie wagst du mit dunkelen Waffen zu nahen,
Wie welk ist dein Schild und dein Schwert nur
   ein Schilfhalm.
Ein Stoßwind sie rollet zusammen wie Wolken;
Dein Nachtwerk verderbet sich selber, du
   Nachtbild.«
»Du dürftest mir dräuen«, erwidert die Stimme,
»Es neigen die Völker die Stirne vor meiner,
Ein Schütteln der Braunen erwecket, versenket
Die zweifelnden Schlachten, die rüstigsten
   Jagden.
Ich komme aus grauer, verahndeter Ferne,
Entschleudre im Winde die Blitze des Todes,
Die Stürme im Blicke, die Blitze in Händen,
Doch über den Wolken ist milde mein Wohnen,
Auf blauem Gefild sind Gefährten der Ruh.«
»So wohn dort in Freuden«, befiehlt ihm da
   Oskar,
» Vergesse dort Fingals stets ruhlosen Sohn,
Noch nimmer ich streckte zu dir in die Wolken
Den blinkenden Speer! Was runzelst du heftig
Die Stirne, noch nimmer ich flohe den Starken.«
Der Geist ihn nun warnte: »Entfliehe dem Lande
Empfange die Winde mit wendendem Steuer,
Und daß du mich kennest, die unstete Göttin,
Die alle verehren, die je sie veloren,
Und daß du mir trauest, ihr nennet mich Jugend,
Dem Schoß mir entsteigen die Augen der Kinder,
Mein Atem sie nähret, sie ziehn ihn zum Herzen,
Ich bilde in ihnen und breite wie Äste
Neugierige Hände zur Kühnheit der Helden,
Ich schütze die Kühnheit, mein Liebling ist
   Cormalo;
Mein Oskar, ich lieb dich, entfliehe dem Lande,
Das sorgsam getrennet vom tobenden Meere,
Die unstete Sonne sich schneller nicht decket,
Als fliehet die Jugend, als fliehet ihr
   Glück.
Er rufet: »Ich schiffe zu Taten der Zukunft,
Entfliehe O Jugend, nie altert der Ruhm«,
Und Oskar legt vorwärts die Klinge des
   Schwertes,
Er fühlet die dunkelen Speere des Geistes,
Er schneidet sich strahlende Wege durchs
   Dunkel.
Der Geist auf den Wolken gestaltlos entfliehet,
Wie Säulen des Rauchs vom verlöschenden
   Feuer,
Zerteilend sie jaget der Finger des Knaben,
Doch rühret ihn fern noch die drohende Stimme,
Ein rollender Felsen. Die Krieger erwachten,
Sie fragten der Ursach des mächt'gen Getönes;
Er zeigte der Sonne hochprächtigen Wagen
Die tausend der Wellen auf glänzendem Rücken

Sie trugen mit Jubel, und trugen den Helden
Zur nahenden Küste des schimmernden Ruhms.
Es ahnden die sausenden Wälder die Stürme,
Sie sammeln dann dichter dir wankenden
    Häupter,
So weckte der zornige Nachtgeist die Feinde;

They came over the desert like stormy
clouds, when the winds roll them along the
heath; their edges are tinged with lightning;
the echoing groves foresee the storm!
The horn of Oscar's battle is heard; Lano
shook over all its waves. The children of the
lake convened around the sounding shield
of Cormalo. Oscar fought as he was wont in
war.

Bald höret auch Cormalo hallen das
    Schlachthorn
Von Oskar, und sammelt die Kinder des Sees
Am tödlichen Wasser,

das schrecklich erdampfet
Im lieblichen Sommer, als frör es im Winter.
Und Oskar verkündet die blutige Rache
Für Argon und Ruro und fordert die Schwester.
Kaum ist es gesprochen, so stürzen beim Namen
Mit eilenden Schritten zusammen die Heere;
Als wär es ein Küssen, so eng sie sich drängen,
Wie leuchtendes Feuer, so funkeln die Waffen,
Als säten sie Menschen, so fallen die Helden,
Sie streiten wie Stürme in rollenden Wogen,
Da trennt sie der tobende Oskar, der suchet den
    König
Sucht Cormalo, findet ihn balde, der mutig
    voran,
Und staunend dem Kampfe entsinken die Hände
Den rasenden Völkern, sie warten des Ausgangs.
Es sprangen die Helme, es borsten die Schienen,
Da lief in das Schwert des Oskar verblendet
    Sich Cormalo, blind in der frevelnden Seele.

Cormalo fell beneath his sword:

the sons of dismal Lano fled to their secret
vales!

Es legen die Seinen vor Oskar die Waffen
Hernieder und bringen
die klagende Königin.
Mit herrlichen Schiffen, mit rötlichen Segeln
So kehret daheim nun der siegende Oskar,
Er bringet zu Annirs lautschallenden Hallen
Die Tochter, die einz'ge; sie deckte die Augen.
Das Antlitz des Alten war glänzend vor Freude
Er führet die Tochter, er führet die Sieger,
Läßt tragen die Beute zum Grabe der Söhne.
Da klagte in Tränen die Tochter, die Witwe:
»O höret ihr Winde, ich höre euch Quellen,
Die heimlich hier fließen, aus Gräbern der
    Brüder.
So sehet die Tränen, die strömend sich drängen;
Ihr Bruder, so herrlich, du Argon und Ruro
Ihr waret ja alle, mir alle so lieb.
Doch Cormalo liebt ich vor allen so innig;
Was hast du erschlagen die herrlichen Brüder
Was hast du erschlagen, du Fremdling, den
    Liebling?«

Oscar brought the daughter of Inis-Thona to
Annir's echoing halls.
The face of age is bright with joy; he blest
the king of swords.

So jammert sie lange, so starb sie in Tränen
Und löschte die Flamme der ewigen Rache.
Und als sie da ruhet erbleichet am Grabe,
Da schauet erst Oskar die lichtenden Wangen,
Nun sieht er sie liebend und sieht sie nicht
    wieder,
Und sehnt sich die herrlichen Taten zu löschen
Mit schmerzlichen Tränen, und scheuet den
    Glückwunsch.
Er kehrt wohl zurück zu mir und zu Fingal,
Wir freuten des Sieges uns immer allein,
Die Dämpfe des tödlichen Wassers ihn hatten
Im Keime ersticket, die Jugend zerknickt;
So saß er am Ufer und starrte hinunter,
Die Wellen sie kamen, die Wellen sie gingen,
Oft rief er: »Ich sehe ein Eiland da ferne,
Da springen die Brunnen der Jugend so helle,
Ein einziger Tropfen vom leuchtenden Springe
Gibt Jugendgenesen, wie Frühling die Blätter.«
Und einstens ganz heimlich, da stößt er sein
    Schifflein
Vom Sande ins Wasser, ich sah ihn erst fern,
Am Himmel ich sahe mit dampfenden Waffen,
Mit funkelnden Augen den Nachtgeist der
    Jugend,
Die Stimme ein Donner, der ferne verhallet,
Vom Sturme gezogen ihr Mantel tropft flatternd
Vom fließenden Regen und Oskar sog sehnlich
Die Tropfen mit durstendem Munde in sich,
Und streckte die Hände so sehnlich, so zart,
Wie Säuglinge tun zu der nahenden Mutter,
Und rief sie, und nannte sie Quelle der Jugend,
Sie reicht ihm die blitzende zuckende Hand.
Die Winde sie stürmten mit Wut an den Felsen,
Ich hörte am Ufer viel Stimmen auf Wolken,
Am Morgen ich sahe sein Schiff ach verkehrt,
Auf Klippen zerspalten, da lag's wie sein Schild.
Wo Oskar geblieben, kein Stein mir verkündet,
Auf Heiden kein Jäger kann suchen sein
    Grabmal.
Doch Fingal er sagte: »Die Quelle der Jugend,
Er hat sie getrunken in hellem Gesang.«
Entweichet, entfliehet ihr drückenden Wolken,
Nicht Schmerzen allein nur, auch Freuden sie
    dauern,
Oft denk ich des Tages, des Tages der Heimkehr
Des stattlichen Oskar von Inisthona,
Des kommenden Frühlings von Inisthona.
Wie groß war die Freude; der erste ich sahe
Die Segel des Oskar, wie leuchtende Wolken
Dem irrenden Wandrer erscheinen im Morgen.

Wir führten ihn singend durch Hallen des
    Schlosses,

How great was the joy of Ossian, when he
beheld the distant sail of his son! It was like
a cloud of light that rises in the east, when
the traveller is sad in a land unknown:
and dismal night with her ghosts, is sitting
around in shades!
We brought him with songs to Selma's halls.

Fingal spread the feast of shells. A thousand

bards raised the name of Oscar: Morven answered to the sound.
The daughter of Toscar was there; her voice was like the harp,
when the distant sound comes, in the evening, on the soft rustling breeze of the vale!
O lay me, ye that see the light, near some rock of my hills! Let the thick hazes be around, let the rustling oak be near. Green be the place of my rest; let the sound of the distant torrent be heard. Daughter of Toscar, take the harp, and raise the lovely song of Selma; that sleep may overtake my soul in the midst of joy; that the dreams of my youth may return, and the days of the mighty Fingal. Selma! I behold thy towers, thy trees, thy shaded wall! I see the heroes of Morven; I hear the song of bards: Oscar lifts the sword of Cormalo; a thousand youths admire its studded thongs. They look with wonder on my son: they admire the strength of his arm. They mark the joy of his father's eyes; they long for an equal fame, and ye shall have your fame, O sons of streamy Morven! My soul is often brightened with song; I remember the friends of my youth. But sleep descends in the sound of the harp! pleasant dreams begin to rise! Ye sons of the chase, stand far distant nor disturb my rest. The bard of other times holds discourse with his fathers! the chiefs of the days of old! Sons of the chase, stand far distant! disturb not the dreams of Ossian!

Sie tönten von hohen Gesängen der Tochter.
Sie tönen wie Harfen des Abends hernieder,

Es winket das Licht noch an rauschenden
     Buchen,
Durch Eichen es strahlet, es ziehet auf Strömen;
Jetzt singe, O Tochter, die lieblichen Lieder,
Daß Schlaf mich umnachte inmitten der Freude,
Daß Jugend mir kehre zurück im Gesange!
Wie lieblich es säuselt von Tönen der Tochter,
Es tönet der Schild, den Oscar erkämpfte,
Die herrliche Sonne sich schauet darin!
Auch mich trieb die Jugend in tobende
Schlachten,
O stört nicht ihr lärmenden Freunde der Seher,
Wie unstete Sonne, so wandelt die Vorzeit
Bald auf und bald unter, wie Frühling im
     Grünen;
Du weckest mich Frühling mit Tropfen des
     Himmels,
Doch nahen die Stürme, die bald mich
     entblättern,
Es kommet der Wandrer, er sah mich erblühen,
Er sieht mich verwelken. Nun seh ich dich Fingal
In hangenden Wolken, die Augen sind Sterne,

Dein Schild ist ein Vollmund, dein Schwert ist ein
     Rotstreif:
Dein Oskar der jaget ganz nahe bei dir,
Er stehet in ewiger jugend bei dir.
Im grünenden Tale vom Strome durchwunden
Da sonnen sich Hirsche, es flattern die Adler,
Die Knospen sich öffnen, welch Murmeln ist
     droben,
Es sinken die Winde, du rufest mich Fingal:
»Komm Ossian ziehe hinauf. Wie hebt sich der
     Müde du dir?
Wir gehen«, so sprichst du, »auf eilenden
     Strahlen,
Die Jugend ist einmal und schnelle und kurz,
Von unseren Schlachten der Boden wird
     schwarz,
Wird finster und schweigend und quellig und
     kalt:
Ein Grabstein, der gibt dir die Ruhe, komm
     Ossian,
Komm Ossian, komme, gern hören wir Sang.«
Ich komme, ich komme, bald sehet ihr nimmer
Den Fußtritt im Sande, die Harfe im Schwunge,
Dann säuseln mir Winde am Morgen im
     Grauhaar
Und wecken nicht wieder den Barden der Lieder.
Geschlechter sich heben, wie Wellen im Meere,
Es bringet viel frische Geschlechter der Morgen,
Am Ufer zerschellen sie Abends ermüdet,
Ich sehe die wogenden Bäume des Ufers,
Es sinket ein Kranz auf das sinkende Haupt:
O Jugend wie gleichst du den Träumen des
Alters.

# Bibliography

Achim von Arnim, Ludwig. *Achim von Arnims Sämmtliche Werke* 2. Berlin, 1857. Reprinted by Georg Olms Verlag, Hildesheim, 1982. Rebound as Vol. 6 (incl. vols. 11, 12 of 1857 edition).

Alexander, Franz G., and Sheldon T. Selesnick. *The History of Psychiatry: An Evaluation of Psychiatric Thought and Practice from Prehistoric Times to the Present.* New York, 1966.

Allroggen, Gerhard. "Die Opern-Ästhetik E. T. A. Hoffmanns." In *Beiträge zur Geschichte der Oper,* edited by Heinz Bekker, pp. 25–34. Regensburg, 1969.

Archangeli, Melanie. "Magister Tinte: The Evil Force in 'Das fremde Kind.' " Unpublished paper, Pennsylvania State University, 1986.

Aretin, Karl Otmar Freiherr von. *Vom deutschen Reich zum Deutschen Bund* 2, *Deutsche Geschichte: Frühe Neuzeit.* Göttingen, 1985.

Ascanasius, or The Young Adventurer; Containing an Impartial History of the Rebellion in Scotland. Edinburgh, 1802.

Auhuber, Friedhelm. *In einem fernen dunklen Spiegel: E. T. A. Hoffmanns Poetisierung der Medizin.* Opladen, 1986.

Behrman, Alfred. "Zur Poetik des Kunstmärchens: Eine Strukturanalyse der 'Königsbraut' von E. T. A. Hoffmann." *Erzählforschung* 3 (1978): 107–34.

Beardsley, Christa-Maria. *E. T. A. Hoffmann: Die Gestalt des Meisters in seinen Märchen.* Bonn, 1975.

———. *E. T. A. Hoffmanns Tierfiguren im Kontext der Romantik.* Bonn, 1985.

Bechtold, Arthur. *Kritisches Verzeichnis der Schriften Johann Michael Moscherosch.* Munich, 1922.

Berchtenbreiter, Irmgard. *Achim von Arnims Vermittlerrolle zwischen Jakob Böhme als Dichter und seiner Wintergartengesellschaft.* Munich, 1972.

Berkowski, Naum J. *Die Romantik in Deutschland.* Translated from the Russian by Reinhard Fischer. Leipzig, 1979.

Betz, Otto, and Veronika Straub. *Bettina und Arnim: Briefe der Freundschaft und Liebe, 1806–08* 1. Frankfurt, 1986–87.

Bleiler, E. F., ed. *The Best Tales of Hoffmann.* By E. T. A. Hoffmann. New York, 1967.

Bobertag, Felix, ed. *Gesichte Philanders von Sittewald von Hanß Michael Moscherosch* 32. In the series Deutsche National-Litteratur, ed. Joseph Kürschner. Berlin and Stuttgart, 1882.

Böhme, Jakob. *Theosophia Revelata oder Alle Göttlichen Schriften Jacob Böhmens (1730)* 9. Ed. Will-Erich Peuckert. Stuttgart, 1956.

Börne, Ludwig. *Gesammelte Schriften* 6. Vienna, 1868.

Brinker-Gabler, Gisela. "Tiecks Bearbeitungen altdeutscher Literatur. Produktion, Konzeption, Wirkung." Diss., Cologne, 1973.

Brundage, James A. "Prostitution in the Medieval Canon Law." In *Sexual Practices and the Medieval Church*. Ed. V. L. Bullough and James A. Brundage, pp. 149–60. Buffalo, 1983.

Bulfinch, Thomas. *Bulfinch's Mythology, The Age of Fable*. New York.

Burger, Heinz Otto. "Arzt und Kranker in der deutschen schönen Literatur des 19. Jahrhunderts." In *Der Arzt und der Kranke in der Gesellschaft des 19. Jahrhunderts*. Edited by Walter Artelt and Walter Rugg Artelt, pp. 98–106. Stuttgart, 1967.

Casper, Bernhard. "Der historische Besen oder über die Geschichtsauffassung in E. T. A. Hoffmanns *Serapionsbrüdern* und in der katholischen Tübinger Schule." In *Romantik in Deutschland, ein interdisziplinares Symposium*, edited by Richard Brinkmann, pp. 490–501. Stuttgart, 1978. In the series Deutsche Vierteljahrsschrift für Literaturwissenschaft und Geistesgeschichte.

Colonna, Francesco. *Le songe de Poliphile*, traduction libre de l'italien, J. G. Le Grand. Paris, 1804.

Conrad, Horst. *Die literarische Angst: Das Schreckliche in Schauerromantik und Detektivgeschichte*. Düsseldorf, 1974.

Coville, A. "France: Armagnacs and Burgundians (1380–1422)." In *A Cambridge Medieval History* 7, pp. 368–92. Edited by J. R. Tanner et al. Cambridge, 1968.

Cramer, Thomas. *Das Groteske bei E. T. A. Hoffmann*. Munich, 1970.

Cronin, John. *Die Gestalt der Geliebten in den poetischen Werken E. T. A. Hoffmanns*. Bonn, 1967.

Dämmrich, Horst. *The Shattered Self: E. T. A. Hoffmann's Tragic Vision*. Detroit, 1973.

DeLoecker, Armand. *Zwischen Atlantis und Frankfurt*. Frankfurt, 1983.

Diepgen, Paul. *Geschichte der Medizin: die historische Entwicklung der Heilkunde und des ärztlichen Lebens*. 2, 1. Hälfte. Berlin, 1959.

Dobat, Klaus. *Musik als romantische Illusion*. Tübingen, 1984.

Dörner, Klaus. *Bürger und Irre: Zur Sozialgeschichte und Wissenschaftssoziologie der Psychiatrie*. Frankfurt, 1969.

Ellis, John M. "E. T. A. Hoffmann's 'Fräulein von Scuderi.' " *Modern Language Notes* 64 (1969): 340–50.

———. *Narration in the German Novelle: Theory and Interpretation*. Cambridge, England, 1974.

Faber du Faur, Curt von. *German Baroque Literature: A Catalogue of the Collection in the Yale University Library*. New Haven, 1958.

Feldges, Brigitte, and Ulrich Stadler. *E. T. A. Hoffmann: Epoche-Werke-Wirkung*. Munich, 1986.

Fischer, Bernd. *Literatur und Politik. Die 'Novellensammlung von 1812' und das 'Landhausleben' von Achim von Arnim*. Frankfurt, 1983.

Frankenberg, Abraham von. *Bericht von dem Leben in Abschied des in Gott seligruhenden Jacob Böhmens, dieser Theosophischen Schriften eigentlichen Authoris und Urhebers*. Amsterdam, 1682.

Freud, Sigmund. *Collected Papers 1917* 4, 1959. Translated by Joan Riviere.

Freund, Winfried. *Die deutsche Kriminalnovelle von Schiller bis Hauptmann*. Paderborn, 1980.

Gajek, Bernhard. "Achim von Arnim: Romantischer Poet und preußischer Patriot (1781–1831)." In *Sammeln und Sichten: Festschrift für Oscar Fambach zum 80. Geburtstag.* Ed. Joachim Krause, Norbert Oellers, and Karl Konrad Polheim, pp. 264–82. Bonn, 1983.

Garlington, Aubrey, "E. T. A. Hoffmann's 'Der Dichter und der Komponist' and the Creation of the Germanic Romantic Opera." In *The Musical Quarterly* 65 (1979): 26–47.

Gibson, H. B. *Hypnosis: Its Nature and Therapeutic Uses.* London, 1977.

Göres, Jörn. " 'Was soll geschehen im Glücke' Ein unveröffentlichter Aufsatz Achim von Arnims." *Jahrbuch der deutschen Schillergesellschaft* 5 (1961): 196–221.

―――. "Das Verhältnis von Historie und Poesie in der Erzählkunst Achim von Arnims." Diss., Heidelberg, 1956.

Gorski, Gisela. *E. T. A. Hoffmann: Fräulein von Scuderi.* Stuttgart, 1980.

Grimmelshausen, Jacob Christoffel von. *Der seltzame Springinsfeld.* Tübingen, 1969.

Grundmann, Herbert. *Geschichtsschreibung im Mittelalter.* Göttingen, 1965.

Grunwald, Stefan. *A Biography of Johann Michael Moscherosch 1601–69.* Bern, 1969.

Gunzel, Klaus, ed. *Die Serapionsbrüder. Märchendichtungen der Romantik.* Cologne, 1986.

Haase, Frank. "Carl Pistor: Eine Marginalie zu E. T. A. Hoffmanns Novelle *Rat Krespel.*" MHG, vol. 31 (1985), pp. 15–17.

Harich, Walter. *E. T. A. Hoffmann: Das Leben eines Künstlers.* Berlin, 1923.

Harms, Wolfgang. "Das Interesse an mittelalterlicher deutscher Literatur zwischen der Reformationszeit und der Frühromantik." *Akten des VI. Internationalen Germanistenkongresses* 1, pp. 60–83, Basel, 1980.

Hausner, Gertrud, "Achim von Arnim und die Literatur des 17. Jahrhunderts." Diss., Vienna, 1934.

Heinisch, Klaus J. *Deutsche Romantik: Interpretationen.* Paderborn, 1966.

Hemmerich, Gerd. "Verteidigung des 'Signor Formica.' Zu E. T. A. Hoffmanns Novelle." In *Jahrbuch der Jean-Paul-Gesellschaft* 17 (1982): 113–28.

Hewitt-Thayer, Harvey. *Hoffmann: Author of the Tales.* Princeton, 1948.

Himmel, Helmut. "Schuld und Sühne der Scuderi." MHG, vol. 7 (1960), pp. 1–15.

Hoermann, Roland, *Achim von Arnim.* Boston, 1984.

―――. "Symbolism and Mediation in Arnim's View of Romantic Fantasy." *Monatshefte* 54 (1962): 201–15.

Hoffmann, E. T. A. *Die Elixiere des Teufels.* ed. W. Kron. Munich, n.d.

―――. *E. T. A. Hoffmann: Gesammelte Werke,* Ed. Hans Joachim Kruse. Berlin-Weimar, 1978.

―――. *E.T.A. Hoffmanns Sämtliche Werke.* Vols. 5–8. Ed. G. von Maassen. Munich-Leipzig, 1912.

―――. *E.T.A. Hoffmanns Werke.* 5. Teil, *Die Serapionsbrüder.* Ed. Georg Ellinger. Berlin n.d.

―――. *Hoffmanns Werke.* Ed. Nino Erné. Hamburg, 1964.

―――. *Fantasie- und Nachtstücke.* Ed. W. Müller-Seidel und W. Kron. Munich, n.d.

―――. *Lebens-Ansichten des Katers Murr.* Ed. Wolfgang Kron. Munich, n.d.

―――. *Nachlese.* Ed. Friedrich Schnapp. Munich, n.d.

―――. *Schriften zur Musik, Aufsätze und Rezensionen* 5. Ed. Friedrich Schnapp. Munich, 1977.

———. *Die Serapionsbrüder*. Ed. Walter Müller-Seidel and Wulf Segebrecht. Munich n.d.

———. *Die vier großen Gespräche und die kleinen Schriften über Literatur und Theater*. Weimar, 1924.

———. *Tagebücher*. Ed. Hans von Müller and Friedrich Schnapp. Munich, 1971.

Hoffmann, Werner. *Clemens Brentano: Leben und Werk*. Bern, 1966.

Hoffmeister, J. *Der ketzerische Schuster: Leben und Denken des Görlitzer Meisters Jakob Böhme*. East Berlin, n.d.

Holbeche, Yvonne. "The Relationship of the Artist to Power: E. T. A. Hoffmann's 'Das Fräulein von Scuderi.' " *Seminar* 16 (1981): 1–11.

Jacobs, Monty. "Arnims 'Altdeutsche Landsleute.' " *Euphorion* 16 (1909): 179–80.

Jenisch, Erich. "Zacharias Werners Mutter." *Euphorion* 31 (1930): 95–119.

Jennings, Lee B. "The Downward Transcendence. Hoffmanns *Bergwerke zu Falun.*" In *Deutsche Vierteljahrsschrift* 59 (1985): 278–89.

Johnes, Thomas, trans. *Chronicles of England, France, and Spain and the Adjoining Countries*. New York, 1901.

Kaiser, Gerhard R. *E. T. A. Hoffmann*. Stuttgart, 1988.

Karoli, Christa. "E. T. A. Hoffmann und Zacharias Werner." MHG, vol. 16 (1970), pp. 43–61.

———. "E. T. A. Hoffmann und Zacharias Werner: Ein Beitrag zum romantischen Genieproblem." *Vergleichen und Variationen: Festschrift für H. Motekat*. Ed. A. Goetze and G. Pflaum, pp. 147–69. Munich, 1970.

Kleßmann, Eckart. *E. T. A. Hoffmann oder die Tiefe zwischen Stern und Erde*. Stuttgart, 1988.

Kluge, Carl Alexander Friedrich. *Versuch einer Darstellung des animalischen Magnetismus, als Heilmittel*. Berlin 1811.

Knaack, Jürgen. "Achim von Arnim—Nicht nur Poet: Die politischen Anschauungen Arnims in ihrer Entwicklung." Diss., Hamburg, 1976.

Koehn, Lothar, *Vieldeutige Welt: Studien zur Struktur der Erzählungen E. T. A. Hoffmanns und zur Entwicklung seines Werkes*. Tübingen, 1966.

Kolkenbrock-Netz, Jutta. "Wahnsinn der Vernunft-juristische Institution-literarische Praxis. Das Gutachten zum Fall Schmolling und die Erzählung 'Der Einsiedler Serapion' von E. T. A. Hoffmann." *Wege der Literaturwissenschaft*. Ed. Jutta Kolkenbrock-Netz et al., pp. 122–144. Bonn, 1985.

Kosch, Wilhelm. *Deutsches Literaturlexikon* 1. Bern, 1968.

Kovach, Thomas A. "Mythic Structure in E. T. A. Hoffmann's 'Das Fräulein von Scuderi': A Case Study in 'Romantic Realism.' " *Sprache und Literatur: Festschrift für Arval L. Streadbach zum 65. Geburtstag*. Ed. Gerhard P. Knoop et al., pp. 121–28. Bern, 1981.

Kratzsch, Konrad. "Die Vorlagen zu Achim von Arnims 'Wintergarten" aus den Beständen der Arnim Bibliothek in der Zentralbibliothek der deutschen Klassik." *Marginalien: Blätter der Pirkheimer Gesellschaft* 29 (1968): 29–44.

Kratzsch, Konrad. "Untersuchungen zur Genese und Struktur der Erzählungen Ludwig Achim von Arnims." Diss., Jena, 1968.

Kuttner, Margot. *Die Gestaltung des Individualitätsproblems bei E. T. A. Hoffmann*. Hamburg, 1936.

Lazare, Christopher, ed. *Tales of Hoffmann*. New York, 1946.

Leibbrand-Wettley, Annemarie. "Die Stellung der Geisteskranken in der Gesellschaft des 19. Jahrhunderts." In *Der Arzt und der Kranke in der Gesellschaft des 19. Jahrhunderts* (Stuttgart, 1967), pp. 50–69.

Leibbrand, Werner. *Romantische Medizin.* Leipzig, 1939.

Lettenhove, Baron Kervyn de. *Oeuvres de Froissart.* Brussels, 1972.

Lichtenhahn, Ernst. "Zur Idee des goldenen Zeitalters in der Musikanschauung E. T. A. Hoffmanns." In *Romantik in Deutschland.* Edited by Richard Brinkmann, pp. 502–12. Stuttgart, 1978.

Lindken, Hans Ulrich. *E. T. A. Hoffmann: Das Fräulein von Scuderi, Erläuterungen und Dokumente.* Stuttgart, 1979.

Lockemann, Fritz. *Gestalt und Wandlungen der deutschen Novelle.* Munich, 1957.

Lomas, Peter. "The Significance of Post-partum Breakdown." In *The Predicament of the Family.* Ed. Peter Lomas, pp. 126–39. London, 1967.

Maassen, Carl Georg von, ed. *E. T. A. Hoffmanns Sämtliche Werke* 5–8. Munich and Leipzig, 1912.

MacPherson, James. *The Poems of Ossian.* New York, n.d.

Marsch, Edgar. *Die Kriminalerzählung: Theorie, Geschichte, Analyse.* Munich, 1972.

Matt, Peter von. *Die Augen der Automaten. E. T. A. Hoffmanns Imaginationslehre als Prinzip seiner Erzählkunst.* Tübingen, 1971.

Matzker, Reiner. *Der nützliche Idiot: Wahnsinn und Initiation bei Jean Paul und E. T. A. Hoffmann.* Frankfurt, 1984.

Mayer, Hans. "Die Wirklichkeit E. T. A. Hoffmanns." In *Romantikforschung seit 1945.* Ed. Klaus Peter, pp. 116–44. Königstein, 1980.

McGlathery, James M. "Der Himmel hängt ihm voller Geigen: E. T. A. Hoffman's *Rat Krespel, Die Fermate* and *Der Baron von B.*" *German Quarterly* 51 (1978): 135–49.

———. *Mysticism and Sexuality: E. T. A. Hoffmann. Part 1: Hoffmann and His Sources.* Las Vegas, 1981.

———. *Mysticism and Sexuality: E. T. A. Hoffmann. Part II: Interpretations of the Tales.* Bern, 1985.

Mesmer, Franz Anton. *Mesmerismus: Oder System der Wechselwirkungen, Theorie und Anwendungen des thierischen Magnetismus als die allgemeine Heilkunde zur Erhaltung des Menschen.* Ed. Karl Christian Wolfart. Berlin, 1814. Reprinted in Amsterdam, 1966.

Meyer, Herman. *Der Sonderling in der deutschen Dichtung.* Munich, 1963.

Migge, Walther, ed. *Achim von Arnim: Sämtliche Romane und Erzählungen* 1 (1974), 2 (1963). Munich.

Mistler, Jean. *Hoffmann le Fantastique.* Paris, 1950.

Möllers, Eva R. *Ernst Theodor Amadeus Hoffmann als Darsteller aktueller rechtlicher Fragen.* Vienna, 1934.

Möllers, Gerhard. "Wirklichkeit und Phantastik in der Erzählweise Achim von Arnims." Diss., Münster, 1971.

Momberger, Manfred. *Sonne und Punsch: Die Dissemination des romantischen Kunstbegriffs bei E. T. A. Hoffmann.* Munich, 1986.

Morgenblatt, March 25, 1817 (Jahrgang 11).

Moscherosch, Johann Michael. *Wunderliche Wahrhaftige Gesichte Philanders von Sittewald, das ist Straffschriften.* Straßburg, 1666.

Motekat, Helmut. "Vom Sehen und Erkennen bei E. T. A. Hoffmann." *MHG,* vol. 19 (1973), pp. 17–27.

Mühlher, Robert. *Deutsche Dichter der Klassik und Romantik.* Vienna, 1976.

———. "Gedanken zum Humor bei E. T. A. Hoffmann." In *Gestalt und Wirk-*

lichkeit: Festschrift Ferdinand Weinhandl. Ed. Robert Mühlher and Johann Fischl, pp. 505–19. Berlin, 1967.

Mühlpfordt, Herbert M. "Vererbungs- und Umwelteinflüße auf die Brüder J. L. und E. T. A. Hoffmann." *Jahrbuch der Albertus Universität zu Königsberg* (Würzburg), 17 (1967): 80–146.

Müller, Dieter. "Zeit der Automate: Zum Automatenproblem bei Hoffmann." MHG, vol. 12 (1966), pp. 1–8.

Müller, Hans von. *Gesammelte Aufsätze über E. T. A. Hoffmann.* Ed. Friedrich Schnapp. Hildesheim, 1974.

Müller, Hans von, and Friedrich Schnapp. *E. T. A. Hoffmanns Briefwechsel 2* (1814–22). Munich, 1968.

Musäus, J. K. A. *Volksmärchen der Deutschen.* Munich, n.d.

Negus, Kenneth. *E. T. A. Hoffman's Other World.* Philadelphia, 1965.

Nehring, Wolfgang. "Die Gebärdensprache E. T. A. Hoffmanns." *Zeitschrift für deutsche Philologie* 89 (1970): 207–21.

Nettesheim, Josefine. *Poeta doctus oder Die Poetisierung der Wissenschaft von Musäus bis Benn.* Berlin, 1975.

Nipperdey, Otto. "Wahnsinnsfiguren bei E. T. A. Hoffmann." Diss., Cologne, 1957.

Nudow, Heinrich. *Versuch einer Theorie des Schlafs.* Königsberg, 1791.

Ochsner, Karl. *E. T. A. Hoffmann als Dichter des Unbewußten: Ein Beitrag zur Geistesgeschichte der Romantik.* Frauenfeld, 1936.

Olbrich, Karl. "E. T. A. Hoffmann und der deutsche Volksglaube." In *E. T. A. Hoffmann.* Ed. Helmut Prang, pp. 56–88. Darmstadt, 1976.

Oppeln-Bronkowski, Friedrich von. *David Ferdinand Koreff: Serapionsbruder, Magnetiseur, Geheimrat, und Dichter.* Berlin, 1928.

Peters, Diana Stone. "E. T. A. Hoffmann: The Conciliatory Satirist." *Monatshefte* 66 (1974): 55–73.

Pfotenhauer, Helmut. "Exoterische und Esoterische Poetik in E. T. A. Hoffmanns Erzählungen." In *Jahrbuch der Jean-Paul-Gesellschaft* 17, pp. 129–44. Munich, 1982.

Pikulik, Lothar. *E. T. A. Hoffmann als Erzähler: Ein Kommentar zu den Serapionsbrüdern.* Göttingen, 1987.

———. "Das Wunderliche bei E. T. A. Hoffmann: Zum romantischen Ungenügen an der Normalität." *Euphorion* 69 (1975): 294–319.

Pinel, Philippe. *Traité médico-philosophique sur l'aliénation mentale, ou la manie.* Paris, 1801.

Planta, Urs Orland von. *E. T. A. Hoffmanns Märchen "Das fremde Kind."* Bern, 1958.

Post, Klaus D. "Kriminalgeschichte als Heilsgeschichte." *Zeitschrift für deutsche Philologie* 95 (1976): 132–56.

Prang, Helmut, ed. *E. T. A. Hoffmann: Wege der Forschung.* Darmstadt, 1976.

Preisendanz, Wolfgang. "Eines matt geschiliffenen Spiegels dunkler Widerschein: E. T. A. Hoffmanns Erzählkunst." *Zu E. T. A. Hoffmann,* pp. 40–54. Stuttgart, 1981.

Randl, Olga. *Das Dämonische als Stilform in den literarischen Werken E. T. A. Hoffmanns.* Munich, 1912.

Rasch, Wolfdietrich. "Achim von Arnims Erzählkunst." *Der Deutschunterricht* 7 (1955): 38–55.

Reber, Natalie. *Studien zum Motiv des Doppelgängers bei E. T. A. Hoffmann.* Giessen, 1964.

Reichl, Anton, "Über die Benutzung älterer deutscher Literaturwerke in Achim von Arnims 'Wintergarten.' " *Schulprogramm Arnau.* Böhmen, 1889–90. 1, 2.

Reil, Johann C. *Über die Erkenntniß und Cur der Fieber* 4. Vienna, 1802.

———. *Rhapsodien über die Anwendung der psychischen Curmethode auf Geisteszerrüttungen.* Halle, 1803.

Reimann, Olga. "Das Märchen bei E. T. A. Hoffmann." Diss., Munich, 1926.

Reuchlin, Georg. *Das Problem der Zurechnungsfähigkeit bei E. T. A. Hoffmann und Georg Büchner. Zum Verhältnis von Literatur, Psychiatrie und Justiz im frühen neunzehnten Jahrhundert.* Frankfurt, 1985.

Reuter, Christian. *Schelmuffskys wahrhaftige, curiöse und sehr gefährliche Reise: Beschreibungen zu Wasser und Lande in zwei Theilen curiösen Liebhabern vor Augen geleget, und mit zweyen Lust und Trauerspielen versehen.* Frankfurt and Leipzig, 1750.

Ricci, Jean. *E. T. A. Hoffmann: L'Homme et l'oeuvre.* Paris, 1947.

Rickmann, Christian. *Von der Unwahrheit des Versehens.* Jena, 1770.

Riley, Helene M. Kastinger. *Achim von Arnim in Selbstzeugnissen und Bilddokumenten.* Hamburg, 1979.

———. *Ludwig Achim von Arnims Jugend- und Reisejahre.* Bonn, 1978.

Rippley, La Verne J. "The House as Metaphor in E. T. A. Hoffmann's 'Rat Krespel.' " *Papers on Language and Literature* 7 (1971): 52–60.

Robson-Scott, W. D. *The Literary Background of the Gothic Revival in Germany.* Oxford, 1965.

Rölleke, Heinz. "Anmerkungen zu 'Des Knaben Wunderhorn.' " *Clemens Brentano: Beiträge des Kolloquiums im Freien Deutschen Hochstift, 1978.* pp. 276–94. Tübingen, 1980.

Rosteutscher, Joachim. *Das ästhetische Idol im Werke von Winckelmann, Novalis, Hoffmann, Goethe, George und Rilke.* Bern, 1956.

Roth, Friedrich. "Dr. Adalbert Friedrich Marcus, der erste dirigierende Arzt des allgemeinen Krankenhauses zu Bamberg." *Festschrift zum 100jährigen Jubiläum des allgemeinen Krankenhauses zu Bamberg.* Bamberg, 1889.

Rothschuh, Karl E. "Naturphilosophische Konzepte der Medizin aus der Zeit der deutschen Romantik." In *Romantik in Deutschland.* pp. 243–66.

Rowley, Brian. "The Novelle." In *The Romantic Period in Germany.* New York, 1970. Ed. Siegbert Prawer, pp. 121–40.

Safranski, Rüdiger. *E. T. A. Hoffmann.* Munich, 1984.

Sanders, Volkmar. "Realität und Bewußtsein bei E. T. A. Hoffmann." In *Studies in Germanic Language and Literature.* Ed. R. Fowkes and Volkmar Sanders. New York, 1967.

Scher, Steven. *Zu E. T. A. Hoffmann.* Stuttgart, 1981.

Schmidt, Peter. "Gesundheit und Krankheit in romantischer Medizin und Erzählkunst." In *Jahrbuch des Freien Deutschen Hochstifts,* pp. 197–228. Tübingen, 1966.

Schnabel, Johann Gottfried. *Wunderliche Fata einiger Seefahrer, absonderlich Albert Julii, eines gebohrnen Sachsens.* Nordhausen, 1736.

Schnapp, Friedrich. "Der Seraphinenorden und die Serapionsbrüder E. T. A. Hoffmanns." *Literaturwissenschaftliches Jahrbuch* 3 (1962): 99–112.

———. *Dichter über ihre Dichtungen: E. T. A. Hoffmann* 13. Munich, 1974.

———. *Der Musiker E. T. A. Hoffmann: Ein Dokumentband.* Hildesheim, 1981.

Schnapp, Friedrich, and Hans von Müller. *E. T. A. Hoffmanns Briefwechsel, Königsberg bis Leipzig 1794–1814* 1. Munich, 1967.

Schneider, Karl Ludwig. "Künstlerliebe und Philistertum in Werk E. T. A. Hoffmanns." In *Die Deutsche Romantik*. Ed. Hans Steffen, pp. 200–218. Göttingen, 1978.

Schneider, Peter. "Verbrechen, Künstlertum und Wahnsinn. Untersuchungen zur Figur des Cardillac in E. T. A. Hoffmanns *Das Fräulein von Scuderi.*" MHG 26 (1980), pp. 34–50.

Schubert, Gotthelf Heinrich. *Ansichten von der Nachtseite der Naturwissenschaft.* Darmstadt, 1967.

———. *Symbolik des Traumes.* Heidelberg, 1968.

Schumm, Siegfried. *Einsicht und Darstellung: Untersuchung zum Kunstverständnis E. T. A. Hoffmanns.* Göppingen, 1974.

Schütz, Christel. "Studien zur Erzählkunst E. T. A. Hoffmanns." Diss., Göttingen, 1955.

Schweitzer, Christoph E. "Bild, Struktur und Bedeutung: E. T. A. Hoffmanns 'Die Fermate.' " MHG 19 (1973), pp. 49–52.

Scott, Walter. *Minstrelsy of the Scottish Border.* Ed. Thomas Henderson. New York, 1931.

Segebrecht, Wulf. *Autobiographie und Dichtung: Eine Studie zum Werk E. T. A. Hoffmanns.* Stuttgart, 1967.

———. "E. T. A. Hoffmann." In *Deutsche Dichter der Romantik.* Ed. Benno von Wiese, pp. 391–415. Berlin, 1971.

———. "E. T. A. Hoffmanns Auffassung vom Richteramt und Dichterberuf." *Jahrbuch der deutschen Schillergesellschaft* 11 (1967): 62–138.

———. "Heterogenität und Integration bei E. T. A. Hoffmann." *Zu E. T. A. Hoffmann*, pp. 10–21. Stuttgart, 1981.

———. "Krankheit und Gesellschaft: Zu E. T. A. Hoffmanns Rezeption der Bamberger Medizin." In *Romantik in Deutschland*, pp. 267–90.

———. "Die Thematik des Krieges in Achim von Arnims Wintergarten." *Aurora* 45 (1985), pp. 310–16.

Shears, Frederich S. *Froissart: Life and Work.* London, 1930.

Slocum, Linda, "E. T. A. Hoffmann's 'Nußknacker und Mausekönig': Thematic Threads in Divided Worlds." Unpublished paper, Pennsylvania State University, 1986.

Smith, Albert H. "Variations on a Mythical Theme: Hoffmann, Gautier, Queneau and the Imagery of Mining." *Neophilologus* 63 (1979): 179–86.

Speyer, Friedrich, and Carl Moritz Marc. *Dr. A. F. Marcus nach seinem Leben und Wirken.* Bamberg, 1817.

Spring, Pauline. "E. T. A. Hoffmann's 'Der unheimliche Gast': Magnetism and the Sinister Personality." Unpublished paper, Pennsylvania State University, 1986.

Stegmann, Inge. "Deutung und Funktion des Traumes bei E. T. A. Hoffmann." Diss., Bonn, 1973.

Steig, Reinhold. *Achim von Arnim und die ihm nahe standen.* Vol. 1. *Achim von Arnim und Clemens Brentano.* Stuttgart, 1894. Vol. 2. *Achim von Arnim und Bettina Brentano.* Stuttgart, 1913.

Steinecke, Hartmut. "Der beliebte, viegelesene Verfasser . . . : Über die Hoffmann-Kritiken im 'Morgenblatt für gebildete Stände' und in der 'Jenaischen Allgemeinen Literatur-Zeitung.' " MHG 17 (1971), pp. 1–16.

Sternberg, Thomas. *Die Lyrik Achims von Arnim.* Bonn, 1983.

Sucher, Paul. *Les Sources du merveilleux chez E. T. A. Hoffmann.* Paris, 1912.

Sucher, Paul, translator. *Le Vase d'or, Les mines de Falun.* Paris, 1947.

Taylor, Ronald. "Music and Mystery: Thoughts on the Unity of the Work of E. T. A. Hoffmann." *Journal of English and Germanic Philology* 75 (1976): 477–91.

Thalmann, Marianne. *Das Märchen und die Moderne.* Stuttgart, 1961.

————. *Der Trivialroman des 18. Jahrhunderts.* Liechtenstein, 1967.

————. "Meisterschaft: Eine Studie zu E. T. A. Hoffmanns Genieproblem." In *Der Gesichtkreis: Festschrift Joseph Drexel.* Munich, 1956.

Thurnher, Eugen, ed. *Thomas Lirer: Schwäbische Chronik.* Bregenz, 1962.

Toggenburger, Hans. *Die späten Almanach-Erzählungen E. T. A. Hoffmanns* (Bern, 1983).

Trautwein, Wolfgang. *Erlesene Angst-Schauerlituratur im 18. und 19. Jahrhundert. Systematischer Aufriß; Untersuchungen zu Bürger, Maturin, Hoffmann, Poe und Maupassant.* Munich, 1980.

Tsouypoulos, Nelly. "Die neue Auffassung der klinischen Medizin als Wissenschaft unter dem Einfluß der Philosophie im frühen 19. Jahrhundert." *Berichte zur Wissenschaftsgeschichte* 1 (1978): 87–100.

Vitt-Maucher, Gisela. "E. T. A. Hoffmanns Die Königsbraut. 'ein nach der Natur entworfenes Märchen.' " MHG 30 (1984) pp. 42–58.

————. "Hoffmanns Rat Krespel und der Schlafrock Gottes." *Monatshefte* 64 (1972): 51–57.

Vietta, Silivo. "Das Automatenmotiv und die Technik der Motivschichtung im Erzählwerk E. T. A. Hoffmanns." MHG 30 (1984), pp. 25–33.

Voerster, Jürgen. *160 Jahre E. T. A. Hoffmann-Forschung (1805–1965).* Stuttgart, 1967.

Vordtriede, Werner. "Achim von Arnim." In *Deutsche Dichter der Romantik.* Ed. Benno von Wiese, pp. 317–33. Berlin, 1983.

Walter, Jürgen. "Das Unheimliche als Wirkungsfunktion. Eine rezeptionsästhetische Analyse von E. T. A. Hoffmanns Erzählung 'Der Sandmann.' " MHG 30 (1984), pp. 15–33.

Weise, Christian. *Die drei ärgsten Ertz-Narren in der ganzen Welt/ aus vielen närischen Begebenheiten hervor gesucht/ und allen Interessenten zu besserem Nachsinnen übergeben.* 1676.

Weiss, Hermann. "Achim von Arnim, Writer in Transition: Themes and Techniques in Short Prose Narratives." Diss., Princeton, 1968.

————. "Achim von Arnims Harmonisierungsbedürfnis: Zur Thematik und Technik seiner Novellen." *Literaturwissenschaftliches Jahrbuch* 15 (1974): 81–99.

————. "The Labyrinth of Crime: A Reinterpretation of E.T.A. Hoffman's 'Das Fräulein von Scuderi.'" *Germanic Review* 51 (1976): 180–89.

————. *Unbekannte Briefe von und an Achim von Arnim aus der Sammlung Varnhagen und anderen Beständen.* Berlin, 1986.

Wellek, René. *Confrontations.* Princeton, 1965.

Werner, Hans Georg. "Der romantische Schriftsteller und sein Philister-Publikum: Zur Wirkungsfunktion E. T. A. Hoffmanns." in *Zu E. T. A. Hoffmann.* Ed. Steven P. Scher, pp. 74–97. Stuttgart, 1981.

————. *E. T. A. Hoffmann: Darstellung und Deutung der Wirklichkeit im dichterischen Werk.* East Berlin, 1971.

Winter, Ilse. *Untersuchungen zum serapiontischen Prinzip E. T. A. Hoffmanns.* The Hague, 1976.

Wirz, Jacques. "Die Gestalt des Künstlers bei E. T. A. Hoffmann." Diss., Basel, 1961.

Wittkop-Ménardeau, Gabrielle. *Hoffmanns Leben und Werk in Daten und Bildern*. Frankfurt, 1968.

Wittkowski, Wolfgang. "E. T. A. Hoffmanns musikalische Musikerdichtungen 'Ritter Gluck,' 'Don Juan,' 'Rat Krespel.' *Aurora* 38 (1978): 54–74.

Wunderlich, Gesa. "Krankheits- und Therapiekonzepte am Anfang der deutschen Psychiatrie." Diss., Berlin, 1981.

Wüstnei, D. H. G. *Versuch über die Einbildungskraft der Schwangeren in Bezug auf ihre Leibesfrüchte zur Beantwortung der Frage: "Können Schwangere sich wirklich versehen?"* Rostock, 1809.

Index

Bending the Frame in the German Cyclical Narrative was composed by World Composition Services, Inc., Sterling,Virginia, in 10/13.5 Meridien Medium; printed and bound by Thomson-Shore, Inc., Dexter, Michigan; and designed and produced by Kachergis Book Design, Pittsboro, North Carolina